Level 5

Diploma in Leadership for Health and Social Care and Children and Young People's Services

- Tina Tilmouth
- Jan Quallington

HODDER
EDUCATION
AN HACHETTE UK COMPANY

Orders: please contact Bookpoint Ltd, 130 Milton Park, Abingdon, Oxon OX14 4SB. Telephone: (44) 01235827720. Fax: (44) 01235400454. Lines are open from 9.00 – 5.00, Monday to Saturday, with a 24 hour message answering service. You can also order through our website www.hoddereducation.co.uk

If you have any comments to make about this, or any of our other titles, please send them to educationenquiries@hodder.co.uk

British Library Cataloguing in Publication Data

A catalogue record for this is available from the British Library

ISBN: 978 1 444 1 56089

First Edition Published 2012
Impression number   10 9 8 7 6 5 4 3
Year   2015 2014 2013

Hachette UK's policy is to use papers that are natural, renewable and recyclable products and made from wood grown in sustainable forests. The logging and manufacturing processes are expected to conform to the environmental regulations of the country of origin.

Cover photo © Daly and Newton/Getty Images
Typeset by Pantek Media
Printed in Dubai for Hodder Education, an Hachette UK Company, 338 Euston Road, London NW1 3BH

Level 5

Diploma in Leadership for
Health and Social Care
and Children and Young
People's Services

Contents

Contents

Acknowledgements and Photo Credits

Every effort has been made to acknowledge ownership of copyright. The publishers will be glad to make suitable arrangements with any copyright holders whom it has not been possible to contact.

Pages 1–3 and 7–8 contain public sector information published by the Health and Safety Executive and licensed under the Open Government Licence v1.0. Pages 25–26 contain public sector information published by the Scottish Government and licensed under the Open Government Licence v1.0.

Photo credits

The authors and publishers would like to thank the following for the use of images in this volume:

Page 7 © David J. Green / Alamy; page 9 © Tony Baggett – Fotolia.com; page 19 © ERproductions Ltd/Blend Images/Corbis; page 40 (top) © Ferenc Szelepcsenyi – Fotolia.com; page 40 (bottom) © CandyBox Images – Fotolia.com; page 76 © George Doyle / Getty Images; page 90 © John Phillips / Photofusion Pictures; page 97 © carlosseller / Fotolia.com; page 100 © Mary Evans / Peter Higginbotham Collection; page 102 © Vehbi Koca / Photofusion; page 138 © Jan Schuler – Fotolia.com; page 150 © www.imagesource.com; page 160 © Crown Copyright; page 164 © Dean Mitchell / Fotolia.com; page 167 © Simone van den Berg – Fotolia; page 181 © Chris Schmidt / iStockphoto; page 183 © moodboard / Alamy; page 186 © Alain Machet (1) / Alamy; page 188 © Ocean/Corbis; page 194 © Maggie Murray / Photofusion Pictures; page 195 © Medical-on-Line / Alamy; page 197 (top) © Hulton-Deutsch Collection/CORBIS; page 197 (bottom) © gwimages – Fotolia.com; page 199 © AJ PHOTO/SCIENCE PHOTO LIBRARY; page 212 © Crown Copyright; page 213 © iofoto – Fotolia.com; page 216 © Manu29 – Fotolia.com.

Introduction

Leadership and management, when practiced effectively and with integrity, lead to teams which are cohesive and businesses which are successful. This book has been designed with aspiring and existing leaders and managers in mind to enable them to develop the skills, knowledge and competencies required to engage with the workforce and to produce successful outcomes for the care setting and the client.

The authors of this book have been in leadership/management roles in both health care and educational settings and are well placed to provide insight into the issues health care managers currently face.

The content of the book reflects the most common topics needed for those who manage staff and who are undertaking further training in leadership/management roles.

Chapter 1: The health and safety of our clients, staff and ourselves is a legal requirement in any workplace and is the responsibility of everybody. Without exception, all care managers are required to know and practise the legal aspects of health and safety in order to deal with staff, clients and patients in a safe manner. This chapter will remind you of the legislation that affects you in your workplace and the responsibilities you have with respect to yourself, your environment and your clients. In addition, there are assessments for you to undertake to test your knowledge, understanding and skills required for health and safety and risk management, including the development of policies, procedures and practices in health and social care or children and young people's settings.

Chapter 2: The government agenda to ensure that integrated 'joined-up' services are offered to all means that, as managers of care settings, it is necessary to understand the whole premise of what it means to work in partnership with other care professionals. In this chapter we will look at how we can promote effective partnership working by establishing good working relationships with the care services we deal with on a daily basis, our own colleagues and the families of the people we care for. One of the main aims for a health care service of the future is the need to make sure that health and social services work together and share information to give 'joined-up' care to the people they work for. Services sharing information about the people in their care so that health, housing, benefits and other needs are considered together will enhance the experiences of everybody who needs care at some point in their lives.

Chapter 3: Effective interpersonal skill demands that we know ourselves well and are aware of what we bring to the relationship and how we might impact on those we communicate with. Understanding what it is the other person is saying rather than assuming we know is a most useful skill to develop in management. Our aim should be to finish the interaction leaving someone feeling better than they did before we met them. In this chapter we revisit the systems of communication we use in care work and in particular in managing a care setting. In any relationship, be it personal or working, effective interpersonal skills play an essential part and being able to communicate well is one of the most important aspects of your role as a leader and manager. Misunderstanding and misinterpretation of the message can lead to team conflict and disruption to the smooth running of the organisation. Moreover, it can lead to ineffective delivery of services and unproductive teamwork. Being an effective communicator holds the key to successful working.

Chapter 4: People receiving care services must be confident that they can trust those who deliver care to not only know what to do, but also to know how to do it well. That requires continually updating and extending your own knowledge and skills and to ensure that your team is also equipped with appropriate knowledge and skills in order to fulfil their roles effectively. In this chapter we look at personal professional development and help you to reflect on the fundamental importance of these activities in contributing to the management and enhancement of high quality care service. The activities in this chapter will help you to identify and reflect on different strategies to enhance your own development and will assist you to devise strategies to promote and develop professional attitudes, knowledge, skills and behaviours in those that you lead.

Chapter 5: The importance of understanding the positive values of equality, respect for diversity and inclusion in care work cannot be over-estimated. The circumstances that bring individuals into contact with carers suggest that recipients of care are likely to be vulnerable in one way or another. Inevitably, caring for others and engaging with them in decisions about their lives often involves the exercise of power, which has the potential to be misused and abused. How the care worker understands and approaches the responsibilities of their role will have a direct impact on either increasing equality and nullifying discrimination and disadvantage, or helping to reinforce, perpetuate or even increase inequality, discrimination and disadvantage. The purpose of this chapter is to enable you to reflect on the importance of respecting difference and individuality. The activities and assessments in this chapter will assist you to develop strategies for implementing and leading excellent practice in respect of equality, diversity and inclusion within the care context

Chapter 6: Person-centred planning and practice has been described as 'a process of life planning for individuals based around the principles of inclusion and the social model of disability'. (The Circles Network (2008)). In this chapter we look at the skills and knowledge you need to promote and implement person-centred practice. By looking at how care has changed over the last 150 years we address the changing perceptions about how health care must be delivered to improve the quality of life of vulnerable people. From a service-led provision to the development of the personalisation agenda, we can see how this has changed the face of care in the UK. We also deal with aspects of consent and what this means for clients as well as the issues of active participation which recognise an individual's right to participate in the activities and relationships of everyday life as independently as possible. The individual as an active partner in their own care or support is given a voice in today's health service and is no longer regarded as a passive recipient.

Chapter 7: The most important person in your team is the service user or client and they are central to any team working. An effective team is one in which the development of a positive and supportive culture is shared and only in this way can we expect staff to be supportive of a shared vision to meet the agreed objectives for a health and social care or children and young people's setting. In this chapter you will learn how to lead and manage a team and enhance their performance in a health and social care or children and young people's setting. You will be introduced to team functions and the roles that are adopted in teams and will examine models of leadership relevant to the health and care sector. The activities have been designed to encourage you to examine strategies of team working and leadership in order to identify your own strengths, responsibilities, learning needs and to reflect on best practice within the care context.

Chapter 8: Supervision provides professional support and learning for staff to enable them to develop knowledge, skills and competence in their work. In this way we can ensure that the experience of the service user/patient/client is enhanced and in turn the quality and safety in the care setting is improved. In this chapter we will cover the purpose and processes of professional supervision together with performance management and dealing with conflict.

Chapter 9: In an attempt to ensure that all individuals requiring care are dealt with holistically and with their needs being met, the 'personalisation'agenda was introduced into recent government documentation. A system of care and support tailored to meet the needs of the individual has replaced the 'one size fits all' approach previously in vogue and outcome-based practice, also referred to as outcomes management, and outcomes-focussed assessment is one such approach to achieving desired patient care goals. The purpose of this chapter is to enable you to gain the skills and knowledge required in the process of planning and achieving positive outcomes that underpin the personalisation agenda. It also explores the role of the manager/senior worker in providing a supportive environment for individuals to achieve positive outcomes.

Chapter 10: One of the key steps in safeguarding is to work in partnership with other organisations in order to achieve the best possible outcomes and this chapter will help you to address this area of your work. It will enable you to learn how to engage with issues related to the protection and safeguarding of vulnerable adults and to understand the legal and regulatory basis for safeguarding.

Chapter 11: The emphasis on person-centred care has seen a rise in a number of initiatives to enable people to live as independently as possible. There are, however, some groups of people who may require support of a more substantial nature and who therefore need to move into residential accommodation and group living arrangements. In this chapter we look at the various options for care, not only for the elderly adult but also for children and young people. From small residential homes for the elderly or young people with learning disabilities to sheltered accommodation or Extra Care housing, there are numerous options available now for group living and the activities in this chapter will help you to increase your knowledge of the alternatives to residential accommodation.

Chapter 12: You may not work directly with children but you are required to have some understanding of the safeguarding protocols and procedures with children. In this chapter you will be introduced to the policies and procedures for safe working with children and the ways in which to respond to evidence of abuse and harm in children.

Chapter 13: This chapter addresses the different forms of assessment in the context of partnership working and looks at how you can manage the whole process of carrying out, reviewing and planning assessment for clients. Reference is made to three models of assessment and their uses and the Single Assessment process, as suggested by the National Service Framework for Older People (2001), is introduced and discussed. Throughout the chapter a series of activities will help you to build a portfolio of evidence to cover the learning outcomes of the unit.

1

Unit M1 Develop health and safety and risk management policies, procedures and practices in health and social care or children and young people's settings

Occasionally, we may be less than complimentary about the Health and Safety rulings we hear about from time to time. We often hear the expression 'it's health and safety gone mad' and I am sure you can give examples of such madness! However, without exception, *all* care managers are required to know and practise the legal aspects of health and safety in order to deal with staff, clients and patients in a safe manner.

In this chapter you will be reminded of the health and safety legislation that affects you in your workplace and the responsibilities you have with respect to yourself, your environment and your clients. In addition, the purpose of the diploma unit is to assess your knowledge, understanding and skills required for Health and Safety and Risk Management, including the development of policies, procedures and practices in health and social care or children and young people's settings. As such, the chapter will address these areas.

Learning outcomes

By the end of this chapter you will:

1. Understand the current legislative framework and organisational health, safety and risk management policies, procedures and practices that are relevant to health and social care or children and young people's settings.

2. Be able to implement and monitor compliance with health, safety and risk management requirements in health and social care or children and young people's settings.

3. Be able to lead the implementation of policies, procedures and practices to manage risk to individuals and others in health and social care or children and young people's settings.

4. Be able to promote a culture where needs and risks are balanced with health and safety practice in health and social care or children and young people's settings.

5. Be able to improve health, safety and risk management policies, procedures and practices in health and social care or children and young people's settings.

1 Understand the current legislative framework and organisational health, safety and risk management policies, procedures and practices relevant to health and social care or children and young people's settings

1.1 Explain the legislative framework for health, safety and risk management in the work setting

Take a look at the following headline articles taken from the Health & Safety Executive website.

Care home in court after resident dies from drinking toilet cleaner

15th February 2011

A Sheffield care home operator has admitted breaching safety laws after an elderly resident died after inadvertently drinking toilet cleaner.

Retired accountant, Derek Johnson, 80, died on the same day he was found to have drunk the dangerous chemical.

The liquid had been left unattended for several hours in his room at Newfield Care Home, Cat Lane, Sheffield. He had been living at the home for just over a month before his death in July 2009. He was frail, registered blind and had symptoms of dementia.

The Health and Safety Executive (HSE) prosecuted the care home operator, Palms Row Healthcare Ltd, because they put vulnerable

▶

people, including Mr Johnson, at risk by failing to properly manage the use of cleaning fluids.

Sheffield Magistrates' Court heard that Mr Johnson began vomiting blue liquid and was taken to Northern General Hospital where he died just hours later. The liquid was later found to be toilet cleaner which had been noticed in his room earlier that day but not removed.

The HSE investigation found the company had an inadequate system to control such chemicals and to prevent access to areas of risk by vulnerable people. Inspectors discovered that trolleys carrying hazardous substances were often left unattended, sometimes for considerable periods, and there were no proper procedures in place for cleaners to check trolley contents were intact.

The investigation also showed it was too easy for vulnerable residents to get into areas such as the laundry and kitchen which should have had controlled access.

Following the incident, HSE served Palms Row Healthcare with three Improvement Notices as well as bringing the prosecution.

HSE Inspector Carol Downes said:

'Mr Johnson's death was a terribly tragic one, particularly as it could have been easily avoided by simply locking away the chemicals.

'There was no excuse for Palms Row Healthcare's failure to protect the vulnerable people in its care. It is imperative that care home owners consider the risks to people they are looking after and manage those risks to prevent incidents like this.'

Mr Johnson's brother, Ray, who was in court with his daughter, Liz Smith, said:

'The loss of Derek was a huge shock to the family, particularly to me as his brother. Derek was placed in a nursing home for his own safety and yet my very act of trying to keep him safe resulted in his death. I cannot reconcile this feeling and battle with it daily. I am still trying to come to terms with what I see as the untimely death of my big brother.

'We hope that lessons will be learned from what happened to Derek so that other families do not have to suffer the same heartache and loss that we are still suffering.'

Palms Row Healthcare Ltd, of Westbourne Road, Sheffield, admitted breaching Section 3(1) of the Health & Safety at Work etc Act 1974. The company was fined £15,000 and ordered to pay costs of £14,472.02.

www.hse.gov.uk/press/2011/coi-yh-2511.htm

Training failures led to patient death

21 December 2010

A care home operator was today fined £80,000 for serious training failures following the death of a patient as a result of 'inappropriate and dangerous' restraint techniques.

Forty-two-year-old Anthony Pinder, who had learning and behavioural issues, was physically restrained for around 90 minutes by staff at the Old Vicarage nursing home in Stallingborough, near Grimsby, on 1 October 2004. He was eventually released and crawled unaided to his room, but was found dead a short time later.

Leeds Crown Court heard that Health and Care Services (UK) Limited, part of the Craegmoor group, failed to ensure staff were adequately trained to carry out the safe physical restraint of residents.

The measures used to control Mr Pinder were described as 'poor, inappropriate and dangerous' during the case, although those engaged in the restraint were not blamed because the court heard they were simply doing what they felt was necessary under difficult circumstances. The failure to train staff in safe restraint techniques rested with management.

The Commission for Social Care Inspectorate highlighted an urgent need for safe restraint training just five months prior to Mr Pinder's death, which prompted a written promise from senior management at Health and Care Services that improvements would be made.

However, the investigation found that no such training was given. The company therefore failed to comply with a regulatory requirement, and failed to take all reasonably practicable steps to protect patients at the Old Vicarage – a breach of section 3(1) of the Health and Safety at Work Act 1974.

In addition to the £80,000 fine for pleading guilty to the breach, Health and Care Services (UK) Limited was also ordered to pay £40,823 in costs.

Following the conclusion of the case, HSE Inspector Brian Fotheringham said:

'Anthony Pinder was a vulnerable person whose death was entirely avoidable. Health and Care Services (UK) Ltd position themselves as a market leading specialist care provider through Craegmoor, and Anthony and his family had a right to expect that he would be properly cared for. But they were badly let down.

'Senior management knew that staff at the Old Vicarage often had to physically intervene and restrain residents, but they failed to ensure that staff were trained in appropriate and safe restraint techniques.

'This failure is inexcusable given that this lack of training had been drawn to the attention of the company following an inspection of the home by the Commission for Social Care Inspection five months before Anthony's death. Despite the fact that the Commission produced a report requiring this training to be provided, it was not delivered.

'It is shameful that even after Anthony's death the company did not train the staff. This was only done after I forced the issue by serving an enforcement notice shortly after commencing my investigation.

'The company says that steps have been taken to prevent a repeat of this incident. I hope Anthony's tragic and untimely death and the subsequent prosecution sends an important message to all care sector companies.'

www.hse.gov.uk/press/2010/coi-yh-2140.htm

These headlines clearly demonstrate the sorts of tragic events that can happen when the legal aspects of care work are either treated with disdain or ignored. Failure to uphold the law will inevitably lead to consequences not only to our clients but also to the staff and the care establishment as a whole.

In your role as a manager and leader in health care, whatever sector you are employed in, your knowledge of the law and how it is to be implemented by your staff in their practice must underpin your practice. Undoubtedly you will already have a good working practice of the legal aspects of care work but it is wise to revisit this from time to time.

Activity 1.1.1

You are to give a lecture at the local college about the legal aspects of health care and how they apply to the health and social care or children and young people's settings.

To make a start, see if you can list the laws you are familiar with and explain what the purpose of them are and what your responsibilities are with respect to implementing them. Now see if you can add to your list from a sector you are unfamiliar with.

We came up with the following:

- The Health and Safety at Work Act 1974 (HASAWA)
- Health and Safety (First Aid) Regulations 1981
- Mental Health Act 1983
- Electricity at Work Regulations 1989
- Food Safety Act 1990 and the Food Hygiene Regulations 2006
- Manual Handling Operations Regulations 1992 (MHOR)
- Workplace (Health, Safety and Welfare) Regulations 1992
- Personal Protective Equipment at Work Regulations 1992 (PPE)
- Reporting on Injuries, Diseases, and Dangerous Occurrences Regulations 1995 (RIDDOR)
- Disability Discrimination Act 1995 (DDA)
- Provision and Use of Work Equipment Regulations 1998 (PUWER)

Figure 1.1 Put policies in place to avoid accidents

- Data Protection Act 1998
- Management of Health and Safety at Work Regulations 1999 (MHSWR)
- Control of Substances Hazardous to Health Regulations 2002 (COSHH)
- Regulatory Reform (Fire Safety) 2005
- Corporate Manslaughter and Homicide Act 2007
- Health and Social Care Act 2008.

In other areas such as those dealing with the care of children and young people there are also the following to bear in mind:

- Family Law Reform Act 1969
- Children Act 1989 and Children Act 2004
- Mental Capacity Act 2005.

Table 1.1 shows the purpose of the laws and your responsibility with respect to each and you can check your answers here.

Table 1.1 Legislation, purpose and your responsibilities

Legislation	Purpose	Your responsibilities
The Health and Safety at Work Act 1974 (HASAWA)	Anyone affected by work activity must be kept safe.	To ensure all staff are aware of their part in Health and Safety and to regularly check the policies in place meet all needs. Ensure that written policies are in place.
Health and Safety (First Aid) Regulations 1981	To ensure that everybody has access to immediate first aid care in the workplace.	To maintain first aid training of designated first aiders and to supply resources for first aid.
Mental Health Act 1983	This act allows compulsory action to be taken, where necessary, to ensure that people with mental disorders get the care and treatment they need for their own health or safety or for the protection of other people.	Ensure staff are aware of the reason for the Act.
Electricity at Work Regulations 1989	To minimise the risk due to electricity in the workplace.	To maintain upkeep and ensure regular safety checks are made.
Food Safety Act 1990 Food Hygiene Regulations 2006 Manual Handling Operations Regulations 1992 (MHOR)	To minimise the risk due to food handling in the workplace. To minimise the risk due to moving and handling food.	Ensure good personal hygiene procedures are upheld. Ensure any hazards are identified and controlled. Ensure staff are trained in moving and handling protocols.
Workplace (Health, Safety and Welfare) Regulations 1992	To minimise the risk due to working conditions in the workplace.	Ensure that standards for heating, lighting, sanitation and building upkeep are maintained.
Personal Protective Equipment at Work Regulations 1992 (PPE)	To minimise the risk of cross-infection in the workplace.	To ensure staff are aware of infection control procedures and are trained in dealing with potential cross infection. To supply work wear and PPE.

Reporting on Injuries, Diseases, and Dangerous Occurrences Regulations 1995 (RIDDOR)	Ensure that procedures are in place for the reporting of injury and illness to the HSE or local authority where appropriate.	Maintain the policy in the workplace and ensure that accident forms and reports are in place.
Disability Discrimination Act 1995 (DDA)	Ensure that access and exits to the workplace are safe for those with disabilities in the event of the need to evacuate the premises.	Update premises and ensure policy is known to staff and visitors.
Provision and Use of Work Equipment Regulations 1998 (PUWER)	Risks due to the use of equipment must be minimised.	Train staff in use of equipment and ensure upkeep of equipment is maintained and safe to use.
Data Protection Act 1998 Management of Health and Safety at Work Regulations 1999 (MHSWR)	Ensure that personal information is kept private and safe. Carry out risk assessments to minimise any risks to safety.	Check policy on confidentiality and arrange to undertake regular risk assessments.
Control of Substances Hazardous to Health Regulations 2002 (COSHH)	Minimise the risk from the use of substances that may be hazardous to health.	Carry out risk assessments and ensure staff are trained in use of hazardous substances.
Regulatory Reform (Fire Safety) 2005	Minimise fire hazards.	Regular checks of fire safety procedures in the workplace.
Corporate Manslaughter and Homicide Act 2007	If the death of somebody occurs in suspicious circumstances then an organisation may be convicted of negligence.	Ensure staff are aware of duty of care and are following policy.
Family Law Reform Act 1969	Reduced the age of majority from 21 to 18 and provided for the maintenance for children under guardianship to continue to the age of 21. Also allowed consent by persons over 16 to surgical, medical and dental treatment.	
Children Act 1989 Children Act 2004	The Act set boundaries and gave help for local authorities to regulate official intervention in the interests of children. It also made changes to laws that pertain to children.	
Mental Capacity Act 2005	Provided a legal framework for acting and making decisions on behalf of adults who lack capacity to make particular decisions for themselves.	
Health and Social Care Act 2008	Highlighted significant measures to modernise and integrate health and social care.	

All the laws in Table 1.1 will be enshrined in the policies and procedures you are required to have in your workplace and these will cover a variety of laws. In this chapter we will be addressing the Health and Safety policy.

Policies set out the arrangements you have for complying with the law and procedures identify the activity surrounding practice in order to implement the policy. As a manager, one of your roles is to ensure that staff are aware of the importance of carrying out practice according to policy. Failure to do so can have major consequences for the client, the organisation and the member of staff, as we shall see in the next section.

1.2 Analyse how policies, procedures and practices in own setting meet health, safety and risk management requirements

If you work in a setting where there are more than five employees then you are required to have a written Health and Safety Policy in place. The National Minimum Standards for Care (Number 11.2) states that:

'The agency delivering the care has a comprehensive health and safety policy written procedures for health and safety management defining:

- individual and organisational responsibility for health and safety;

- responsibilities and arrangements or risk assessments under the requirements of the Health and Safety at Work Regulations (1999)(management regulation).'

DOH, 2000

Activity 1.1.2

Take a look at that policy in your work setting now and see whether it details the following points:

- A commitment to ensuring the safety of all employees, patients/clients and visitors to the organisation.

- A statement of intent to that purpose.

- An implementation plan which shows how this will be achieved.

- A list of procedures with respect to action to be taken in the event of accidents or need to evacuate premises.

Write a reflective account to show your understanding of the policy and how it meets health, safety and risk management requirements.

The HSE, or Health and Safety Executive, is part of the government Health and Safety Commission (HSC) and these bodies are responsible for the control and monitoring of the risks within the workplace to ensure that workers remain safe. The belief that 'prevention is better than cure' informs their mission statement, being '...to protect people's health and safety by ensuring that risks in the workplace are properly controlled' (www.hse.gov.uk).

Failure to comply with the legislation and guidelines for Health and Safety as laid down by the HSE can result in prosecution of the employer. This makes it imperative to ensure that all your policies and procedures are complied with by staff and that a responsible attitude towards health and safety is demonstrated by all.

2 Be able to implement and monitor compliance with health, safety and risk management requirements in health and social care or children and young people's settings

2.1 Demonstrate compliance with health, safety and risk management procedures

2.2 Support *others* to comply with legislative and organisational health, safety and risk management policies, procedures and practices relevant to their work

One of your duties as an employer is to ensure policies are in place and, more to the point, being used. In addition, you will need to carry out risk assessments for the premises and then put into place risk control measures. Compliance with the Safety Representative and Safety Committee Regulations (1977) and the Health and Safety Consultations with Employees Regulations (1996) (www.hse.gov.uk) is part of the employer's role and, as a manager, you need to ensure that staff are aware of their responsibility when it comes to compliance with the legal aspects of health and safety.

It is likely that one way in which you have done this is to have Health and Safety as a regular agenda item for your team meeting. In this way, staff can be updated as to training opportunities, risk assessments and their outcomes and general safety in the workplace issues. A poster which gives details of the staff who are designated safety officers and first aiders is also useful since it displays relevant information for staff and visitors to the area.

Figure 1.2 Health and Safety

As a manager, you need to ensure that everyone in your team understands that they are responsible for their own safety and also of anybody with whom they interact in the workplace. By demonstrating good practice in a consistent manner, you will inspire others to follow your lead.

Activity 1.2.1

Write a reflective account to show how you comply with the policies and how you ensure others are also following protocol.

2.3 Explain the actions to take when health, safety and risk management, procedures and practices are not being complied with

All your staff need to be aware of the responsibility they have to update their knowledge and to attend health and safety training on a regular basis. It is your responsibility to ensure that the opportunity to do this is available and that staff are encouraged to take time to attend training courses. Failure to comply could mean the staff member would be put at risk of losing their job and there will also be consequences for the organisation.

Inspectors from the Health and Safety Executive (HSE) and from the local authority enforce health and safety law and have the right to enter any workplace without giving notice. More often than not, notice is given however and on a normal inspection visit an inspector would expect to look at the workplace, the work activities, your management of health and safety, and your compliance with health and safety law. Often valuable guidance or advice is given and, occasionally, improvement notices may be served and action taken if there is a risk to health and safety which needs to be dealt with immediately.

On finding a problem and a breach of health and safety law, action is taken according to the principles set out in HSE's Enforcement Policy Statement. The guidance is set out in the box below.

Informal

If the matter is relatively minor, the employer will be advised as to what to do to comply with the law and the inspector will write to confirm any advice given, and will outline what constitutes a legal requirement from best practice advice.

Improvement notice

An improvement notice is served when there is a more serious breach of the law. In this case, the inspector may advise the employer to do something to comply with the law. The following process is generally followed:

■ The inspector discusses the improvement notice and clarifies understanding.

■ The notice will identify what needs to be done, why, and by when.

■ At least 21 days is given in which to take the remedial action. This allows the employer time to appeal to an Industrial Tribunal if they so wish.

Prohibition notice

In a situation which constitutes a risk of serious personal injury, the inspector may serve a prohibition notice. This means the activity will be prohibited immediately or after a specified time period, and will not be allowed to be resumed until remedial action has been taken. If, for example, your form of transport for your clients or residents is unsafe then this sort of action may be taken.

Prosecution

This occurs when the inspector considers that it is necessary to initiate a prosecution and the decision to do so is informed by the principles in the HSE's Enforcement Policy Statement. We have recently seen prosecutions of care homes for the neglect and cruelty meted out to residents and these were extreme cases. However, failure to comply with an improvement or prohibition notice carries a fine of up to £20,000, or six months' imprisonment, or both.

Appeals

Of course the employer does have recourse to law if they feel they have been treated unfairly and they have a right to appeal to an Industrial Tribunal when an improvement or prohibition notice is served.

It is clear then that health and safety in the workplace should not be taken lightly. Not only must you take care of yourself, your staff, clients and visitors to your workplace, you also have a responsibility to ensure that health and safety policies are up to date, current and being used.

Activity 1.2.2

Explain the actions you would take when health, safety and risk management, procedures and practices are not being complied with in your own setting.

2.4 Complete records and reports on health, safety and risk management issues according to legislative and organisational requirements

You already know the importance of good record keeping and this is highly important in dealing with issues of health and safety. Should an accident happen at work, years later you may be required to attend court if there has been a claim for compensation. If your records are less than accurate you may find yourself in a difficult situation.

Any records maintained need to be:

- accurate
- ordered
- up to date
- safe.

The last point is one of the most important points to remember since it is a legal requirement to protect any data we may have on our clients or staff and maintain it in a confidential way. Any use of such information in an unsuitable way or any breach of confidentiality needs to be dealt with promptly and must be reported to the person in charge. The security of information is a safeguard for vulnerable clients and any breach of that security can be detrimental to clients.

Figure 1.3 Keeping records

Compliance with the Data Protection Act (1998) is an imperative. This act gives individuals the right to access their records whether they are stored as paper files or on computers.

It is worth revisiting the eight principles concerning data the act refers to.

- Data must be secure.
- Data must not be kept for longer than necessary – you will need to check the requirements in your own organisation for the length of time. (For example, antenatal records are kept for 25 years.)
- Data must be accurate.
- Data must be fairly processed.
- Data must not be transferred without protection.
- Data must protect individuals' rights.
- Data must be processed for limited purposes only.
- Data must be adequate, relevant and not excessive.

The National Minimum Standards for care require that all organisation records relating to Health and Safety matters are accurate and kept up to date.

You will be familiar with accident records and may have had to complete these from time to time. We can become blasé about these but we rely on these records, and if years later the case becomes part of a legal process, we need to be able to return to the records to remind us of what actually was done at the time.

Records then do the following:

- Provide an account of the care given.
- Give a record of continuous care (in the case of nursing and medical records).
- Provide a source of reference for care.
- Provide an audit and quality assurance trail.
- Are a legal requirement.

Unfortunately we live in a highly litigious society and in order to protect ourselves when we are being held accountable for the care we give, we need to be aware of the place records have. If a complaint is made against us then we would be hard pushed to answer if we had inadequately prepared records. If negligence or a breach of health and safety is suspected in any care setting, any records and statements pertaining to the case will be taken and scrutinised.

Figure 1.4 Going to court

Dimond (1997) highlighted the major areas of concern in such care reports. She revealed that in many records there were major omissions, including:

- No dates
- Illegibility
- Use of abbreviations
- Callers' and visitors' names not included
- No signatures
- Inaccuracy with respect to dates and times
- Delays in record writing
- Inaccuracies about clients
- Unprofessional language being used.

Our responsibility with respect to record keeping is clear. We need to make records on clients and patients but the way in which we use and store that information is paramount.

We must handle all information effectively and be aware of the need to maintain confidentiality of that information. The checklist to follow may be useful to ensure that you and your staff are aware of good record keeping.

Have I written legibly?

Have I put information in time order, as it happened?

Have I got dates and times in the record?

Have I put in signs and symptoms? I might even have written how the patient/client is feeling.

Did I carry out a risk assessment?

Have I included names of other people involved?

Have I written in a professional manner?

Have I signed the forms/records?

Activity 1.2.3

Write a short account of how you maintain records in your own setting and how you comply with the eight principles shown in the box on page 8.

3 Be able to lead the implementation of policies, procedures and practices to manage risk to individuals and others in health and social care or children and young people's settings

3.1 Contribute to development of policies, procedures and practices to identify, assess and manage risk to *individuals* and others

3.2 Work with individuals and others to assess potential risks and hazards

3.3 Work with individuals and others to manage potential risks and hazards

In writing policies and procedures you will be aware of how detailed and prescriptive these documents can be. They describe the who, what, when, where and how of activities in a very strict and rigid manner and can be very time consuming to write. However, once written they merely need to be updated every 12 months so it is a useful exercise to undertake the task well in the first place so that no major changes need to be made each year.

The HSE have produced a free leaflet called *An Introduction to Health and Safety: Health and safety in small businesses.* You are advised to look at this now and you can access it online by typing the title into your search engine.

This document gives you a statement of general policy based on your responsibilities with respect to the Health and Safety at Work Act 1974. You are also able to record your organisational responsibilities and your arrangements to ensure the health and safety of your employees within the sections supplied. There are also notes and references for further information and, if you haven't got a policy in place, it also contains a template in order for you to develop your own policy.

Your policy should contain the following:

- The responsibilities of the staff who work in the area with respect to the day-to-day running of the workplace and its specific areas.

- The health and safety risks – what they are, action needed to remove or control, who is responsible, time for review.

- Details about who the employee representatives are with respect to health and safety and first aid, etc.

- Details of staff responsible for identifying when maintenance is needed, who draws up maintenance procedures, who to report problems to, who purchases new equipment.

- The procedures with respect to safe handling and use of substances including medicines and who is responsible for identifying hazardous substances and carrying out COSHH assessments, informing employees, and reviewing assessments.

- Details of who supervises and trains new recruits and young workers in Health and Safety.

- Details of where the Health and Safety Law poster is to be displayed.

- Details about the staff members who provide induction training, job-specific training and keep training records.

- Details about the staff who arrange and keep records of health surveillance, accidents, first aid and work-related ill health and those who are responsible for keeping records and reporting under RIDDOR.

- Details about where the first aid equipment is stored and the name of the appointed person/first aider.

- Details about the monitoring of conditions and safe working practices, and the names of people who investigate accidents and work-related sickness.

- Details about staff responsible for carrying out fire risk assessments, and how often checks are made on escape routes, fire extinguishers, alarms, evacuation procedures.

Under the Management of Health and Safety at Work Regulations, you have a responsibility to carry out risk assessment in the workplace in order to eliminate and reduce hazards and risks.

A health and safety risk can be anything that is hazardous. We often work in close contact with chemicals, medication and equipment, all of which may cause harm in some way. The environment with its stairs, lifts, hallways, beds, and even the people in it, may be potentially risky. As a manager you need to be able to identify potential risk and eliminate it as

Activity 1.3.1

Evaluate your own Health and Safety policy and determine its relevance in identifying assessing and managing risk to individuals and others.

far as you are able to. In some instances you will not be able to eliminate the risk entirely but you need to make sure you have identified it and put into place actions to minimise the possibility of harm occurring.

We may view the risk assessment as a somewhat onerous task but we need to carry out such assessment prior to any activity being undertaken. The key stages within the process seek to address the following areas:

Step One: Looking for hazards

An investigation of the premises, activity or procedure needs to be undertaken. The hazards you identify will depend very much on the type of work being carried out. The risk assessment in a school is unlikely to be the same as that in a restaurant or a saw mill.

Step Two: Identifying who could be harmed and how

This seeks to show special arrangements for the types of hazards that people may come into contact with, either through their daily work in an area or even as clients. We are all familiar with hard hats being worn by anybody entering a building site. In your own organisation your risk may be more to do with moving and handling patients or could be to do with issues around infection control. Care homes may need to risk assess their policy on security and entrances to the home.

Step Three: Evaluation of the risk

In this part of the assessment you are making a judgement as to the arrangements already in place for dealing with a potential problem area. An example might be simply changing storage arrangements to free up the fire exit or identifying safer ways to transport clients to outpatient appointments.

Step Four: Record the findings

A record needs to include checklists identifying the hazards, the people likely to be at risk, and arrangements to reduce the hazard.

Step Five: Assess the effectiveness of the precautions in place

Following any dangerous occurrence, staff are expected to complete accident forms and sometimes to inform the HSE. If this occurrence shows up several times then clearly the risk assessment needs to be revisited and safer actions put into place.

The HSE provides an online risk assessment for office workers but with some changes you can use it for your work area also. Go to the HSE website for further help with this activity.

Activity 1.3.2

Complete a risk assessment with a member of your staff for an activity in the workplace and document the process.

4 Be able to promote a culture where needs and risks are balanced with health and safety practice in health and social care or children and young people's settings

4.1 **Work with individuals to balance the management of risk with individual rights and the views of others**

Care settings vary in type and, as such, the risks associated with them will differ. The rights of individuals in our care can occasionally be in conflict with health and safety issues and we need to be prepared to address such occasions. For example, a new client in a care home may wish to go out shopping by themselves or may wish to go along to the local pub in the evening. The client is clearly not imprisoned in the home and there should be no reason to deny them that right, but at the same time the staff may well have some concerns as to the client's safety when they are not in their care. The CSCI (Commission for Social Care Inspection) document *Rights, Risks and Restraints: An exploration into the use of restraint in the care of older people* (2007), although concerned mainly with how some older people have been restrained in some care settings, does, however, make some useful points.

'Respecting people's basic human rights to dignity, freedom and respect underpins good quality social care. People may need support in managing their care and making decisions but they have the right, whether in their own home or in a care home, to make choices about their lives and to take risks.

'Social care services have responsibilities to keep people safe from harm and to ensure their safety. It is this need to balance people's rights to freedom and to make choices with ensuring people are safe that is at the heart of this exploration into the use of restraint in the care of older people.'

It is a case then of balancing the client's safety whilst also respecting their rights.

4.2 Work with individuals and others to develop a balanced approach to risk management that takes into account the benefits for individuals of risk taking

Think about the risks you take on a daily basis. Did you perhaps pull out rather quickly into a busy road in the path of an oncoming car? Perhaps you had to run to catch the bus and didn't look too carefully at the road. Maybe it was simply a case of standing on a chair in order to retrieve something from a high cupboard.

Our attitude to risk is likely to be different when it comes to risking our own personal safety. As care professionals, though, we are bound by law and have a duty of care to our clients and this is likely to change our attitude to risk management. We may be more careful when dealing with clients and take the view that as 'vulnerable adults' they need to be protected in some way. But is this a fair assessment of the people we care for or merely a stereotypical view? Titterton (2005) in his work *Risk and Risk Taking in Health and Social Welfare* takes the view that care workers tend to focus upon what the clients cannot do and therefore take what he calls a 'safety first approach' to risk.

Figure 1.5 Completing a risk assessment

This type of approach focuses on the person's physical problems and disability and tends to ignore other needs. This type of treatment then leads to loss of self-esteem and denies the right to choice and an increase in independence. In this way, there is a danger that the care worker becomes more controlling of the client and person-centred approaches become less of a reality.

Risk in this instance then is thought of in terms of danger, loss, threat, damage or injury and the positive benefits of risk-taking are lost and therefore a more balanced approach needs to be adopted.

The Department of Health agrees with this. In their 2007 paper, *Independence, choice and risk: a guide to best practice in supported decision making,* they make the point that a 'safety first approach' may 'not be necessarily the best option for the person and may be detrimental to quality of life and a risk to maintaining independence'.

A more intelligent option is that proposed by Titterton in his Positive Risk approach. In this approach, risk is seen as positive and enhancing, and recognises the needs of individuals. It demonstrates that choice and autonomy are important and promotes the rights of vulnerable people. Steve Morgan (2004) summarises the approach:

> 'Positive risk-taking is: weighing up the potential benefits and harms of exercising one choice of action over another. Identifying the potential risks involved, and developing plans and actions that reflect the positive potentials and stated priorities of the service user. It involves using available resources and support to achieve the desired outcomes, and to minimise the potential harmful outcomes. It is not negligent ignorance of the potential risks…it is usually a very carefully thought-out strategy for managing a specific situation or set of circumstances.'

If we are to provide real choice and control for our clients we need to enable individuals to take the risks they choose, with support from the staff. This means allowing the individuals using our service to define their own risks and to plan and monitor any activity they wish to undertake which may entail some form of risk.

Activity 1.4.1

Provide evidence to show how you promote a culture where needs and risks are balanced and show how you help your staff to develop such a culture.

4.3 Evaluate own practice in promoting a balanced approach to risk management

4.4 Analyse how helping others to understand the balance between risk and rights improves practice

Risk assessment and risk management are an essential part of adult social care but it is often difficult to balance empowerment with the duty of care we owe our clients. For individuals to be able to lead independent lives, the risks they choose to take need to be constantly weighed up against the likelihood of significant harm arising from that choice and the situation in question.

In assessing the seriousness of risk you may like to address the following areas in your workplace.

■ The sorts of factors that increase exposure to risk, e.g. environmental, social, financial, communication and recognition of abuse.

■ The existence of support to minimise risk.

■ The nature, extent and length of time of the risk.

■ The impact the risk may have on the individual and on others.

In addition to the above, you are also bound by law as stated in Section 3(1) of the Health and Safety at Work Act 1974, which clearly states:

'It shall be the duty of every employer to conduct his undertaking in such a way as to ensure, so far as is reasonably practicable, that persons not in his employment who may be affected thereby are not thereby exposed to risks to their health or safety.'

Unfortunately, this can make us risk averse and you may have staff who err constantly on the side of caution and fail to allow clients to undertake certain activities that they consider to be a risk to safety. This sort of professional risk aversion will undoubtedly lead to a lack of choice for the clients, together with a loss of control and independent living. This will, of course, have an adverse effect on care and is potentially bad practice. Staff, then, need to be supported in carrying out risk assessment that they feel confident about.

Activity 1.4.2

Provide an account of your own practice to show how you promote a balanced approach to risk taking for your own workplace. Write a short account of how you have helped staff in your area to carry out risk assessments that support a positive risk taking approach. Say how this practice has improved the care in your area.

5 Be able to improve health, safety and risk management policies, procedures and practices in health and social care or children and young people's settings

5.1 Obtain feedback on health, safety and risk management policies, procedures and practices from individuals and others

It is essential to evaluate the quality of your service with respect to health and safety on a continual basis and there are a number of ways in which this may be done. First undertake the following activity.

Activity 1.5.1

How do you evaluate the quality of service in your own workplace? List the various measures you use.

You may have identified these according to organisational, team and individual measures of performance.

From an **organisational** point of view, there are a number of ways in which we are able to measure our performance on any aspect of health care.

The Care Quality Commission (CQC) is responsible for registering, inspecting and reporting on social care services in England and its main role is to improve social care and stamp out bad practice. In order to be able to do this, they require all registered adult social care services to submit Annual Quality Assurance Assessment (AQAA). This is a legal requirement and in the assessment, care providers describe what they are doing well, what they could improve and how they are going to improve.

There is also a section on 'barriers to improvement' and providers can indicate what they feel may hinder their improvement. The document also requires the service provider to include a description of the evidence of their claims and where the evidence can be found. They are not required to attach the actual evidence itself but it must be available for inspection.

Your own complaints and compliments procedure can also provide a very good indication of the areas of practice that are working well or badly. In a climate in which people feel able to complain without fear of recrimination this is a useful way to check practice and to act upon the areas which require some work.

You need to be aware that a low number of complaints do not necessarily mean that there are no issues. It may be that individuals feel unable to comment for fear of being victimised and this in itself needs investigation.

Service user and focus groups may also be a part of your quality assurance strategy. The former are structured to gain the views of the people who actually use the service and additionally may provide an avenue of support by peers. If it is possible it should be a service user who runs the group and in this way the clients in the group feel more empowered.

Focus groups can be set up to look at areas of practice and to give feedback on procedures or systems. These may be made up of staff, clients and even visitors or family and are a way of gathering opinions in an open environment. These sorts of meetings are really useful for gathering information that is crucial for the running of your setting and, as such, should be well conducted, with members of the group being clear about what they are being asked to do in a climate that is positive and welcoming. It is important to keep the members informed of the outcomes of the meeting.

At a **team** level, your regular team meeting will provide much needed information on health and safety issues and, as mentioned earlier, it would be most useful if you had this as an agenda item for every meeting. In that way you can ensure that at least once a week there is a discussion about issues that may require attention and staff can be informed of any changes that require their consideration. The minutes of the meeting can be a part of the AQAA evidence which must be made available to inspectors when they visit.

Staff appraisals and supervision sessions provide feedback at an **individual** level and give staff the chance to evaluate their own performance over time and to set goals for the future. This is covered in more detail in Chapter 8.

Other ways in which you can gain feedback about how your setting is performing with respect to health and safety might be to audit the accident records, the COSHH (Control of Substances Hazardous to Health) file, and the training records of staff to ensure that all are up to date and any problems are dealt with.

5.2 Evaluate the health, safety and risk management policies, procedures and practices within the work setting

Activity 1.5.2

Undertake an evaluation of the health and safety activities within your own work setting and compile a folder of evidence for your next AQAA.

5.3 Identify areas of policies, procedures and practices that need improvement to ensure safety and protection in the work setting

5.4 Recommend changes to policies, procedures and practices that ensure safety and protection in the work setting

When identifying areas for improvement and recommending change, you need to consider the following:

■ What has changed in legislation or what recent innovations in care practice require the construction of new policies or procedures?

■ Are all staff fully aware of the health and safety procedures within the workplace or is more training needed to ensure they have up-to-date knowledge?

■ How will you go about recommending the changes needed and what will you need to do to ensure the changes are accepted?

By undertaking a review of your processes and your behaviour with respect to health and safety on a regular basis, you are in a good position to identify weak points and potential areas for improvement. In this way you can ensure that the policies you have in place are effectively protecting the individuals who come into contact with your setting.

Activity 1.5.3

Identify an area of practice that needs improvement to ensure safety and make a recommendation for change to a particular policy.

Document the process you undertake to do this and keep in your portfolio for assessment.

Summary

Having completed the activities in this chapter you may now have a very different view of health and safety and its place in the work setting. The Health and Safety rulings we hear about from time to time which detail issues of neglect or unsafe practice may make us think more carefully about the way in which we carry out health and safety processes in our own settings. It is true that often we may hear of some settings and organisations that have taken a very literal approach to some health and safety rulings and this can often lead to ridicule. This somewhat 'risk averse' attitude can be changed with the implementation of excellent risk assessment strategies and training for staff to help them to be confident in the use of such tools.

It goes without saying that without exception, *all* care managers must know and practise the legal aspects of health and safety in order to deal with staff, clients and patients in a safe manner.

In this chapter you have been reminded of the health and safety legislation that affects you in your workplace and the responsibilities you have with respect to yourself, your environment and your clients. In addition, your understanding required of Health and Safety Risk Management, including the development of policies, procedures and practices in health and social care or children and young people's settings, has been addressed through the activities you have undertaken.

Learning outcomes	Assessment criteria
1 Understand the current legislative framework and organisational health, safety and risk management policies, procedures and practices that are relevant to health and social care or children and young people's settings	**(1.1)** Explain the legislative framework for health, safety and risk management in the work setting **Activity 1.1.1, p.3** **(1.2)** Analyse how policies, procedures and practices in your own setting meet health, safety and risk management requirements **Activity 1.1.2, p.6**
2 Be able to implement and monitor compliance with health, safety and risk management requirements in health and social care or children and young people's settings	**(2.1)** Demonstrate compliance with health, safety and risk management procedures **Activity 1.2.1, p.7** **(2.2)** Support others to comply with legislative and organisational health, safety and risk management policies, procedures and practices relevant to their work **Activity 1.2.1, p.7** **(2.3)** Explain the actions to take when health, safety and risk management, procedures and practices are not being complied with **Activity 1.2.2, p.8** **(2.4)** Complete records and reports on health, safety and risk management issues according to legislative and organisational requirements **Activity 1.2.3, p.9**
3 Be able to lead the implementation of policies, procedures and practices to manage risk to individuals and others in health and social care or children and young people's settings	**(3.1)** Contribute to development of policies, procedures and practices to identify, assess and manage risk to individuals and others **Activity 1.3.1, p.10** **Activity 1.3.2, p.11** **(3.2)** Work with individuals and others to assess potential risks and hazards **Activity 1.3.1, p.10** **Activity 1.3.2, p.11** **(3.3)** Work with individuals and others to manage potential risks and hazards **Activity 1.3.1, p.10** **Activity 1.3.2, p.11**

4 Be able to promote a culture where needs and risks are balanced with health and safety practice in health and social care or children and young people's settings	**(4.1)** Work with individuals to balance the management of risk with individual rights and the views of others **Activity 1.4.1, p.12**
	(4.2) Work with individuals and others to develop a balanced approach to risk management that takes into account the benefits for individuals of risk taking **Activity 1.4.1, p.12**
	(4.3) Evaluate own practice in promoting a balanced approach to risk management **Activity 1.4.2, p.13**
	(4.4) Analyse how helping others to understand the balance between risk and rights improves practice **Activity 1.4.2, p.13**
5 Be able to improve health, safety and risk management policies, procedures and practices in health and social care or children and young people's settings	**(5.1)** Obtain feedback on health, safety and risk management policies, procedures and practices from individuals and others **Activity 1.5.1, p.13**
	(5.2) Evaluate the health, safety and risk management policies, procedures and practices within the work setting **Activity 1.5.2, p.14**
	(5.3) Identify areas of policies, procedures and practices that need improvement to ensure safety and protection in the work setting **Activity 1.5.3, p.15**
	(5.4) Recommend changes to policies, procedures and practices that ensure safety and protection in the work setting **Activity 1.5.3, p.15**

References

CSCI (2007) *Rights, Risks and Restraints: An exploration into the use of restraint in the care of older people.* CSCI.

Department of Health (2000) *Domiciliary Care – National Minimum Standards.* London: HMSO.

Department of Health (2007), *Independence, Choice and Risk: a guide to best practice in supported decision making.* London: HMSO.

Dimond, B. (1997) *Legal Aspects of Care in the Community.* Basingstoke: Macmillan.

HSE (2010) *An Introduction to Health and Safety: Health and safety in small businesses.* Sudbury, Suffolk: HSE. (www.hse.gov.uk/pubns/indg259.pdf)

Morgan, S. (2004) 'Positive risk-taking: an idea whose time has come'. Health Care Risk Report, **10**(10), pp.18–19.

Titterton, M. (2005) *Risk and Risk Taking in Health and Social Welfare.* London: Jessica Kingsley Publishing.

Titterton, M. (2010) *Positive Risk Taking.* Edinburgh: Hale.

www.haletrust.com

www.hse.gov.uk/pubns/indg163.pdf

2

Unit M2c Work in partnership in health and social care or children and young people's settings

'One of our main aims for the future is to make sure that health and social services will work together and share information to give "joined-up" care to the people they work for. Services will share information about the people in their care so that health, housing, benefits and other needs are considered together. By 2008, anyone with long-term health and social care needs should have an integrated Personal Health and Social Care Plan, if they want one. All Primary Care Trusts and local authorities should have joint health and social care managed networks and/or teams for people with complex needs. We will also be building modern NHS community hospitals, which will offer integrated health and social services.'

Department of Health, 2006

The government agenda to ensure that integrated 'joined-up' services are offered to all, as outlined in the quote above, means that as managers of care settings, it is necessary to understand the whole

premise of what it means to work in partnership with other care professionals.

In this chapter we will look at how we can promote effective partnership working by establishing good working relationships with all care services we deal with on a daily basis, our own colleagues and the families of the people we care for.

You are also advised to look at Chapter 7 on teamwork, which will also be useful in completing the activities for this unit.

Learning outcomes
By the end of this chapter you will:

1. Understand partnership working.

2. Be able to establish and maintain working relationships with colleagues.

3. Be able to establish and maintain working relationships with other professionals.

4. Be able to work in partnership with others.

1 Understand partnership working

1.1 Identify the features of effective partnership working

Before we look specifically at partnership working we should remind ourselves of the wider organisation in which we work. We will deal with the NHS as the main service although we are aware that some of you may also work in partnership with the education system and local authorities.

As one of the largest employers in the world with over 1.3 million staff, the National Health Service (NHS) is the biggest health service provider in Europe. You will appreciate then that within such a large organisation there will be many different types of groups and teams working together in an effort to ensure that the best health service is achieved.

Figure 2.1 outlines the structure of the NHS in England since April 2002.

The Secretary of State for Health is the government minister in charge of the Department of Health, and this minister is responsible for the NHS, social work and social care in England and is appointed by the Prime Minister. Responsibility for the overall planning of the health service and for taking forward health and social care policies falls to the Department of Health and the NHS Executive. The 28 Strategic Health Authorities provide the link between the Department of Health and the NHS and plan health care for the population of the region they cover.

You will be aware of the terms 'primary' and 'secondary' health services. Primary care services include general medical practitioners (GPs), community midwives, district nursing, dentists, opticians, practice managers, pharmacists, amongst others, and these are all provided locally, near to where patients live.

The World Health Organization (WHO, 1978) defined primary health care as:

'the first level contact of individuals, the family and the community with the national health system which brings health care as close as possible to where people live and work.'

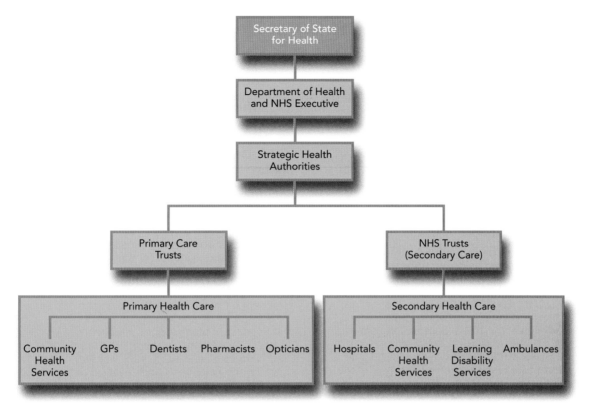

Figure 2.1 Structure of the National Health Service
Office of Health Economics (2009)

'Secondary care' refers to the more specialised services, including hospitals but also ambulances and specialised health services for the mentally ill and the learning disabled.

Figure 2.2 An example of secondary care

These are under the authority of the NHS Trusts whereas the Primary Care Trusts provide primary care services. In addition, the Primary Care Trusts are also responsible for buying almost all of the health care, both primary and secondary, required by the local populations they serve. They do this by using allocated funds from the Department of Health and must decide how much to spend on which health care services for the local population (Office of Health Economics, 2009).

The White Paper *Equity and Excellence: Liberating the NHS* highlights a newer structure for 2011 when a more streamlined NHS would be in place.

The document states:

> 'As a result of the changes, the NHS will be streamlined with fewer layers of bureaucracy. Strategic Health Authorities and Primary Care Trusts will be phased out. Management costs will be reduced so that as much resource as possible supports frontline services. The reforms build on changes started under the previous Government.'

Department of Health, 2010

At time of writing, the Health and Social Care Bill is making its way through parliament but is currently not as widely accepted by politicians and health care professionals as first thought and we await further developments. The Bill proposes to create an independent NHS Board, promote patient choice, and to reduce NHS administration costs. Some of the key things it hopes to accomplish are:

- The establishment of an independent NHS Board to allocate resources and provide commissioning guidance.
- To increase GPs' powers to commission services on behalf of their patients.
- To strengthen and improve the role of the Care Quality Commission.
- To develop Monitor, a body that is responsible for regulating NHS foundation trusts, into an economic regulator which will oversee aspects of access and competition.
- To cut the number of health bodies in order to reduce NHS administration costs by a third, including abolishing Primary Care Trusts and Strategic Health Authorities.

In essence the Health and Social Care Bill plans to devolve commissioning of health care to GP commissioning consortia from 2013 when the PCTs will disappear. With this change the local authorities would need to extend existing partnership arrangements and make new arrangements with GP commissioning consortia. As a result there will be a joint commissioning of pathways, services and systems and also further integration of multi-disciplinary staff teams. Partnership working will be extended throughout the NHS.

As you will appreciate, with such a huge number of people all delivering services at different areas and locations, joint working with other health professionals is paramount if the client is to receive the best service. We will look later at evidence where this has not happened, with dire consequences.

Partnership working has been described as a joint working arrangement where the partners all agree to achieve a common goal for the client despite being independent bodies. In order to do this there is a need to create a new organisational structure or process which is separate from their own organisation and in which they plan and implement a jointly-agreed programme, sometimes with joint staff or resources. There is a sharing of relevant information and a culture of shared ownership and common working arrangements across organisational and professional boundaries.

This sort of working is now integral to the way local authorities have developed community strategies with partners. The sharing of information has enabled councils and their partners to reach a better understanding of local problems and has helped to improve the efficiency of support services.

Activity 2.1.1

Demonstrate your understanding of effective partnership working by writing a reflective piece.

1.2 Explain the importance of partnership working with

- **colleagues**
- **other professionals**
- **others.**

Partnership working has been set up to improve the experience and outcomes of people who use the service and this can be achieved by minimising barriers between different services.

In 2002 the National Service Framework heralded the extension of such working with the recommendation for 'more formalised structures and systems for achieving joint aims.'

Through the use of Health Improvement and Modernisation Plans (HIMPs), partnership working between the NHS, local agencies and communities became the main focus and three-year strategic plans on how all partners were to address health improvement, health inequalities and NHS modernisation were written. PCTs became the key health organisation to represent health within wider partnership working but this is likely to change in the future.

This way of working has benefits for all involved in the care process. For clients it has meant a more 'joined up' approach to the care they receive. Having a single assessment process instead of multiple assessments by different agencies has been well received by clients and extends their choice.

The service users are ultimately our customers and they are at the centre of designing and delivering health and social care services. The Department of Health has actively promoted the involvement of service users and the public in decisions about the planning, design, development and delivery of local services and service users see themselves as having a particular role to play, not least because they are 'experts in their own experience'.

For health professionals, partnership working has improved the quality of the service they offer and has proved to be more cost effective, thus securing jobs. By recognising common goals, a 'whole person' approach can be taken to care and there has been a growth in the understanding of other care professionals' roles and mutual respect is therefore built.

Family carers also play a huge role in caring for their own family members, and are a major part of the partnership in care. It is important for health professionals to recognise and respect the role of lay carers and to support the role. Over the last 20 years or so there has been greater recognition of the benefits of family members providing care, particularly if it helps to maintain the family member in their own home. With detailed knowledge of their loved ones' preferences, illness, culture and value systems, these lay carers are better equipped to provide the loving support the client needs. In the past, however, lay carers were rather a neglected species and felt isolated and unsupported. Health professionals need therefore to ensure that the relatives of clients are involved in care planning processes and assessments.

Activity 2.1.2

Identify the features and importance of effective partnership working for your own organisation.

1.3 Analyse how partnership working delivers better outcomes

When two high profile legal cases hit the headlines and revealed problems in health and social care due to poor communication between care services, it became apparent that the lack of working together in partnership was having tragic consequences. In June 1998, a public inquiry into the management of children receiving cardiac surgical services at Bristol Royal Infirmary was undertaken. Following a higher than expected number of deaths of children, there had been concern raised about the surgery. It was evident that more children died in Bristol than anywhere else in the country following the same operation.

The inquiry made a number of recommendations, one of which was to improve the communication between patients and colleagues. In respect of the way of working, it was further recommended that the development of teamwork and effective leadership should be paramount and there should be a greater focus on multi-disciplinary working or better partnerships.

The final statement revealed that effective teamwork and partnership working did not exist and that the relationships between various professionals were on occasions poor and there was a lack of clinical leadership.

In Section 59 of the recommendations, the inquiry authors stated the following:

'The culture of the future must be a culture of safety and of quality; a culture of openness and of accountability; a culture of public service; a culture in which collaborative teamwork is prized; and a culture of flexibility in which innovation can flourish in response to patients' needs.' The Bristol Royal Infirmary Inquiry, 2001

The inquiry made the suggestion that a multi-professional team should share responsibility and this is just what partnership working involves, a collective, collaborative effort of all those concerned with the care of the patient. Patients do not belong to any one profession but are the responsibility of everybody who comes into contact with them to provide care. See the following website for further information: www.bristol-inquiry.org.uk/final_report/index.htm

It was the death of Victoria Climbié (2003) that forced a further inquiry and highlighted concern about how social services, health and the police co-operated with each other and local education and local authorities. (For full details of the report go to www.education.gov.uk/publications/ and search for 'Victoria Climbié'.)

Again, recommendations 14, 15 and 16 are all concerned with team working, communication and inter-agency working and further advised that improvements in the way information is exchanged within and between agencies are imperative if children are to be adequately safeguarded.

Integration is seen as the assimilation of organisations and/or services into single entities, allowing for greater transparency between partners as well as enhanced benefits for service users (Tilmouth et al., 2011).

The two cases above have shown us how poor communication led to tragic consequences and spurred the movement on towards a more cohesive approach to care. Partnership working enables the strategic goals and vision of the organisation in which we work to be jointly discussed and understood. It enables agreement to be reached on how the care for a client can be implemented in the best interests of that client and their families, as well as the staff.

The Social Partnership Forum's website highlights the benefits of good partnership working as being:

- trust and mutual respect
- openness, honesty and transparency
- top-level commitment
- positive and constructive approach
- commitment to work with and learn from each other
- early discussion – no surprises
- confidentiality when needed.

www.socialpartnershipforum.org/Pages/home.aspx

Working in partnership therefore provides safe, quality care from a range of providers who have the client/patient at the centre of the whole process.

Activity 2.1.3

Using an example from your own practice, show how partnership working has delivered better outcomes.

1.4 Explain how to overcome barriers to partnership working

Health and social care professionals work together at three levels:

- Strategic – planning and sharing information.
- Operational management – policies that demonstrate partnership.
- Individual care – joint training and a single point of access to health care.

However, all these working arrangements involve individuals from different professional backgrounds, and locations, with different funding and resources and philosophies of care and as such are potentially prone to challenges.

Armistead and Pettigrew (2004) made the point that:

> 'It is important to recognise that the very term "partnership" might increasingly be perceived pejoratively, synonymous with lengthy, fruitless meetings, forced upon unwilling organisations by... government policy.'

Various authors have demonstrated what barriers have been described with respect to partnership working and these include lack of role clarity.

Lack of role clarity

The various roles which come together in partnerships can make joint working difficult particularly where there are perceived differences in status between occupational groups. Some practitioners may feel that their professional status is threatened and this can lead to problems in coming to joint decisions.

In addition, joint employment conditions between different organisations can also be a barrier to joint working, particularly where new patterns of working are being requested at the same time. This can lead to resistance to change with resulting poor staff morale and poor morale from other partners – particularly service users and the community.

Financial barriers

When professionals have different pay scales according to their professional group and their role within it, this can cause conflict and barriers to the way in which a partnership will work. In addition, if staff notice that money is used to employ staff from one group to provide a service normally provided by their own staff, resentment sets in. Staff shortages can also damage interaction and the groups will start to withdraw in an attempt to limit demands that are being made.

Different resources

The barriers that exist can be divided into three areas: money, information and time. Where money is in short supply for some partners, this can become a huge issue when establishing budgets and costs for various initiatives.

Partnership working involves costs and this can be frustrating and lead to barriers forming.

Information also poses constraints and these revolve around, not only reluctance to share data, but also linking incompatible IT systems and the way in which records are kept in each organisation.

Time is another area where barriers are widespread. With increasing numbers of partnerships developing, the time spent on meetings and travelling can be an issue and may lead to the outcomes achieved being much less than originally perceived.

Different priorities and cultures

Staff working in different disciplines prioritise the care they give in a variety of different ways. If we lack understanding of how a service works and constantly question the way in which they carry out care, this can lead to barriers forming. In addition, our whole ethos of working may be vastly different to that of the partner and this can lead to questioning of the care they give. An underlying lack of understanding about how care can be delivered in different ways could damage the partnership.

There have been a number of initiatives to try to break down barriers and we can learn a lesson from education here. It has long been a tradition to segregate students in universities based on their chosen professional pathway, but it has been shown that this way of teaching can lead to 'professional arrogance' (Leathard, 1994) and the notion that some groups and degrees are 'better than others'.

Postgraduate education has addressed this and now offers a significant number of Master of Science (MSc) and Master of Arts (MA) level programmes which encompass multi-professional participation. This active development to include a varied studentship has led to a greater understanding of other disciplines with which we may not usually come into contact. The same could be true of multi-disciplinary working. By working in close contact with someone from another professional area, we are able to enhance our knowledge of their role and can better understand how they approach care from a different perspective.

A further way in which barriers can be broken down is simply to address the communication systems between professional groups. Successful collaboration depends on open and transparent discussion. Traditionally, communication has relied on written formats – referral forms, feedback forms, case notes, care plans, letters and faxes. However, whilst quality record-keeping and evidence-based policies and procedures are necessary, there does need to be more one-to-one collaboration and active participation in meeting with partners on a regular basis.

By engaging the family in all decision making and supporting them in their aims to help their loved ones, barriers to the partnership can become a thing of the past. The whole ethos of care put forward by the government document *Putting People First* encouraged 'person-centred care' and this requires complete recognition of the needs and choices of the person receiving care. By ensuring that support is available to families and the client and by listening to those on the receiving end of care, a better quality of life can be expected.

Activity 2.1.4

Explain how you have managed to overcome barriers to partnership working within your own work area.

2 Be able to establish and maintain working relationships with colleagues

3 Be able to establish and maintain working relationships with other professionals

2.1 Explain own role and responsibilities in working with colleagues

3.1 Explain own role and responsibilities in working with other professionals

As we noticed in the last section, in working in partnership you will be working alongside different people from a variety of disciplines, as well as members of the client's family and colleagues within your own team. One of the responsibilities you have then is to maintain an open mind about the way in which other services work and respect the roles of others in the care they give. For your colleagues you also need to create a working environment which promotes national policies with respect to partnership working.

In the White Paper *Equity and Excellence: Liberating the NHS* (2010) the emphasis is on collaborative working within the public sector as stated below:

'We want a sustainable adult social care system that gives people support and freedom to lead the life they choose, with dignity. We recognise the critical interdependence between the NHS and the adult social care system in securing better outcomes for people, including carers. We will seek to break down barriers between health and social care funding to encourage preventative action.'

Department of Health, 2010

The Government White Paper *Our Health, Our Care, Our Say: A new direction for community services* sets out a number of key priorities for health and social care.

The statement is printed below:

'There should be more co-ordination between the health service, social care and the local authority. There needs to be more communication between them.

'One of our main aims for the future is to make sure that health and social services will work together and share information to give "joined-up" care to the people they work for. Services will share information about the people in their care so that health, housing, benefits and other needs are considered together. By 2008, anyone with long-term health and social care needs should have an integrated Personal Health and Social Care Plan, if they want one. All Primary Care Trusts and local authorities should have joint health and social care managed networks and/or teams for people with complex needs. We will also be building modern NHS community hospitals, which will offer integrated health and social services'.

Department of Health, 2006

Effective working in health and social care requires collaboration. In addition, effective team work enhances patient care and safety as members of the team coordinate and communicate their activities and have the patient at the centre of the care.

One of your main roles will be to act as a link person in the partnership, whether it is with families or other professionals and also to develop a climate of trust between all partners.

Trust is such an important issue in management and leadership and is at a premium in today's working climate. If partnerships are to work, you need to ensure that you have created trust in your organisation by being open and reliable in your decision making and by articulating a commitment to the way in which the partnership is to work. Jobs are being lost on a daily basis, and there is a climate of downsizing and outsourcing of work which will all have had an effect on your workforce and the partners with whom you work.

When there is a lack of trust, the result is fear, suspicion and insecurity and this all leads to lowering of morale in general with resultant resistance to change and reduced productivity.

The Authentic Leadership approach developed by George (2003) focussed on characteristics of good leaders. He found that authentic leaders have a strong desire to serve others and demonstrate five basic characteristics.

1. They have a purpose.

2. They have strong values and are clear about the right thing to do.

3. They establish trusting relationships.

4. They demonstrate self-discipline.

5. They are passionate about their mission.

George (2003) further noted that individuals wanted their leaders to be open with them and to become more transparent, thus softening the boundary between roles. A trusting relationship with the leader leads to greater commitment to the mission and also loyalty.

As a manager your role in this will be to create a high-trust culture which ensures that your staff and the people in the partnership feel safe and valued. Communication again is important and in an atmosphere where trust is central to the workings of the team, individuals will feel able to contribute fully.

The document *Partnerships: A literature review* (2007) published by the Institute of Public Health in Ireland had this to say:

'For most partnerships, building trust between partners is the most important ingredient in success. This may be particularly difficult if the problem that the partnership is addressing stems from a legacy of mistrust or conflict between different agencies. It also takes time. One large urban regeneration partnership holds regular "away days" for partners to have a frank exchange of views on the partnership's progress. These help to develop trust by encouraging partners to understand their policy differences more fully, but they do represent a substantial investment of time. However, a high level of trust within the partnership is one of the best ways of avoiding the risk of excessive bureaucracy that can arise when partners feel that they must all be involved in every detail of the partnership's operations.'

Activity 2.2.1

Reflect upon your own role and responsibilities in working with colleagues and other professionals.

Provide evidence of partnership working you have been involved in and comment upon its success. What might you change in the future?

2.2 Develop and agree common objectives when working with colleagues

3.3 Agree common objectives when working with other professionals within the boundaries of your own role and responsibilities

You will be familiar with the notion of setting objectives in order to achieve aims. Part of your role as a manager and leader will be to educate your staff and, as such, you set objectives as to what you hope the learners attending your session will gain as a result of being there. So too with partnership working. There needs to be a good balance between developing the partnership and its objectives in order for it to be successful.

It is all too easy to get carried away with the actual work that needs to be done within the partnership without recognising the differences that might exist between all concerned. For example, we may make assumptions about the way in which other organisations or individuals work and lose sight of what we are actually there for.

Partnership objectives need to be consistent with those of the partner organisations, and other representatives, and we also need to be fully aware of where the boundaries lie between the partnership's work and their own organisation's activities.

In making a more effective partnership, it is essential to invest in building good objectives from the outset. The following set of objectives may be useful:

- Define the partnership role and purpose – What are we here for? What is the partnership actually supposed to do?

- Agree who is to be involved – Who should be invited onto the partnership and how will we select them?

- Establishing protocols and procedures – What structures underpin the partnership?

- Ground rules and behaviour – Set your standards for behaviour and language to build trust and respect.

- Who is in charge? Sharing power and engaging minority interests – ensure that equal parity is given to all groups.

- How will we ensure our activity is widely known? Communication and accountability – letting those outside the partnership know what's going on.

Part of your role as a manager is to encourage others to work effectively and one way to achieve this is to work towards the same goals and to cooperate with the decisions made. When properly managed and developed, such teamwork improves processes and produces results quickly and economically through the free exchange of ideas and information (Tilmouth *et al.*, 2010).

2.3 Evaluate own working relationship with colleagues

3.4 Evaluate procedures for working with other professionals

Activities 2.2.2

Look at the way in which you work with people in your own team and with other professionals and identify your own strengths and weaknesses in these arrangements.

Ask colleagues and other professionals to comment upon your assessment. Write a reflection of what you might do to improve your working arrangements.

We hope that you got some useful feedback from staff and other professional colleagues in undertaking the last activity. However, you may have found some concerns with respect to the ways in which working relationships change as a result of partnership development.

In any environment where there are a range of groups working together from a variety of locations, problems can occur. Pearson and Spencer (1997) commented on this issue and said that the complexity of this way of working was not always good for building inter-professional relationships. This way of working means that the team has too many members to be an effective size and planning meetings can be problematic, trying to get all professionals together at the same time.

With your own staff you may have had a more positive response. Being in close proximity to your team makes it so much easier to communicate and work together, making this type of working more stable and predictable.

2.4 Deal constructively with any conflict that may arise with colleagues

3.5 Deal constructively with any conflict that may arise with other professionals

We cover this particular subject in Chapters 7 and 8 and you are advised to refer to these now.

The *Partnership Working – How To Guide* provided by the Scottish Centre for Regeneration (www.communitiesscotland.gov.uk/stellent/groups/public/documents/webpages/cs_011414.hcsp) provides a useful list of The Top Ten Partnership Killers and potentially the things most likely to cause conflict. We précis this document here.

1. **Outliving their usefulness.** A partnership that lives on beyond its purpose will either wither slowly, creating dissatisfaction among those who stick to the bitter end, or create an excuse for people to leave the office for useless meetings!

    The solution: Have a definite end date and exit and know when the job is done and what you might leave in place.

2. **Competition** between organisations can be useful but too much can lead to blame and self-righteousness.

    The solution: Spend time on team building and developing a sense of shared purpose – build relationships between organisations to blur the boundaries.

3. **The wrong person as representative** in the partnership may make decision making a lengthy process. For example, if representatives from other organisations have to go back to their parent organisations for decisions, a partnership will be powerless.

    The solution: Ensure the people on your partnership have the authority to decide much of the business at the meetings.

4. **Pulling rank.** Non-parity with respect to hierarchical positions may see the higher paid or higher graded officers pulling rank around the table and effectively silencing others who have just as much to give.

    The solution: Maintain the principle of 'equality around the table' and write this into your terms of reference.

5. **Going off the point.** Often a partnership where people are working well will come up with other ideas beyond the partnership's original brief. This will slow the work down.

    The solution: Agree a clear vision and underpin this with a clear focus on five to six priorities.

6. Many organisations will be **attracted to a partnership by money** and this motivation alone can kill a partnership through representatives unwilling to volunteer for shared activities, for instance.

    The solution: Set out clear, shared common ground from the start and focus on your shared priorities and outcomes.

7. **Set targets around the vision.** Don't be vague about what you hope to achieve. Many partnerships will come together around a

good idea but fail to set real targets around the shared vision.

The solution: Set clear targets to support and chart your progress – agree a simple but shared performance management system that everyone signs up to so you're all speaking the same language.

8. **Endless business meetings** that no-one wants to attend will result in non-attendance.

The solution: Keep business meetings short and focussed on what you need to do – not endless report-backs from people who are basically saying 'my project is better than yours'.

9. **We know what's best for you** partnerships which are based on consultation but fail to engage. 'Building your workplan on historical information is not enough – those meant to benefit may not want what you are offering!'

The solution: Base your partnership on a solid foundation of genuine consultation and ensure that you have built-in activities that continually engage your client group.

10. **Lack of communication** between partners will breed suspicion and resentment.

The solution: Set up good processes to network and share information.

From www.communitiesscotland.gov.uk

Conflict may arise at any time in any partnership and should not always be viewed as a negative occurrence. For example, it may highlight an important issue and lead to a better outcome for all concerned. The main aims in any conflict resolution is to communicate, listen and keep an open mind about the situation.

3.2 Develop procedures for effective working relationships with other professionals

4.2 Develop procedures for effective working relationships with others

The most important thing you can do to develop effective working relationships is to build your reputation as being a professional who is trustworthy and inspires confidence. In this way you can show that you provide other professionals with information, advice and support within the boundaries of your role and expertise and as such can develop the procedures for partnership working which is fair to all parties involved.

In working with families and carers there are a number of ways that health and social care organisations develop their procedures to ensure they meet the needs of carers. Some of these may be:

- To identify a mentor within the organisation who will be the first point of contact for carers and will take primary responsibility for making sure that carers' needs are considered.

- Provide 'carer awareness' training for all staff to ensure they understand what role the care will be taking.

- Develop links to local carers' organisations to explore ways of working together.

- Develop a Carers' Charter to ensure that best practice guidelines for working with carers and staff are identified and that staff are aware of these.

- Start up a staff carers' network.

- Make sure information for carers is available and well publicised.

- Involve carers in service planning and development.

- Provide training for carers in areas such as lifting and handling, continence care, use of equipment, stress management and maximising their own health and well-being.

4 Be able to work in partnership with others

4.1 Analyse the importance of working in partnership with others

We have seen from the previous text that the primary purpose of partnership working is to improve the experience and outcomes of people who use services and this is achieved by minimising organisational barriers between different services. In addition partnerships work by:

- delivering co-ordinated packages of services to individuals

- reducing the impact of organisational fragmentation

- bidding for, or gaining access to, new resources

- meeting a statutory requirement.

The rest of this section will be delivered by means of a summary activity.

You need to compile a case study which shows how you have set up a partnership with either a client and their carer or another organisation and show the whole process of that venture.

Activities 2.4.1/2/3

4.3 Agree common objectives when working with others within the boundaries of own role and responsibilities

Using an example from your own practice, reflect on how you set objectives for either a client and their family (carer) or for a new partnership development with another organisation.

Say how you established the working relationship and what process you went through in setting objectives.

4.4 Evaluate procedures for working with others

Use the GROW model as shown in Chapter 7 or undertake a SWOT analysis to show how you might make changes to the whole process as a result of your evaluation.

4.5 Deal constructively with any conflict that may arise with others

Did you experience any conflict throughout the process? Reflect on how you dealt with it and what you learned from your activity.

Summary

In this chapter we have addressed the government agenda to ensure that integrated 'joined-up' services are offered to all, and what this means to you as managers of care settings and your work as partners with other care professionals and clients' families, as well as the client themselves.

Effective partnership working can be promoted by establishing good working relationships with all care services we deal with on a daily basis, our own colleagues and the families of the people we care for.

As a productive way of achieving more efficient and effective use of resources, partnership working can be a powerful tool. It can also be fraught with difficulties and conflict.

Learning outcomes	Assessment criteria
1 Understand partnership working	(1.1) Identify the features of effective partnership working **Activity 2.1.1, p.20**
	(1.2) Explain the importance of partnership working with ■ Colleagues ■ Other professionals ■ Others **Activity 2.1.2, p.21**
	(1.3) Analyse how partnership working delivers better outcomes **Activity 2.1.3, p.21**
	(1.4) Explain how to overcome barriers to partnership working **Activity 2.1.4, p.23**

Learning outcomes	Assessment criteria
2 Be able to establish and maintain working relationships with colleagues	**(2.1)** Explain own role and responsibilities in working with colleagues **Activity 2.2.1, p.24**
	(2.2) Develop and agree common objectives when working with colleagues **See p.24 for guidance.**
	(2.3) Evaluate own working relationship with colleagues **Activity 2.2.2, p.25**
	(2.4) Deal constructively with any conflict that may arise with colleagues **See p.25 for guidance.**
3 Be able to establish and maintain working relationships with other professionals	**(3.1)** Explain own role and responsibilities in working with other professionals **Activity 2.2.1, p.24**
	(3.2) Develop procedures for effective working with other professionals **See p.26 for guidance.**
	(3.3) Agree common objectives when working with other professionals within the boundaries of own role and responsibilities **See p.24 for guidance.**
	(3.4) Evaluate procedures for working with other professionals **Activity 2.2.2, p.25**
	(3.5) Deal constructively with any conflict that may arise with other professionals **See p.25 for guidance.**

4 Be able to work in partnership with others

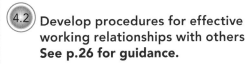

4.1 Analyse the importance of working in partnership with others
See p.26 for guidance.

4.2 Develop procedures for effective working relationships with others
See p.26 for guidance.

4.3 Agree common objectives when working with others within the boundaries of own role and responsibilities
Activity 2.4.1, p.27

4.4 Evaluate procedures for working with others
Activity 2.4.1, p.27

4.5 Deal constructively with any conflict that may arise with others
Activity 2.4.1, p.27

References

Armistead, C. G. and Pettigrew, P. (2004) 'Effective Partnerships: Building a sub-regional network of reflective practitioners', *The International Journal of Public Sector Management*, 17(7), pp.571–85.

Audit Commission (1998) *A Fruitful Partnership – Effective partnership working.*

Boydell, L. (2007) *Partnerships: A literature review.* Dublin: Institute of Public Health in Ireland.

DfE (2004) *Removing Barriers to Achievement: the Government's strategy for meeting special educational needs.* London: HMSO.

Department of Health (2002) *National Service Framework: A practical aid to implementation in primary care.* London: HMSO.

Department of Health (2006) *Our Health, Our Care, Our Say; a New Direction for Community Services.* London: HMSO.

Department of Health (2007) *Putting People First: A shared vision and committment to the transformation of adult social care.* London: HMSO.

Department of Health (2010) *Equity and Excellence: Liberating the NHS.* London: HMSO.

George, B. (2003) *Authentic Leadership: Rediscovering the secrets to creating lasting value.* San Francisco: Jossey-Bass.

Leathard, A. (1994) *Going Inter-professional: Working together for health and welfare.* Routledge: London and New York.

Office of Health Economics (2009) *The NHS – organisation and structure* (http://oheschools. org/ohech4pg2.html)

Pearson, P. and Spencer, J. (1997) *Promoting Teamwork in Primary Care: A research-based approach.* London: Arnold

Tilmouth, T., Davies-Ward, E. and Williams, B. (2011) *Foundation Degree in Health and Social Care.* London: Hodder Education.

Whitmore, J. (2003) *Coaching for Performance: GROWing people, performance and purpose* (3e). London: Nicolas Brealey.

The World Health Organization (WHO) (1978) *Declaration of Alma Ata* www.who.int/hpr/NPH/docs/declaration_almaata.pdf

The Bristol Royal Infirmary Inquiry (2001) www.bristol-inquiry.org.uk/final_report/report/Summary.htm

www.socialpartnershipforum.org/PartnershipWorkingInTheNHS/Benefits/Pages/Workforceqipp.aspx

3

Unit SHC 51 Use and develop systems that promote communication

When we first meet somebody or when we are dealing with work issues we need to be able to put people at ease so that they feel able to communicate their concerns. Understanding what it is the other person is saying rather than assuming we know is a most useful skill to develop in management. Our aim should be to finish the interaction leaving someone feeling better than they did before we met them. Effective interpersonal skill demands that we know ourselves well and are aware of what we bring to the relationship, and how we might impact on those we communicate with.

The purpose of this chapter is to revisit the systems of communication we use in care work and in particular in managing a care setting. In any relationship, be it personal or working, effective interpersonal skills play an essential part and being able to communicate well is one of the most important aspects of your role as a leader and manager. Misunderstanding and misinterpretation of the message can lead to team conflict and disruption to the smooth running of the organisation. Moreover, it can lead to ineffective delivery of services and unproductive teamwork. Being an effective communicator then holds the key to successful working.

By completing the activities for the unit which are included in the chapter, your knowledge, understanding and skills of communication systems will be developed and assessed. The challenges and barriers to communication and the importance of effective management of information will be addressed, as will types of communication and the means of working in partnership with others.

Learning outcomes

By the end of this chapter you will:

1. Be able to address the range of communication requirements in own role.

2. Be able to improve communication systems and practices that support positive outcomes for individuals.

3. Be able to improve communication systems to support partnership working.

4. Be able to use systems for effective information management.

1 Be able to address the range of communication requirements in own role

1.1 **Review the range of groups and individuals whose communication needs must be addressed in own job role**

Communication is the basis of interaction and skills in speaking, writing and, in particular, listening are essential in health and social care. Most of the therapeutic interactions and communication we carry out within health and social care settings are with vulnerable people or their families and with staff and visitors. An important point to remember is the fact that sometimes you will be communicating with a person who is going through personal crisis or is feeling upset in some way and this therefore requires excellent skills in making sure the person feels supported and valued.

The effectiveness of your communication skills as a manager and leader within the care setting will undoubtedly lead to the success of the organisation and the team with which you work.

But to whom will you be communicating in your own particular setting?

Activity 3.1.1

Think about and make a list of all the relationships and contacts you may have within the course of your managerial role.

Figure 3.1 displays some of the relationships and contacts you may have.

Figure 3.1 Relationships and contacts

You may even have more but the point is, that with such a diverse group of people interacting with you each day, there is a need for the use of a variety of communication skills, all highly dependent on the position of the person and the context in which the communication takes place. The recognition of this is paramount since many barriers to communication arise out of the use of inappropriate language and terminology being used which effectively means the message is lost. For example, the delivery of factual information can be quite impersonal and may be totally inappropriate when dealing with a vulnerable child or adult who requires an empathic response to a problem. However, a member of the medical staff may require just such a response. There needs to be flexibility when recognising the type of communication needed in various situations. Research in this area has been well documented and over the last 30 years or so we have seen some ground-breaking research from Macleod-Clark's work back in 1984, which noted the poor information giving and listening skills of nurses leading to breakdown in communication. This led to more research such as that by Davis and Fallowfield (1991) reporting on the general failure of communication and lack of empathy, Graham (1991) describing breakdown in respectful relationships leading to poor communication, and the work by Hewison in 1995, highlighting the power relationships and barriers to communications. You are advised to be aware of more recent texts which deal with communication and interpersonal skills by Burnard (1996) and Donnelly and Neville (2008).

Defining communication

To be skilled in communication requires us to be able to use a variety of interpersonal techniques and before we address these, let's look at some definitions of communication.

'Communication involves the reciprocal process in which messages are sent and received between two or more people.'

(Bazler Riley, 2008)

As we mentioned above, in order for the message to be received and understood there must be a matching of the appropriate communication with the individual to whom we are speaking and the circumstances in which the interaction takes place. Just imagine for a moment speaking to a four-year-old child in the way you might address a member of your staff. There would be a distinct lack of understanding on the part of the child and, if the situation were reversed, a feeling of being patronised for the member of staff! We will come back to this later on in the chapter.

Another definition coined by Crawford, Brown and Bonham (2006) suggests that:

> 'Communication is something we do in our internal world of thoughts and in our external world by speaking, writing, gestures, drawing, making images and symbols or receiving messages from others.'

So effective communication is the means by which we deliver and receive a message and both need to be congruent in order for the communication to work.

The next section gives more detail as to how we can do this

1.2 Explain how to support effective communication within own job role

Three-skill management approach

Robert Katz's skills approach to management and leadership has had a far-reaching effect in shaping our thinking about what constitutes the skills required by a good and effective leader. Katz (1955) suggested in his Three-Skill Approach that three basic personal skills, technical, human and conceptual, were competencies all leaders and managers could acquire, quite separately from the traits or qualities that many researchers had focussed on. These three skills were achievable through learning and not innate, as some leadership skills are often thought to be.

It is to the human skills we now turn our attention but throughout the book we will return to the skills approach.

In Katz's model, human skills refer to how we work with people effectively, creating an atmosphere of trust and cooperation, and being sensitive to the needs of others, involving them in the planning and decision making of the organisation where possible. The way in which we interact with each other in this respect will go a long way to achieving this.

When we look at the skills identified for leaders and managers we are made aware of the importance of communication.

Skills for Care (2006) published the diagram shown in Figure 3.2 to emphasise this.

Of all the skills involved in leading and managing, communication crosses both divides. Being effective in this then is crucial.

When we communicate effectively, we invariably use a variety of skills but more importantly, it is how we develop our relationships with others in the setting that is paramount to getting the message across and being effective.

In management roles we communicate with people who may be in a subordinate position to ourselves, those in more senior roles, peers and others such as visitors or other service providers. The direction of the communication will have a bearing on how you address these groups. For example, have a look at Figure 3.3.

There are a number of reasons for communicating as a manager and leader and these include the following:

- Delegation of work
- Conducting meetings
- Presentations
- Supervision and appraisal
- Report writing
- Building the team
- Negotiation
- Interviewing.

All of these tasks in themselves are detailed and can be further broken down to reveal more complex levels. An example might be helpful to explain what we mean here.

For example, let's look at supervision. Before undertaking such roles we need to be aware of what they entail. Our list might look like this:

- Function of supervision
- Who requires it?
- Mechanics of how it is carried out
- Record-keeping policies
- Conduct of the interview
- Evaluating the process.

Whatever the communication need or type, a good working relationship is essential, and one which demands that there is trust and the ability to be able to talk openly and honestly. In all communication that occurs in the course of your daily work you will undertake a variety of roles and will therefore need to adjust your communication to each circumstance. It is therefore important to know what role you are fulfilling in any interaction in health and social care settings. As we mentioned above, the different mix of people to which you will have access will require a different type of communication and you may find yourself

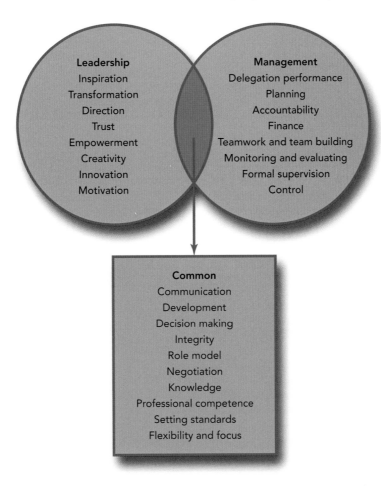

Figure 3.2 Leadership and management structures

undertaking the following throughout a span of duty:

- advising
- instructing
- welcoming
- assessing
- observing
- informing
- counselling.

↓ Discussing with or instructing a member of staff about work

↑ Providing senior staff with information

→ Sharing information with peers and those on same level as yourself

↗ Requesting and giving of information between departments and individuals of different hierarchical levels

Figure 3.3 Direction of communication (Gopee and Galloway, 2009, p.20)

Effective communicators make appropriate choices when it comes to deciding how they intend to interact and when they are clear about the purpose of the interaction.

Activity 3.1.2

In order to cover the criteria for this part of the unit undertake to do the following and keep your findings in your portfolio.

Keep a communication diary for one span of duty. Using the following questions show how you have undertaken the different types of communicating as shown below:

- advising
- instructing
- welcoming
- assessing
- observing

- informing
- counselling.

What context did the communication take place in?

What purpose did it have?

How successful was it?

You may have been surprised at how varied the types of communication which took place for you have been, and by now you will be realising that effective communicators are those people who adapt their communication style to the situation and respond in sensitive and empathetic ways to the needs of those to whom they are communicating. In supporting others to become effective communicators, it is necessary for you as a leader to be an effective role model and, where you are able, to reflect effectively on how you are communicating your messages.

Good and effective communicators are just as much aware of the skills and types of communication as they are of the need to affirm the self-worth of the person with whom they are interacting. What do we mean by this?

Anyone who has taken part in training as a counsellor will have come across the term 'unconditional positive regard and empathy' (Rogers, 1980).

Empathy is the ability to 'put yourself in the shoes of others' or to understand the client's frame of reference, and active listening skills are the best way to show this. This is different from showing sympathy which might make a person feel pitied. Unconditional positive regard is similar but goes a little further.

If we support all our communication by accepting and valuing the people with whom we interact in the expression of warmth and a non-judgemental attitude, we will improve our communication skills no end.

Have you ever been dealt with in a manner in which you felt judged by someone or who you felt was not listening to you? In this sort of situation it is very difficult to be open and honest about our feelings and needs. If we judge the people with whom we are interacting, whether they are staff or clients, then they may feel they are unable to open up to us in ways which might be detrimental to the organisation's aims and objectives. In other words your failure to communicate effectively will lead to lack of success.

We fully realise that occasionally it is difficult not to judge someone or at least dislike what they are saying or doing. Dealing with this in

an honest way shows that, although we may disagree with a point of view or an action, we still value them as an individual.

So, effective communication can be supported by you as a manager and leader by ensuring that your staff are all aware of the need to be flexible in the way in which they communicate within varied contexts and to engage in communication which is empathic and values the people with whom they interact. However, so often communication is challenged and breaks down and in the next section we will analyse how this happens.

1.3 Analyse the barriers and challenges to communication within own job role

Having looked at what makes for effective communication we can easily identify areas where barriers block communication. Sometimes when we feel that we are not communicating well we need to reflect on the reasons for the problem. A common complaint in large organisations is one of poor communication which often leads to conflict. It can be a major issue in whether or not the job gets done!

Activity 3.1.3

Think for a moment about a time when you felt your message just wasn't being received.

List the factors both internal and external that may have been the reasons for the blocks or barriers in communication.

You may have come up with some of the following reasons for blocks in communication or even more:

- Difference in culture and values.
- Negative feelings about the person you are speaking to or getting upset about what they are saying, leading to conflict.
- Difficulties in own life, making it difficult to concentrate.
- Feeling unsafe, due to person's demeanour or behaviour.
- Not listening effectively.
- Tiredness.
- Feeling unwell.
- Noise.
- Inappropriate environment.

Let's take the main ones from this list and look in more detail at how they affect our interactions.

Difference in culture and values

In health work we talk at length about 'fostering equality and diversity' and the importance of respecting the differences we may come across in people. We are talking not only about cultural differences but also about the differences in values that people hold. This can have a huge impact on our ability to communicate.

Living in a multi-cultural society it is important to be culturally aware in our interpersonal interactions. Miller (2006) says that defining the term culture is complex. When we talk about race, we often confuse the term with ethnicity and culture. Ethnicity, gender and social class, whilst all being relevant, should additionally include religious beliefs, sexuality, rationality, skin colour and experience of oppression (Miller, 2006).

Miller (2006) suggests that by developing a respectful curiosity about the beliefs and practices within all service users' lives, we are able to communicate in more meaningful ways (p.6).

Negative feelings about the person you are speaking to or getting upset about what they are saying

We occasionally meet with people who, for whatever reason, we just don't 'click' with. As a manager and leader you cannot be expected to like everybody you work with. As we mentioned earlier, we work in settings where there is a diverse population of people and we come into contact with all types of characters. Just like ourselves, others have their own feelings, values and attitudes and sometimes these may clash with how we see the world. We may not share their views or particularly like the stance the person takes, but as the manager and leader in a setting we do have to show tolerance of these views (providing they are not contravening any anti-discrimination policy) and, in this instance, we need to be fully aware of how we come across to those we are communicating with. It is possible that we may communicate our own dislike of somebody through our body language or the way we speak to them; this will have a negative effect on the interaction and may lead to conflict in the workplace.

Body language and non-verbal communication (NVC)

One of the things that we often do not pay enough attention to is our body language. Argyle (1978) pointed out that non-verbal communication can have as much as five times the impact on a person's understanding compared to the words spoken, so if we are displaying negative non-verbal signals this can prove problematic. Communication can be broken down as follows:

- 7% is what you say in words
- 38% is contributed to how you say it (volume, pitch, tone, rhythm, etc.)
- 55% reflects your body language (facial expressions, gestures, posture, etc.).

It is also good to remember that clients in a health and social care setting may have communication difficulties and may not pick up the non-verbal cues communicated (Crawford *et al.,* 2006).

The way in which we present ourselves can have as much if not more impact on whether our message is listened to and understood.

When communicating:

> 'our attention is focused on words rather than body language. But our judgement includes both. An audience is simultaneously processing both verbal and non-verbal cues. Body movements are not usually positive or negative in and of themselves; rather, the situation and the message will determine the appraisal.'
>
> (Givens, 2000, p.4)

It is therefore vital to ensure that our bodily actions match our speech in order to get our message across. Awareness of the way in which we conduct our communications through our non-verbal communication is just as important as what we say in some cases.

Conflict and resistance to change causing upset

When we come across a situation that is causing some conflict, this again may cause us to have negative feelings about a person.

Look at the following Case Study.

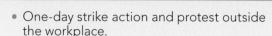

Case Study

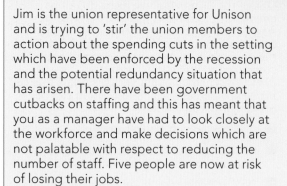

Jim is the union representative for Unison and is trying to 'stir' the union members to action about the spending cuts in the setting which have been enforced by the recession and the potential redundancy situation that has arisen. There have been government cutbacks on staffing and this has meant that you as a manager have had to look closely at the workforce and make decisions which are not palatable with respect to reducing the number of staff. Five people are now at risk of losing their jobs.

Jim has sent out an e-mail to all Unison members and is seeking the following commitment from union members:

- One-day strike action and protest outside the workplace.
- Non-cooperation at meetings, with all the Unison members turning their chairs to face the back of the room, staging a protest whilst being present.

Think about the following:

1. Comment *honestly* on how this makes you feel about Jim and his potential disruptive influence.

2. What is your initial response to the actions?

3. Now reflect on the above and say why you reacted this way and how you will respond to the situation.

Conflict is often viewed as a negative issue and becomes a problem when it affects our work, causes inappropriate behaviour and lowers morale, impacting on the workforce and the clients.

It is possible that your own thoughts about Jim are negative and it would be very difficult to have any sort of dialogue with him that can be positive at the present time. Perhaps you feel his actions are unjust and unfair; the cuts are not your fault, after all, but a result of a government drive to reduce costs in the NHS. You may even take this stance personally.

Your reactions are perfectly reasonable in such a situation but as a manager you have to now detach yourself from the subjective emotions of the situation, i.e. the personal feelings about Jim, and deal in a more objective way with the task at hand, that of reducing the impact of these actions and raising staff morale. A tall order!

John Adair in his book *Effective Teambuilding* (2000) came up with the following five strategies for dealing with conflict:

1. **Competing** – forcing your own ideas through because you believe your way is right.

2. **Confronting/collaborating** – by bringing all the issues into the open and exploring all feasible options you are showing an openness to change.

3. **Compromise** – negotiating halfway.

4. **Avoid** – opt out altogether and avoid taking up any position.

5. **Accommodate** – allowing the change to happen in order to not hurt feelings.

Having seen the above which will you opt for?

In dealing with any conflict, four key steps can be identified:

1. Describe the actual conflict and define it well.

2. Listen actively to all parties to fully understand the issues.

3. Emphasise the benefit of finding a way forward and the negative consequences of not doing so in order to secure the commitment of all parties to resolve the conflict by…

4. Reach(ing) an agreement.

In the incident above, the conflict is about the budget cuts impacting on your workforce. It is unavoidable and therefore you are unable to change it. But the way in which you approach the inevitable redundancies and unrest will go a long way to securing a happier outcome in the long run. The strategy which appears to be the most useful will be that of collaboration and confronting the issue and employing the views of all the workforce in exploring all the options.

What is happening here is a huge change to the way in which the people in this organisation are operating and any change is a difficult area to deal with. We will return to the theory and practice of change in Chapter 7 but a brief word here.

Craine (2007) comments that:

'People facing change often go through a cycle of emotions similar to those experienced when faced with the death of a loved one. Thus, by understanding the "grieving" process people use to deal with change, it may be possible to reduce some of the potentially damaging consequences.' (p.44)

In our scenario the people in the organisation face a loss in a small way similar to that suggested above and, as such, your understanding of the emotions they are feeling will help you in dealing with how to face the changes in an effective way.

With effective communication that encourages the person/team within the institution to accept and understand the reason for the change, you can move to a new way of working that is embraced by everyone (Cole, 2011).

Buono and Kerber (2010) further state that:

'It is important to create a climate of trust, honesty, and transparency. Persuasive and ethical communication is critical, ensuring both the clarity of the message and the honesty and trustworthiness of managers and executives. If organisational members do not trust the change implementer and his or her message, their acceptance of the change is unlikely.' (p.1)

We will return to this later on in the book.

Not listening effectively

Have you ever engaged in a conversation and been aware that the person you are speaking to is not listening? Undertake Activity 3.1.4 for evidence for your portfolio.

If we are to understand our staff and clients and be able to communicate, we need to be able to attend and listen to what they are saying and this is a very difficult skill to do well.

Active listening shows that our staff and clients have been heard and the way in which we do this is with the following skills:

- Acknowledging and reflecting feelings
- Body language
- Restating
- Paraphrasing
- Summarising
- Questioning.

Acknowledging and reflecting feelings

When we undertake this activity, all we are doing is repeating back to the person a word, phrase or sentence that they have spoken and, by doing so, they become aware that we are paying attention to what they are saying and are inviting them to continue with the conversation.

Body language

We mentioned the importance of this briefly above and we now turn to the work of Egan, who gave us the acronym **SOLER** (see Table 3.1)

Activity 3.1.4

Think of a time when you know that you were not being listened to and heard.

- What was going on at that time?
- How did it affect the interaction?
- What do you think was going on for the person you were trying to communicate with at that time?

Table 3.1 Explanation of 'SOLER'

S	Sit squarely	Sit slightly opposite the other person so that you are either side of an imaginary corner. This allows you to see all aspects of non-verbal communication which you may not see if you were sitting side by side and is less threatening than sitting face on. When working in a mental health setting, I was encouraged to take my personal safety seriously – it is advisable to arrange the seating so that you have easy access to the exit.
O	Open position	Sit with uncrossed arms and legs; this conveys to the client that you are open and not defensive.
L	Lean slightly towards the client	Leaning slightly towards the client shows that you are interested and want to understand their problem.
E	Eye contact	It is important to get the balance right. The client will feel uncomfortable if you stare and will think that you are not interested if you do not look at them at all.
R	Relax	If you are relaxed you can concentrate on listening rather than worrying about how to respond to the clients.

in order to help us remember how to create a good relationship with reference to our non-verbal communication. You may have come across this before.

Restating

Restating involves repeating back to the person words or short phrases which they have used and this can show that they have been heard and understood. In addition, it can encourage the person to continue with the conversation and explore what they are saying more deeply.

Paraphrasing

In order to show a person that you understand their concerns from their point of view, you rephrase what you understood to be the core message of their communication. By doing so, you are able to check your understanding of what the person has said.

By using such phrases as 'It sounds like...' or, 'It seems that...' or 'I'm wondering if you mean' and 'I have got it right that...', you are testing your accuracy and perception of what is being said.

Summarising

When we summarise we gather together the person's statements and try to identify their thoughts and feelings. This helps us to get a grasp on the main problem. A summary is simply a longer paraphrase that enables you to bring together the important aspects of what the person is saying. It can help us to clarify content and feelings, review what has been said and bring the communication to an end.

Questioning

Questioning is an essential skill but we need to be aware that too many questions can make the person we are communicating with feel as though they are being interrogated. You will be aware of the types of questions but here is a reminder:

- Open questions – these are the 'what', 'where', 'how', and 'who' questions. 'Why' might also be included but it can be a difficult one for somebody to answer and puts pressure on them to justify their position. Think about the last time you were asked why you felt that or did that.

- Open questions can be useful as they involve the person more and encourage exploration and thoughtfulness.

- Closed questions – these non-exploratory type questions elicit only 'yes' or 'no' answers and may shut down the communication.

The way in which we ask the question is also important and we can be:

- Direct
- Concise – i.e. specific and brief
- Clear – saying precisely what we mean.

Silence

There are different kinds of silences: thoughtful silences, which give us space to process our thoughts, or angry, tense silences, where the same thing is happening but is hard to bear for any length of time.

To be useful we need to be aware of what kind of silence it is and allow the person space to process their thoughts before stepping in to help by breaking the silence.

By being aware of eye contact or body language, we can ascertain if the silence is uncomfortable.

Listening is an art and active listening leaves people with whom we interact with much the same feeling as expressed by Rogers (1980):

> 'When I have been listened to and when I have been heard, I am able to perceive my world in a new way and to go on. It is astonishing how elements that seem insoluble become soluble when someone listens, how confusions that seem irredeemable turn into relatively clear flowing streams when one is heard. I have deeply appreciated the times that I have experienced this sensitive, empathic concentrated listening.'

Difficulties in own life making it difficult to manage or lead

Under this heading we are going to concentrate on emotions and how they impact on communication.

In all management and leadership situations you will be dealing with your own issues, as well as those of others, and sometimes this can affect the way in which you are perceived, understood or viewed. You may well have come across situations which touch you because they reflect a problem you may have yourself. Or you may simply be dealing with a person you find particularly difficult, perhaps even aggressive. In Chapter 7 we look at how to deal with anger and conflict. You may well recognise the effect that a bad mood has on a workforce! Have you ever worked in a team where the manager arrives in a foul mood, storming in and slamming the office door? Immediately everybody is on their guard because they know the boss is in a bad mood! What has been communicated in a simple action will affect the way in which people interact for the rest of the day. As a manager then you do have a responsibility to ensure that your communication is positive where it can be and this requires a certain amount of self-awareness. Being aware of who you are will have an impact on others. This means you need to attend to your own personal growth and development.

Emotional intelligence

Daniel Goleman (1995) argued for the usefulness of his work on emotional intelligence.

He stated that emotional intelligence is:

> 'the capacity for recognising our own feelings and those of others for motivating ourselves, for managing emotions well in ourselves as well as others.'
>
> (Goleman, 1995, p.137)

Along with self-awareness, Goleman highlighted four other areas which make up the theory of emotional intelligence:

- self-management
- social awareness
- relationship management
- motivation.

For Goleman, self-awareness was about knowing our own emotions and recognising those feelings as they happen.

Self-management highlights the need to manage those emotions we feel and to handle them appropriately. So we may feel angry at something somebody has said but, as a manager and leader, showing that anger inappropriately will have a negative effect on relationships. Think back to the manager who slammed the office door and the sorts of repercussions that action will have had on the staff.

Social awareness refers to the empathy and concern we have for others' feelings; the acknowledgement that people under threat in an organisation may show aggression and anger. During times when decisions affecting people's jobs have to be made, this sort of respect is sometimes lacking and the manager sees only the task in hand, failing to acknowledge the sort of effect this is having on those at risk and those who have to continue to work in such a climate of change.

Relationship management is the ability to handle relationships competently in order to best deal with conflict, and to develop collaboration in the workforce.

Finally, Goleman refers to motivation particularly of ourselves to enable the workforce to meet goals.

Take a look at the Case Study below and reflect on how this person showed emotional intelligence and deflected a potentially threatening outcome.

Tom could have responded by standing his ground and defending his stance. If he had said, 'I am looking at nothing', then this could be misconstrued and cause offence. We might say it didn't matter since the other man was drunk but it might have escalated feelings and could have ended up in a scuffle breaking out. He could have ignored the man with the same sort of outcome. Instead, he calmly put the man off his guard and responded in a friendly way, clearly not what the man was expecting.

So what can we take from this? In a management situation our awareness of the impact of our actions and responses can go a long way to defusing situations that might be potentially threatening. We may not be feeling very happy or friendly ourselves but being in a position of authority demands that we have some awareness of the feelings of others. A good manager is one who has a level of emotional intelligence about them.

Case Study

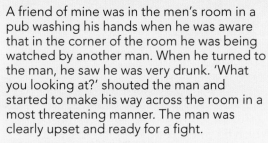

A friend of mine was in the men's room in a pub washing his hands when he was aware that in the corner of the room he was being watched by another man. When he turned to the man, he saw he was very drunk. 'What you looking at?' shouted the man and started to make his way across the room in a most threatening manner. The man was clearly upset and ready for a fight.

Tom looked at him, smiled and put his hand out to invite the other to shake it. 'Hi, I'm Tom, how are you?' he said, smiling.

The man was taken aback and shook Tom's hand in response, clearly uncertain about what had just happened.

Both men emerged from the men's room laughing and joking.

(Thanks to Tom Barber for use of this story.)

Activity 3.1.5

You are aware that a member of your staff has recently undergone a traumatic separation from her husband. She has three small children and is struggling to make ends meet. She finds it difficult to get to work on time and has been late a number of times recently. You know she does not have family to help her get the children to school.

When you ask to see her to try to resolve some of her issues, she is aggressive and quite rude. How would you respond?

The situation in Activity 3.1.5 is difficult since you are likely to feel quite angry yourself, particularly when you are trying to come up with a solution for your member of staff. However, fighting anger with anger does not work and hopefully you perhaps would have put into place some of the following actions.

Perhaps you would have empathised with her plight and asked her how she might see a way forward. Likely, she has been unable to take time out to note the decline in her work or her lateness. You might suggest a change in hours to help her to get to work on time or a reduction in her hours of work until she can settle her children into a more favourable routine. Perhaps she might work the same number of hours but at times when the children are at school.

The way in which you deal with the situation will have an effect on the whole workforce.

Inappropriate environment

Another area where communication is apt to break down is being in an inappropriate environment. You will be aware of the need for privacy when carrying out sensitive types of communication, breaking bad news or reprimanding someone. But have you thought about the impact your own setting will have on others?

The initial impact of a room or building can have a huge effect on how people feel when they enter the building and can influence the success of an interaction.

Have a look now around the room in which you are sitting. How does it make you feel? Think about it for a moment. Is it welcoming, untidy, too busy, crammed, too large, are the chairs too far apart? I once remember attending an informal interview and was asked to sit in an easy chair. The interviewer sat in an upright chair next to me and towered over me. The effect this had on me, as I sank down into the

soft cushions, was of being vulnerable. I am sure the interviewer had not intended for me to feel that way but it certainly changed the way in which I responded to his questions.

It is as well to take a good look at where and when you conduct important communications with staff. Noisy environments may mean your message is not heard, impacting on the outcomes you may have expected.

Have you thought about where you conduct your staff meetings. Again, even the position of the chairs can affect the interactions. For example, look at the two photographs of different types of classroom set-ups.

Which do you prefer? Does the set-up in classroom one bring up memories of school? Perhaps those memories are less than happy? The way that our environment communicates with us is extremely important.

Analyse the communication barriers present in your own working environment and write a short reflective piece to show your understanding of the effects these have. You will need this work for the next section and as evidence for your portfolio.

1.4 Implement a strategy to overcome communication barriers

The activities from the previous section will be useful in detailing how you intend to overcome the problems in your own work area and in this section we can only give a general indication of how you will fulfil this particular part of the unit.

Dealing with communication barriers

Much of the last section highlighted the types of communication barriers and these fall into two groups, internal and external.

The external barriers refer to environmental and cultural barriers and these can be dealt with by making changes to the actual fabric of the environment and improving the general layout of the place in which communication is to occur. The environment where we engage with visitors and staff when we communicate bad news or supervision and team meetings needs to be looked at with more critical eyes. If you feel uncomfortable and unsettled in this setting, then the chances are that your staff and visitors will feel likewise.

With respect to cultural barriers, we are aware that this is about recognising that everybody is different and you may have identified in your own settings areas where there is a shortfall in this aspect. For example, you may have noticed that some of the care workers fail to respond to some of the clients in appropriate ways simply because they lack an understanding of the condition or culture of the client. For example, a deaf client may be excluded from certain social activities or a client who wishes to practise his religion is not given the opportunity.

In ensuring that your staff respond to the differences of their clients, they need to be aware of the responsibilities they have to *all* individuals in the setting. Have you checked your anti-discrimination policy lately? You may need to revise and update the policy to ensure that all staff are aware of how they can implement it in their practice and how they address the issues of cultural sensitivity and diversity.

There may be a need for more training to raise awareness of cultural and religious differences in your workforce. The key here is to determine how well your own setting delivers 'holistic and person-centred care' or care that is user focussed, promoting independence. Only you can say what you need to do in your own workplace.

Review the continuing professional development programme in your setting and the policies which relate to client care and holistic practice.

The internal factors pertaining to communication barriers require you to be aware of your own emotions and feelings about how you are dealing with the problems which you come across. Our awareness of the way in which we portray ourselves to others can only come about with a true reflection of ourselves, and this can sometimes reveal uncomfortable traits. We sometimes need to move out of our comfort zone and identify areas for our own self-development in terms of how we communicate. Donnelly and Neville (2008) comment that being aware of oneself enables you to review your personal values against the professional standards that you are now expected to work within.

In an effort to improve our management and leadership skills, we also need to be aware of the way in which we communicate.

Take time to reflect on and evaluate your own skills in communication.

Consider the next communication you have with each of the following:

- Client
- Member of staff.

Write a brief description of the circumstances in which the interaction took place. Comment upon the following:

- Your own body language with respect to SOLER
- Your listening skills
- Your ability to show unconditional positive regard and empathy.

Reflect on your strengths and areas for improvement and develop a strategy to show how you intend to undertake these improvements. Keep this work in your file as evidence of your completion of assessment criteria for 1.4.

According to Geldard and Geldard (2003), through the development of your self-awareness you can resolve past and current issues and, by doing so, you can improve on your skills in the role of manager.

1.5 Use different *means of communication* to meet different needs

In this section we deal with the actual communication methods we have at our disposal. We have touched on this briefly earlier but now address in more detail the various aspects of what constitutes interpersonal skills.

In the study of communication we might come across the following three terms:

■ Interpersonal communication, which involves non-verbal, paralinguistic and verbal communication.

■ Environmental communication, which involves the way in which our environment affects our interactions. We touched on this previously.

■ Intra-personal communication, which takes place within ourselves or 'self talk'. We addressed this in the last two sections where we dealt with feelings and emotions and their effects on interaction.

So we now focus on interpersonal communication. Table 3.2 shows the types of non-verbal communication we use and this will be revision for you.

Activity 3.1.9

Think briefly about your own non-verbal communication. What areas would you like to improve on to make your own communication more effective?

Paralinguistic communication

When we moderate our speech, for example, changing the pitch, volume, rhythm, tone of voice and timing, occasionally lapsing in to the odd grunt, ums and ahs, we are using paralinguistic communication. The words we use are very important but the way we say something is of equal importance and can affect how our message is perceived. Yawning, sighing, coughing, tutting, laughing and groaning can also be mentioned here as forms of paralinguistic communication. How do we communicate these aspects of language in written communication though? In such cases we may change the colour or size of the font or use capital letters and exclamation marks.

Paralinguistic communication can offer us a clue to how a person is feeling and this can help in our dealings with them.

Verbal communication

Verbal communication can be complex since the meaning of words changes between cultures and generations and on its own can be an ineffective form of communication. For example, words such as 'wicked', and 'bad' mean something very different to the youth of today than they did to my grandmother! There are many more examples of how words change. The words we use alter depending on the situation and the people involved and, because of this, we can never be sure that a word has the same meaning for two people (Porritt, 1990). This is particularly important when communicating feelings, as the strength of the word may differ between people.

Our choice of words is important and we need to be careful not to use jargon and abbreviations that our clients or staff may not understand. Similarly, we should avoid the use of euphemisms which we might refer to as 'double speak', such as saying someone has 'passed away' instead of died. For weeks as a student nurse I lacked understanding about the term 'she has gone to Rose Cottage' and thought the patients I had nursed had all been taken to a care home of that name! In fact they had died.

One of the things that can be most annoying and might alienate your staff can be the use of cliché and management-type speak. Terms such as 'thinking outside the box', 'blue-sky thinking', 'scoping' and other such clichés can sound over used and inauthentic and may also be misunderstood.

Written communication

Written reports, notes, e-mail and other forms of electronic communication are all important forms of communication and being able to maintain clear and accurate records is a legal requirement.

As Donnelly and Neville (2008) point out, written communication should be accurate, in detail, up to date, non-judgemental and legible so that others are able to read it. We also need to comply with confidentiality guidelines and, as such, all forms of written communication must be kept safely.

As a manager you will undoubtedly favour one form over another but you do need to be aware of the advantages and disadvantages of written communication.

I like to use e-mail a lot and find it to be quick, convenient and with the added bonus that people can respond immediately or when it is convenient to them. As a written record of a communication, it can be accessed afterwards for evidence in a way that a telephone communication cannot be used. We can also add attachments and links into the mail to relevant internet sites, allowing the respondent to go straight to the information. There is no postage to pay and it can save on journey time to and from meetings.

The mainly impersonal nature of the e-mail and the fact that people communicating cannot pick up on paralinguistic and non-verbal signs are disadvantages, however. Short and to the point e-mails can sometimes appear rude and there is also the tendency for people to not reply to e-mails they do not understand, so you could be waiting for a while for an answer!

Table 3.2 Non-verbal communication

Facial expression	Our facial expression communicates emotions unless we train ourselves to mask our feelings. Burnard (1996) argues that it is important to be congruent – if you say you are angry while smiling, it gives a confusing mixed message.
Eye contact and gaze	The way we look into another person's eyes during conversation is what is known as eye contact. If somebody can hold eye contact through a conversation, it can communicate a level of confidence and willingness to communicate fully. Some of the people we communicate with will have a very low level of eye contact which might communicate a lack of ease with the conversation or a lack of confidence. It is a good idea to reduce the level of our eye contact to reflect theirs, otherwise it can feel threatening. The appropriateness of maintaining eye contact differs according to culture.
Gestures	Gestures are movements of your arms and hands that accompany speech. Gestures can help communication, for example, pointing at the direction a person needs to go in can add emphasis to the communication. However too much gesturing can be distracting.
Body position, posture and movement	The body position of a client can tell you a lot about how they are feeling – if they are hunched over, with arms and legs crossed, they are probably feeling quite anxious. Rogers (1980) recommends that we relax and it is important not to appear too formal and distant. However, if we are too laid back in our posture, we could appear disinterested. Sitting with our arms and legs crossed can appear closed off and defensive. However, in some circumstances, it may be a good idea to mirror the body posture of the person we are with.
Personal space and proximity	Two to three feet in distance between the chairs is about right for me; however I have noticed that some clients push their chairs back as soon as they sit down in the prearranged chairs. I assume the space does not feel comfortable to them. People seem to have their own invisible boundaries which change according to who they are interacting with and how comfortable they feel. Porritt (1990) calls it a bubble that surrounds us.
Clothes	The clothes we choose to wear say a lot about us. Dressing too informally and too formally can alienate us from our clients.
Therapeutic touch	Touch can be a contentious subject. On the one hand there is evidence of touch having therapeutic benefits; on the other it can be misinterpreted and seen as an invasion of a person's personal space. Bonham (2004) suggests it may be appropriate and supportive for staff to touch when clients are distressed as it may validate the degree of their suffering. He suggests that appropriate places to touch in this situation are hands, forearms, upper arms and shoulders.

From Tilmouth, T. *et al.*, 2011

Confidentiality is another important consideration, with the potential for confidential information going to the wrong person by mistake or accidentally forwarded on by the respondent to someone who would not be included by the first writer.

2 Be able to improve communication systems and practices that support positive outcomes for individuals

 Monitor the effectiveness of communication systems and practices

In monitoring something, we take the decision to diagnose whether there are any deficiencies to address in a system and to forecast whether, in the future, changes may need to be made due to new initiatives coming on line (McGrath, 1985).

To gain an accurate understanding of the state of affairs with respect to your own communication system, you need to do two things:

1. Search for information to support the current level of function with respect to communication.

2. Analyse and interpret that information to decide on a plan of action.

The next activity is designed to help you to do just that.

Activity 3.2.1

Obtain feedback from the following groups of people about your communication systems in place at this time:

■ clients

■ staff

■ visitors

■ other professionals you deal with.

You might design a questionnaire or carry out group meetings to get feedback. Keep the work for your portfolio.

 Evaluate the effectiveness of existing communication systems and practices

Having collected the information, you now need to analyse and evaluate it. To carry out an evaluation you need to determine the value of something or judge its worth and, in this case, there is a need to evaluate just how well your communication systems work.

This can be carried out on an informal basis where you obtain casual feedback from individuals as to how well your systems work. However, it is far better to collect information that may be used in auditing your service and can provide evidence to external bodies of your continual progress and quality assurance in the organisation.

Activity 3.2.2

How do you evaluate the quality of the performance of the communication systems in:

■ the organisation

■ the team

■ yourself.

What standards do you use?

There are a number of useful ways in which you can formally ask for feedback. For example, you may use client forums and meetings when the quality of these services can be discussed and minuted. This provides valuable information as to how the clients and service users feel about the organisations. Other ways may be through a complaint and compliment system, questionnaires, appraisal and focus groups.

The care you give and the way you deliver the care has a significant impact, not only on the users of the service but also on staff morale and, as such, any feedback is essential to measuring the quality of that care.

2.3 Propose improvements to communication systems and practices to address any shortcomings

2.4 Lead the implementation of revised communication systems and practices

This section is one which requires you to put into practice any changes you may need to improve the communication system in your organisation.

3 Be able to improve communication systems to support partnership working

 Use communication systems to promote partnership working

The NHS Reorganisation Act in 1973 placed a statutory duty on local authorities and the NHS to collaborate with each other through Joint Consultative Committees. Further reform in 1976 led to Joint Planning teams and collaboration with respect to finance in order to provide better social care and, in 1990, the delivery of care was via a market-based approach with purchasing and providing of services to enhance social care provision.

Partnership working is an important means of making improvements in health care for people and depends on effective partnerships between the different professions and organisations involved in commissioning and delivering services and interventions.

From 2013, the Health and Social Care Bill devolves commissioning of health care to GP commissioning consortia and PCTs will disappear. In the event of this happening, there will be a need to change existing partnership arrangements and make new arrangements with GP commissioning consortia. This is likely to result in joint commissioning of pathways, services and systems and also integration of multi-disciplinary staff teams.

One of the key things you as a manager will need to do is to recognise that partnership working is going to change and as such you need to ensure you are aware of the implications of the Health and Social Care Bill, including the newly proposed Health and Wellbeing Boards and the importance of establishing good, early working relationships with GPs in your area and in their new commissioning roles.

All partnership working depends on effective communication and good working relationships. As part of a care team that goes beyond the boundaries of your own organisation, you need to be aware of the need to build team links with external bodies.

Effective health and social care is that which is provided in collaboration and partnership with others, either in the same team or across a range of different agencies and disciplines within the care sector. You will therefore be involved in several different teams in your work setting.

In the last 20 years or so there has been a greater emphasis put on multi-disciplinary team working where groups of people from different professions work together, with the client at the centre of the project. This came about after the publication of the Laming report (2003) which highlighted the importance of working closely with people from other professional groups and agencies. When people work physically close together, they communicate more, they know each other better and understand each other's values and procedures better and therefore work more effectively together. This will have a good effect on the relationships we have with patients and clients and the care they receive will be improved.

At this current time health services are divided between 'primary' and 'secondary'. Primary care services include:

- general medical practitioners (GPs)
- dentists
- pharmacists
- opticians
- district nursing
- practice managers
- community midwives
- other services.

Primary health care is defined, according to the World Health Organization (WHO, 1978), as:

'the first level contact of individuals, the family and the community with the national health system which brings health care as close as possible to where people live and work.'

The more specialised services, or 'secondary care', are those services we use less often and are provided in fewer locations. This includes hospitals, ambulances and specialised health services for the mentally ill and the learning disabled.

The partnerships you have at this present time may well include those from primary as well as secondary care, yet all will change after 2011 when we can expect to see a more streamlined NHS Service. The 2010 White Paper 'Equity and Excellence: Liberating the NHS' states:

> 'As a result of the changes, the NHS will be streamlined with fewer layers of bureaucracy. Strategic Health Authorities and Primary Care Trusts will be phased out. Management costs will be reduced so that as much resource as possible supports frontline services. The reforms build on changes started under the previous Government.'
>
> (Department of Health, 2010)

From 2013 further changes will be made and your current partnerships will need to be reviewed further.

From 2013 the Health and Social Care Bill comes into force and will devolve the commissioning of health care to GP commissioning consortia and PCTs as we know them will disappear.

By extending existing partnership arrangements with GP commissioning consortia, local authorities should be able to engage in the joint commissioning of services and systems with the knock-on effect of integrating multi-disciplinary staff teams. With broader partnerships of statutory agencies (for example, leisure, learning, employment, transport, housing and benefits) emerging, we will be able to ensure that patients and clients are able to access these functions and not be forced into segregated health and care services. This will result in a more coherent approach to care.

With the local authorities and their NHS partners actively working towards closer working relationships, the management and delivery of structures, including shared officers and staff, will result in better service delivery.

The way we work with others demands that we are open about what we do and effective in sharing information. As an integral way of working, local strategic partnerships have been able to share information and sometimes services to enable clients to be cared for in a more effective way.

We want to ensure that the service we offer improves the experience and outcomes of the people who use that service. This can only be done by minimising the barriers between different services and ensuring that the lines of communication are not blurred.

All this is likely to impact upon your partnership working. Use the checklist in Activity 3.3.2 to determine your commitment to the changes ahead.

Activity 3.3.2

Planned actions	Tick box	Action needed
Do I understand the new concept of local partnerships and the implications of the Health and Social Care Bill?		
Have I an understanding of Health and Wellbeing Boards?		
Am I already establishing good working relationships with GPs in their proposed new commissioning role?		
What is happening locally with the formation of GP consortia?		
Do I know which partnerships exist that are relevant to my service and understand how I link into these – for example, by way of chairing, membership, or receiving feedback?		
Can I have a more front seat role in the planning of new partnerships?		

3.2 **Compare the effectiveness of different communication systems for partnership working**

3.3 **Propose improvements to communication systems for partnership working**

Activity 3.3.3

This section requires you to carry out a small research study and relates to Activities 3.3.1 and 3.3.2.

Having undertaken to determine where you are now with respect to partnership working, you now need to do the following.

Compile a questionnaire or set up an action research group to determine the effectiveness of your current working across partnerships with respect to the communication. The following questions may be helpful:

- Where does communication break down?

- What is good about our communication?

- What needs to be changed?

- Is there anything that we are missing?

When you feel you have the information you need, set down some proposals to improve what you do already.

Link in with Activity 3.3.2 and ensure you are moving towards the changes proposed for the future.

---

4 Be able to use systems for effective information management

4.1 **Explain legal and ethical tensions between maintaining confidentiality and sharing information**

Beauchamp and Childress (1994) defined confidentiality as 'keeping secret' information given to a person by another. Infringement occurs when that information is disclosed to someone else without the giver's consent.

Health and Social Care staff are required to maintain confidences obtained via their work and you as a manager need to meet this requirement with respect to the staff you deal with. However, if there is a public interest issue at stake then confidence may be broken. For example:

- If a crime has been committed or you believe it is about to be.

- If malpractice has occurred.

- If child abuse is suspected

- In order to prevent suicide.

- If professional misconduct has occurred.

If a breach of confidentiality occurs within your workplace then you as the manager are obliged to take disciplinary action and/or legal action.

From a legal point of view you as a manager are obliged to follow the laws associated with maintaining confidentiality and these are:

- Data Protection Act 1998

- Human Rights Act 1998

- Clinical governance requirements

- Caldicott recommendations

- Skills for Care guidelines.

From an ethical point of view, in maintaining confidentiality, health professionals explicitly or implicitly make a promise to their clients to keep confidential the information they provide them with, thus respecting the autonomy of the client. But problems arise when decisions need to be made as to the sharing of certain personal information. For example, Article 10 of the Convention on Human Rights and Biomedicine states, 'everyone has the right to respect for private life in relation to information about his/her health care' (European Parliament & Council of the European Union, 1995).

In disclosing their HIV status, an individual under this law can expect for this information not to be disclosed and his/her privacy respected. This would be in the patient's best interests and upholds the ethical principle of beneficence. However, the competing principle of justice seems to work against the former since it might be in the public interest to disclose such information in order to protect others.

Another of the tensions with respect to confidentiality lies with the use of information and its safekeeping. The report entitled 'Information for Health: an information strategy for the modern NHS 1998–2005' stated that:

> 'A modern and dependable NHS needs accurate and instantly accessible information. This is vital for improving care for patients, for improving the performance of the NHS, and the health of the nation.'
>
> (NHS Executive, 1998, p.5)

In an effort to improve the effectiveness and efficiency within health care work, the information strategy proposed included electronic health records for all patients, enabling 24-hour access to patient records, and thus seamless care for patients contacting general practitioners, hospitals and other services. Risks and concerns over the security and confidentiality of patient information thus became an issue.

The legal and ethical tension then lies in the need to optimise the quality of patient care by sharing information across a number of professional groups and the need to keep patients' information confidential and secure. In the next section we shall look at how we might balance such potential conflicts.

4.2 Analyse the essential features of information sharing agreements within and between organisations

The Department of Health's (1996) *The Protection and Use of Patient Information* identifies the best practice for information sharing and as a manager you need to be aware of its contents. In principle, the guidance outlines the need to keep personal information about patients, 'not just for delivering personal care and treatment, but also for general public health care and administrative purposes.'

It also gives guidance as to the following:

■ The use of patient information and the duty of confidence.

■ The need to keep patients informed about why the information is required.

■ How the information will be used.

■ How the patient may access it.

Within this paper there is also guidance about safeguarding information and the security measures, and requirements for inter-agency coordination and the passing on of information are also highlighted.

The recommendations within the Caldicott Report should also be taken into account here.

In 1997 the government appointed a committee to recommend how the information collected for patient records should be processed. The principles produced by the committee became part of the Data Protection Act in 1998 and recommended the appointment of a person in every organisation to be responsible for the maintenance of confidentiality. In care homes this would be a senior staff member (or manager) who would be legally required to ensure that a policy was in place to protect the individual in the home.

The most important of the principles outlined were:

■ The purpose of the information and the transfer of such had to be clearly justified.

■ Client identifiable information should be limited if possible.

■ Reduction of client identifiable information should be worked towards.

■ Accessibility – staff should be permitted to access information on a need-to-know basis only.

■ Staff should be made aware of their responsibilities with respect to confidentiality.

■ All information kept on the client must conform to law.

(Tilmouth *et al.*, 2011)

Any patient information you keep may be passed on for a particular purpose with the patient's consent or on a need-to-know basis. You also need to ensure that the patient is fully informed about how the information about them may be used.

The guidance also stresses the importance of anonymising personal information wherever possible in order to minimise the risk of security breaches into our systems. Threats to security can be accidental and due to human error or due to system failure or naturally occurring events such as fire, or from deliberate breaches from external hackers.

The responsibility for maintaining confidentiality lies with the manager and you need to be convinced that your policies and procedures are appropriate and operational within your area.

Activity 3.4.1

Write a reflective account, explaining the legal and ethical tensions between maintaining confidentiality and sharing information in your own organisation and analysing the essential features of information sharing between your own and other organisations.

4.3 Demonstrate use of information management systems that meet legal and ethical requirements

All organisations must show that they act responsibly in relation to their staff, and clients, and must obey the law in key areas such as health and safety, employment, finance and company law.

In addition the health industry must adhere to specific regulations for their industry and ethical frameworks.

Activity 3.4.2

The following is adapted from the National Occupational Standards for Managers Unit B8: Ensure compliance with legal, regulatory, ethical and social requirements.

Evaluate your own performance against these standards and then ask a colleague or your manager to verify your judgement. Keep the completed work in your portfolio as evidence.

Management standard (adapted text)	How do I do this and what evidence do I have to show on completion?	Verification by manager or colleague	Further action needed
What are the national and international legal, regulatory, ethical and social requirements of my area and how do I monitor them? What effect do they have on my area of responsibility, and what will happen if we don't meet them?			
What are the policies and procedures which make sure my organisation meets all the necessary requirements?			
How do I make sure relevant people have a clear understanding of the policies and procedures and the importance of putting them into practice?			
How do I ensure that policies and procedures are put into practice and provide support?			
How do I encourage a climate of openness about meeting and not meeting the requirements?			
What failures to meet the requirements have I identified and corrected?			
What reasons have I identified for not meeting requirements and how have I adjusted the policies and procedures to reduce the likelihood of failures in the future?			
Have I provided full reports about any failures to meet the requirements to the relevant stakeholders?			

It is not possible to determine how you may have answered the task in Activity 3.4.2; however, one of the main legal requirements in any information system deals with the quality of the reports collected and the way in which the system is implemented. As a manager there are four key areas which you need to monitor and evaluate:

1. **Purpose** – clarity about why you need to collect data.

2. **Collection** – the processes by which data is collected.

3. **Storage** – the processes and systems used to store and maintain patient information and notes.

4. **Analysis** – the process of translating data into information that can be used to improve the organisation and its care-giving.

Taking this a step further, the actual information that is collected must also comply with legal requirements of accuracy.

Dimond (2005) highlighted the major areas of concern in care reports. She revealed that in many records there were major omissions, including:

- no dates
- illegibility
- use of abbreviations
- callers' and visitors' names not included
- no signatures
- inaccuracy with respect to dates and times
- delays in record writing
- inaccuracies about clients
- unprofessional language being used.

(Tilmouth *et al.*, 2011)

The need to document accurately what happened provides an account then of what actually was done at the time and what took place.

We rely on these records, and if years later the case becomes part of a legal process, we need to be able to return to the records to remind us of what actually was done at the time.

Records then do the following:

- Provide an account of the care given (although they do not show what the quality of that care was).
- Give a record of continuous care (in the case of nursing and medical records).
- Provide a source of reference for care.
- Provide an audit and quality assurance trail.
- Are a legal requirement.

Unfortunately we live in a highly litigious society and in order to protect ourselves when we are being held accountable for the care we give, we need to be aware of the place records have. If a complaint is made against us, then we would be hard pushed to answer if we had inadequately prepared records. If negligence is suspected in any care setting, any records and statements pertaining to the case will be taken and scrutinised.

Summary

This chapter has sought to reacquaint you with the range of communication requirements for your own role, to help you to improve communication systems and practices that support positive outcomes for individuals and for partnership working and to enable you to use systems for effective information management.

The need to be an effective communicator in dealing with staff, clients and partners is evident. Complaints tend to focus on the breakdown in communication as being the potential reason for poor service.

In this chapter we have looked at the need to, first of all, know ourselves well and to be acutely aware of what we bring to the relationship, and how we might impact on those we communicate with. Taking the time to really understand what it is the other person is saying, rather than assuming we know, is a most useful skill to develop in management. Our aim should be to finish the interaction leaving someone feeling better than they did before we met them.

By revisiting and revising the systems of communication we use in care work and in particular in managing a care setting, we are able to ensure that misunderstanding or misinterpretation of the message, which can lead to team conflict and disruption, becomes a thing of the past.

Being an effective communicator holds the key to successful working.

Learning outcomes	Assessment criteria
1 Be able to address the range of communication requirements in own role	**1.1** Review the range of groups and individuals whose communication needs must be addressed in own job role **Activity 3.1.1, p.30** **1.2** Explain how to support effective communication within own job role **Activity 3.1.2, p.33** **1.3** Analyse the barriers and challenges to communication within own job role **Activity 3.1.3, p.34** **Activity 3.1.4, p.37** **Activity 3.1.5, p.40** **Activity 3.1.6, p.41** **1.4** Implement a strategy to overcome communication barriers **Activity 3.1.7, p.41** **Activity 3.1.8, p.41** **1.5** Use different means of communication to meet different needs **Activity 3.1.9, p.42**
2 Be able to improve communication systems and practices that support positive outcomes for individuals	**2.1** Monitor the effectiveness of communication systems and practices **Activity 3.2.1, p.44** **2.2** Evaluate the effectiveness of existing communication systems and practices **Activity 3.2.2, p.44** **2.3** Propose improvements to communication systems and practices to address any shortcomings **Activity 3.2.3, p.45** **2.4** Lead the implementation of revised communication systems and practices **Activity 3.2.3, p.45**

Learning outcomes	Assessment criteria
3 Be able to improve communication systems to support partnership working	**(3.1)** **Use communication systems to promote partnership working** **Activity 3.3.1, p.45** **Activity 3.3.2, p.46** **(3.2)** **Compare the effectiveness of different communication systems for partnership working** **Activity 3.3.3, p.47** **(3.3)** **Propose improvements to communication systems for partnership working** **Activity 3.3.3, p.47**
4 Be able to use systems for effective information management	**(4.1)** **Explain legal and ethical tensions between maintaining confidentiality and sharing information** **Activity 3.4.1, p.48** **(4.2)** **Analyse the essential features of information sharing agreements within and between organisations** **Activity 3.4.1, p.48** **Activity 3.4.2, p.49** **(4.3)** **Demonstrate use of information management systems that meet legal and ethical requirements** **Activity 3.4.2, p.49**

References

Adair, J. (2000) *Effective Teambuilding: How to make a winning team*. London: Pan Macmillan.

Alton Barbour, A. and Koneya, M. (1976) *Louder Than Words: Non-verbal communication*. Columbus, Ohio: Merrill.

Argyle, M. (1978) *The Psychology of Interpersonal Behaviour* (3e). Harmondsworth: Penguin.

Bazler Riley, J. (2008) *Communication in Nursing*. Missouri: Mosby Elsevier.

Beauchamp, T. L. and Childress, J. F. (1994) *Principles of Biomedical Ethics*. Oxford: Oxford University Press.

Bonham, P. (2004) *Communication as a Mental Health Carer*. Cheltenham: Nelson Thornes.

Buono, A. F. and Kerber, W. K. (2010) 'Creating a Sustainable Approach to Change: Building organizational change capacity'. [Online] journal article: *SAM Advanced Management Journal*, Vol. 75.

Burnard, P. (1996) *Acquiring Interpersonal Skills: A handbook of experiential learning for health professionals* (2e). London: Chapman and Hall.

Cole, J. (2011) *We Know Why, But Do We Know How?* Unpublished essay submitted for MSc in Educational Management and Leadership, Worcester University.

Craine, K. (2007) 'Managing the Cycle of Change'. [Online] *Information Management Journal*, 41, 5, 44–50. Academic Search Complete, EBSCO*host*, [accessed 14.6.11].

Crawford, P., Brown, B. and Bonham, P. (2006) *Communication in Clinical Settings*. Cheltenham: Nelson Thornes.

Davis H. and Fallowfield, L. (eds) (1991) *Counselling and Communication in Health Care.* Cirencester: Wiley.

Department of Health (1996) *The Protection and Use of Patient Information.* London: TSO.

Department of Health (2010) *Equity and Excellence: Liberating the NHS.* London: HMSO

Dimond, B. (2005) *Legal Aspects of Nursing* (4e). Harlow: Pearson Education.

Donnelly, E. and Neville, L. (2008) *Communication and Interpersonal Skills.* Exeter: Reflect Press.

European Parliament & Council of the European Union (1995) Directive 95/46/EC of the European Parliament and of the Council of 24 October 1995 on the protection of individuals with regard to the processing of personal data and on the free movement of such data. *Official Journal,* **L281,** pp.31–50.

Geldard, K. and Geldard, D. (2003) *Counselling Skills in Everyday Life.* London: Palgrave Macmillan.

Givens, D. B. (2000) 'Body Speak: What are you saying?' *Successful Meetings.* (October) 51.

Goleman, D. (1995) *Emotional Intelligence.* New York: Bantam Books.

Gopee, N. and Galloway, J. (2009) *Leadership and Management in Health Care.* London: Sage.

Graham, R. J. (1991) 'Understanding the Beliefs of Poor Communication'. *Interface.* 11, pp.80–2.

Hewison, A. (1995) 'Nurses' Power in Interactions with Patients'. *Journal of Advanced Nursing.* 21, pp.75–82.

Katz, R. (1955) 'Skills of an Effective Administrator'. *Harvard Business Review.* 33(1), pp.33–42.

Lord Laming (2003) *The Victoria Climbié Inquiry: Summary report of an inquiry.* Cheltenham: HMSO.

Macleod-Clark, J. (1984) 'Verbal Communication in Nursing' in Faulkner, A. (ed.) *Recent Advances in Nursing 7. Communication.* Edinburgh: Churchill Livingstone.

McGrath, J. E. (1985) 'Critical Leadership Functions' in Hackman, J. R. and Watson, R.E. (1986) *Leading Groups in Organisations,* P.S. Goodman and Associates (eds) San Francisco: Jossey-Bass.

Miller, L. (2006) *Counselling Skills for Social Work.* London: Sage Publications.

NHS Executive (1998) *Information for Health. An Information Strategy for the Modern NHS 1998–2005.* London: NHS Executive.

Porritt, L. (1990) *Interaction Strategies: An Introduction For Health Professionals* (2e). London: Churchill Livingstone.

Rogers, C. (1980) *A Way of Being.* New York: Houghton Mifflin.

Rogers C. (2002) *Client-Centred Therapy.* London: Constable.

Skills for Care (2006) *Leadership and Management Strategy: Strategy for the social care workforce.* Leeds: Skills for Care.

Tilmouth, T., Davies-Ward, E. and Williams, B. (2011) *Foundation Studies in Health and Social Care.* London: Hodder & Stoughton.

World Health Organization (WHO) (1978) *Declaration of Alma-Ata.* www.who.int/hpr/NPH/docs/declaration_almaata.pdf

4 Unit SHC 52 Promote professional development

The purpose of this chapter is to assist you to reflect on the fundamental importance of professional development in contributing to the management and enhancement of high quality care service. The activities in this chapter will help you to identify and reflect on different strategies to enhance your own development and will assist you to devise strategies to promote and develop professional attitudes, knowledge, skills and behaviours in those that you lead.

People receiving care services must be confident that they can trust those who deliver care to not only know what to do, but also to know how to do it well. That requires you to continually update and extend your knowledge and skills and, as a manager, to ensure that your team is also equipped with appropriate knowledge and skills in order to fulfil their roles effectively. Personal professional development is a journey that you should be on for the whole of your life. It does not end with the completion of a course or a specific activity but should, ideally, be an 'activity of daily living'. The secret of successful personal development is to learn to be reflective and questioning, both about the things we know and the things we do not know.

In this chapter, and in completing the activities in this unit, your understanding of professional development, professionalism and the responsibilities that these concepts entail will be examined and assessed. You will develop your reflective and individual planning skills in order to help you to determine how you can most effectively support your own and others' development and you will evaluate strategies to overcome barriers.

Expectations of standards of care are set out in codes of practice and codes of conduct. These codes articulate the standards of care that the public can expect to receive. Care is a complex, multi-dimensional activity and encompasses more than simply performing a skill. Whilst technical competence gained through developing knowledge and skills is important it is not sufficient on its own. Good and excellent care can only be achieved when technical competence is accompanied by also developing appropriate attitudes, those characteristics in the affective domain that relate to feelings values and the manner in which activities are carried out. Professional development must, therefore, also take account of enhancing and developing those attitudes and behaviours that are value driven and which exemplify 'caring' (Cuthbert and Quallington, 2008, p.2). Seedhouse (1998, p.35) suggests that to care is 'a moral endeavour' and that any intervention should be 'purposive, thoughtful and intended to do good'. An essential component of any professional development activity, therefore, is reflection on your own and others' performance in order not only that knowledge and skills are enhanced but also that the highest standards of care are attained.

Learning outcomes

By the end of this chapter you will:

1. Understand principles of professional development.

2. Be able to prioritise goals and targets for own professional development.

3. Be able to devise a professional development plan.

4. Be able to improve performance through reflective practice.

1 Understand principles of professional development

What is professional development? What is the manager's role in developing themselves and promoting the professional development of others?

1.1 Explain the importance of continually improving knowledge and practice

There are many definitions of professional development, but this simple statement:

> 'Professional development is a planned process of improving and increasing capabilities of staff'

encompasses the key elements that must be endorsed by proactive, forward-thinking organisations. Health and care are service focussed rather than product driven, consequently it is the people who work within the organisation who determine its success. Success is therefore inextricably linked to capabilities and attitudes of the staff and the development and enhancement of knowledge and skills. Professional development can, therefore, be said to be an essential component of organisational success.

The success that an organisation aspires to is normally expressed by way of a vision. An organisational vision will seek to articulate something about the underpinning values of the organisation; it will identify the standards of the service that can be expected and it will usually express the values and commitment that it owes to its clients and its workforce. The vision can be further supported by ensuring that the professional development of the workforce is appropriately designed to meet the challenges faced by the service. Professional development enables an organisation to keep up to date and to change proactively so that their service is relevant and appropriate. Firstly, it is important to note that to get the most out of investment in professional development it should be planned in line with an organisational vision. It is recognised that those organisations that embed personal professional development into their culture are best able to respond to day-to-day challenges and pressures and are more resilient and able to transform in response to changing situations and requirements (Schon, 1973, p.28; Harrison, 2009).

Whilst *ad hoc* training may be valuable, if that is the only development that is undertaken it is likely to be a disparate set of activities that provide the participant with packages of knowledge but which do not contribute to the greater whole. Planned development in contrast is intended to achieve specific outcomes that may be either focussed on the needs of an individual and/or may contribute to the learning needs of an organisation. For example, if an individual identifies the need for training in a particular area, such as 'break-away training', this request should be assessed both in terms of individual needs but also the on-going needs of the organisation. More benefit could be accrued by selecting an individual to attend a 'train the trainers' course in this area and to develop specialist skills and knowledge which they can then use to train other staff. Whilst this may be a greater initial investment, it future-proofs the organisation. This way both organisation and individuals benefit.

Secondly, professional development is a process. This implies that it is an on-going activity and needs to be thought about as something that is incremental with the different elements contributing to a larger whole. Thirdly, personal professional development increases the capabilities of staff. If it is tailored to individual needs, it should bring about personal enhancements and opportunities as individuals expand their personal tool box of skills. The image of 'The Knowledge and Skills Escalator' articulated in the *Knowledge and Skills Framework for the NHS* (DoH, 2004) is a powerful one. It effectively illustrates the idea of professional development being about continual movement. It generates the image of individuals having access to a range of education and development opportunities at different levels which can be individually selected and which can be packaged in many different ways. It supports the idea that professional development can be undertaken either in a traditional, linear way, starting at the bottom and moving through the levels to the top, but that it is also equally valid for an individual to get off the escalator at any point and move around on that level in order to access a whole package of different activities before re-joining the escalator. The direction of travel may take an individual up a floor to extend previous knowledge, or down a floor to access new learning. It also suggests that there should be no limit to opportunities, that even if you start at the bottom you have the opportunity to move to the top. As a manager it is important that you and your organisation capitalise on the benefits that professional development brings by ensuring that it is purposive and planned to meet the individual needs of your staff and to address organisational needs.

Activity 4.1.1

Think about the range of professional development activities that you and your team have participated in over the last year. (Think about the informal activities as well as attendance at formal training and education events.)

- Make a list.
- Were they planned, and if so, by whom?
- Were they part of a development plan for the organisation or focussed on individual needs?
- What is the evidence that they have resulted in positive outcomes?
- Give examples.

If an organisation is investing in staff development, it is important that the investment both financial and human is of value. When planning personal professional development it is important to think about what the desired outcome from the activity should be.

Professional development can be achieved through providing one-to-one individual support, access to education and/or training opportunities, formally or informally, either in the workplace or outside the organisation. It should be a sustained activity which, when embedded into the culture of an organisation, will increase staff morale as well as enhance the quality of their performance and which will result in positive and measurable outcomes for the organisation.

1.2 Analyse potential barriers to professional development

Why do we need to engage in professional development? Professional development is an essential activity for all staff working in health and care settings in order to safeguard the health and well-being of the public. Knowledge is not static. Things we thought we knew for a fact may turn out to be wrong, limited or less effective than new ways of doing things. Research and development is a key feature of health care. The outcomes of research generate new knowledge which results in improved treatments, enhanced equipment and different ways of approaching care. In addition, individual user needs and expectations, political priorities and requirements mean that practitioners must be able to review and modify practice appropriately in the light of emerging evidence.

The requirement for care workers to engage in professional development is articulated in legislation through the expectation of the 'duty of care'. The term 'duty of care' has both a legal and moral foundation. It is the basis for the obligations that we owe to those in our care. It is based on the moral principles of respect for persons and the moral duty to prevent harm and to promote good. It also has long-standing legal

precedence, the following definition being commonly accepted in tort law:

'You must take reasonable care to avoid acts or omissions which you can reasonably see would be likely to injure your neighbour.'

(Lord Atkins at p.580, *Donaghue* v *Stephenson* [1932])

In this context 'neighbour' refers to someone with whom you have a professional relationship and for whom you owe a duty of care. The duty of care imposes an obligation on the care-giver to ensure that their care meets **reasonable** and **agreed standards**, the expectation being that care provided will be at least as good as care provided by other similar practitioners at that level of experience, and additionally, that current relevant guidelines, procedures and protocols have been appropriately accorded with. Neither ignorance, nor omission, on the part of the care-giver is an excuse for sub-standard care if it is judged that the care-giver should reasonably have been expected to know something. For example, failure to attend scheduled updates on infection control or failure to follow revised care practices could expose the individual and/or the organisation to legal challenge if harm results to clients.

The requirement for professional development is further reinforced in professional codes and standards of conduct, such as the General Social Care Council Code of Practice for Social Care Workers (GSCC, 2010); the Health Professions Council (2008) Standards of Conduct, Performance and Ethics; the Nursing and Midwifery Council (2008) The Code: Standards of conduct, performance and ethics for nurses and midwives; and articulated in various National Occupational Standards.

These documents articulate the standards that the public can expect from those delivering care. All codes and standards of practice make explicit reference to the need for those providing care to work within their levels of knowledge and experience and to address any knowledge deficits. Merely attending mandatory training updates such as Manual Handling and Resuscitation, for example, are important but unlikely to be sufficient to meet the responsibility and breadth of expectations for personal and professional development implied in the law and in codes of conduct.

Each individual is also accountable for their professional development and you may be required to identify to your managers, to your profession and/or to a legal authority how you have maintained this. As a manager and leader of others, it is your responsibility to ensure that those you manage are appropriately equipped to effectively fulfil their roles. This requires you to assess each individual's capabilities against their job description to ensure that there are no deficits in the knowledge and skills they possess against those that are necessary to do their job.

Activity 4.1.2

Look at your own job description (if you do not have one, or if it no longer accurately describes your role, write a list of the duties that your role entails) then write a list of the essential skills and qualities necessary for someone to fulfil that role effectively.

Are there any requirements in the role that you feel less confident of your skills to fulfil adequately? These are some areas for professional development.

You can repeat the exercise for individuals you manage. This provides you with the opportunity to reflect on roles and responsibilities, as well as providing an opportunity to rectify any deficits. It also ensures that your staff are clear about the expectations that you have of them and to discuss ideas you both may have of extending or developing the role.

Tip: Once you understand others' strengths, weaknesses and personal interests, you can use these to identify champions. These individuals may be asked to take responsibility to lead and develop expertise in different subject areas in order to support their own and others' development. If presented as an opportunity that is not threatening, commitment from participants is likely to be high. Importantly, individuals must not be forced into positions in which they will feel intimidated or threatened. Those not comfortable with even small group presentations should be encouraged to share their knowledge in different and less threatening ways.

Whilst a deficit model, that of identifying and addressing knowledge gaps, is important in ensuring that essential training requirements are met, this is a limited model. Development implies something that is positive and proactive and failure to capitalise on the potential benefits of a coherent staff development plan is a missed opportunity. Each of us has different strengths and weaknesses. Identifying what these are in yourself and in your team is an important first step in planning professional development. Development should be a positive activity focussed on enhancement and should be used as an opportunity to get the best from the team as a whole in order that the organisation gains the most benefit.

Consequently, if you have a good understanding of the team you can focus development on individuals' skills and strengths and so you not only increase individual knowledge but you also harness others' skills to benefit the team as a whole, to increase job satisfaction and responsibility for individuals.

Conquering potential barriers to professional development

The need for professional development is not contentious and it is not difficult to mount a convincing argument for its integration into organisational culture, yet when times are busy and challenging, it can be the first thing to drop off the agenda. However, I would argue that staff development is not an optional luxury but rather is an essential requirement for any service seeking to provide care for others. The challenge for the manager, therefore, is to find ways of overcoming the barriers. Barriers are little more than hurdles to get around. Whilst they may seem insurmountable, ingenuity, creativity and a positive attitude may be sufficient to overcome them. Barriers should be viewed as problems to be solved rather than as overwhelming obstacles.

When planning personal professional development, it will be important for you as a manager to engage the expected participants in the process as partners. If the participant is receptive to the development opportunity they are less likely to think up 'yes, but…' scenarios and will be more likely to find solutions to their own barriers. For example, if attendance at a course is difficult because of someone's personal commitments, a discussion with them about how this could be overcome or different ways of studying could resolve the issue. It is important that individuals are engaged and understand the need for the activity and the benefits and opportunities that might result from it.

Managers do not have to think of all the possible solutions. More importantly, you need to create an environment that encourages and expects the

Activity 4.1.3

Think about your team and make a list of the different strengths and attributes that each individual brings. Include yourself in this. Can you identify any ways that you could use and develop these different attributes?

team to share the responsibility and to think up creative solutions and support each other. You may have to set parameters on this such as costs, time frames, numbers of staff and so forth, in order that solutions are realistic and achievable.

Managing time is an important component of developing an effective staff development programme. It takes time to identify individual needs and interests and to assess what things will bring about most benefit to the team and the organisation, but if done effectively, this will be time well spent. It is important to account for interests as well as organisational needs, although the latter may take priority. If staff feel their individual interests are supported, it will help maintain motivation and morale in the team. In addition, staff need to feel that the activity is valued for its own sake and is not just another chore to be squeezed in around more important routine activities. Consequently staff need the encouragement to put their learning into practice.

As a manager you will be aware that there is never enough resource to meet everybody's needs and wants and it is important that planning is realistic to avoid disappointment and disillusion. It is also important to ensure that the resource is used as efficiently and fairly as possible; time spent researching different means of achieving goals, such as on-line or blended learning, may substantially reduce costs and increase flexibility.

When times are difficult it may be necessary to reduce the amount of development that can be supported. Trying to do too much runs the risk of adding additional stress on staff and possible loss of good will. It is your responsibility to be able to justify decisions. Sorting your activities into priority categories with identification of associated risks if an activity is not done is one way of prioritising development.

Jasper (2006, p.32) suggests a simple mnemonic which you can use to assess the practicality of professional development activities: 'REACT'. That is:

Is the planned activity:

- Relevant?
- Easily defined?
- Achievable?
- Cost effective?
- Timely?

Even when an essential training need has been identified, there are times when the ability to authorise training may not fall within your sphere of authority. A useful skill to learn as a manager is to be able to articulate a convincing argument to support your case to the authorising individual (group). This may best be achieved through the development of a brief report. This may be presented orally but a report has a number of benefits. It will demonstrate that you have taken the issue seriously and that you have taken time to research and present this professionally; it will ensure that you do not forget anything; and it will enable the individual to reflect on it once your presentation is over. A report has a specific function and style and to get most impact from it, you should meet the basic criteria outlined below. Further guidance can be gained in a number of guides such as that written by Bowden (2004). An outline of key points is summarised below:

- Assess your audience and identify what they will wish to know.
- Set a clear objective.
- Research your topic.

Activity 4.1.4

	Activity	Expected outcome and date for completion	Potential risk if not undertaken
Essential			
Desirable			
Opportunity			

- Prioritise your findings.
- Write your report.

Reports must be concise, accurate, clear and well structured. The opening paragraphs should clearly include:

- **Terms of reference** (a definition of the task; your specific objective and purpose of writing).
- **A brief summary** (a very brief overview of the report including a statement of: aims, key findings and main conclusions and recommendations).
- **The main body of the report** (including an introduction identifying context, main body which is a discussion of findings and evidence to support those findings, a conclusion which will normally be clear about a desired course of action, and recommendations about how this can be achieved).
- **References** (these give credibility to the evidence that you are presenting).

Activity 4.1.5

Think about something you would like to implement in your own organisation and try to write a report that will persuade your manager to support your initiative.

As discussed at the beginning of this section, barriers are often not insurmountable and one of your roles as manager is to identify strategies for overcoming barriers.

1.3 Compare the use of different *sources and systems of support* for professional development

Not all professional development will be achieved by attendance at formal training or education events. There are various forms of informal support that are of significant value in developing others' capabilities.

It has been said that the richest resource that any organisation possesses is the people who work within it. An organisation will only evolve and change if people make it happen. Individuals are interested in, and motivated by, different things and this includes their motivation to learn something. Consequently, everyone's knowledge base and skill set is different, even when similar levels of formal training have been undertaken. If we could pool and share this knowledge, everyone including the organisation would benefit. A key role for a manager is to utilise the existing skill set within a team in order to enhance knowledge and skills of others. The following paragraphs introduce a few means of achieving this with very limited investment.

Presentations and sharing good practice

It is acknowledged that formal presentations, even those between close knit teams of people, can be intimidating and time consuming to prepare and deliver. However, creating an opportunity to discuss a 'best kept secret' in an informal, five-minute contribution may be less threatening and an effective way of sharing good practice. All, or a small number of, team members can be invited to come to a meeting and must be warned to be prepared to share with their colleagues an issue of practice, taking only five minutes. This could be something that they think they do well, and should briefly include evidence that demonstrates that this is good practice. They may want to discuss new knowledge such as highlighting a change in standard treatment. Alternatively they could present a problem and invite their colleagues to suggest solutions or ways of finding solutions. This type of activity stimulates discussion and provides an opportunity for everyone in the team to learn something new, to reflect on their own practice and knowledge, and to identify those things which should be investigated further, or those things which the team would wish to implement and develop. Whilst these vignettes do not provide sufficient information to initiate a change of practice in other practitioners, it is an effective way of sharing headlines so that anyone who is interested in taking this further can contact an identified individual. Alternatively, staff can be invited to present to colleagues a summary of knowledge gained at formal training events, or to present and initiate discussion of client case studies to reflect on and evaluate care management. Inevitably the success will be dependent on the commitment of those involved.

This kind of development activity is more likely to be sustained if all members are expected to contribute in rotation. It should be planned and co-ordinated by one team member and occupy a regular slot so that staff see it not as an addition to work, but very much as another element of the expectation of everyday work.

Whilst a team is a very valuable and often untapped resource, it is also important that staff have access to up-to-date resources that can provide answers to professional questions. In the past it was necessary for organisations to purchase books and whilst books have their place for reference, in many cases, particularly in respect of clinical management, these quickly become out of date. Therefore, books need to be purchased judiciously and updated regularly.

Good quality and easily accessible information is increasingly available through electronic means, either through search engines on the internet or through access to electronic and digitised resources and journals. CD training packs which support learning in key elements of your provision are an ideal means of delivering training to a large number of staff without the additional expense of covering attendance and cover for study days.

Appraisal

Requests for and the identification of the need for more formal methods of personal professional development are often generated through formal appraisal processes. Appraisal is a key strategy for managers to assess performance and needs against organisational requirements and aims. Appraisal is a formally constituted, annual activity that should be booked with all staff. Appraisal is normally conducted by a manager but can be conducted by peers if its focus is on developmental needs rather than role performance. Whichever model is adopted, individuals need warning about what it will involve in order that they can prepare for it in advance. Ideally they should see examples of any documentation that will be used so that they can plan responses to the questions that will be asked. Appraisal offers a vehicle for structured, personal development planning that can have positive outcomes for both individuals and the organisation. It may help develop a strategy for an individual to

Activity 4.1.6

Think about which of the following functions of personal development planning are important within your organisation.

Function of personal development planning	Tick	Does your PDP enable this function to be realised?
Assessment of competence to undertake a role against pre-determined criteria (e.g. role descriptor)		
Opportunity to enhance effectiveness and performance		
Planning for the future (short, medium and long term)		
Clarification of values and behaviours		
Evaluation of service		
Means of enhancing service		
Increase staff motivation		
Opportunity for self-reflection		
Identification of strengths and areas for improvement		
Strategy to solve problems		
Provide a structure for and commitment to staff training and development		
Opportunity to manage and respond to change		
Increase team capabilities		
Manage underperformance		
Provide a structure for individual feedback		

meet personal goals and objectives, both short and long term. It will help the manager to match individuals and their training needs against organisational aims and it will also enable managers to assess the fairness of the training and development allocation across the staff team. Where necessary it also provides a process for managing staff performance, as it encourages managers to measure individual performance against role competency criteria.

Most of us would admit to sometimes day-dreaming about the future and imagining that things were different or better, that we had more knowledge about something, or that we had the courage to change direction in life. For many, these dreams are nothing more than dreams. However, for others these dreams become reality. That may be luck or good fortune but to wait for good luck may be too optimistic for many of us. Personal development planning is an opportunity to begin to take control of the future by providing individuals with a deeper understanding of their performance, their skills, their needs and their dreams.

Ideally, appraisal is a shared activity that is conducted in partnership and it should result in some kind of individual personal development planning. To maximise its potential it should not be seen as a top-down process that only relates to the manager's assessment of job performance, even if this is a necessary component. Personal development planning (PDP) can have a number of different purposes and it is important that the method that you select for PDP meets your needs as a manager, as well as the individual staff member's needs. It takes time and effort to implement a successful appraisal and development process and it must be planned and used as a basis for decision making if it is going to have any significant impact.

It is important that the tool that you design or utilise addresses those purposes that you have identified as important for your organisation. If you do not have an appraisal process in your organisation you may want to consider writing a proposal to implement one.

Writing personal development plans will be addressed later in this chapter.

Mentoring

Mentoring is an invaluable tool for supporting staff development and is a powerful means of individual empowerment. Clutterbuck and Megginson (1999, p.17) describe mentorship as being like 'standing in front of a mirror with a trusted other, who can help you see things that you do not know how to see, or that have become too familiar for you to notice'.

Mentoring can be defined simply as a helping relationship between an individual with potential and an individual with expertise. The role of the mentor is to guide the mentee. Knowledge, experience and organisational

perspective are shared candidly within a context of mutual respect and trust. The mentoring relationship is multi-dimensional and is characterised as a partnership between two people (mentor and mentee) normally working in a similar field or who share similar experiences and who can support each other. It is important to distinguish mentorship from a manager–employee relationship. Mentorship can exist within, or between, organisational role structures and can be conducted across different organisations. It is an effective way of helping people to progress in their careers and is becoming increasing popular as its potential is realised. A number of roles of the mentor have been listed by Bolton (2010, p.193): role model, enabler, teacher, encourager, counsellor, befriender, facilitator, coach, confidante, supporter and 'un-learner'.

If mentorship is to be successful, it is important that roles and responsibilities of the parties involved are clarified and that mentors and mentees are matched appropriately and that both parties understand what is expected of them.

Mentorship can be used to meet a number of development purposes: to induct new staff, to support and guide learners or junior staff in their roles, to share expertise and specialised knowledge and skills within a team. Mentorship exists formally over a defined period although many such relationships progress informally beyond this if it is mutually beneficial to the participants.

Coaching

Coaching, although sometimes used interchangeably with mentoring, is in fact a distinct activity, although there are some similarities. Coaching is an activity designed to help individuals fulfil their potential and thus is an ideal strategy for some elements of professional development. Coaching can be defined as a process that supports and enables an individual to unlock and maximise their own potential, to develop and improve performance. It is a process of helping them to learn rather than teaching them. Coaching requires a belief that individuals are capable of addressing and resolving their own issues and needs. Not only are they capable but coaching implies that they are best suited to take responsibility for their own decisions and actions and solutions; coaching can therefore be said to be a leadership style. Coaches use a range of different tools and models to support their coachee. Coaching requires an attitude of positive regard and good communication skills in order to provide the right prompts to enable the coachee to reach their own resolutions and conclusions. A coach may or may not have experience or expertise in the coachee occupation. The skill of the coach is in asking the coachee appropriate prompt questions in order to enable them to think clearly and coherently about their own issues.

Coaching is an excellent way of improving performance through reflection. It not only supports an individual to reflect on an issue to find their own solutions, it also builds capacity in a team. Coaching can be done through the appraisal process, as a planned and formal activity in its own right, or informally in day-to-day practice. The 'GROW' model of coaching (Whitmore, 2009) provides a simple and structured model for the coach.

G = Goal setting asks questions to encourage the coachee to clarify what they want and where they want to get to. The coach will encourage the coachee to explore what achievement would look like to them.

R = Reality promotes questions that require reflection on now. What is the situation currently? What is stopping you achieving your goals? What do you need to achieve your goals? What is a realistic time scale? What do you enjoy and why? What are the key risks?

O = Options. This stage of the model encourages the coachee to explore different means of achieving the goal. Questions that might be asked include: What are all the different ways that you could achieve your goal? What else could you do? What are the pros and cons of different options? What would happen if...? Which of the options would bring about the best result?

W = Way forward. Finally, the coach will encourage the coachee to make an action plan. Questions that might be useful include: What are you resolved to do, and by when? What support do you need? What commitment do you have? When should we/you review progress?

Coaching enables control and development to remain squarely with the coachee, with the effective coach acting merely as a key to help them unlock their own potential.

Appreciative inquiry

A strategy that is gaining significant interest in recent years in developing teams and organisations is 'appreciative inquiry' (Cooperrider, Whitney and Stavros, 2003). Appreciative inquiry focusses on the positive features of an organisation and its workforce, rather than a deficit model. It directs energy to identifying and building on strengths rather than trying to compensate for or to rectify weaknesses. Appreciative inquiry aims to generate a collective image of a new and better future organisation, in which all of the workforce have an investment and a contribution to make. The practice of appreciative inquiry is to explore best practice, past and present, within the organisation and to concentrate on defining those positive values, practices and processes which improve and enhance best practice.

Cooperrider, Whitney and Stavros suggest 4Ds to guide appreciative inquiry:

- **Discovery** – Seeking that which is 'best' including staff.
- **Dream** – Developing a collective vision.
- **Design** – Identifying strategies that can achieve the vision and revising these until the vision can be achieved.
- **Destiny** – Engendering and supporting new ways of working that can enable the vision to be realised and sustained.

Activity 4.1.7

Look up Cooperrider, Whitney and Stavros' model. How useful would this be as a strategy for professional development?

1.4 Explain factors to consider when selecting opportunities and activities for keeping knowledge and practice up to date

Inevitably, investing in opportunities to enable staff to keep up to date is associated with costs and it would be unrealistic and irresponsible not to consider these costs seriously. However, it is important to balance these investment costs against risks and costs associated with the risk of not engaging in development activities.

It is tempting to see staff development as a luxury, non-essential activity when times are tight, but in an environment in which treatments, practices and expectations are constantly changing, that would be a mistake. What is important is to ensure that any development budget is spent appropriately and that key risks are prioritised over other less important activities. As with any risk assessment, it is important to evaluate risks in the light of both their likely probability and the extent of their potential impact.

For example, failing to ensure that staff gain appropriate training in relation to manual handling would leave the organisation vulnerable to litigation and potentially expensive compensation claims from both staff and possibly clients. Given the nature of care work that requires moving and handling to take place, it is highly likely that an incident will occur and it is also likely to have a high impact. This would result in a high risk score which should alert the manager that there is a need to do something urgently to rectify the deficit. Risks can be plotted on a chart so that it is easy to get a visual image of where key areas need to be addressed.

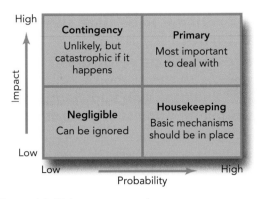

Figure 4.1 Risk assessment chart

Activity 4.1.8

Think about your own organisation and the range of risks that you are subject to. You may have identified risks such as the employment of new staff; the effective implementation of Care Quality Commission's standards and the effectiveness of evidence to illustrate compliance with these standards; introduction of new care standards or key priorities such as a national focus on infection control, or reduction in pressure areas or increased attention on nutrition; the risk of not sustaining staff motivation and morale; ensuring viability and popularity; introduction of new practice or processes.

All of these risks could be lessened by appropriate staff development. In any organisation it is necessary to address priorities. Categorise your risks using Figure 4.1. Does this provide you with information on which to begin to make choices?

In making decisions about priorities, it is important to draw on a range of evidence to ensure that your money and time will be well spent. Whilst this is a time-consuming activity, it can be part of an annual review of quality. Staff development should be directed towards those areas where there are gaps or where improvements are needed. Consequently, undertaking an analysis of client complaints or staff turnover and individual staff perceptions could indicate areas of underachievement or staff insecurity. More proactively drawing up a chart of the staff's wish list for development arising from appraisals may be useful.

Building on existing development and developing expertise that can be shared rather than spreading the budget too thinly may be a more effective strategy. Additionally, it is important to know how good staff development is. If you have already sent staff to particular activities/providers, it is important to reflect on how well the experience went and whether it has had an impact on service provision. As a manager, value for money and ability to achieve the objectives set must be key evaluative questions.

Managers in the care environment have a professional responsibility to keep up to date. They need to be aware of changes to practice requirements; these could result from changes in government policy or new initiatives, the publication of new standards for practice, or new knowledge that requires different behaviours. Being aware of current issues and practices in your sector enables the manager to be proactive. If a report or publication relating to poor practice is published about another provider in the sector, it provides the manager with an opportunity to review practices in their own organisation and address any shortcomings. Ignorance and complacency are not defendable. In situations of rapid change and in competitive markets, it is a fact that only those organisations that are able to be flexible, adaptive and productive will excel. The survival and sustainability of your organisation may depend on its ability to respond effectively and quickly to change, to become what Senge (1990) identifies as a 'learning organisation'.

According to Senge, learning organisations are:

'...organisations where people continually expand their capacity to create the results they truly desire, where new and expansive patterns of thinking are nurtured, where collective aspiration is set free, and where people are continually learning to see the whole together'.

(1990, p.3)

While all people have the capacity to learn, the structures in which they have to function are often not conducive to reflection, engagement and learning. Furthermore, people may lack the tools and understanding to make sense of the situations they face. Organisations that are continually expanding their capacity to control and create their future require a fundamental shift of mind-set among their members. The manager's role is to 'discover how to tap into people's commitment and capacity to learn at all levels' (Senge, 1990, p.4).

Senge (1990) identifies five key dimensions for a successful learning organisation:

1. **Systems thinking** – requires decisions to be made within a bigger picture framework, acknowledging impacts on other areas of the business, and over long-term thinking.

2. **Personal mastery** – organisations learn through individuals which requires us to deepen knowledge by reflection and questioning what we know.

3. **Mental models** – requires us to test out assumptions.

4. **Building shared vision** – develop a shared vision of what you want to achieve in your team and think creatively about how that can be achieved.

5. **Team learning** – creating dialogue within a team to ensure that learning is able to result in shared understanding within the team as a whole.

The Institute of Management Services similarly notes that organisations that are exemplars for the training and development of their workforces demonstrate a number of key characteristics:

■ Value individual and organisational learning as a prime means of delivering the organisational mission.

■ Involve all its members through continuous reflection in a process of continual review and improvement.

■ Structure work in such a way that work tasks are used as opportunities for continuous learning.

(www.ims-productivity.com/page.cfm/
content/Learning-Organisation)

Looking at these characteristics, one can see that the concept of a learning organisation shares many of the attributes that could be said to characterise a quality organisation.

Activity 4.1.9

Look at the characteristics identified by Senge (1990) for a learning organisation and those noted by the Institute of Management Services above.

How well does your organisation reflect these characteristics?

Think about why they do or do not.

What changes need to be made to more closely align your organisation to the principles identified above?

Organisations that have characteristics of learning organisations (Senge, 1990) experience increased reputation, increased effectiveness, increased staff motivation and staff satisfaction, higher levels of staff retention, increased staff flexibility and are more able to respond to change and consequently better prepared to compete with competitors, which in turn increases business opportunities. Perhaps most important of all, learning organisations have the most satisfied 'customers'.

2 Be able to prioritise goals and targets for own professional development

2.1 **Evaluate own knowledge and performance against *standards and benchmarks***

Earlier in the chapter you should have completed an activity to enable you to map your personal knowledge and skills against your job description. However, the job description may be only one of the measures that can be used to identify any development needs. Individuals working in the care industry will also be subject to a range of professional codes, expectations and standards of performance that are set by external organisations. For example, the Nursing and Midwifery Code of Conduct, the GSCC Code of Practice for Care Workers or various National Occupational Standards.

Activity 4.2.1

Make a list of the codes and standards that guide and govern your role.

When did you last review and reflect on your work against these standards?

How is your work influenced by these codes and standards?

Evaluate your performance in the light of these standards.

Evidence from a number of studies on ethical leadership suggest that the single most important factor in ensuring high standards and ethical practice is the ethical value-led behaviour of the leaders in that organisation.

As well as identifying the standards of care to be achieved, codes of practice articulate the manner in which care should be delivered. All recipients of care should expect to receive competent care. An organisation that strives for excellence will also ensure that attention is paid to the value base of care provision which facilitates good and excellent practice as opposed to merely competent or safe practice.

Activity 4.2.2

Complete the learning organisation questionnaire, then reflect on how well you think your organisation demonstrates the characteristics of a learning organisation.

2.2 Prioritise development goals and targets to meet expected standards

The preceding sections should have provided you with an opportunity to:

- reflect on your own strengths and weaknesses
- review your role and its requirements
- review the requirements of those in your team

- identify the key risks to your organisation
- reflect on education and training deficits in relation to roles
- think about a range of different ways of developing the team
- identify barriers to professional development
- reflect on the value base of your organisation.

You should now be ready to pull all of this information together in order to draw up a professional development plan for yourself. Once you have done this it is important that you assist members of your team to write their plans. This will then enable you to draw up an organisational plan and assess the viability and the contribution that development activities could make to the enhancement of the organisation.

As a manager it is your responsibility to ensure that staff development meets both organisational needs and priorities, as well as supports and motivates individual team members' personal and professional development. A good development plan will fulfil both requirements. It will seek to address and avert potential risks resulting from knowledge or skills deficits. It will seek to enhance service delivery and to develop personal and professional capacities of staff. It should be realistic but also strive to be ambitious. It is important to achieve a balance between what can properly be supported and to devise creative strategies to achieve more. It must be fair; opportunities must be fairly distributed across the team and across all levels of staff. It must result in tangible outcomes and consequently staff who are developed must be enabled to share and/or implement their learning. Consequently, when designing your plan, you will need to build in evaluative measures to ensure that you are fulfilling your obligations and objectives.

3 Be able to devise a professional development plan

3.1 Select learning opportunities to meet development objectives and reflect personal learning style

Having identified your own strengths, deficits, training needs and ideas for service enhancements, it is important that these are transformed into tangible actions that can be articulated as objectives. Objectives are statements that describe what the end point of an activity will be. Objectives should be written with the **SMART** acronym in mind; that is they should be **S**pecific, **M**easureable, **A**ttainable,

Relevant and Timebound. When writing your objectives you should have the end in mind before you start. Think of it as a journey – it is not often that you set out on a journey not knowing where you want to end up. When travelling you also plan how you are going to get there and you reflect, albeit informally, on how successful your plan was. You may choose a tried and tested means of getting to an important occasion but if you have a lot of time and no specific arrival time, you may be a little more adventurous in selecting your mode of transport. Setting learning objectives is analogous to planning a journey. Your plan must be able to deliver what you set out to do and you must evaluate how successful you have been. Consequently, the more information on which you can base your plan should secure the best chance of success.

What information do you need in order to develop a good plan?

Firstly, what do you know about yourself? How do you like to learn? Individuals learn in different ways and you should think about the method that suits your preferred learning style so that, where possible, you can select appropriate learning activities. Individuals learn in different ways and if possible you should think about the method that suits your preferred learning style.

Think about different learning activities you have participated in. Do you like discussion and working with others? Do you prefer tutor guidance? Do you like exploring and learning on your own? Are computer programs a style of learning that you enjoy? If you enjoy the process of learning you are more likely to stick with it, particularly if it is over a period of time.

3.2 Produce a plan for own professional development, using an appropriate source of support

Once you understand how you like to learn, you now need to articulate what you need to learn and identify how this can be achieved. Identifying needs and areas for improvement can amount to nothing more than a 'wish list' – 'wouldn't it be nice if....'. Time spent reflecting on these wishes will help you to prioritise your development needs. Once you have identified your needs these must be articulated as objectives. It is important that objectives are prioritised and committed to paper in the form of a plan.

Developing a formal plan serves a number of purposes. It enables you to structure and prioritise your learning and development. It allows you to set short- and long-term goals which enable you to think about your development as a whole and should thus ensure

---

Activity 4.3.1

What is your preferred learning style?

Try to remember your most satisfying and least satisfying learning experiences. What was it that made them satisfying or not?

Honey and Mumford (1992) developed a questionnaire that enables participants to distinguish between four key ways of learning. Many have a dominant style but equally many have more than one.

Activist – I prefer to work intuitively, be flexible and spontaneous, generate new ideas and try things out. I like to learn from problem solving, discussion, group work and experience.

Reflector – I like to watch/listen and reflect, gathering data and taking time to consider options and alternatives. I like lectures, project work and information research.

Theorist – I prefer to go through things thoroughly and logically, step by step. I like guidelines. I prefer to learn from books, problem solving and discussion.

Pragmatist – I learn by 'trying things out'. I am practical and realistic. I like work-based learning and practical application in real settings.

Is it helpful to identify your preferred style?

Think about the characteristics of your team. Can you identify their different learning styles?

If individuals can be matched with their preferred style it will make learning easier for them, inevitably these cannot always be fully accommodated but knowing one's style will help appropriate planning.

more overall benefit and should enable you to include ambitions as well as needs. Planning enables you to address those things that you must do, such as to update your knowledge and skills, but it also helps you to start to devise a more creative and personalised plan. The short-term goals may or may not contribute to the longer-term ones. Writing your objectives in a plan adds weight and structure to them and they are more likely to be acted on, especially if the plan is shared with another such as a line manager who may commit to supporting it.

When prioritising your objectives, think about how much you want to do something. Personal/professional development is not something that happens to you, it is something you normally actively choose or agree to participate in. Before embarking on development activities, you should be clear about what you are prepared to invest in achieving the goals that you set. This may include decisions about your personal motivations, the time you are prepared to make available, which is likely to be in addition to anything your employer will

Activity 4.3.2

Using the template below develop your professional development plan. Ensure that you write objectives that can be measured and evaluated. Clearly articulate the evidence that will demonstrate whether or not you have achieved your objectives.

Overall learning development need	What specifically do you need to know/learn?			
Objectives	**Date for achievement**	**How will you achieve your objective?**	**Support required**	**Evidence and outcomes**
What specific end or steps do you have in mind? You must include a measureable verb in each objective statement in this column, e.g. Pass an accredited First Aid course.	When will you assess progress? When will you have achieved your objective?	How will you meet your objective?	Human? Financial? Time? Learning resources?	What evidence will you have to confirm your achievement?
Avoiding barriers and blockers	What positive steps can you take to avoid barriers?			
Example *Develop IT skills to enable effective forward planning and publication of staff rotas for off-duty cover.*	September this year	Complete course on using Microsoft Excel	Either day release to attend course or time to undertake online programme	Publication of all off-duty rotas using computerised support packages. Staff cover will be effective and planned and produced four weeks in advance.
Avoiding barriers and blockers	What positive steps can you take to avoid barriers and blockers? Identify need and actual and potential benefits for the organisation. Research and present different methods of achieving goal with pros and cons identified. Discuss with and gain commitment from line manager through signed agreement or financial support to enable attendance/completion of the course. Report progress.			

provide. You must be realistic about resources and in particular the financial burdens and who will be responsible for them. It is also important to acknowledge the potential impact that education and development can have on those around you, both at home and at work. This can be as a result of support that others must provide or in view of the change that may occur in you as a result of the development. You must be realistic about these factors but that does not mean you should not also have aspirations and set an ambitious plan.

A successful professional development plan will clearly specify how the objectives will be achieved and will also identify the timeframes and milestones against which progress can be measured. Finally it will suggest criteria against which the activity can be evaluated.

You may need support from your managers for some aspects of personal professional development and a well worked through plan with clear objectives and outcomes may help you seek the support you need. If you can demonstrate that you expect to achieve benefits for the organisation as well as yourself, you may have a greater chance of success.

3.3 Establish a process to assess the effectiveness of the plan

As discussed in the previous section, any professional development activity involves costs either for the organisation or for the individual. It is important that these costs are worthwhile. Evaluating the effectiveness of staff development enables the manager to assess the value of the investment and make responsible decisions for the future.

Firstly, you should establish whether the objectives you set have been met. Secondly, what evidence do you have that they have been met? If the activity was designed to teach the acquisition of a skill, it is relatively easy to assess whether the activity was successful. However, some educational development activities are more intangible, more difficult to assess and may take longer to see any benefit, such as changes in attitude, behaviour and practice. You may be able to assess specific elements of learning, for example, an increased knowledge base.

However, knowing something does not necessarily mean that the learning has been beneficial. What is more important may be to assess whether it has resulted in a change in behaviour. Education that results in behaviour change is deeper level learning and is most likely to be the kind of learning that has high impact and can be sustained over time. However, it can also be threatening for others who may feel challenged by new practices. Such behaviour change may have to overcome the very strong influence of habit and accustomed practice. In order to assess how effective a new practice is, it

must have an opportunity to be used effectively and its implementation may need to be trialled and supported within the workplace. If the learning requires a change in behaviour or practice, the conditions need to exist to enable that change to be implemented. As a manager you need to think of strategies that can support that change and, where relevant, demonstrate to others the benefits of that change.

If the development activity has failed to meet the objectives set, it is equally important to assess why these have not been achieved. Were the objectives realistic? If they were, question why they have not been successful. Questions such as the following may help to identify what went wrong. What was the motivation, ability or commitment of the participants? Did the participants enjoy it? What did they like/dislike about it? Did the activity fail to engage participants? Was it delivered in a way that was suitable for the participants? If not, what would have helped? Did it deliver value for money? Is there a better way of achieving the same outcomes? Was it worthwhile in a different way from that which was originally conceived?

Development plans are living documents. Priorities for training and education needs are not static but must be revised and rewritten on the basis of changing requirements, new practice and research evidence and altered expectations, as well as following completion or review of objectives. Plans can be formally reviewed at appraisal meetings but can also be updated to take account of *ad hoc* learning opportunities which occur. Many practitioners are required by their profession to keep records of their personal professional development in order to demonstrate their fitness to practise. A well worked through plan will provide good evidence of on-going and concurrent engagement with continuing professional development requirements.

4 Be able to improve performance through reflective practice

4.1 Compare models of reflective practice

Reflective practice is an essential element of personal development. It provides an opportunity to stop and take stock. Bolton (2010, p.4) identifies a number of applications for reflective practice.

Reflective practice enables you to:

- Identify what you know but do not know that you know.

- Identify what you want to know but do not know.

- Reflect on what you think feel, believe, value.

- Examine how well actions match up to beliefs.

- Reflect on barriers to practising the way that you would wish to practise.

- Think about what you should/can change in your work context and how this could be achieved.

- Learn how to value others' perspectives even when they differ from your own.

- Examine your personal behaviours and responses and seek ways to make these more productive.

Jasper (2006, p.40) sees reflective practice as an essential means of professional growth and development that enables practitioners to develop basic skills and knowledge into expert skills and knowledge. Inevitably simple repetition of a skill should enable a practitioner to be more competent in its performance. However, reflective analysis about that performance enables you to identify more quickly specific areas for improvement or gaps in your knowledge. A good analogy is to think about the strategies used by elite sportsmen and women; they record, replay and analyse both their own and others' performance in order to identify their strengths and improve them and eliminate less good practice. Reflection in care work provides a similar opportunity to assist practitioners to improve their own performance and that of the teams that they work with. Whilst it is not undertaken by video analysis, it can be done by writing a record of events or by analysing current practice against desired practice.

Reflective practice is a conscious activity that results in positive decisions. Reflection has gained significant weight in recent years in the care arena and a number of models have been developed to assist practitioners to reflect. Reflective practice was first coined by Donald Schon (1983). He identified that learning in practice could be enhanced by two different kinds of activity: reflection in-action and reflection on-action.

Reflection in-action requires practitioners to 'think ahead', to critically reflect on what one is doing whilst one is doing it and to revise actions in the light of that reflection (Greenwood, 1993).

Reflection on-action is a retrospective activity that requires practitioners to interpret and analyse recalled information from activities that they have been engaged with (Boyd and Fales, 1983; Fitzgerald, 1994; Atkins and Murphy, 1994). Different models of reflection suit different learning styles and different purposes. A model is a tool to provide structure to an activity and it is important that you select one that suits your style. The significant thing to remember is that, whichever model is selected, it is the learning that results from the activity that is the

significant thing: learning that is either confirmation that behaviour is appropriate or learning that suggests a need to gain more information or change practice.

Models of reflection are normally illustrated as cyclical activities such as those depicted in Figure 4.2 and Figure 4.3.

Figure 4.2 Model of reflection

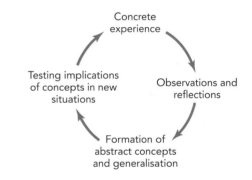

Figure 4.3 Model of reflection

Many models are constructed around the use of structured questions to prompt reflection in a logical and systematic manner (Johns, 1995). These questions are often focussed on incident analysis as the key method of reflecting (Gibbs, 1988). This approach entails practitioners selecting a significant incident, writing about it in detail and then analysing what happened, asking why, identifying what additional knowledge would have enabled the practitioner to behave differently. It requires the reflector to explore what evidence there is that similar things have been addressed by others more effectively and to establish what learning can be drawn from the experience.

This approach enables practitioners to be better prepared when faced with similar experiences in the future, as well as providing an opportunity to identify shortcomings in knowledge or skills which can be rectified. This reflection on-action is obviously a valuable tool – it enables individuals to reflect on their experiences, both positive and negative, and learn from them. As a manager of a team, teaching and encouraging staff to be self-reflecting is very important. However, reflection need not just relate to isolated and specific incidents. Reflection in-action can be a powerful tool. It can be used to improve practice by supporting individuals to question their routine work as they carry it out. They may measure their behaviour against their values and the values of the organisation to ensure that these are consistent. Or they may try a new approach to an activity and evaluate its success. Encouraging staff to become self-governing and to take responsibility for their own work standards is an important element of a successful learning organisation. Reflective practice provides an opportunity for all practitioners to check their own standards of work and enhance practice.

Activity 4.4.1

Examine different models of reflective practice and reflect on their benefits and drawbacks. Which do you think you would find most useful in your professional context?

4.2 Explain the importance of reflective practice to improve performance

4.3 Use reflective practice and feedback from others to improve performance

Reflective practice is invaluable as a staff development tool. Once individuals learn to be reflective they can begin to take responsibility for their own learning and to identify their own learning needs. That is not to suggest that reflective practice does not need managerial support to enable you to take the outcomes from reflective practice forward; it often does.

Reflective practice is a tool that can be used by all practitioners, individually, to enhance their own practice. It can also be used as a management tool enabling managers to guide and support staff to reflect on key elements of their role and their performance. Prompts such as 'You did that really well. What was it that made that such a successful activity?' are useful. This approach develops individuals' self-esteem, confidence and a questioning and critical approach to their work. Reflection provides an ideal vehicle of learning that can be shared within the wider team. Teams can reflect as a group, particularly if they are keen to examine or change an aspect of practice which they have in common.

Inevitably when we reflect, no matter how candid we try to be, it is difficult to see the world from anything other than our own perspective. Reflection may require that we seek opinions and information from others to validate our reflections. Whilst information gained in this way can be seen as threatening, if managed and used sensitively, 360-degree reflection and feedback can be very illuminating and can challenge and refocus our perceptions of reality.

360-degree reflection asks us to reflect on our behaviours and performance once we have gathered information from a range of individuals, both those in positions of authority and those over whom you have authority. You contain the threat by selecting those people who will be honest but who can be trusted to feed back responsibly and constructively. It is important that you do not only ask your friends; they are likely to tell you what you want to hear rather than what you need to know. To gain the most from the activity, you need to know how different people experience you and your actions. Learning about how others perceive and experience you, your actions, attitudes and behaviours can be very empowering. Getting all round 360-degree feedback may provide you with insight about the following:

- **A façade** – information which suggests that you are better or worse at something than you think you are.

- **A blind spot** – information that you did not know about yourself.

- **A suggestion** about something that you could easily do which would make a positive difference.

- **An opportunity** to stop doing something.

360-degree feedback is usually built around a questionnaire as this helps the individual to control the areas that they want feedback on.

The criteria for choosing the wording of questionnaires for 360-degree feedback reflect general principles for designing performance appraisal systems and criteria, and include the following points:

- Questions should be relevant to the recipient's job.

- Each question should be concise, use plain English and omit qualifiers, such as 'when appropriate' and 'as necessary'. Vague and complex questions rarely produce clear feedback.

- Each question should relate to a clearly-defined competency or function to avoid muddled feedback.

- Questions should set clear and appropriate standards. For example, 'makes decisions' is a poor criterion as the decisions made could be unclear, late or wrong. A better statement might be 'makes timely and effective decisions'.

Open questions provide the opportunity to add comments in support of the answers to the rated questions and, as such, can be particularly helpful. The recipient is able to look for frequently used words or phrases and for common themes. When wording such questions, it is important to use clear language, for example, 'what does the recipient do well?', and 'what does the recipient need to improve?' (CIPD, 2011)

Activity 4.4.2

Think about the values which underpin care work.

Which values would you say are most important in your organisation? You may want to reflect on values such as respect for people, justice and fairness regardless of age, sex, gender, intelligence and disability. Or the importance of developing and sustaining independence and autonomy, or the entitlement to receive high standards of care, etc.

How are the organisational values that underpin work in your organisation communicated to your clients and to your team?

If your team were asked to rank the most important values in the organisation would they mirror yours?

The Chartered Institute for Personnel and Development (CIPD) provides a range of free and very useful resource materials and guidance for the implementation of 360-degree feedback. It can be accessed by entering CIPD in a good web search engine, or by accessing www.cipd.co.uk/hr-resources/factsheets/360-degree-feedback.aspx#link_furtherreading.

Team reflection

Another powerful tool is team reflection. So much more can be achieved by a group of individuals than by one person alone. Reflecting on performance as a team has enormous potential in identifying strengths and gaining commitment to change. The process is the same as for any other reflective process. The reflecting focusses on team strengths and deficits, although inevitably individual contributions to a team are of enormous significance. Ideally team members should contribute different strengths so that they complement each other and make a successful whole. Team reflection helps to identify and understand others' strengths in order that these can be utilised to their full potential.

4.4 Evaluate how practice has been improved through:

- **reflection on best practice**
- **reflection on failures and mistakes**

There is a great deal of emphasis on evidence-based practice and best practice. This is another means of reflection. It has involved somebody identifying an issue and researching it in order to generate evidence. Best practice is the analysis of different ways of doing things in order to identify if there is a preferred way of undertaking the activity. Access to up-to-date learning resources is important in supporting staff to keep abreast of new evidence and best practice.

Inevitably, identifying mistakes or near mistakes and assessing whether or not these could have been avoided is an important activity. It is important that these are seen as a productive activity and not a punitive one. Its primary focus is about learning from an incident or set of behaviours in order that changes can be made to improve issues. The most significant examples of this are big public inquiries which are called when serious failures and mistakes in public services are identified, such as Alder Hey, the mid-Staffordshire Enquiry, Baby P, etc. In each case it has been identified that staff failed to follow procedures and protocols, that there were lapses in expected standards of care and that there was a failure in anyone taking responsibility and reporting these lapses. Ideally if organisations and individuals practise reflectively then public inquiries of this type should never be needed.

On a smaller scale, investigations into minor mistakes and accidents are designed to enable learning from reflection on the circumstances that allowed an accident or mistake to happen. Importantly, getting the balance between investigation, reflection and assigning blame is crucially important. If staff feel they are going to be unfairly blamed or punished for mistakes, it may prevent them from reporting them or coming forward with concerns. An organisation that supports its staff to raise concerns, to acknowledge deficits and to report mistakes is much more likely to be a learning organisation than one where this is not the primary culture. An open organisation provides the conditions for someone to acknowledge and investigate what went wrong and to reflect on how things can be improved or done differently.

Activity 4.4.3

Think about the opportunities that exist in your organisation for staff to raise concerns, question practices or acknowledge mistakes. Are these formal or informal?

If you can draw on a real example of a failure, mistake or required change of a standard of practice, answer the following:

- What happened?
- Was the incident reported to senior staff?
- If the incident was reported to senior staff, who did they report it to and why that individual?
- How was the individual perceived?
- What actions resulted from the incident?
- Are policies and protocols fit for purpose?
- If a similar thing occurred again are you confident that employees feel sufficiently well supported to report the issue?
- What changes could you make in order to make it easier for staff to raise issues that can improve service and help to manage risks?

Summary

On completion of this chapter you should be able to discuss the importance of personal/ professional development and reflect on the role of this in creating a learning organisation.

You will have identified and reflected on your own knowledge and skills and developed a personal development plan. You will have identified strategies to embed staff development planning within your organisation to improve the capabilities of the workforce and you will be able to identify different forms of reflection and use these to increase the capacity of individuals and the team you manage.

Learning outcomes	Assessment criteria
1 Understand principles of professional development	**(1.1)** Explain the importance of continually improving knowledge and practice **Activity 4.1.1, p.55** **(1.2)** Analyse potential barriers to professional development **Activity 4.1.2, p.57** **Activity 4.1.3, p.57** **Activity 4.1.4, p.58** **Activity 4.1.5, p.59** **(1.3)** Compare the use of different sources and systems of support for professional development **Activity 4.1.6, p.60** **Activity 4.1.7, p.62** **(1.4)** Explain factors to consider when selecting opportunities and activities for keeping knowledge and practice up to date **Activity 4.1.8, p.63** **Activity 4.1.9, p.64**
2 Be able to prioritise goals and targets for own professional development	**(2.1)** Evaluate own knowledge and performance against standards and benchmarks **Activity 4.2.1, p.64** **Activity 4.2.2, p.64** **(2.2)** Prioritise development goals and targets to meet expected standards **See p.65 for guidance.**
3 Be able to devise a professional development plan	**(3.1)** Select learning opportunities to meet development objectives and reflect personal learning style **Activity 4.3.1, p.66** **(3.2)** Produce a plan for own professional development, using an appropriate source of support **Activity 4.3.2, p.67** **(3.3)** Establish a process to assess the effectiveness of the plan **See p.68 for guidance.**

Learning outcomes	Assessment criteria
4 Be able to improve performance through reflective practice	**(4.1)** **Compare models of reflective practice** Activity 4.4.1, p.70
	(4.2) **Explain the importance of reflective practice to improve performance** Activity 4.4.1, p.71
	(4.3) **Use reflective practice and feedback from others to improve performance** Activity 4.4.2, p.71
	(4.4) **Evaluate how practice has been improved through:** ◼ **reflective practice** ◼ **reflection on failures and mistakes** Activity 4.4.3, p.73

References

Atkins, S. and Murphy, K. (1994) 'Reflective Practice', *Nursing Standard* **8** (39), pp. 49–54.

Bolton, G. (2010) *Reflective Practice: Writing and professional development* (3e). London: Sage Publishing.

Bowden, J. (2004) *Writing a Report: How to prepare, write and present effective reports* (7e). Oxford: How to Books.

Boyd E. and Fales, A. (1983) 'Reflective Learning: The key to learning from experience', *Journal of Humanistic Psychology* **23** (2), pp. 99–117.

CIPD (2011) *CIPD Factsheet 360 Degree Feedback*, www.cipd.co.uk/hr-resources/factsheets/360-degree-feedback.aspx#link_furtherreading

Clutterbuck, D. and Megginson, D. (1999) *Mentoring Executives and Directors*. Oxford: Butterworth-Heinemann.

Cooperrider, D., Whitney D. and Stavros, J. (2003) *The Appreciative Inquiry Handbook*. San Francisco: Berrett-Koehler.

Cuthbert, S. and Quallington, J. (2008) *Values for Care Practice*. Exeter: Reflect Press.

Department of Health (2004) *The NHS Knowledge and Skills Framework and Development Review Guidance – Working Draft Version 7*. London: Department of Health. www.dh.gov.uk

Duncan, P. (2007) *Critical Perspectives on Health*. Basingstoke: Palgrave Macmillan.

Fitzgerald, M. (1994) 'Theories of Reflection for Learning' in *Reflective Practice in Nursing*, Palmer, A. and Burns, S. (eds). Oxford: Blackwell Scientific.

General Social Care Council (2010) *Code of Practice for Social Care Workers*. London: GSCC.

Gibbs, G. (1988) *Learning by Doing: A guide to teaching and learning methods*. Oxford: Oxford Further Education Unit.

Greenwood, J. (1993) 'Reflective Practice: A critique of the work of Argyris & Schon', *Journal of Advanced Nursing* **19**, pp. 1183–7.

Harrison, R. (2009) *Learning and Development* (5e). London: Chartered Institute for Personnel and Development.

Health Professions Council (2008) *Standards of Conduct, Performance and Ethics*. London: HPC.

Jasper, M. (2006) *Professional Development, Reflection and Decision-making*. Oxford: Blackwell Publishing.

Johns, C. (1995) 'Framing Learning Through Reflection within Carper's Fundamental Ways of Knowing in Nursing', *Journal of Advanced Nursing* **22**, pp. 226–34.

Nursing and Midwifery Council (2008) *The Code: Standards of conduct, performance and ethics for nurses and midwives*. London: NMC.

Seedhouse, D. (1998) *Ethics: The heart of health care*. Chichester: Wiley.

Senge, P., Kleiner, A., Roberts, C., Ross, R. and Smith, B. (1994) *The Fifth Discipline Fieldbook: Strategies and tools for building a learning organisation*. New York: Doubleday.

Whitmore, J. (2009) *Coaching for Performance. GROWing people, performance and purpose* (4e). London: Nicholas Brealey.

5 Unit SHC 53 Champion equality, diversity and inclusion

The purpose of this chapter is to enable you to reflect on the importance of respecting difference and individuality. The activities and assessments in this chapter will assist you to develop strategies for implementing and leading excellent practice in respect of equality, diversity and inclusion within the care context.

Learning outcomes
By the end of this chapter you will:

1. Understand diversity, equality and inclusion within own area of responsibility.

2. Be able to champion diversity, equality and inclusion.

3. Understand how to develop systems and processes that promote diversity, equality and inclusion.

4. Be able to manage the risks presented when balancing individual rights and professional duty of care.

1 Understand diversity, equality and inclusion within own area of responsibility

1.1 Explain models of practice that underpin equality, diversity and inclusion in own area of responsibility

The importance of understanding the positive values of equality, respect for diversity and inclusion in care work cannot be over-estimated. The circumstances that bring individuals into contact with carers suggest that recipients of care are likely to be vulnerable in one way or another. Inevitably, caring for others and engaging with them in decisions about their lives often involves the exercise of power, which has the potential to be misused and abused. How the care worker understands and approaches the responsibilities of their role will have a direct impact on either increasing equality and nullifying discrimination and disadvantage, or helping to reinforce, perpetuate or even increase inequality, discrimination and disadvantage. It can be argued that discrimination is often perpetuated unwittingly and arises from ignorance, insensitivity or commonly held beliefs that are not challenged. No matter how it is justified, discrimination has no place in care contexts. The role of the care manager is to ensure that anti-discriminatory practice is promoted as a key organisational value. Raising staff awareness about equality, diversity and inclusion, encouraging debate and devising strategies of care that empower rather than disable are essential features of the manager's role.

What does equality mean? It does not mean treating everyone the same. That is because people are all fundamentally unique, unlike inanimate objects; human states and needs are not static. People have different needs and vulnerabilities at different times. If we are to meet these needs effectively, we need to engage with people as individuals, to identify their differences and then to address their specific needs. A useful analogous term which helps the term equality to be understood is 'fairness'. Treating people with equality literally means treating people fairly. Fairness requires that individuals receive that to which they are entitled, and experience equally good standards of service, similar consideration and respect but these similar standards are modified on the basis of need and not on the basis of practitioner preference.

Applying the principle of equality requires practitioners to take a very active stance to ensure that systems, processes and practices do not unduly disadvantage those who receive care. A popular model of promoting equality is through the equal opportunities approach. To understand equality it is necessary to understand that all individuals should have the same opportunities to achieve good outcomes. The equal opportunities approach is based on the idea that, as far as possible, the starting point for all individuals should be the same. This means that disadvantages and barriers must, where possible, be removed, or that positive interventions are implemented to nullify disadvantage caused by those barriers in order that those opportunities can be realised.

An equal opportunities approach also requires that individuals are not treated differently merely on the basis of irrelevant criteria such as age, race, disability, gender or sexuality. For example, it would be discriminatory to impose an age limit as the only criterion for qualifying for physiotherapy treatment. This is because age is irrelevant. If the person has the potential to benefit from the treatment, irrespective of their age, they should have the same opportunity to access it; preventing their access would be unfair. The equal opportunity approach requires practitioners to reflect on potential and actual barriers to opportunities and propose and implement active intervention to overcome these barriers. This approach to managing difference and diversity has had significant success in improving equality and inclusion. Much of this improvement has been brought about by anti-discriminatory legislation such as the Sex Discrimination Act 1975, Equal Pay Act 1970, Race Relations Act 1976, Disability Discrimination Act 1995 and Equality Act 2006.

However, the equal opportunities approach has also been criticised (Thompson, 2011). Critics suggest that social structures and behaviours are so deeply discriminatory that, even when opportunities are equalised, some individuals will still be unable to overcome barriers and realise their potential and will continue to remain marginalised and disempowered. Critics also focus on the fact that an equal opportunities approach is rule based, overly intrusive, controlling and heavy handed, particularly because equal opportunities are so often supported by legislation which sets targets and penalties for failure to comply. Whilst, as discussed, this has had a positive impact on many discriminatory practices, there has been a change in approach to equality which is focussing much more positively on celebrating difference and diversity rather than seeing inequality as a barrier to be overcome. Humans are all unique, which entails that all have a personal set of attributes, skills, needs and preferences which comprise our differences. Historically, some differences have come to be more significant than others, but there is no real rational reason for this to be embraced or continued. To suggest that someone is less valuable because of the colour of their hair (Cuthbert and Quallington, 2008, p.23) is easily recognised as ridiculous, and yet on examination, it is no more ridiculous than discrimination on other equally spurious grounds such as age, race or sexuality.

Diversity and equality can be seen as two sides of the same coin. Equality involves fairness and diversity involves valuing difference (Thompson, 2011, p.9). As Thompson points out, what connects equality and difference is not the level of equality or the fact that something is different, it is because of the discriminatory response that the inequality or difference provokes in others. So to go back to the example of different

Figure 5.1 Equal opportunities in the workplace

coloured hair, difference does not matter if nobody responds badly to it. Difference only matters when you are treated less well on the basis of that difference. The difference and diversity model encourages people to see difference as something to celebrate rather than something to be threatened by.

Walker (1994, p.212, *adapted*) identified that the difference and diversity model is based on four key principles:

- People *function* best when they feel valued.
- People feel more valued when they believe their individual and group differences have been taken into account.
- The ability to learn from those who are different is the key to becoming empowered.
- When people are valued and empowered they can work independently and together to build relationships and *build capacity*.

Activity 5.1.1

Think about the approach taken to equality, diversity and difference in your own organisation. Is it a model based on rules that sees inequality as barriers to be overcome, or does it frame equality as a celebration of difference?

What do you think are the advantages and disadvantages of the two approaches in your organisational context?

A word of caution in adopting an approach focussed on the celebration of difference is the risk of failing to take the impact that difference can result in sufficiently seriously, so that difference is celebrated superficially but little is done to tackle the social inequalities and barriers that construct difference as a problem.

1.2 Analyse the potential effects of barriers to equality and inclusion in own area of responsibility

Ensuring that equality, diversity and inclusion are effectively embedded within an organisation requires that all staff in all roles embrace and implement these principles. The role of the manager is crucial in identifying and removing barriers to the implementation of these principles.

All organisations have their own culture or, as Thompson (2011, p.199) suggests, a 'symbolic universe' in which a shared set of meanings, beliefs, values, norms and practices are based. The organisational culture provides the parameters within which an individual operates. Consequently, it is important that managers are aware of their organisational culture and subcultures and try to implement a culture based on the desired values of the organisation.

It is important that an organisational culture is developed which reflects and reinforces a commitment to valuing diversity. The challenge is to ensure that everybody knows what the values of the organisation are and understands that they are expected to adopt these in their work, rather than merely comply with them. However, staff cannot be expected to enact values that they are not aware of. An explicit and transparent statement of values must be discussed with staff and made available to the public, thus providing a clear indication of expectations of behaviours. Secondly, discussion of what this actually means in practice is important in raising awareness and helping staff to make the link from expressed values, which may seem intangible, into real practice. Research into successful organisations demonstrates that there is a clear correlation between espoused values and the ethical leadership of that organisation's leaders on the successful realisation of values within an organisation (Renz and Eddy, 1996). That is to say that it is essential that the leaders are perceived to really live and enact the values rather than just pay lip-service to them.

Barriers

Our values, beliefs and attitudes are usually deeply ingrained and they are reinforced by our cultural context which leads us to believe that they are true. It is only when these values and beliefs are challenged, either by new information or different experiences that demonstrate that those beliefs may be flawed, that many people's values are reflected on and, where appropriate, changed. Even when individuals' views can be shown to be discriminatory or inconsistent with other values that they hold, deeply held beliefs may be resistant to change. A prejudice is an attitude or belief that is based on a faulty and inflexible generalisation. Many of the prejudices that are held lead to negative emotions and discriminatory actions, although prejudice does not necessarily cause one to discriminate unfairly. However, examining beliefs and values and questioning why we might hold a particular belief is the first step in breaking down prejudice.

The second step is to redefine views in the light of new information. Thirdly, to change behaviour in the light of those views and, fourthly, to challenge others who articulate similar prejudices. None of these steps is easy, particularly the latter; however, raising awareness and challenging can have a significant impact on breaking down discrimination and prejudice. The fact that prejudice is often not only an individual issue but represents views that might be more widely held makes this a difficult issue to eliminate. When it is a strong, culturally held belief, challenge is difficult and individuals may fear ridicule, victimisation or reprisals. In an organisation it is important that everyone is aware that prejudice cannot be tolerated and that individuals are encouraged, supported and protected to speak out against it. Creating a culture of discussion and tolerance is important in developing an open-minded community.

Prejudice can lead to unacceptable behaviours, from harassment and bullying to a substantial abuse of power over others, which leads the perpetrators to violate and infringe others' rights. If this is found to occur there must be penalties for failing to comply with organisational values. However, it is not just individuals and groups that can be prejudiced and discriminatory. As Thompson (2011, p.32) points out significant structural barriers exist that discriminate negatively on individuals. For example, there may be an unwritten policy and agreement that women in their 20s and 30s are not employed in managerial posts because of the potential for them to leave or take maternity leave when they have children. Alternatively, the organisation that fails to provide accessible toilets for those in wheelchairs is discriminatory and in breach of the law.

Many organisations are constrained by the premises and resources available to them in developing completely fair facilities. However, this is not an excuse for doing nothing. The expectation is that modifications must be made and that these may be constrained by the environment but they must also be fit for purpose.

1.3 Analyse the impact of legislation and policy initiatives on the promotion of equality, diversity and inclusion in own area of responsibility

The promotion of equality, diversity and inclusion has been supported by a number of legislative changes to ensure that people comply with anti-discriminatory practices. The following list reflects the major pieces of relevant legislation.

- Articles 1, 2 and 14 of the Human Rights Act (1995)
- Sex Discrimination Act (1975)
- Equal Pay Act (1970)
- Race Relations Act (1976)
- Disability Discrimination Act (1995)
- Disability Rights Commission Act (1999)
- Race Relations Act (2000)
- Employment Equality (Religion or Belief) Regulations (2003)
- Employment Equality (Sexual Orientation) Regulations (2003)
- Disability Discrimination Act (2005)
- Equality Act (2006).

In addition to the major anti-discrimination Acts, there are clauses within other Acts which focus on anti-discrimination requirements. For example:

- The Children's Act 1989 which requires authorities to take special account of children's disabilities and the support needed to enable them to live as near normal lives as possible.

- Guidance in the form of 'No secrets' (DoH, 2000) which sets out adult protection policies and recognises adult discrimination as abuse.

- The document *Working Together to Safeguard Children* (Department of Education, 2010) which requires practitioners to guard against 'myths and stereotypes'.

2 Be able to champion diversity, equality and inclusion

2.1 Promote equality, diversity and inclusion in policy and practice

The culture of an organisation will have a powerful and pervasive influence over the behaviour and practices of the people within that organisation (Mullins, 2009). The organisation in which you work can be instrumental in preventing or addressing discrimination and inequality, through supportive policies, or it can tolerate, turn a blind eye and reinforce discriminatory behaviours.

Organisations are complicated places, where complex interactions occur between individuals and groups and between the management of an organisation and the employees. The complexity and interdependency of relationships supports an environment in which conflicts of interest and power differentials can be abused if appropriate policies, practices and guards are not in place to counteract this.

Activity 5.1.2

In each of the following cases identify whether you think discrimination has occurred and whether there is a law in this case which might be appealed to in order to support anti-discriminatory practice. In each case where you think discrimination has occurred, identify what strategies could have been in place to ensure discrimination does not happen.

Mary, 62, applies for a job as a care assistant. In spite of having previous experience in this area of work, she is not offered an interview. On asking why, she is told that she does not meet the essential criteria for the position because of her age.

Perminder attends a day centre. Whilst there she overhears another attendee making racist comments about her to a member of staff.

Gemma has a long-standing disability and uses a wheelchair. She is required to attend meetings for the care company that she works for, but these meetings are always held in an upstairs room in an old building with no lift. She finds being carried upstairs humiliating and has stopped attending the meetings. Her manager is adamant that she must attend.

John has had a stroke and lives in a care home where he depends on care from others for his daily activities. He has been a cross-dresser for many years. Since his stroke, the care staff have refused to dress him in (his own) women's clothing, because they feel it will cause distress and upset to the other residents.

Wendy, a white middle-class woman of 40, has applied for a post in a women's refuge set up specifically to cater for young Asian women. The refuge is funded by the local Asian community. The advertisement specifically identified being Asian as a necessary characteristic.

Julie has been off sick with depression for five months. Whilst still on sick leave and a week before she is due to return to work, Julie is invited for an interview with her manager who suggests that she should hand in her resignation.

Formal power structures are necessary in most organisations. These structures are supported by policies and procedures and they provide a framework for everyone to understand their role and responsibilities. Power can be exercised through management structures and is evident in an organisational hierarchy, role, and position and sometimes by virtue of specialist knowledge or experience. Within this system, each layer has some exercise of power over those below them and this is acknowledged and understood by both those leadership roles and those who are subordinates. Where individuals step outside the responsibilities of their role, those in leadership positions are legitimately empowered to take appropriate sanctions to ensure the smooth and effective running of the organisation. This type of power is legitimate and provides a framework for the effective running of the organisation. However, power operates also on an informal level.

Informal power is more difficult to understand because it is insidious, operates beneath the surface and is not formally acknowledged by anyone. Such power is not related to role or position. Some people are natural leaders and have an innate ability to influence others, and this may be entirely independent of their position within the organisation. Where this is a positive, value-based influence support from this individual can be invaluable to the manager in ensuring good practice. Equally, if the powerful personality leads others to exploit their power, cut corners, bend rules or manipulate situations for their own advantage, then the manager must recognise the impact of this and find strategies to minimise their influence. Informal power structures may be most prevalent at times of change or high workloads within an organisation when people feel stressed or threatened. The ability to recognise and work constructively with informal power relations is an essential skill of a manager.

Activity 5.2.1

Identify various ways in which power may be exercised over others inappropriately.

2.2 Challenge discrimination and inclusion in policy and practice

In order to challenge discrimination, it is first necessary to understand what discrimination is and how it manifests itself. At its most simple, discrimination can mean simply distinguishing differences between one or more things. This simple definition confers no value, neither good nor bad, in identifying difference. However, when used in the context of inequality it is associated with negative attribution (Thompson, 2011), that is to say it is used to discriminate against someone. Discriminating against someone generally implies disadvantage or oppression of that individual which impacts negatively upon their self-concept, their dignity, their opportunities or their ability to get social justice. Discrimination takes many forms:

- stereotyping
- marginalisation
- invisibilisation
- infantilisation
- medicalisation
- dehumanisation
- trivialisation.

Activity 5.2.2

Define what these forms of discrimination mean and identify examples of discrimination that could occur in your own context in each of these categories.

Common categories of discrimination include race and racism, gender and sexism, age and ageism, educational disadvantage, economic disadvantage and disability discrimination. However, it should be noted that discrimination can exist outside of these well publicised categories. Negative discrimination occurs when the identification of difference results in someone being treated unfairly on the basis of that difference. This may be as a result of personal prejudice from another or because of structural, cultural or political processes and systems that foster and support inequality.

There is irrefutable evidence that discrimination continues to occur in the health sector (Cuthbert and Quallington, 2008, p.28; Beecham et al., 2008; Help the Aged, 2007; Disabilities Rights Commission, 2006).

All Codes of Practice for care workers include statements about the requirement to treat others equally and fairly and to engage in non-judgemental and anti-discriminatory practice and yet discrimination continues to exist.

Organisations must develop, implement and monitor policies that support anti-discriminatory practice. These help to raise awareness about unacceptable behaviours and provide a structure for individuals to challenge such behaviours. This includes the responsibility of management to ensure that all staff work within the policy and respect the difference of others. Most organisations will have a policy which addresses issues around the responsibility of staff to respect the dignity of others, and the right of all staff to equality and inclusion in respect of practice and opportunity. Many policies also encompass clauses in relation to bullying or harassment.

Activity 5.2.3

Access your own organisation's equality policies. What categories does the policy cover? How well publicised is it?
Undertake a small pilot and ask different staff members in different levels of the organisation how familiar they are with the policy and what this means for them and their behaviour.

2.3 Provide others with information about:

- **the effects of discrimination**
- **the impact of inclusion**
- **the value of diversity**

The effects of discrimination

Discrimination usually means that one group or person gains unfair advantage over another group or person. It causes people to feel devalued, worthless, angry, hopeless and powerless. All of these emotions are negative and unproductive and, on an individual human basis, are completely unacceptable and unnecessary. From an organisational perspective, this can have a significant impact on the efficacy of the workforce. Discriminatory practice is likely to result in poor performance, poor staff relations and a missed opportunity to benefit from the different attributes and potential of all the staff employed.

Discrimination may be a result of individual prejudice or cultural or structural causes. Prejudice is a belief that one group of people, or one person, is better or worse than others on the basis of a particular characteristic, which may be nothing more than a characteristic of birth and could, in life's lottery, have been a feature of anyone. For example, gender or race. The belief is based on false or incomplete information. It often manifests itself as a generalisation, for example, a belief that 'all people with blond hair are...'. Clearly, the only thing that can be said about all people with blond hair is that they are all blond.

However, false beliefs may be widely held and deeply ingrained; they are not easily changed, even in response to evidence to the contrary (Thompson and Thompson, 2008). If the belief is not successfully challenged, it may be accepted as a fact and this then may invoke an emotional response which may be dislike or dismissal of the person or individuals associated with the belief. Discriminatory, unfair behaviour often follows – inequitable treatment, exclusion, dismissal, becoming the butt of humour, being ridiculed, deliberately being marginalised, threats and violence are extreme forms of discriminatory behaviour. Importantly, in the workplace much discriminatory behaviour is covert and dressed up in the forms of humour. Perpetrators are able to justify and trivialise the action by statements such as, 'It's just a bit of fun', 'She's got no sense of humour', 'He's so sensitive'. This makes it difficult to address as individuals do not want to be seen to be making a fuss about nothing. A clear policy is required that identifies that singling out an individual's characteristics and using these to ridicule or humiliate them is completely unacceptable.

Discrimination is not restricted to prejudice but can be equally excluding and disabling when it is the result of structural causes. For example, the difficulty those with disabilities may have in securing employment. It is only in recent years that changes are being required to public buildings to make them appropriately accessible to all. Excuses are used such as 'the appropriate facilities to support people with disabilities in this workplace do not exist, therefore, even if this person is the best candidate for the job, we cannot employ them'. There is no understanding that this type of behaviour is discriminatory. The facilities are seen as a barrier and there is a failure from others to take responsibility for ensuring that these barriers do not exist or that creative solutions are needed to overcome them, to ensure that equal opportunities exist for all.

The main outcome of discrimination, whether it be by individuals or by discriminatory structures, is oppression. Oppression is causing harm or injury as the result of unjust use of power. The harm need not be physical harm, in fact the harm is much more likely to be insidious and less easily assessed. Oppression, as a result of discriminatory practice, does however result in significant harm. It may manifest as another's loss of confidence, or undermining of one's self-belief and self-esteem; it may cause stress, anxiety or depression, all of which may then impact on work performance and subsequent work opportunity. If the individual is unable to successfully challenge the oppression, there is a risk that the prejudicial belief or disabling structure takes on the significance of a fact that then results in the oppressed person responding defensively by avoiding situations and people that discriminate against them by trying to keep a low profile, and a negative cycle begins.

Activity 5.2.4

Imagine yourself in a parallel world in which you are seen as an inferior being. You have similar capabilities to others and yet these are dismissed because your characteristics mark you out as being of lesser value. You are constantly overlooked, marginalised and given the worst and dirtiest jobs to do. You do not have access to the developmental opportunities afforded to others. You are good humouredly ridiculed for the amusement of others. If anything goes wrong it is assumed that you are responsible.

What sanctions do you think are appropriate to improve the situation and bring about a more equal environment? What are the risks, if any, of imposing sanctions?

If nobody stops or challenges the above then the perpetrators continue and the victimised have to learn strategies to cope. This is clearly unfair.

The impact of inclusion

So far much of the discussion has been focussed on the impact of discrimination, that is, identifying discriminatory practice, understanding what it feels like to experience it and implementing strategies to prevent it, or to apply sanctions to those that perpetrate it. Whilst this is extremely important, all of these anti-discriminatory approaches are focussed on the negative acceptance that discrimination is a fact of life and that energy should be spent on mitigating the effects. Inclusion, on the other hand, takes a more positive approach. A

philosophy of inclusion is concerned with how things should and could be. Energies are spent on becoming better members of a community, by creating new visions for the community. The emphasis for inclusion is not on justifying reasons why someone should be included and developing policies and procedures to support this; inclusion starts from an assumption that everyone should have equal rights and opportunities and that these should only differ when there is appropriate reason to do so. It is not a replacement for anti-discriminatory policies but, if it is used effectively, it can help to minimise the use of such policies because the focus is on enhancement and making the workplace better for all.

The value of diversity

No two people are alike, even identical twins will have different skills and attributes. When building a team, Belbin (2010) suggests that the most effective teams are those in which the participants have different and complementary skills and attributes in order that the team is balanced and able to effectively fulfil all of its responsibilities. Belbin described a team inventory against which different team members' skills and attributes could be measured in order that they could be used most effectively; additionally the inventory enables the team to identify gaps that may need to be filled.

You can use Belbin's model to analyse your team, as a basis for developing your team's strengths, managing its weaknesses, and for gaining new or absent skill sets when you have an opportunity to recruit. Whilst teams are unlikely to be perfectly balanced, developing a team with a diversity of skills, attributes and strengths makes for a much more effective team than if everyone is the same. Diversity is a strength and if we appreciate it rather than fear it, there is an opportunity to capitalise on it.

Action-oriented roles	Shaper	Challenges team to improve
	Implementer	Puts ideas into action
	Completer finisher	Ensures thorough, timely completion
People-oriented roles	Co-ordinator	Acts as chairperson
	Team worker	Encourages cooperation
	Resource investigator	Explores outside opportunities
Thought-oriented roles	Plant	Presents new ideas and approaches
	Monitor evaluator	Analyses the options
	Specialist	Provides specialised skills

Figure 5.2 The value of difference illustrated by Belbin's team roles

Belbin's work illustrates, in a very practical way, how difference and diversity can be used to enhance the capabilities of staff and teams within organisations to improve organisational outcomes. Teams in which everyone wants to be a leader or teams where everyone is overly concerned with detail to the detriment of strategy and bigger pictures are dysfunctional teams. Celebrating difference and diversity is not something that is just desirable but rather is something that is essential for an organisation to grow and develop. Organisations need to employ a diverse workforce if they are going to maximise their potential. There are many benefits to this. The organisation does not only benefit in terms of having the right skill mix; when the workforce is diverse, a different range of perspectives will be represented and this creates the opportunity for new, different and possibly enhanced ways of doing things. Increasingly the client base that any organisation serves is diverse and it is necessary to be able to understand and reflect the needs of the whole population that is served.

2.4 Support others to challenge discrimination and exclusion

The first step in supporting others to challenge discrimination and exclusion is to accept that it exists and to acknowledge that discrimination is a significant factor in inhibiting equality. As managers it is important to communicate to staff that discrimination is fundamentally wrong and that it cannot be tolerated within an organisation that values its entire workforce.

Challenging discrimination is not easy and no one is exempt from prejudice or exclusive practices. What is important is that individuals are open to recognising that and are committed to change. It takes practice and time. It will be helped by publicising and promoting policies that clearly set out expectations of behaviour to others and which remind staff that they risk disciplinary sanctions should they breach the policy. However, whilst it might be possible to get staff to comply with these policies to a greater or lesser degree, that is only part of the picture if it does not change hearts and minds. The risk is that if only compliance is achieved, when you take your eye off the ball, the behaviour will revert to that which perpetuated inequality. For many people, understanding the consequences and impacts of their actions will cause a change in behaviour and encouragement for others to change.

Like it or not, we are all products of our culture, our life experiences and to some extent our education. Discrimination and exclusion may not be intentional but may be the result of the belief that everyone experiences life the way I do. If I have never been conscious of discrimination, it may be that I do not see it when it happens to others. Equally, I may be very conscious of discrimination and attitudes

that relate to my experience. For example, as a working mother I have always been very sensitive to individuals who make value-based assertions about the negative effect of working mothers on their children. You need to be able to relate to another's experience in order to begin to get a sense of the injustice that is felt by unfair and exclusionary treatment. It is not possible to be somebody else, in their shoes, but it is possible to ask them how it feels and to try to imagine what that is like. Sometimes it is useful to try to assume the role of the impartial observer, setting aside emotion and experience and asking whether something is right or not. This approach enables you to make a judgement on the 'ethicality' of a particular behaviour.

It is also important to take a critical look at ourselves, our values and attitudes to others. Where do these values and attitudes come from and are they consistent with the values that one would choose to have, if selecting from a value set? Reflective practice is an excellent vehicle for self-reflection.

The most simple reflective model asks three questions:

- What happened?
- Why?
- So what?

Gibbs' (1988) Model of Reflection is particularly useful in reflecting on values because it requires the reflector to engage with their feelings and to consider and evaluate the morality of their thoughts and feelings (see Figure 5.3).

Activity 5.2.5

Using an incident analysis model of reflection, such as the one in Figure 5.3, reflect on thoughts, feelings and behaviours regarding situations in which you may have been tempted to label someone, or to make assumptions about their capabilities or trustworthiness, or when you may have felt anxious or threatened by someone you do not know.

Try to reflect on what caused you to respond in the way that you did. Was your response reasonable? Could you have behaved differently? What risks would there have been if you had behaved differently? Can you think of strategies to prompt you to behave differently in the future?

Discriminatory behaviour is often hidden, even from ourselves, and unless we take the time to be sensitive to and question our responses to others, and to be aware of the impact of our behaviours, then individuals will continue to be treated unfairly.

As a manager it is important that, as part of awareness raising, you personally are identified as someone who positively challenges discrimination and supports others to do this. This requires that you are very conscious of your own behaviour and that you lead by example.

Promoting equality and inclusion as positive concepts and as everybody's responsibility may help to encourage others to challenge discrimination when they encounter it. However, the way that the manager responds to this could determine whether the individual is willing to do this again in any other situation. Importantly, any challenge should be taken seriously and time must be made to listen to what the individual believes is occurring. The manager has a responsibility to investigate the situation impartially, trying to gain as much evidence as possible in order to ensure that they have the whole picture. This includes talking to others who may be involved or who may have witnessed the discrimination. Confidentiality should be maintained wherever possible to protect those who raise concerns. If the discrimination is found to be a reality, it is important to put an action plan in place to improve the situation and to provide managerial support to ensure that this can be implemented effectively. If discrimination has been found to occur, sanctions should be applied appropriately and proportionally. The purpose of investigating issues of concern is to learn from the situation, resolve the particular situation and, where possible, implement

strategies to prevent something similar happening in the future. If at all possible, staff relations should be supported and protected. Actions should primarily be focussed on enhancing and improving practice rather than on retribution. Having clear flow charts and processes that demonstrate how to raise a concern responsibly provides protection for those who wish to challenge discrimination and for those who may be under investigation.

Douglas (2004), a management consultant, suggests the following approach for managers in his training programme on 'valuing difference':

- Strip away and challenge stereotypes.

- Learn to listen for the differences in people's assumptions (know your staff).

- Build strong relationships with those that are regarded as different.

- Empower oneself to become more open to learning about difference and be able to take advantage of the opportunities that can bring.

- Empower others to change their own views and to challenge inappropriate views and behaviours in others.

- Support those who challenge discrimination.

- Develop systems that are designed to include rather than be seen as barriers.

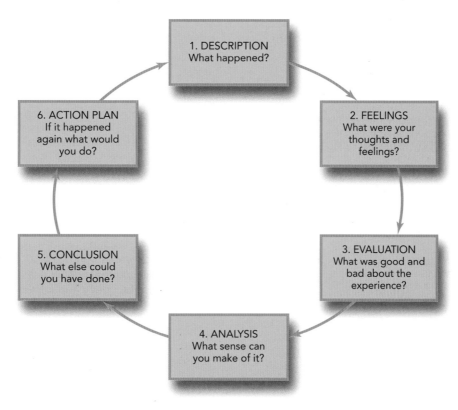

Figure 5.3 Gibb's Model of Reflection

3 Understand how to develop systems and processes that promote diversity, equality and inclusion

3.1 Analyse how systems and processes can promote equality and inclusion or reinforce discrimination and exclusion

The appropriateness and 'usability' of the systems and processes that exist within an organisation will determine whether they help to dispel and reduce discrimination or whether they support and promote it. The first step is to ensure that clear and well understood policies exist that set the standards of the behaviours expected of all employees in the workplace. When designing policies there are three steps to meet if the policy is to be effective.

The policy

The policy must be clear so that there can be no misinterpretation of what is intended. It must address the issue concerned directly and it must reflect current legal requirements. This may require you to ensure that there have been no amendments, extensions or changes to anti-discriminatory laws. A well designed policy is essential in addressing discrimination and promoting a positive culture that celebrates diversity. Where possible, new policies should be agreed or designed in consultation with union or employee representatives.

Policies should:

- give examples of what constitutes discrimination, harassment, bullying and intimidating behaviour including cyber-bullying, work-related events and harassment by third parties;

- explain the damaging effects of discrimination and why it will not be tolerated;

- state that any examples that demonstrate that discriminatory behaviour has occurred will be treated as a disciplinary offence;

- clarify the legal implications and outline the costs associated with personal liability;

- describe how individuals can get help, raise a concern, make a complaint, formally (complaints and grievance procedures) and informally (advice and counselling);

- promise that allegations will be treated speedily (include expected time-frames), seriously and confidentially and prevent victimisation;

- clearly identify steps in the process (who will investigate, how this will be escalated if necessary, identify what other actions could result, e.g. no action as no case to answer, implementation of action plans rather than escalation);

- clarify the accountability of investigators (who, where possible, should be independent of the issue and staff involved), managers and the role and responsibilities of union or employee representatives;

- identify requirements for documentation and record keeping;

- require supervisors/managers to implement the policy and ensure it is understood;

- emphasise that every employee carries responsibility for their behaviour.

The policy should be monitored and regularly reviewed for effectiveness, including:

- records of complaints, why and how they occurred, who was involved and where an analysis of trends will help you to identify if the policy is working or if there are any systemic problems;

- reviews of individual complaints to ensure that action plans were implemented as intended, to identify resolution and to identify if there was any evidence of victimisation for those involved.

Communication

When designing or when reviewing and updating a policy, it is important that a communication strategy is designed at the same time. A policy that nobody knows about is of no value. The strategy needs to include a number of different ways of communicating. For example, telling staff in a staff meeting can be supplemented by alert notices in a staff room under a 'What's New' heading. When alerting staff to a policy, it is helpful to write a short paragraph clarifying what this means for them. This makes it very personal and emphasises their personal responsibility.

These days many organisations have staff intranet sites so a pop-up alert here is a good way of raising awareness. This also allows you to add a link to the policy and allows you to highlight changes. It also enables you to add additional information behind this. For example, you could add a 'Frequently Asked Questions' page or some examples or cases to illustrate how this policy may be applied in practice.

Policies should be communicated so that all employees:

- have been made aware – through induction, training and other processes – about their rights and personal responsibilities under the policy and understand the organisation's commitment to deal with harassment;

- are aware of who to contact if they want to discuss their experiences in order to decide what steps to take;

- know how to take a complaint forward and the timescales for any formal procedures.

You can check out the effectiveness of your communication by doing informal and random checks to see if staff are aware of the policy.

Training

Awareness-raising, although crucially important, is not sufficient. Equality, diversity and anti-discrimination policies need to be supported by training. This helps people to look at themselves and their own responses to different situations and provides examples of different ways of responding to situations. It will also ensure that staff are up to date with the legal context in which they work. There are many ways of ensuring that training occurs and these can be in group face-to-face sessions that are planned as part of the staff development programme or they can be via an on-line package. Many organisations require individuals to engage with equality and diversity training at induction. However, further opportunities for training are important.

In a reflective and learning organisation, the ideal situation is to try to identify issues before they become grievances or complaints. Consequently, a well publicised and confidential opportunity to receive advice, support and counselling should be a feature of how organisations engage with diversity and equality. One way of supporting this is to recruit a number of advisors, trained to help any person who believes they are being discriminated against, to talk through their situation and look at all the options before they take precipitous action. Often talking through the issue and being believed and supported in this way is enough to enable the individual to draw on their own reserves and tackle the issue directly or use strategies to change the situation indirectly. This level of support must be independent of line management, which involves a different level of formality and responsibility, and independent of anyone who may subsequently be asked to investigate an issue if it is escalated. It must also utilise individuals who can be relied on to be impartial to provide information and options but not to make decisions for the complainant. It is also essential that they can maintain confidentiality. All employees should have access to someone with whom to speak in confidence about an

issue they may have. This could be via an employee helpline or be a nominated person who may be a trained volunteer colleague. This can help complainants decide what course of action to take by exploring their options. The decision to progress a complaint should rest with the individual.

Having a champion (or champions) for diversity will help to keep issues on the agenda and will help to ensure that the organisation is able to reflect on best practice in other organisations. It is not necessary for the manager to take on this role. It can be an opportunity for someone interested in this area to extend their skills and develop their role.

The aim of any activities that you instigate is to support compliance with equality legislation and to eliminate harassment, sexual harassment and discriminatory treatment.

Anti-harassment and sexual harassment policy and procedures

Secure and use the Equality Authority 'Code of Practice on Sexual Harassment and Harassment in the Workplace'.

Anti-discrimination policy and procedures

Secure and refer to *Guidelines for Employment Equality Policies in Enterprises* published by Congress, IBEC and the Equality Authority.

Disciplinary policy and procedures

Ensure that the disciplinary policy includes reference to complaints of discrimination, harassment and sexual harassment.

Ensure that a proper disciplinary policy, along with appropriate procedures and sanctions, is in place to deal with situations where complaints of sexual harassment, harassment and discrimination are upheld after investigation.

All policies

Take steps to ensure the policy and procedures are accessible to those who do not speak fluent English.

If it is communicated that equality and diversity are everybody's responsibility, it confers an obligation of employees to challenge or report discrimination if they encounter it. This can be very daunting for employees who have to continue to work in an organisation in which an investigation, suspension or prosecution occurs as a result of the challenge. Whilst the expectation is that individuals should raise challenges and concerns, it is imperative that they can do this in a supportive and protective environment. Most challenges should be able to be dealt with inside the organisation which should, with appropriate guidance, support and sanctions if appropriate, be able to resolve the situation. However, there are occasions when a practice is widespread and resistant to change or of such a serious nature that a more radical approach is required. In such circumstances, workers who witness such activities or who have reason to believe malpractice is occurring will be protected in law for making this public. However, this does not mean that the individual has a right to go to the press or other public forum to expose an organisation.

Whistle-blowing means 'making a disclosure in the public interest'.

Protection for 'blowing the whistle'

A whistle-blower is protected if they:

■ are a 'worker'

■ believe that malpractice in the workplace is happening, has happened in the past or will happen in the future

■ are revealing information of the right type (a 'qualifying disclosure')

■ reveal it to the right person, and in the right way (making it a 'protected disclosure').

Protected disclosures

For disclosure to be protected by the law, it should be made to the right person and in the right way. Disclosure must meet the following criteria:

■ The disclosure must be in good faith (which means with honest intent and without malice).

■ The whistle-blower must reasonably believe that the information is substantially true.

■ The whistle-blower must reasonably believe they are making the disclosure to the right 'prescribed person'.

If a qualifying disclosure is made in good faith to an employer, or through a process that the employer has agreed, the whistle blower is protected.

Activity 5.3.1

Check whether you have a whistle-blowing policy in place and identify whether the responsibilities contained within it clearly identify for the worker what is expected of them in this situation.

If a worker feels unable to make a disclosure to their employer, then there are other 'prescribed people' to whom a disclosure can be made. Disclosure can be made to the person

responsible for the area of concern. For example, it would be reasonable to raise concerns about discrimination to a dignity advisor.

To make a protected disclosure to others, the whistle-blower must:

1. reasonably believe their employer would treat them unfairly if the disclosure was made to the employer or a prescribed person, or

2. reasonably believe that the disclosure to the employer would result in the destruction or concealment of information about the wrong-doing, or

3. have previously disclosed the same or very similar information to the employer or a prescribed person.

An Employment Tribunal must also think it was reasonable for the whistle-blower to make the disclosure. The Employment Tribunal will take into account the following:

■ The identity of the person you made the disclosure to (e.g. disclosing to a relevant professional body may be more likely to be considered reasonable than to the media).

■ The seriousness of the wrong-doing.

■ Whether the wrong-doing is continuing or likely to occur again.

■ Whether your disclosure breaches the employer's duty of confidentiality (e.g. if information was made available that contains confidential details about a client).

■ If the whistle-blower made a previous disclosure, whether they followed any internal procedures then.

The term 'worker' has a special wide meaning in the case of whistle-blowing. As well as employees, it includes agency workers and people who aren't employed but are in training with employers. Some self-employed people may be considered to be workers for the purpose of whistle-blowing if they are supervised or work off-site.

If 'whistle-blowers' become the subject of an investigation, or if they are ridiculed or dismissed or not taken seriously, then the culture of the organisation will support collusion and silence which will in turn allow poor practice to thrive.

3.2 Evaluate the effectiveness of systems and processes in promoting equality, diversity and inclusion in own area of responsibility

It is important as a manager that you are not complacent about the effectiveness of policies and procedures that have been designed to support a culture that promotes and assures equality and respect for diversity. An annual assessment of effectiveness is a good way of checking whether this issue remains at the forefront of people's minds and in their practice. The types of activities that can be used to monitor the effectiveness of your policies include:

- User surveys – you can use a quick questionnaire or short question and answer interview to assess how well the users of your service feel that their difference is respected and equality promoted by your staff.

- When you work alongside others or have an opportunity to witness staff interactions, you can do this in a purposive way and concentrate on how well staff promote equality and respect diversity.

- Reflective practice, including incident analysis, allows you and your team to reflect on behaviours, interactions and incidents and to identify ways of enhancing or improving practice. Do not forget that reflective practice also allows you to identify good practice and share this more widely.

Activity 5.3.2

Design a tool that will enable you to monitor the commitment to and implementation of equality and diversity within your organisation.

Pilot the tool and summarise your results.

Draw up an action plan based on the results.

3.3 Propose improvements to address gaps or shortfalls in systems and processes

The results gained from implementing and trialling your assessment tool should enable you to determine whether you have sufficient information to make judgements about staff knowledge and compliance with equality and diversity policies and procedures. It should also help you to assess whether these are embedded in the culture or whether staff pay 'lip-service' to these. If you are unable to determine these or need further information regarding a particular aspect because you have identified an area that is not complied with or gives rise to a trend, then it is important that you do some further monitoring using a different tool.

Action plans must be based on firm and reliable evidence. Possible actions may be raising awareness or further staff development, and in some cases may lead to disciplinary action.

4 Be able to manage the risks presented when balancing individual rights and professional duty of care

Health care environments are believed by both clients and workers to exist on the premise that they are concerned with 'doing good' by supporting and promoting individuals' health and well-being. However, this assertion can be interpreted differently by different stakeholders and can be the subject of a dilemma. Care workers owe a responsibility to and are accountable to various people: their patients or clients, their employers, their professional or regulatory body, the law. At times the duties to these different stakeholders can come into conflict. It is widely accepted that those in receipt of care and those providing care have both rights and responsibilities; although the responsibilities of clients in care interactions are not well documented and the rights of workers in respect of interactions with clients are not frequently discussed. However, it is normally acknowledged that rights and responsibilities go hand-in-hand. Rights do not exist without a correlating responsibility to protect or action that right. Rights can also be referred to as entitlements (Buchanon, 1984). These entitlements may be universal or refer to a defined group on the basis of specified criteria. Universal rights are those that have been agreed by the international community and which are protected under the Human Rights Act (1998) which sets out 16 basic rights that are applicable to anyone in the UK. Where these rights are violated or restricted, an individual has a legal right to challenge the infringement.

There are a number of rights that relate specifically to those receiving care in care services. These rights are articulated in health policy, care standards documents, patients' charters and professional codes of conduct. Equally in upholding these rights, obligations are placed on care practitioners to ensure that entitlements are met.

Activity 5.4.1

Review a range of documents, e.g. policies, standards, codes of practice, relevant to your work context. What rights are articulated in these?

4.1 Describe ethical dilemmas that arise in own area of responsibility when balancing individual rights and duty of care

If good was a universally understood and agreed concept, it would not be difficult to ensure that patients and users of services received their entitlements for good care and support aimed at supporting and promoting health and/or well-being. However, if we accept in principle that difference and diversity are a 'good' thing, then we must also accept that different interpretations of good are also a good thing. It is this apparent conflict that can cause a dilemma for care workers. For example, if I believe that someone's health will be greatly improved if they stop smoking, is it my responsibility as a care worker to ensure that they are denied the opportunity to smoke? That is certainly one way of managing the situation and justifying to myself that I am acting in their best interests. However, the opposing argument to that is that what is of overriding importance is the need for individuals to make good decisions about their own health and lives. This is more sustainable because it brings about attitude change, as well as behaviour change, and it means that individuals are encouraged to take responsibility for their own lives, which is the right and, it can be argued, the obligation of all adults, unless there is evidence that they are unable to do this.

The dilemma that the practitioner must reconcile is how far someone's right to make decisions for themself can be supported when it is in conflict with a professional obligation. In the example given above, the solution must be in enabling an individual to make choices for themself, even when these are not agreed with by the staff, as long as the staff have used the opportunity to educate the individual on the dangers of undertaking their course of action and have identified the risks in doing this. Inevitably this relies on the expertise of the practitioner to provide comprehensive and accurate information in an accessible and understandable manner. The duty of the care worker is not to control others' lives but to inform them and support them in order that they can make good decisions for themselves.

- An individual who does not want confidential information to be shared with their daughter.
- A client who you see being treated disrespectfully by one of your colleagues does not want the incident reported.
- A staff member who wants time to attend Mass when on duty on a Sunday.
- A client who does not want to be supported to meet their hygiene needs.

A useful 'rule of thumb' is to encourage and support individual decision making, as far as is reasonably possible, as long as this does not infringe the rights of others. The reason that these kinds of situations are called dilemmas is that there are often no wholly satisfactory solutions that will appease all parties; rather it requires a workable compromise that all parties feel can be acceptable to them. The challenge for practitioners, when there are no clear and obviously right answers, lies in intelligently applying good judgements, based on strong values which support good principles of practice. These principles should underpin all care practice: respect for dignity and autonomy, promotion of equality and diversity, fairness and justice, management of risk and protection from harm, and sound judgement and compassion.

Embedding a culture of care within an organisation which is principle based rather than rule based can be difficult, particularly in those organisations that have a high number of non-professional staff who are more used to applying protocols, rules and procedures than making independent decisions. Staff must be trained and understand the limits of their responsibilities. Values and expected standards must be clearly articulated and understood by all staff and appropriate support strategies must be in place to enable staff to seek help and advice. The impact and influence of the values demonstrated by the manager cannot be overestimated in modelling the expectations of care behaviours. A number of recent reports, suggest that care practitioners do not always respond appropriately to the individual needs of those in their care, particularly the Francis Report relating to lapses in care at Mid-Staffordshire NHS Foundation Trust (2010), 'Care and Compassion', the Report by the Ombudsman into the care of older people (Parliamentary and Health Service Ombudsman, 2011), and the Care Quality Commission Report (CQC, 2011). It is a manager's responsibility to ensure staff understand expectations and that these expectations are implemented and sustained.

Activity 5.4.2

Here are some examples of activities where duty of care and responsibilities come into conflict. Should they be supported and on what basis is this justified?

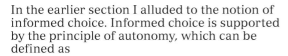

What checks could you implement in order to reassure yourself that values and standards are being met? How frequently is it necessary to implement these?

These could, for example, involve discussions with clients, self-assessment by staff or observations of practice in relation to a particular standard.

4.2 Explain the principle of informed choice

In the earlier section I alluded to the notion of informed choice. Informed choice is supported by the principle of autonomy, which can be defined as

'Self-rule that is free from both controlling interferences by others and from personal limitations that prevent meaningful choice, such as inadequate understanding.'

(Beauchamp and Childress, 2001, p.58)

There are at least four elements necessary for autonomous decision-making:

- Understanding the value of respect for persons and their differences.

- The ability to be self-governing and being able to determine one's own personal goals, desires and preferences.

- The capacity or competence to make choices or decisions based on deliberation and reason.

- The freedom to make choices for oneself and then to act on these.

(Cuthbert and Quallington, 2008)

Informed choice and autonomous decision making require more than the simple articulation of preferences in order to meet the requirement for informed choice. In making an informed choice, an individual must be given a choice of alternatives, even if that choice is simply to do, or not to do, something. Making a meaningful choice also entails that you understand what those choices mean and what the impact of those choices could signify. It is the responsibility of the practitioner to ensure that the individual has sufficient information, which has been provided in an understandable way to enable them to make good choices. If the individual does not understand the information, the onus is on the practitioner to find an alternative way of explaining it. It is not sufficient to claim that, because you told them something, they were adequately informed. Checking understanding about what they think

they are being told by questions and getting them to summarise what you have said is a useful way of assessing this.

For informed choice, it is a requirement that an individual has the capacity to manipulate the information that they have been given in order for them to reach a decision. I will discuss capacity more in the following section. However, an individual's capacity should be assumed unless there is evidence to demonstrate that they are unable to understand the alternatives before them. A further requirement is that the choice is their choice and should not be unduly influenced by those around them. That is not to say that they cannot be guided if they ask for help, but guidance should be in the form of benefits and risks rather than directives which tell others what to do. It is very easy to think that you know what is best for another individual, particularly when you have encountered similar situations before. However, understanding the principles of respect for dignity, equality and diversity means that each individual should have the same opportunity to make decisions for themselves, even if this results in less good outcomes, as long as they are able to do so in full knowledge of the risks.

Another condition of informed choice is the requirement for opportunity for deliberation and time for reflection. This is often a condition which is overlooked. How often, in an attempt to be helpful or to meet others' expectations and agendas, have you agreed to do something which you have later wished you had not agreed to? Given time to reflect on various risks and potential outcomes, individuals may decide on a choice that is quite different from the one they originally thought they may select.

The final condition of informed choice is that individuals must be able to implement the choices they have been given. Being offered a choice means that this should then be respected and actioned as this is an essential element of trust in any therapeutic relationship. It is this element of informed choice that can make practitioners nervous, as it requires individuals to balance risks and their own responsibilities against the rights and choices of those in their care.

4.3 Explain how issues of capacity may affect informed choice

The necessary condition of capacity was briefly discussed above. Anything that affects an individual's capacity to weigh up information and make choices may compromise their ability to make those choices. Decisions about capacity are judged on the basis of competence. Factors that compromise an individual's ability to make decisions may be either internal to that individual, for example, mental ability, intellectual capacity, anxiety or pain, or they can be as a result of external factors such as control or paternalistic and protective behaviour of others, lack of adequate information, or not being presented with real choices.

Activity 5.4.4

Think about your own work context.

What factors can impact on the ability of those you care for to make decisions for, and about, themselves?

List the different strategies which are used in your work environment to support decision making for those whose capacity is either permanently or temporarily impaired.

What strategies could be used to help people better understand the information necessary to make choices and to better understand the choices that they do have?

You may have identified the need for information in appropriate languages or visual information. If it is a commonly occurring situation, you may want information sheets. Sometimes it is as simple as someone who can sit with the individual and patiently explain the situation and the choices in front of them. If it becomes clear following assessment that an individual is unable to make choices for themselves, the next best thing is to reflect the choices that they would have made, had they been able to make a choice. Any indication that individuals have previously expressed choices about an issue must be taken seriously into consideration. Families and significant others may be able to help here but, unless they have legal rights to make decisions, they should not be the only source of information, as not all families and significant others have benevolent motives or necessarily share the views of the incapacitated person.

Figure 5.4 Information should be provided in appropriate languages

Competence is not easy to define or to assess and yet it is an important element of determining the level of decision making that should be supported. Standards of competence in health care tend to be focussed on the ability to make choices and therefore assessment is not dissimilar from assessing the conditions required for informed consent. Beauchamp and Childress (2001) suggest that competence to make some decisions may not require such high standards as those that are required for informed consent. For example, an individual who may not be able to make judgements about complex treatment decisions may still be able to express a preference about what they would prefer to eat. Beauchamp and Childress (2001, p.73) present a table aimed at identifying abilities and inabilities which can be used as a basis for determining competence.

Table 5.1

Type of ability or skill	Inabilities used to judge competence
Ability to state a preference	Inability to express or communicate a preference or choice
Ability to understand information and appreciate one's situation	Inability to understand one's situation and its consequences Inability to understand relevant information
Ability to reason about a consequential life decision	Inability to give a reason Inability to give a rational reason Inability to give risk/benefit-related reasons Inability to reach a reasonable decision (as judged by the Reasonable Person's Standard)

The values and duties expected in care practice regarding the standards and assessment of capacity have been set out in legislation. The Mental Capacities Act (2005), which was enacted in 2007, is intended to:

'Be enabling and supportive of people who lack capacity, not restricting or controlling of their lives. It aims to protect people who lack capacity to make particular decisions, but also to maximise their ability to make decisions, or to participate in decision-making as far as they are able to do so.'

(Department for Constitutional Affairs, 2007, p.19)

The associated Code of Practice (Department for Constitutional Affairs, 2007) provides examples and guidance about how the principles of the Mental Capacity Act (2005) can be applied in practice.

The Mental Capacity Act (2005) sets out five statutory principles that underpin the legal requirements. These are the values that care managers must ensure are embedded within the practices in their organisations.

1. A person must be assumed to have capacity unless it is *(formally)* established that they do not have capacity.

2. A person is not to be treated as unable to make a decision unless all practicable steps to help *him* do so have been taken without success.

3. A person must not be treated as unable to make a decision, merely because *he* makes an unwise one.

4. An act done, or decision made, under the Act for and on behalf of a person who lacks capacity must be done, or made, in *his* best interests.

5. Before the act is done, or the decision is made, regard must be had to whether the purpose for which it is needed can be as effectively achieved in a way that is less restrictive of the person's rights or freedom of action.

It is important to understand that, in many cases, a person's ability to make decisions may fluctuate. A person's capacity or lack of capacity refers specifically to their capacity to make a decision at that time and in that circumstance (Cuthbert and Quallington, 2008). Consequently it may be necessary to review and revisit capacity decisions.

Activity 5.4.5

'Reflection in action'

Reflect on how well you think that the principle of informed consent is embedded as a fundamental principle guiding the work of the staff in your organisation.

 4.4 Propose a strategy to manage risks when balancing individual rights and duty of care in own area of responsibility

Balancing individual rights and the duty that is owed to those in your care in terms of protecting them from harm is complex. In focussing on the duty to protect those in our care from harm, it is all too easy to focus on the negative and potential risks that can befall someone, rather than concentrating on the benefits that could be accrued and developing a strategy to manage them. When the fear of disciplinary action or public investigation for any harm that occurs is added to this, it is not surprising that care practitioners tend to err on the side of caution in managing risks and that this 'over protection' can take precedence over individual rights.

It is important to remember that the risk that is taken belongs to the individual and this is why informed consent is such an important element of care decisions. It is essential that, where possible, individuals have had an opportunity to assess the level of risk that they wish to take in relation to the preference to do, or not to do, a particular thing. A good example to illustrate this is the extent to which an individual who is relatively frail and unstable, but of sound mind, is enabled to be independent. Any risk assessment will clearly determine that the individual poses a higher risk of falling than the average person. That does not, however, mean that they should be unnecessarily restricted. In fact to restrict their mobility poses its own risk. Rather it becomes the responsibility of the care worker to analyse what the highest risk areas are, and to try to provide strategies that will reduce the likelihood of the risk occurring. So, for example, is the person prepared to utilise a stick or a walking frame to reduce the likelihood of falling? Can the environment be managed to eliminate unnecessary risks, for example, rugs or cables that may cause an individual to trip can be removed. Will the individual agree to call for support when they need to move, and crucially, as part of this assessment, could the support always be provided? It is not helpful to offer support and then put the individual in a difficult situation when everyone is too busy to help. Working with individuals to identify preferences and strategies that are most acceptable to them helps to ensure that they will utilise them, but more importantly, the locus of control for their care remains with them.

As a manager you will be familiar with the need to conduct risk assessments. When these concern individuals, it is important that these are conducted specifically in relation to individual clients. It is only in this way that differences, choices and preferences can be properly accommodated. A blanket approach to risk assessment that applies to all people will be unnecessarily restrictive for some and present risks for others. When doing a risk assessment and a subsequent action plan to manage that risk, it does not require that all potential and actual risks must be eliminated. It does mean that all serious risks must be considered and where possible, a plan to reasonably manage the degree of risk should be designed in partnership with the person affected.

Risk prediction is not a precise art and is influenced by many things: personal experience, particularly negative experiences, the recency of a similar event, the degree of damage if the risk comes to pass, the degree of fear or anxiety generated by the potential risk, the personality of the individual analysing the risk and whether they are naturally risk averse, or welcome risk taking (Cuthbert and Quallington, 2008, p.130).

> 'Risk perception involves people's beliefs, attitudes, judgements, experiences and feelings, as well as wider social or cultural values and dispositions that people adopt towards hazards and their benefits.'
>
> (Pidgeon *et al.*, 1992, p.89)

There are many different assessment tools available for assessing risk and, as identified before, these tend to focus on the negative aspects of risk and the potential for harm. Few emphasise the positive benefits of managing risk in a way that fosters and protects individual rights as a fundamental principle and also enables practitioners to demonstrate that they have fulfilled their obligations in respect of a duty to care.

Activity 5.4.6

Compare, contrast and evaluate two different risk assessment/risk management tools and evaluate how effectively they support practitioners to take a positive approach to risk management and the protection of individual rights.

NB For further information, read chapters on risk management in Cuthbert and Quallington (2008) or Titterton (2005).

Practitioners, when they enter into a contract of care with an individual, assume duties and obligations in relation to that contract. These obligations include those issues that have been discussed in this chapter such as respect for dignity and diversity and promotion of equality and fairness. Practitioners have an obligation to 'do good and promote the interests' of their patients and clients, and avoid and protect those in their care from harm. However, the law is equally clear that this does not involve acting 'paternalistically' and overriding an individual's rights and opportunities to make choices for and about themselves; even when the motives of those wishing to impose their decisions on another are beneficently motivated and intended to be in the best interests of the client. The only person who should judge what is in their best interest is the individual themselves. The practitioner should support and facilitate this through trying to help the individual think through the situation, by providing them with additional information and by answering questions. The role of the practitioner should be more aligned to the role of coach than someone who takes a controlling parental role and tells the individual what to do.

Management of care is inherently unpredictable and risky. It is not possible to predict the outcome of interventions and therefore the requirement for effective care cannot be focussed on outcome alone. If called to account, the practitioner must be able to demonstrate that the activity was within their scope of knowledge and responsibility, that they had performed the activity based on best or accepted practice standards, that they had assessed the individual risks in this situation and tried to manage these appropriately, and that they had, wherever possible, involved and sought informed consent from the individual affected by the activity. Accidents and unfortunate outcomes can still occur but all reasonable action must have been taken to try to avoid them. Where accidents or mishaps do occur, it is important that reflection occurs to see if anything could be learned that could prevent something similar happening in the future.

Summary

The promotion of equality, diversity and inclusion is essential in an organisation that is committed to treating those in their care with respect and dignity and these principles are also essential to ensure that individual differences, needs and preferences can be accommodated.

The care manager must ensure that they lead by example and demonstrate a strong commitment to these principles through their own behaviours. This includes ensuring that the policies and procedures on equality, diversity and inclusion are fit for purpose, well publicised and understood by the staff and utilised appropriately. Good processes both set standards and expectations and protect all those that use them or are subject to them when standards are called into question.

Learning outcomes	Assessment criteria
1 Understand diversity, equality and inclusion within own area of responsibility	**(1.1)** Explain models of practice that underpin equality, diversity and inclusion in own area of responsibility **Activity 5.1.1, p.76**
	(1.2) Analyse the potential effects of barriers to equality and inclusion in own area of responsibility **See p.77 for guidance.**
	(1.3) Analyse the impact of legislation and policy initiatives on the promotion of equality, diversity and inclusion in own area of responsibility **Activity 5.1.2, p.78**
2 Be able to champion diversity, equality and inclusion	**(2.1)** Promote equality, diversity and inclusion in policy and practice **Activity 5.2.1, p.79**
	(2.2) Challenge discrimination and inclusion in policy and practice **Activity 5.2.2, p.79** **Activity 5.2.3, p.80**
	(2.3) Provide others with information about: ■ the effects of discrimination ■ the impact of inclusion ■ the value of diversity **Activity 5.2.4, p.81**
	(2.4) Support others to challenge discrimination and exclusion **Activity 5.2.5, p.82**
3 Understand how to develop systems and processes that promote diversity, equality and inclusion	**(3.1)** Analyse how systems and processes can promote equality and inclusion or reinforce discrimination and exclusion **Activity 5.3.1, p.86**
	(3.2) Evaluate the effectiveness of systems and processes in promoting equality, diversity and inclusion in own area of responsibility **Activity 5.3.2, p.87**
	(3.3) Propose improvements to address gaps or shortfalls in systems and processes **See p.87 for guidance.**

Learning outcomes	Assessment criteria
4 Be able to manage the risks presented when balancing individual rights and professional duty of care	**Activity 5.4.1, p.87** (4.1) Describe ethical dilemmas that arise in own area of responsibility when balancing individual rights and duty of care **Activity 5.4.2, p.88** **Activity 5.4.3, p.89** (4.2) Explain the principle of informed choice **See p.89 for guidance.** (4.3) Explain how issues of capacity may affect informed choice **Activity 5.4.4, p.90** **Activity 5.4.5, p.91** (4.4) Propose a strategy to manage risks when balancing individual rights and duty of care in own area of responsibility **Activity 5.4.6, p.92**

References

Beauchamp, T. and Childress, J. (2001) *Principles of Biomedical Ethics*. Oxford: Oxford University Press.

Beecham,J., Knapp, M., Fernández, J-L, Huxley, P., Mangalore, R., McCrone, P., Snell, T., Winter, B. and Wittenberg, R. (2008) *Age Discrimination in Mental Health Services*. Discussion Paper Personal Social Services. May.

Belbin, R. (2010) *Management Teams: Why they succeed or fail* (3e). London: Butterworth Heinemann.

Buchanon, A. (1984) 'The right to a decent minimum of health care', *Philosophy and Public Affairs*, 13(1), pp.55–78.

Care Quality Commission Report (2011) *National Report on Dignity and Nutrition Review*. 13 October. London: CQC.

Cuthbert, S. and Quallington, J. (2008) *Values for Care Practice*. Exeter: Reflect Press.

Department for Constitutional Affairs (2007) *Mental Capacity Act 2005 Code of Practice*. London: The Stationery Office.

Department of Health (2000) *No Secrets: Guidance on developing and implementing multi-agency policies and procedures to protect vulnerable adults from abuse*. London: The Stationery Office.

Department of Education (2010) *Working Together to Safeguard Children*. London: The Stationery Office.

Directgov website (2011) *Protection for Whistleblowers*, www.direct.gov.uk/en/Employment/ResolvingWorkplaceDisputes/Whistleblowingintheworkplace/DG_10026552 (accessed Oct 2011).

Douglas, L. (2004) Chapter 9 in Harrison, R. *Learning and Development* (5e). London: Chartered Institute for Personnel and Development.

The Francis Report (2010) *Inquiry Report into Mid-Staffordshire NHS Foundation Trust*. London: Department of Health.

Gibbs, G. (1988) *Learning by Doing: A guide to teaching and learning methods*. Oxford: Oxford Further Education Unit.

Mullins, L. (2009) *Management and Organisational Behaviour* (8e). Harlow: Prentice Hall.

Ombudsman's Report (2011) 'Care and Compassion', *Report of the Health Service Ombudsman on Ten Investigations into the Care of Older People*. London: Parliamentary and Health Service Ombudsman.

Pidgeon, N., Hood, C., Turner, B. and Gibson, R. (1992) *Risk Analysis, Perception and Management*. Report of a Royal Society Study Group. London: The Royal Society.

Renz, D. and Eddy, W. (1996) 'Organisations, Ethics and Healthcare: Building an ethics infrastructure for a new era', *Bioethics Forum*, 12 (2), pp.29–39.

The Mental Capacity Act (2005) Department for Constitutional Affairs at http://webarchive. nationalarchives.gov.uk/+/http://www.dca.gov. uk/legal-policy/mental-capacity/mca-summary. pdf (accessed October 2011).

Thompson, N. (2011) *Promoting Equality: Working with diversity and difference* (3e). Basingstoke: Palgrave Macmillan.

Thompson. N and Thompson, S. (2008) *The Critically Reflective Practitioner*. Basingstoke: Palgrave Macmillan.

Titterton, M. (2005) Risk and Risk taking in Health and Social Welfare. London: Jessica Kingsley Publishing.

Walker, B. (1994) 'Valuing Differences: The concept and a model' in Mabey, C. and Iles, R. *Managing Learning*. Buckingham: Open University Press.

6 Unit HSCM1 Lead person centred practice

The purpose of this chapter is to enhance the manager's knowledge, understanding and skills required to promote and implement person centred practice. The Circles Network (2008) described person centred planning (and practice) as:

> 'a process of life planning for individuals based around the principles of inclusion and the social model of disability.'

The Department of Health subscribes fully to the social model of disability and in this chapter we will look at how care has changed over the last 150 years in an attempt to address the changing perceptions about how health care must be delivered to improve the quality of life of vulnerable people. From a service-led provision, we look at how the development of the personalisation agenda has changed the face of care in the UK.

We also deal with aspects of consent and what this means for clients and address the issues of active participation as a way of working that recognises an individual's right to participate in the activities and relationships of everyday life as independently as possible. The individual as an active partner in their own care or support is given a voice in today's health service and is no longer regarded as a passive recipient.

Learning outcomes
By the end of this chapter you will:

1. Understand the theory and principles that underpin person centred practice.

2. Be able to lead a person centred practice.

3. Be able to lead the implementation of *active participation* of individuals.

1 Understand the theory and principles that underpin person centred practice

 Explain person centred practice

In 2004 Stephen Ladyman, former Parliamentary Under-Secretary of State for the Community, described person-centred practice as follows:

> '... by "person-centred" I mean we have to move away from mass-produced services. Services that too often created a culture of dependency and move towards a future that seeks to develop the potential that is in every single individual.'
>
> (Ladyman, 2004)

Social care services in the UK have promoted person centred practice and it remains today high on the national policy agenda, often being hailed as representing best practice with respect to care.

The Government publication *Putting People First: A shared vision and commitment to the transformation of adult social care* was published in 2007 and outlined its personalisation agenda – the Government's vision of enabling individuals to live independently with complete choice and control over their lives.

Personalisation is about allowing individuals to build a system of care and support tailored to meet their own individual needs and designed with their full involvement. Historically, a 'one size fits all' approach to care was in practice and this meant the individual having to fit into and access already existing care services, whether they were appropriate or not. Now individuals can access their own budget and decide on which services they will spend that budget.

The term 'person centred care' has not been consistently used in literature and is often applied to elderly people and those with disabilities. Agreement has been reached, however, and the term is now used to describe care which is user focused, promoting independence and autonomy. Collaborative and partnership approaches to care often use the term 'person-centred' to describe their ethos (Innes *et al.*, 2006).

Figure 6.1 Discussing a care plan

Activity 6.1.1

Explain person centred practice and describe its benefits.

You may have described some of the following in your answer above.

■ It is a way of caring for a person as an individual with unique needs and differences.

■ It is an empathetic type of care since you are caring for an individual by being aware of how they might be feeling.

■ The care you give is 'individual' and is very different from treating everybody the same.

Person centred practice then refers to a variety of specific ways in which we can help people who use social care services to plan their own futures (Stalker and Campbell, 1998).

1.2 Critically review approaches to person centred practice

We can clearly see the benefits of the philosophy behind person centred care but despite extensive support by government, policy-makers, practitioners, and clients and their families, there remain difficulties with implementation.

Person centred practice has resulted from 30 years of investigation into the development of quality care, the origins of which can be traced to changes that took place in the early 1970s as part of a move to 'normalisation' when long-stay institutions for disabled people began to close down. At this time it was expected that long-term patients previously resident in and under the care of large institutions would be neatly returned to the community and be cared for by community-based services. Mainly aimed at the mentally ill patient, by the late 1960s it became apparent that this was an attempt to 'normalise' the conditions these individuals suffered and to remove stigma attached to such illnesses. With support from the European Convention on Human Rights (1950), the Mental Health Act of 1957 and the Howe Report (1969), recommendations were made in the 1971 White Paper 'Better Services for the Mentally Handicapped' which advocated a 50% reduction of hospital places by 1991. In addition, health professionals started to reflect different attitudes and contribute to new thinking on learning disability if not other forms of disability.

Figure 6.2 Disability

Unfortunately, the planned changes did not have the desired effects for the clients who were removed to community care. They were expected to fit into the available care services for all and very little personalisation of care was evident at this point in time. In addition to the huge problem of discrimination and the stigma attached to being a physically or learning disabled person or mentally ill person in the community, it became apparent that the health care system was systematically failing these individuals and this led to further criticism of the social care agenda. Research into the problems being encountered at the time revealed major change was needed in the way in which care was being delivered and one critical observation was the use of the Medical Model of care versus the social model debate.

The Medical Model of care describes the disabling condition and focuses on the impairment the individual suffers and how that impairment reduces the individual's quality of life, causing disadvantage. In this model, the emphasis then is on identifying the disability, understanding it and learning to treat and change its course if possible or prevent further deterioration.

An alternative model, the social model of care, took the opposite view and looked rather at the environment and its disabling impact on individuals. In other words, the view supported the notion that society creates disability and that barriers and prejudice, together with the subsequent exclusion by society, are the defining factors for who is disabled and who is not in a particular society. The lack of resources, facilities or the environment which restricted mobility meant that disabled individuals were unable to participate in work or education.

This model reflected the views that whilst physical or mental impairment posed problems these do not necessarily have to lead to disability unless society fails to accommodate these differences.

This change in thinking led to a sea change in the way in which disability was viewed and politicians were forced to address the issues which were arising. It was clear that, in order to improve care, changes to the way in which it was being delivered would need to be high on the agenda.

Over time, there was marked improvement in how society started to accept disabled people, those with learning disabilities, as well as people with mental health problems and older people as equal members of the community. The 'social model' of care enabled this change by forcing the view that society was in fact the problem for such groups because it failed to provide adequate services to meet their needs. The model was hailed therefore as a more person centred approach to care than the Medical Model.

As we have seen above, the approach to person centred care has involved a shift in the way in which care is delivered and it has been linked heavily to the experiences of disabled people in our society. In the past the needs of disabled people were assumed to be a universal need rather than an individual issue. This meant that organisations took decisions for people because they belonged to a particular group and determined how they should live and the nature of the care they would require. Rather than services being designed to fit around the needs of individuals, a 'one size fits all' design was the order of the day.

The outcome of all these changes has not only put the person at the centre of the care process but has also shifted power towards them, enabling them to have more freedom of choice – something which most of us take for granted.

The principles guiding this agenda centre on the notion of equality, choice, independence and inclusion. In order to meet these needs, the services we supply in health care must challenge the unequal power structures that have been evident between service providers and service users. Sanderson (2003, p.20) talks about this change as being the need to operate from a position where they have 'power with' service users rather than 'power over' them.

In trying to implement person centred care, managers need to be clear about how the support to clients will be delivered. It is not merely a case of including clients and families and asking them what they think or what they want. There are processes to guide practice and four tools have been developed for the implementation of person centred planning and practice. You may well be familiar with these which include:

1. **The McGill Action Planning System (MAPS)**, which is a planning process for children with disabilities to enable their integration into the school community. The team in this process includes the child, family members, friends, and regular and special education personnel.

2. **ELP or Essential Lifestyle Planning** are detailed plans used to get to know what is important to someone. When using these types of plans the assumptions behind them are that:

   ■ The individual will have a lifestyle that works for them.

   ■ Our quality of life depends upon how well or badly we achieve that lifestyle.

   As care workers we should help people to live their chosen lifestyle – not try to change the person to fit in with our view of life.

3. **Personal Futures Planning** – the author of this approach, Beth Mount, commented:

   'The person futures planning process suggests a series of tasks and provides a set of tools to help us begin the process with people to uncover their capacities, to discover opportunities in the local community, and to invent new service responses that help more than get in the way.'

   (Mount, 1992)

   This planning process involves:

   ■ Getting to know the person to determine what their life is like now.

   ■ Developing ideas about what they would like to do in the future.

   ■ Taking action to help them to implement this, and exploring possibilities within the community and looking at what needs to change within services.

   (Mount and O'Brien, 1992, see edg. usablewebsites.org/files/Personal_ Futures_Planning.pdf)

4. **PATHS (Planning Alternative Tomorrows and Hope)**. This system was developed by Jack Pearpoint, Marsha Forest and John O'Brien and focusses on what is termed the person's 'North Star' or their dream for the future. This 'dream' is then put into action and reviewed one or two years later.

For a description of the research, see Helen Sanderson (2000) *Critical Issues in the Implementation of Essential Lifestyle Planning Within a Complex Organization: An action research investigation within a learning disability service.* Manchester Metropolitan University. Unpublished Ph.D. thesis.

Health care has come a considerable distance in terms of person centred care. Traditional views of clients as a passive recipient of care are now challenged and the way in which the 'needs of the disabled' were determined, without reference to the individual, have largely disappeared.

Today person centred planning has taken centre stage in services but has not been fully adopted or implemented across social care provision and there needs to be more work carried out.

Campbell (2001) recognises the progress in user involvement, but other writers comment on the slowness of the process. In the next section we shall address how the law has addressed the personalisation agenda.

Activity 6.1.2

Person centred care reflects the values of empowerment and personalisation that underlie contemporary approaches to health and social care in England. Write a reflective account of your own views on this subject and describe how you meet these needs in your own organisation.

1.3 Analyse the effect of legislation and policy on person centred practice

As we noted in the last section, the social model of health has become a major contributor to the change in the way health care is delivered in this country. A report by Beresford *et al.* in 2005 for SCIE and the Department of Health helped inform the formulation of the Green Paper 'Independence, well-being and choice: Our vision for the future of social care for adults in England'. Since then a White Paper, 'Your health, your care, your say', has been published encompassing both children's and adult services and health and social care.

The service users who contributed to this report clearly stated that they favoured a social model approach to care which 'supports people to be independent by ensuring they have the support to live as they wish' (Beresford *et al.*, 2005).

In addition, there is a strong commitment by government to support the personalisation agenda and currently there are moves to push through a new Health and Social Care Bill (2011).

The Government paper 'A vision for adult social care: Capable communities and active citizens', published in November 2010, set out the plans for a new direction for adult social care, putting personalised services and outcomes centre stage, based on six principles. These principles outlined changes to the current policies and are detailed below.

1. **Personalisation:** individuals would take control of their own care with the direct payments to them of personal budgets.

2. **Partnership:** care and support was to be delivered in a partnership between individuals, communities, the voluntary and private sectors, the NHS and councils, together with wider support services, such as housing.

3. **Plurality:** the broad market of high quality service providers would be matched to the variety of people's needs.

4. **Protection:** safeguards against the risk of abuse or neglect would be reviewed so that risk of such would no longer limit a person's freedom.

5. **Productivity:** the delivery of higher quality care and support services would be matched to greater local accountability and more focus on publishing information about agreed quality outcomes would support this.

6. **People:** a workforce who would provide skilled and compassionate support would lead the changes.

Following this publication, in May 2011 a call for the major revamp of adult social care law in England was announced by the Law Commission. It called for a single piece of legislation so people were clear about their rights. This first report of two reviews said that the current framework, covered by more than 40 laws, was 'out-dated and flawed' (BBC News, May 2011). The report on adult social care recommended the most far-reaching reforms of adult social care law seen for over 60 years, with proposals that older people, disabled people, those with mental health problems and carers will, for the first time, be clear about their legal rights to care and support services.

Historically, though, the delivery of health care in this country has not always been service-user friendly and a lot of the debate has been about care for the physically and mentally disabled, and for the elderly. There has been an uncomfortable journey through the years in which governments have tried to address the growing need for help for those who could not work for whatever reason.

The Poor Laws back in 1834 and the development of the Charity Organisation Society (COS) in 1869 tried to address the poverty experienced by some at the time. Individuals were categorised into two groups; those deemed 'worthy and deserving of receiving' charity and those who were classed as 'unworthy or undeserving' of help. The latter group were sent to the workhouse with its terribly dehumanising regime and such treatment was to last for many more years in one way or another. The institutionalisation of people who were disabled or who had mental health problems or learning disabilities was a classic example of the control the medical profession had over individuals who had been classified by their medical condition and kept in large institutional or hospital settings. There was no choice exercised in these places and staff were in complete control. These institutions expanded over the next few years and by 1914 there were over 120 asylums in England.

Figure 6.3 A workhouse

An unfortunate by-product of the institutionalisation of such groups, together with the lack of choice and control, was the discrimination felt by these individuals and the stigma attached to such conditions. It was to take another 50 or so years before this was actually addressed as a problem in society.

Changes to the law in 1927 saw an amendment to the Mental Deficiency Act of 1913 replacing the term 'moral defective' with 'moral imbecile'. It is interesting to note that still the discriminatory language persisted but the latter was put forward as the preferred term.

In the 1940s the Poor Laws were abolished and in 1948 the Welfare State and National Assistance Act were introduced. National Assistance Boards dealt with financial support and local authorities provided basic residential accommodation to disabled and older people. With a public welfare system becoming established as a result of the Beveridge Report, the aim was to provide a 'cradle to grave' system of social insurance and benefits for the disadvantaged in society.

Benefits were to be provided for the unemployed, the sick, the retired and the widowed and, together with an acceptable minimum standard of living in the UK, the whole structure of welfare was being addressed. White Papers on education and the creation of a National Health Service were all under scrutiny at the time and the resultant National Assistance Act of 1948 addressed the needs of disabled people and put a duty of care on local authorities to supply services for such groups. In addition, the National Health Service Act of the same year also ensured that hospitals and long-term care were available for disabled groups. Although these changes were welcomed and positive for those disadvantaged by circumstances, the provision still fell short of providing individualised or person centred care.

The rising tide of dissatisfaction with the care system saw the development of the civil rights movement of the 1960s and 1970s. It was at this time that the Medical Model and the way power was distributed in society came under scrutiny and the disability movement was born.

There was also an emerging 'anti-psychiatry' movement in the late 1960s which criticised the Medical Model in mental health and demanded that individuals with mental health problems had a greater say in decisions about their lives and choices. The closure of psychiatric institutions and former asylums was to become a major government issue, particularly when there were several media reports of inhumane treatment in such places.

The Chronically Sick and Disabled Persons Act (1970) placed a duty on local authorities to provide care and support services for disabled people. The passing of this Act was hailed as a ground-breaking step towards equality and became the first piece of disability legislation in the world which addressed the rights of people with disabilities, seeking to give them an equal place in society.

In the 1980s and 1990s there was a move towards a more individualistic, consumer-led approach to social care and the Conservative government talked of the 'dependency culture' that was in evidence and the need to address this.

The passing of the Social Security Act (1986) saw Supplementary Benefit being replaced with Income Support and the Disabled Persons Act (1986) brought about assessment of needs for disabled persons. With the movement of people out of long-term institutions, there was also the provision of an Independent Living Fund (ILF) which was brought in to increase choice and control in order to promote independent living.

It was in the late 1980s that the concept of the 'mixed economy of care' was introduced. The 1988 Griffiths Report on Community Care advised that social services should use a variety of providers to prevent a 'monopoly' on the provision of care and support. At this time, the use of private sector providers, particularly in homes, domiciliary and day care services, was encouraged and a market economy was introduced.

The 1989 'Caring for People' White Paper paved the way for community care and care management in social work. This gathered momentum and the NHS and Community Care Act (1990) developed the use of a 'needs-led approach' together with assessment and 'individually tailored packages of care'. The emphasis was to be on providing flexible care in people's own homes so that they might live 'as normal a life as possible'.

In the late 1990s new legislation allowing for direct payments came about as a result of the Community Care and Direct Payments Act 1996. This was to enable social service authorities/ departments to make cash payments to disabled people for community care services and in later years this was also made available to older people, people with mental health problems, carers and parents of disabled children.

This major development to ensure that all groups requiring care were empowered and had choice and control was picked up by the New Labour government in the years 2001–9, which was keen to promote independent living. 'Individual budgets' introduced in 2003 brought about a new model of social care provision.

Improving the Life Chances of Disabled People (2005) – individual budgets to improve choice and control over the mix of care and support.

Independence, Well-being and Choice (2005) – social care services help people to maintain their independence by 'giving them greater choice and control over the way their needs are met'.

Our Health, Our Care, Our Say: A new direction for community service (2006) developed the concept of personalised care.

Putting People First: A shared vision and commitment to transformation of adult social care was a commitment to enable people to manage and control their own support through individual/personal budgets.

Care Support Independence: Shaping the future of care together (2009) – consultation on how personalised social care and support can be delivered and funded.

Personal Health Budgets: 'First steps' (2009) introduces the personal health budget to allow people to have more choice, flexibility and control over the health services and care they receive.

The *Valuing People* White Paper (2001) made direct payments available to more people with a learning disability and it is in this paper that we first officially come across the term 'person centred planning'.

Several more White Papers in the following years all contribute to the need for independence, choice and control to be firmly placed in the hands of the service user and these are shown in the box above.

Activity 6.1.3

What other policies and laws relating to person centred practice are you aware of in your own area of practice?

You may have identified some of the following in your answer above:

■ **The National Service Framework and the single assessment process (SAP).** This was introduced on the Older People framework and ensures that the elderly person in care receives appropriate care to meet their own individual needs. The SAP calls for a holistic assessment to be made with the emphasis on partnership working (see Chapter 2).

■ **National Minimum Standards** although not legal requirements are guidelines which instruct the registered manager to 'develop and agree an individual plan' for all service users.

■ **Care Programme Approach (CPA) (1990)** – similar to the SAP, this applies to the individual with mental health problems and ensures that they are fully involved in their own care plan.

■ **The Personalisation Agenda (2008)** defines personalisation as 'the way in which services are tailored to the needs and preferences of citizens to empower citizens to shape their own lives and the services they receive'.

1.4 Explain how person centred practice informs the way in which consent is established with individuals

Person centred care demands that the individual requiring care is fully involved in the whole planning process and, as such, can be deemed to have consented to such arrangements in a verbal way. Any discussion about treatment and care and the proposed treatment must be given in a sensitive and understandable way and the individual should be given enough time to think about the information and to ask questions if they need to. By engaging with the care worker, they have 'implied' that they consent to the process and this is an acceptable way of obtaining consent. Often we ask for written consent and this is certainly true if the case involves any risk. In this case, a written record will remain in the individual notes recording the treatment and care agreed on. The actual process of writing up the notes of the consent must be rigorous, accurately recording all discussions and decisions made relating to obtaining consent.

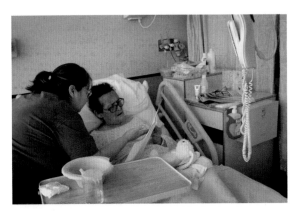

Figure 6.4 Signing a consent form

In approaching the care planning process, the assumption is that every adult must be presumed to have the mental capacity to consent or refuse treatment, unless they are:

- unable to take in or retain information provided about their treatment or care

- unable to understand the information provided

- unable to weigh up the information as part of the decision-making process.

(Nursing and Midwifery Council)

The decision as to whether the individual lacks capacity must be made with the medical staff providing the treatment or care and in consultation with family and care staff. In an emergency situation when a person requires treatment but is unconscious, then treatment to preserve life may be given, as long as it is in the best interests of that person and this is covered in law.

If the individual does not consent to treatment, care workers need to respect that refusal and a record of the refusal to consent made.

But what happens if the person who has refused treatment or care is confused or mentally incapacitated in some way? In this instance, the care staff must make a full and frank assessment of their care and ensure that the individual is safeguarded. The same principles of consent apply to incapacitated people.

If it is felt that a referral to court to obtain permission to treat is necessary, guidelines provided list the following circumstances:

- sterilisation for contraceptive purposes

- donation of regenerative tissue such as bone marrow

- withdrawal of nutrition and hydration from a patient in a persistent vegetative state

- where there is doubt as to the person's capacity or best interests.

(Nursing and Midwifery Council)

Two laws which are useful to know are the Adults with Incapacity (Scotland) Act 2000 and the Mental Capacity Act 2005 (England and Wales). These allow people over the age of 16 to appoint a proxy decision-maker who has the legal power to give consent to medical treatment when the patient loses the capacity to consent. In the case of a person who is detained under mental health legislation, the principles of consent continue to apply and care staff must ensure that the individual is aware of the circumstances and safeguards needed for providing treatment and care without consent.

If you are dealing with a child under the age of 16, then obtaining consent is complex and legal advice needs to be sought. Young people under the age of 16 are considered to lack the capacity to consent or to refuse treatment and that right remains with the parents, or those with parental responsibility. If the child is considered to have significant understanding and intelligence to make up his or her own mind about what is happening to them, then that may be waived.

A child of 16 or 17 is considered to be able to consent for themselves but good practice demands that parents or guardians are involved. Refusal of consent by a child of any age up to 18 years can be overridden by the parents. In exceptional circumstances, it may be necessary to seek an order from the court.

There are a couple of exceptions where a capable individual may be treated without first obtaining their consent. For example, a magistrate can order detention in hospital if a person has an infectious disease that presents a risk to public health – such as rabies, cholera or anthrax (Public Health (Control of Disease) Act, 1984).

Under the National Assistance Act (1948), a severely ill or infirm person who is living in unsanitary (unclean) conditions can be taken to a place of care without their consent.

Finally the Mental Health Act (1983) instructs that people with certain mental health conditions, such as schizophrenia, bipolar disorder or dementia, can be compulsorily detained at a hospital or psychiatric clinic without their consent.

Activity 6.1.4

Reflect and write about the way in which consent is established with individuals in your setting.

1.5 Explain how person centred practice can result in positive changes in individuals' lives

There can be little doubt that person centred practice is good for the soul! The traditional service-led approach was an easy way to deliver care for care workers but meant that people did not receive the help they really needed at the right time.

Personalisation gives more choice and control over lives and ensures that people have wider choice in how their needs are met. They are able to access universal services such as transport, leisure and education, housing, health and opportunities for employment regardless of age or disability (SCIE).

A campaign launched in 2006 entitled Dignity in Care outlines the means by which tolerance of indignity in health care can be eliminated. The Dignity Challenge led by the Department of Health states that high quality care services that respect people's dignity should (amongst other things):

■ Treat each person as an individual by offering personalised services.

■ Enable people to maintain the maximum possible level of independence, choice and control.

Activity 6.1.5

Give examples of how person centred practice has resulted in positive changes in individuals' lives in your care.

2 Be able to lead a person centred practice

2.1 Support *others* to work with *individuals* to establish their history, preferences, wishes and needs

2.2 Support others to implement person centred practice

In this section you need to undertake the activities in order to meet the outcomes and to supply your assessor with evidence-based practice. Each outcome refers to working with and supporting others and in this context 'others' refers to family, friends, advocates, paid workers, as well as other care professionals.

As we have seen, person centred care and planning are key factors in the 'Valuing People' document and this was specifically written with learning disabled people in mind. However, the whole tenet of individualistic care is now considered to be good practice for all care services.

In leading person centred practice you and the others involved in the process need to keep in mind the following points:

■ The central figure in the process is the client.

■ Family and friends are partners in the care process.

■ The care plan is a guide to what is important for the client and shows what support they need.

■ A care plan helps the person to be a part of the community and is not merely about what services they need.

■ The plan is a continuous process and does not stop when it has been written. The people involved continue to evaluate and act within the plan to help the client to achieve the best quality care.

(DOH, 2001)

In order to lead good practice and enable staff and others to be fully involved in care planning that is truly person centred there must be a good support network in place. A study carried out by Innes, McPherson and McCabe (2006) drew together a review of the literature about frontline workers, in particular those working with clients in the community. We believe the findings are appropriate and may be applied to any care setting.

By approaching workers who were involved in planning care, they found the following:

'In discussion groups, frontline workers highlighted their personal commitment to health and social care work and emphasised the importance of having a range of skills that link in complex ways to their gender, age, ethnicity and general experiences. They also felt that managers and others not directly involved in frontline work, however, often relegate personal qualities to second place in favour of formal qualifications.

'They also felt that care managers – and society as a whole – lack awareness of the range of tasks frontline workers perform and generally undervalue frontline care work.'

(Innes *et al.*, 2006)

As a manager leading person centred care, you need to be aware that some of your staff may actually identify with these views and need your support to ensure they have the skills to carry out person centred care to the high standards they favour.

Activity 6.2.1

Write a case study indicating how you have ensured that your staff are supported in person centred care planning. Observe a member of staff undertaking the process with the client and family members and evaluate the process.

2.3 Support others to work with individuals to review approaches to meet individuals' needs and preferences

The Action on Elder Abuse Toolkit provides us with a useful set of questions when undertaking the planning process. It states, in section 3.9 of the document:

'Person centred approaches

Such an approach ties in with an emphasis on person centred approaches, and encourages engagement, time and patience. Key questions for a person centred approach include:

- What is the person communicating about their views? How can we help them understand and communicate more?

- What is life like for this person? How do they experience the world?

- What would it be like to be in their shoes?

- What is important for them?

- What might their hopes and dreams be?'

(Action on Elder Abuse Toolkit)

Activity 6.2.2

Using the questions above, work with a member of staff to review approaches to meet an individual's needs and preferences. Ask the people involved in the process to comment on the questions and their appropriateness in determining the client's care plan.

2.4 Support others to work with individuals to adapt approaches in response to individuals' emerging needs or preferences

This final section requires you to evaluate the whole process carried out in the above activities. In adapting approaches to account for emerging needs, there needs to be an evaluation of the care process that has been undertaken. Person centred practice recognises that needs change over time and this will require a change in the service provision.

Activity 6.2.3

(This activity should be undertaken some weeks following the initial planning session with the client.)

Use the information from the previous activity's work with the client, staff member and family to make a judgement of the care plan and identify what has changed and what requires change in the client's care.

Document the whole process and ask all involved to give feedback on the whole process revealing what they felt was good about it and what needs work.

How successful has the person centred approach been for this client?

3 Be able to lead the implementation of *active participation* of individuals

3.1 Evaluate how *active participation* enhances the well-being and quality of life of individuals

Langer and Rodin (1976) conducted a study to assess the effects of enhanced personal responsibility and choice on a group of nursing home residents. Two groups were studied and, in the experimental group, the residents were given a communication emphasising their responsibility for themselves. The second group, the control group, were told that the staff were responsible for all care. In addition, those residents in the experimental group were given the freedom to make choices rather than having decisions made for them and they were also given a plant to take care of. The opposite arrangements were in place for the control group. The results of the study showed a significant improvement for the experimental group over the control group on alertness, active participation and a general sense of well-being.

The expectation at the start of the study was that the debilitated condition of many of the aged individuals residing in institutional settings is the result of living in a virtually decision-free environment and consequently is potentially reversible.

This is, of course, only one study and an old one at that. However, person centred care has arisen due to the reaction that came about in the early 1960s to the appalling care treatment of residents in long-term care institutions where little respect was afforded to the person in care. It was not that long ago that those considered to be 'severely disabled' were shut away in long-stay hospitals and other institutions. Today, the United Nations Convention on the Rights of the Child and the Children Act of 1989, together with the Human Rights Act, have addressed this situation and an individual's right to 'active participation in the community' is now high on the Government policy agenda.

Being unable to make a decision or to have a dialogue about the care and needs an individual may have inevitably leads to a major reduction in self-esteem and we are fully aware of how this affects health and well-being.

Consider for a moment how you might feel if you were a patient in hospital and never consulted about your treatment. You merely had to accept the decisions made and do as you were told. It would not be very long before you were completely switched off and passive in whatever was being done to you. You might even feel that you were being undervalued with respect to any of your wishes.

The Nursing and Midwifery Council standards of conduct make it very clear that health care workers should listen to the people in their care and respond to their needs as individuals. They should be aware of their preferences and act in accordance with these. The General Social Care Council echoes this and the Code of Practice states that care workers must treat people as individuals and support their right to control their own lives and make informed choices.

Activity 6.3.1

Undertake a small scale study of a group of individuals in your care and ask them to comment on how well active participation in their own care enhances their well-being and quality of life.

3.2 Implement systems and processes that promote active participation

A study commissioned by the Joseph Rowntree Foundation and carried out by Wilcox *et al.* (1994) outlined ten key ideas about active participation and, in particular, community participation.

The publication, *The Guide to Effective Participation*, is worth looking at but we outline in the box below some of the ten key ideas.

---

1 Level of participation

A five-rung ladder of participation relating to the stance an organisation promoting participation may take:

- *Information*: telling people what is planned.

- *Consultation*: offering options, listening to feedback, but not allowing new ideas.

- *Deciding together*: encouraging additional options and ideas, and providing opportunities for joint *decision-making*.

- *Acting together*: not only do different interests decide together on what is best, they form a partnership to carry it out.

- *Supporting independent community interests*: *local* groups or organisations are offered funds, advice or other support to develop their own agendas within *guidelines*.

---

2 Initiation and process

Many problems in participation develop because of poor preparation within the promoting organisation – with the result that when community interest is engaged, the organisation cannot deliver on its promises. There needs to be a process in place to allow others to be involved and to allow the process to be controlled and monitored.

3 Control

The initiator or person in control can decide how much or how little control to allow to others – for example, just information, or a major say in what is to happen.

4 Power and purpose

Power will depend on who has information and money. It will also depend on people's confidence and skills. Many organisations fear loss of control and may be unwilling to allow people to participate. However, working together allows everyone to achieve more than they could on their own. The guide emphasises the difference between power *to* and power *over*. People are empowered when they have the power to achieve what they want.

5 Role of the practitioner

Practitioners control much of what happens and the guide is written mainly for people who are planning or managing participation processes. It may be difficult for a practitioner both to control access to funds and other resources and to play a neutral role in facilitating a participation process.

6 Stakeholders and community

Anyone who has a stake in what happens is a stakeholder and some of these will have influence in the community.

7 Partnership

Partners must trust each other and share commitment.

8 Commitment

People are committed when they want to achieve something, and apathetic when they don't. They care about what they are interested in. If people are apathetic about proposals, it may be that they don't share the interests or concerns of those putting forward the plans and that can be a starting point for dialogue.

9 Ownership of ideas

People are most likely to be interested and committed if they have a stake in the idea. Running brainstorming workshops and helping people think through the practicality of ideas can be useful.

10 Confidence and capacity

Ideas and wish-lists are little use if they cannot be put into practice. Many participation processes involve breaking new ground – tackling difficult projects and setting up new forms of organisations. Training may be needed or the opportunity to learn formally and informally, to develop confidence and trust in each other.

Adapted from the findings of Community participation and empowerment: putting theory into practice, published in 1994 by the Joseph Rowntree Foundation. Reproduced by permission of the Joseph Rowntree Foundation.

The process above is very much a social work model of practice and can be seen in initiatives such as the Sure Start programme. When arranging care packages for clients, it is important to involve as many partners in the community as possible in order to widen choice and options. By having an understanding of community developments, you are better able to refer clients to the right services.

Activity 6.3.2

Show evidence of the systems and processes in your own work that promote active participation.

3.3 Support the use of risk assessments to promote active participation in all aspects of the lives of individuals

The national occupational standards for social work practitioners have identified six key roles, one of which highlights risk assessment.

In key role 4, the social work practitioner is instructed to manage risk to individuals, families, carers, groups, communities, self and colleagues. The standard is outlined in the box opposite.

- Manage risk to individuals, families, carers, groups, communities, self and colleagues.

- Address behaviour which presents a risk to individuals, families, carers, groups, communities, self and others.

- Identify and assess the nature of the risk.

- Balance the rights and responsibilities of individuals, families, carers, groups and communities with associated risk.

- Regularly monitor, re-assess and manage risk to individuals, families, carers, groups and communities.

- Take immediate action to deal with the behaviour that presents a risk.

- Work with individuals, families, carers, groups, communities and others to identify and evaluate situations and circumstances that may trigger the behaviour.

- Work with individuals, families, carers, groups and communities on strategies and support that could positively change the behaviour.

Helping individuals to make choices in their own care means that, occasionally, a choice may involve a risk at some level. Generally we can view risk in two ways:

1. The risk a person poses to other people.

2. The risk a person may be subject to, whether by a chosen action or not.

In the first case, risk assessment focuses on how the person may pose a risk to others. For example, mental health workers and prison officers will have risk assessments in place, together with strategies and procedures which will protect them in the event of a situation developing.

In the second case, the risk is not necessarily viewed as a negative thing and may in fact be positive. If the risk to be taken is life enhancing for the person (e.g. a young cared for person wishes to move away to attend university but is deemed as vulnerable), then the assessment needs to identify what the risks may be and whether they are acceptable to take or not.

In social work there are two types of risk assessment favoured and these are worth studying:

- Actuarial assessment

- Clinical assessment.

Actuarial assessment has been taken from the insurance model of assessment and involves a statistical calculation of the risk. In this type of assessment, the risk is calculated according to the probability of something happening and then expressed in numerical form. You are predicting what might happen, together with the likelihood of that happening and then making a judgement as to whether to take the risk or not.

The clinical assessment of risk fits better with the person centred approach to care in that it is undertaken on a case-by-case basis and is therefore more individual in nature. It also proposes that there is a better understanding of the nature of the risk rather than merely a calculation of the probability.

However, as it is based upon professional judgement and is largely subjective, it may be inaccurate. What I say is a risk to a person may not necessarily register as such with your assessment.

Two forms of error have been cited with clinical assessment and these are false negatives and false positives. Walker and Beckett (2005) make the following points about this.

False negative is where a situation is identified as having a low risk and a harmful event occurs anyway. For example, if a person is left in the care of their family and comes to harm, the risk assessment is deemed to be 'wrong'.

False positives represent situations which are viewed as high risk where a harmful event would not occur, even in the absence of intervention. For example, if the elderly person had remained in their own home, they would not have come to any harm but removing them to a care setting causes distress and therefore harm has been caused.

These cases illustrate the uncertainty of risk assessment and Walker and Beckett (2005) conclude that it is imperative to review any situation in which a mistake has been made in the risk assessment and to determine if there are any factors that should have been noted and were not. Alternatively, it may have been that the situation which emerged could not have been reasonably foreseen and prepared for because 'a bad outcome in and of itself does not constitute evidence that decision was mistaken' (Macdonald and Macdonald, 1999).

So how do you undertake a risk assessment and feel relatively safe in the decisions you have made? One way is to ensure that you can defend each decision you make with respect to the assessment of the individual. You might think about the following questions to guide your assessment.

- Have you taken all reasonable steps in the process?

- Have you used reliable methods?

- Have you collected enough information and looked at it in an evaluative manner?

- Are you working within policy and law?
- Have you recorded all the decisions that were made?

In addition to the above, you might actually take a purely health and safety approach to risk:

- Step 1: looking for hazards.
- Step 2: Identifying who could be harmed and how.
- Step 3: Evaluation of the risk.
- Step 4: Record the findings.
- Step 5: Assess the effectiveness of the precautions in place.

Chapter 1 gives a more detailed account of this approach and you are advised to read this chapter again.

Activity 6.3.3

Undertake a risk assessment for one of your clients and reflect on how you will ensure that active participation is promoted for that person.

Summary

Person centred practice arose out of the reaction to institutional care practices in the late 1950s and 1960s and has been adopted by governments as being the best way forward to improve the quality of life of vulnerable people. From a service-led provision, the development of the personalisation agenda has changed the face of care in the UK.

Active participation is a way of working which recognises an individual's right to participate in the activities and relationships of everyday life as independently as possible.

In a nutshell, person centred care is just that, the person is at the centre of their own care package and as such is respected, viewed as an individual and an expert in their own lifestyle. With changing needs and personal development, care planning needs to be evaluated on a regular basis and will inevitably change over the period of time the person requires care. Partnership working with others in the service industry is also an important element in person centred care and effective working relationships with other service providers are a part of the process in this type of care.

Learning outcomes	Assessment criteria
1 Understand the theory and principles that underpin person centred practice	1.1 Explain person centred practice **Activity 6.1.1, p.97**
	1.2 Critically review approaches to person centred practice **Activity 6.1.2, p.99**
	1.3 Analyse the effect of legislation and policy on person centred practice **Activity 6.1.3, p.101**
	1.4 Explain how person centred practice informs the way in which consent is established with individuals **Activity 6.1.4, p.103**
	1.5 Explain how person centred practice can result in positive changes in individuals' lives **Activity 6.1.5, p.103**

Learning outcomes	Assessment criteria
2 Be able to lead a person centred practice	**(2.1)** Support others to work with individuals to establish their history, preferences, wishes and needs **Activity 6.2.1, p.104**
	(2.2) Support others to implement person centred practice **Activity 6.2.1, p.104**
	(2.3) Support others to work with individuals to review approaches to meet individuals' needs and preferences **Activity 6.2.2, p.104**
	(2.4) Support others to work with individuals to adapt approaches in response to individuals' emerging needs or preferences **Activity 6.2.3, p.104**
3 Be able to lead the implementation of active participation of individuals	**(3.1)** Evaluate how active participation enhances the well-being and quality of life of individuals **Activity 6.3.1, p.105**
	(3.2) Implement systems and processes that promote active participation **Activity 6.3.2, p.106**
	(3.3) Support the use of risk assessments to promote active participation in all aspects of the lives of individuals **Activity 6.3.3, p.108**

References

Beresford, P., Shamash, M., Forrest, V., Turner, M. and Branfield, F. (2005) *Developing Social Care: Service users' vision for adult support.* London: SCIE.

Campbell, P. (2001) 'The role of users of psychiatric services in service development – influence not power', *Psychiatric Bulletin*, Vol. 25, pp.87–8.

Circles Network (2008) www.circlesnetwork. org.uk/index.asp?slevel=0z285&parent_id=85

DOH (2001) *Valuing People: A new strategy for learning disability for the 21st century; planning with people; towards person-centred approaches – accessible guide.* London: HMSO.

DOH (2005) *Improving the Life Chances of Disabled People.* London: HMSO.

DOH (2006) *Our Health, Our Care, Our Say: A new direction for community service.* London: HMSO.

DOH (2006) *Dignity in Care: Becoming a champion.* London: HMSO.

DOH (2007) *Putting People First: A shared vision and commitment to the transformation of Adult Social Care.* London: HMG. www.dh.gov.uk/en/ Publicationsandstatistics/Publications/ PublicationsPolicyAndGuidance/DH_081118

DOH (2009) *Personal Health Budgets: First steps.* London: HMSO.

HM Government (2009) *Shaping the Future of Care Together.* Green Paper.

Innes, A., Macpherson, S. and McCabe, I. (2006) *Promoting Person-Centred Care At The Front Line*. York: Joseph Rowntree Foundation/SCIE.

Ladyman, S. (2004) 'Health and Social Care Advisory Service: New directions in direct payments for people who use mental health services', speech, Department of Health, London, 18 May.

Langer E. J. and Rodin, I. (1976) 'The Effects of Choice and Enhanced Personal Responsibility for the Aged: A field experiment in an institutional setting'. *Journal of Personality and Social Psychology*, **34**(2), pp.191–8.

Macdonald, K. and Macdonald, G. (1999) 'Perceptions of risk' in Parsloe, P. (ed) *Risk Assessment in Social Work and Social Care*. London: Jessica Kingsley.

Sanderson, H. (2000) *Critical Issues in the Implementation of Essential Lifestyle Planning Within a Complex Organization: An action research investigation within a learning disability service*. Manchester Metropolitan University. Unpublished Ph.D. thesis.

Sanderson, H. (2003) 'Implementing person-centred planning by developing person-centred teams', *Journal of Integrated Care*, Vol. 11, No. 3, pp.18–25.

Stalker, K. and Campbell, V. (1998) 'Person-centred planning: an evaluation of a training programme', *Health and Social Care in the Community*, Vol. 6, No. 2, pp.130–42.

Walker, S. and Beckett, C. (2005) *Social Work Assessment and Intervention*. Dorset: Russell House Publishing.

Wilcox, D., Holmes, A., Kean, J., Ritchie, C. and Smith, J. (1994) *The Guide to Effective Participation*. York: Joseph Rowntree Foundation.

www.nmc-uk.org/Nurses-and-midwives/Advice-by-topic/A/Advice/Consent/

Unit LM1c Lead and manage a team within a health and social care or children and young people's setting

The most important person in your team will be the service user or client and they need to be central to any team working. Effective team performance requires the development of a positive and supportive culture in an organisation. Only in this way can we expect staff to be supportive of a shared vision to meet the agreed objectives for a health and social care or children and young people's setting.

In this chapter you will learn how to lead and manage a team and enhance their performance in a health and social care or children and young people's setting. The chapter will introduce you to team function and the roles that are adopted in teams and will examine models of leadership relevant to the health and care sector. The activities in the chapter will encourage you to examine strategies of team working and leadership in order to identify your own strengths, responsibilities and learning needs and to reflect on best practice within the care context.

Team working means taking responsibility for your own work, as well as respecting the contributions of all your colleagues, and good communication is essential to effective team working.

Learning outcomes

By the end of this chapter you will:

1. Understand the features of effective team performance within a health and social care or children and young people's setting.

2. Be able to support a positive culture within the team for a health and social care or children and young people's setting.

3. Be able to support a shared vision within the team for a health and social care or children and young people's setting.

4. Be able to develop a plan with team members to meet agreed objectives for a health and social care or children and young people's setting.

5. Be able to support individual team members to work towards agreed objectives in a health and social care or children and young people's setting.

6. Be able to manage team performance in a health and social care or children and young people's setting.

1 Understand the features of effective team performance within a health and social care or children and young people's setting

1.1 Explain the features of effective team performance

Imagine a group of footballers who have little idea about the rules of the game, what the objectives of the game are and how the position they play works with the rest of the team. Picture the first match and hazard a guess as to the outcome. Of course, it is likely to be a mess, isn't it? With nobody working together and without any direction, the game will be lost.

So too with team performance. Effective teams work together and work towards common goals and objectives.

Figure 7.1 An ineffective team

A team is a group of people who work together (unlike our collection of footballers above!) and a group is a collection of two or more people who communicate together because they have interests in common. From the beginning of time, people have used work groups to get things done and to generate new ideas (Wheelan, 2005). But what is it that makes a group of people a team?

If we coordinate the work of a group of people and develop shared goals, working towards a common aim, then we are almost there. The members in a team need to be able to communicate and collaborate effectively to function effectively.

Pearson and Spencer (1997) suggest that teams are formed because of a belief that having people work on shared goals interdependently will lead to synergy; the aggregate of individuals' performances will be exceeded by the work group's performance (Tilmouth *et al.*, 2011).

Effective teams display certain features and the following are eight characteristics identified by Larson and LaFasto (1989) in their book *Teamwork: What Must Go Right/What Can Go Wrong.*

1. The team must have a clear goal.
2. The team must have a results-driven structure.
3. The team must have competent team members.
4. The team must have unified commitment.
5. The team must have a collaborative climate.
6. The team must have high standards that are understood by all.
7. The team must receive external support and encouragement.
8. The team must have principled leadership.

To sum up then, goals, roles, procedure, relationships and leadership are the essential pre-requisites to effective team working (McKibbon *et al.*, 2008).

1.2 Identify the challenges experienced by developing teams

New teams coming together need to establish themselves and this in itself can prove to be a challenge. Your ability as a manager and leader of a diverse group of staff to develop positive relationships is very important here and requires the ability to communicate effectively with people at all levels within the organisation.

Tuckman's (1965) theory on how groups develop over time demonstrates the process of forming a team. His mnemonic for common stages of group development is one you may be familiar with but we recap below:

The stages of team development
- Forming
- Storming
- Norming
- Performing
- Mourning or Adjourning.

Forming

At this stage the members of the team are new to each other and the group and, as such, are unsure and wary of each other and the purpose of the team. Individual roles are unclear and there is a heavy reliance on the team leader for direction and support. Your approach at this time is very important. Being too directive may result in team members not forming together as a team and this will slow down the process of team cohesion.

Storming

As team members become more familiar with each other, it is here that challenging the team leader occurs. Personality clashes and differences of opinion also occur at this time and the atmosphere within the group changes and it may start to feel uncomfortable. Problems that occur at this time are likely to be blamed on the team leader who may start to emerge as a scapegoat. It is far easier to blame the manager for all of the problems within the team because you are the one who is perceived to be different from the rest of the team. Your position in the team may lead to the problems of the team being transferred to you, the scapegoat, rather than the team as a whole!

Although storming is uncomfortable it is a most important stage.

Norming

In this stage the team begins to find some mutual direction and consensus. The ideas which have been thrown around during the storming stage start to come together and there is a need to move away from the storming stage to a more harmonious state of affairs.

If the storming stage has been allowed to occur, the team starts to feel positive and intimate.

Performing

At this stage the team members start to apply themselves to the job in hand and simply get on with the work that needs to be done. Because they know each other quite well now, they feel safe to take on different roles and activities.

Mourning/Adjourning

This fifth stage was added later in Tuckman's theory and occurs when a team comes to an end. If you're about to leave your team or if a new member is joining, it is likely that you'll go through a stage of mourning. You may look back and review events from the past and you will look forward to future challenges. At this stage it is natural to experience negative feelings for the team as a way of coping and feeling better about leaving them.

Activity 7.1.1

Using Tuckman's stages of development identify the challenges experienced by your team and reflect on how you dealt with them.

1.3 Identify the challenges experienced by established teams

Once the team is established, the major challenge is to ensure that it continues to work towards the objectives of the setting as set out in your strategic plan. For this to happen everyone in the team needs be working to keep operations running smoothly. For you as the manager, this requires keeping the team together and the communication lines open.

It also requires a good knowledge of the individuals who make up your team and the roles they play. Teamwork is not about getting people together and dictating to them your orders, but rather about developing a commitment to the goals by establishing trust and cohesion.

Effective teamwork requires that all team members relate well to each other and as a manager you need to recognise the similarities as well as the differences in the individuals who make up your team. Your biggest challenge is to respect those differences in personality and to work with these to ensure the team does not clash or become dysfunctional.

Belbin's research (1981) on the various roles needed in an effective team is worthy of note here. The study looked at determining how problems could be predicted and avoided in teams by controlling the dynamics of the group.

The results revealed that the difference between success and failure for a team was not dependent on factors such as intellect, but more on behaviour. The research team began to identify separate clusters of behaviour, each of which formed distinct team contributions or team roles (www.belbin.com).

Belbin's nine team roles shown in Figure 7.2 are discussed here.

Plant

These people tend to be highly creative and good at solving problems in unconventional ways. As lateral thinkers and problem solvers, they often find new ways of tackling a problem and better ways of doing things. If somebody, however, favours this role they may have lots of energy at first but, when boredom sets in, be unable to carry things through. This may well lead to not following standard procedures because of boredom and becoming a rebel.

Figure 7.2 Belbin's team roles
The Management Network, 2003

	Team role	Strengths	Allowable weaknesses
Action oriented roles	Shaper	■ Challenging, dynamic, thrives on pressure ■ The drive and courage to overcome obstacles	■ Prone to provocation ■ Offends people's feelings
	Implementer (company worker)	■ Disciplined, reliable, conservative and efficient ■ Turns ideas into practical actions	■ Somewhat inflexible ■ Slow to respond to new possibilities
	Completer finisher	■ Painstaking, conscientious, anxious ■ Searches out errors and omissions ■ Delivers on time	■ Inclined to worry unduly ■ Reluctant to delegate
People oriented roles	Coordinator (Chairman)	■ Mature, confident, a good chairperson ■ Clarifies goals, promotes decision-making, delegates well	■ Can often be seem as manipulative ■ Off loads personal work
	Team worker	■ Co-operative, mild, perceptive and diplomatic ■ Listens, builds, averts friction	■ Indecisive in crunch situations
	Resource investigator	■ Extrovert, enthusiastic, communicative ■ Explores opportunities ■ Develops contracts	■ Over-optimistic ■ Loses interest once initial enthusiasm has passed
Cerebral roles	Plant	■ Creative imaginative, unorthodox ■ Solves difficult problems	■ Ignores incidentals ■ Too pre-occupied to communicate effectively
	Monitor evaluator	■ Sober, strategic and discerning ■ Sees all options ■ Judges accurately	■ Lacks drive and ability to inspire others
	Specialist	■ Single-minded, self-starting, dedicated ■ Provides knowledge and skills in rare supply	■ Contributes only on a narrow front ■ Dwells on technicalities

The monitor evaluator

These are logical, objective people who weigh up the team's options in a dispassionate way but with a tendency to disregard the emotions in the team. In team meetings this person would bring the team back to the task, enabling the team to focus. They are unlikely to be side-tracked by the emotions involved in the situation.

Coordinators

These are the people who delegate work appropriately and have an ability to draw out team members and focus on the team's objectives. With facilitator and leadership qualities, they have a skill in bringing people together, recognising that every member of the team has got a skill. They acknowledge diversity and make sure that everyone's opinions are heard. They know a lot of people and are good at networking.

Resource investigator

If the team is isolated and inwardly focused, this is a good person to have since they will investigate the world outside in order to obtain knowledge about what is happening locally and nationally.

Implementer

This is the person in the team who carries out strategies as efficiently as possible and takes forward and gathers the ideas that have come from the team. This person gets the task done.

Completer finisher

This is the person in the team who polishes the job to the highest result. They may be the perfectionist in the team. If they become too involved at the beginning of the task, they would be interested in getting to the detail but this may make the task laborious and over long. Getting them involved at the end of the task to go over the detail, eradicating the typing errors, would be a good use of their skills.

Team workers

These are the frontline soldiers who carry out the work. Team workers are given an idea and they turn it into action immediately.

Shaper

These are very task-focused people who cannot abide meetings that go on and on as they just want to get out and do the work. They will challenge a team to keep moving and recognise when an idea has had its day and the team need to try another tack. They have an idea of the bigger picture.

Belbin came up with the final, ninth team role called the **Specialist**. Specialists in their particular fields, for example, are those who focus on their own subject only. They can be seen as more independent and not really part of the team.

Each role has its strengths and weaknesses and by being aware of the roles each of your staff exhibit and assigning them duties that fit that role, effective performance can be assured.

Activity 7.1.2

Identify the roles that Belbin identified in a team meeting at work.

1.4 Explain how challenges to effective team performance can be overcome

The reality of modern health and social services is that the care we get depends as much on how health and social care employees work with each other as on their individual competence within their own field of expertise (Tilmouth *et al.*, 2011).

We learned in the previous two sections about the sorts of challenges we might meet with respect to team work. Newly formed teams need to go through a development process and well established teams have to be motivated to perform in roles to which they comfortably fit. Effective teams are those which comprise groups of people who complement each other in the roles they undertake within the team and who are managed and led in an efficient way.

The challenges to team working are many and varied. Consider the divide between social care staff working alongside medical staff who may be separated by geographical boundaries, working in external settings, communication boundaries and status inequalities. These sorts of boundaries can be a source of conflict and as such may undermine team working. They can be frustrating and make the completion of tasks difficult. In addition, the mismatch of cultures, behaviours and understanding of services in the setting can also be challenging and may affect the work we do (see also Chapter 2).

We may also find that there may be a lack of understanding of each other's roles within the team and lack of clarity regarding management roles and responsibilities which may lead to unrest in the team.

A key factor in developing good team working is the ability of the manager to develop positive relationships with the wide range of staff from different disciplines. This requires the ability to communicate effectively with people at all levels within the organisation. In the next section we look at how leadership and management styles can help to overcome such challenges.

Poor communication is an area which is consistently upheld as a reason for underperformance and can also lead to conflict (see Chapter 3) (Yoder Wise, 2003) so it follows that as a manager and leader of a team, you need to hone these skills and improve any deficit where you can. One aspect of communication is that of negotiation.

Much of the manager's day is spent in negotiating with other people and it can become an almost unconscious thing. We may simply be setting up a meeting or planning care with a member of staff but the way in which this is carried out can mean the difference between an effective outcome or a failed one.

We might consider the following points when addressing any challenge to the team effectiveness.

- Empathy. Have we really considered what it feels like to be in the shoes of the particular team worker with a problem?

- Can we seek clarification to make sure that we fully understand the other person's position and their needs?

- Are we calm or taking things personally?

- Are we prepared to support our case?

- Can we keep to the point and not allow ourselves to be side-tracked?

- Can we offer a compromise?

Successful negotiation is linked to assertiveness and we aim to negotiate successfully in an open and flexible manner in order to achieve a successful outcome.

Activity 7.1.3

Reflect on the challenges you experience within your team and detailed in Activity 7.1.1 and determine how you could have improved your approach to them. Apply the above checklist and say how you used those areas and what you might have improved upon. Write up as a reflective account for your journal.

1.5 Analyse how different management styles may influence outcomes of team performance

Whilst the section heading specifically talks about management styles, the wider unit title includes leadership and for this reason we will cover both here.

Leadership and management are terms often used simultaneously but they are different. Management is concerned with process and developing systems which relate to organisational aims and objectives. It is about communicating those systems across the organisations.

Leadership, on the other hand, is about the behaviour and personal style of the person leading.

Stewart in 1997 stated that:

'Management is essentially about people with responsibility for the work of others and what they actually do operationally, whereas leadership is concerned with the ability to influence others towards a goal.'

At team level management, it is unlikely that you are in a position to change very much in the wider organisation and therefore you may function more as a manager but the way you manage can influence others and in this respect it is worth looking at leadership traits.

Gordon Allport's (1936) trait theory suggests that certain characteristics which people possess make them good leaders. The idea that 'leaders are born rather than made' asserts that by identifying those characteristics in a person, we could identify who might be an effective leader. On the other hand, behavioural theory suggests that leadership can be learned and that people may be taught to display the appropriate behaviours. In this theory the assumption is that 'leaders are made not born' and some theorists argue by learning to behave in a manner which makes you a 'good' leader, that it is possible to become a good leader. More on this later.

Contingency theories put forward the view that situations lend themselves to different styles of leadership and that flexibility on the part of the team leader to adapt in response to those situations is key (McKibbon *et al.*, 2008; Fielder, 1967; Martin *et al.*, 2010). Successful outcomes in this respect depend on the leader adopting a style based on several variables: the job in hand, the qualities of those in the team and the context in which the team is working.

Adair (1983), a most influential writer on leadership and management, identified three key roles for leaders, these being:

1. achieving the task

2. developing team members

3. maintaining the team.

These may sound obvious but how often do we become so task orientated we forget the needs of the team?

Team members need to understand the task and be given the resources to achieve that task if the outcome is to be successful. In this respect, team and individual development is critical to ensure that individuals can perform in the team (Martin *et al.,* 2010).

Activity 7.1.4

Write down what you believe to be the characteristics of a good leader.

You may have answered with some of the following:

- Trust
- Respect
- Honesty
- Ambition
- Confidence
- Good interpersonal skills
- Charisma
- Intelligence.

All these are, of course, correct and there are many more you may have included.

Kouzes and Posner's (2003) Leadership Challenge model identifies the following character traits that are generally associated with good leaders:

- Honest
- Inspiring
- Forward-looking
- Competent
- Intelligent
- Dominance
- Consciousness
- Enthusiastic
- Sense of humour
- Integrity
- Courage
- Visionary.

But, the bottom line is that good leaders and managers are able to generate enthusiasm and commitment in others. They lead by example, with consistent values and break down barriers which stand in the way of achievement. Kouzes and Posner (2003) again:

- A good leader will also inspire a shared vision and enlist the commitment of others.

- A good leader will promote collaborative working which builds trust and empowers others.

- A good leader recognises others' achievements and celebrates accomplishments (Tilmouth *et al.,* 2011).

In addition, the social skills needed in different leadership roles vary, and leaders need to adjust their styles at different times to facilitate the group process (Wheelan, 2005).

At times we may need to be more directive and assertive to address and reduce any anxiety in team members, but this needs to be accomplished in a positive and open way. Supplying the resources needed to get the job done helps the team to accomplish their tasks and feel supported. When the team start to work well and demand to participate more, a good leader will recognise this and step back rather than risk resentment due to the undue influence from the leader. At times the leader's competence is questioned and it is important not to take the attacks personally. Ultimately you want the team to take the leadership role on themselves to become more autonomous and responsible.

Whatever qualities we possess or need to develop, we will use these in various ways and adopt certain styles with respect to how we lead and manage.

Lewin *et al.* (1939) described leadership styles and although somewhat dated they remain relevant to team leadership and management today. He identified three very different leadership styles.

Leadership styles

Autocratic/Authoritarian or 'I want you to ...'

Figure 7.3 Autocratic leader

This style demands the leader/manager to make decisions on their own without consulting the team. There is an expectation on their part that the team will follow the decision exactly, thus enabling the task to be accomplished in the least amount of time. Using this style means that instructions have to be clear and concise. Dissatisfaction sets in when the team members have ideas but are unable to voice these and are not consulted on decisions being made. This can make them feel less involved and their commitment to the task is likely to be lukewarm, to say the least.

This type of leadership is good in situations requiring immediate or emergency action. For example, in emergency departments or in a crisis situation decisions have to be made quickly.

Democratic/Participative or 'Let's work together to solve this'

Figure 7.4 Collaborative leader

When the team has been involved in the decision-making process, with the final decision being 'owned' by the whole team, a democratic process has been followed. The democratic style is the most popular style of leadership and management but it also has its drawbacks. Teams are made up of individuals with vastly different opinions and decision making can therefore be a lengthy process. The leader must be prepared in this case to make the final decision in a collaborative way.

Laissez-faire or 'You two take care of the problem while I go'

The team is allowed to make its own decisions and get on with the tasks. This may work well when people are capable and motivated in making their own decisions. In situations where there is no need for a central coordination, for example, in sharing resources across a range of different people and groups, this might be a useful style to adopt. However, one of the problems of this style is the tendency to go off task with the result that the outcome is never achieved. This will lead to the team becoming impatient with the amount of time it takes to make a decision.

Figure 7.5 Laissez-faire manager

Activity 7.1.5

Describe a situation when these leadership styles are used in a health and social care or a children and young people's setting and analyse how different styles may influence outcomes of team performance.

Part of a manager's role is to encourage others to work effectively and whichever style you adopt, you need to be able to rationalise why you chose that way to work. The outcomes will be affected if you fail to recognise the effect your style of leadership is having on the team. An effective team is committed to working towards the same goals and the team members will cooperate with the decisions made. In well managed teams, results are produced quickly and economically where there is a free exchange of ideas and information (Tilmouth et al., 2011).

1.6 Analyse methods of developing and maintaining

- **trust**

- **accountability**

Consider first the managers you have worked for. Picture them in your mind and then reflect on what it is that you either liked or disliked about them. Was it purely their friendly nature or were you a little in awe of them? Did they inspire you with confidence or were you just a little bit scared of them? Did they show an interest in you as a person or were they more task focused?

One thing is certain, the managers and leaders we work for all have the same goal in mind and that is to 'get the job done' and to get results. What differentiates between a good and poor working relationship between the manager/leader and the workforce is how that is achieved and a lot of it is to do with accountability and trust.

Your role as a team leader and a manager is a most important one, particularly in today's climate which demands the delivery of quality care with fewer staff and resources. You are charged with ensuring that staff morale remains high in a care service which changes constantly. So how do you accomplish this?

The American Management Association collected data on the managerial effectiveness of 622 leaders across hundreds of organisations and highlighted three competencies that spanned all industries. This is reflected in work by Terry (1993) and George (2003) on authentic leadership.

The three competencies are:

1. **Building trust and demonstrating personal accountability**

    This is developed by keeping your promises and honouring commitments to the staff. The leader/manager who accepts responsibility for their actions and communicates honestly is not regarded as weak by the staff but as somebody who can be trusted.

2. **Action orientation**

    This really is a case of keeping the momentum up and maintaining a sense of urgency about a project or a piece of work. Staff want somebody to act decisively when a solution is needed and to suggest a solution in a crisis.

3. **Flexibility and agility**

    Working for somebody who has fixed ideas can be demoralising, so if you are able to adjust to the situation and change your behaviour according to the change in circumstances, you demonstrate that you are open to new ways of doing things.

By being authentic in this way you develop a sense of trust with the staff and they can then be held accountable for their actions.

Good management demands that we hold people accountable for what they do or don't do and the way in which you do this can make or break the relationship.

When goals were not met due to something the employee has failed to do, then it is appropriate for them to be held accountable for this failure. But if we are trying to hold employees accountable for things that are out of their control, then this is unreasonable and you will lose the trust you have with the staff.

The key ingredient is consistency and if you follow through on commitments, then your staff will expect to be called to account if goals are not met or jobs are not done. The way in which you do this is also important and we all recognise that being dealt with in a firm but kind way in private, about a performance error, is much better than being berated in public for a misdemeanour.

It is also important that all staff are dealt with in the same way. There is nothing worse than being a part of an organisation where some members of staff seem to be able to fail in aspects of their role and yet are not held accountable for it. The sense of injustice is great and trust is lost.

As a manager there is a distance between yourself and the staff. You are, after all, carrying out a different role to them. But, the leaders and managers who do not take the time to build relationships with staff and who feel that the human element is unimportant will be unable to gain the trust of their staff and may find it difficult to hold people accountable for their work. It is a wise manager who takes time to find out a little about their staff and to share a little about yourself. I will always remember one manager I had as a staff nurse who always asked how my family was and was always happy to share a few words with me.

Trust builds respect and it is that which gets results. We can cultivate trust by being transparent and honest in what we are thinking and doing. We show ourselves to be trustworthy managers by being consistent and the sort of person who can be relied upon.

Activity 7.1.6

Write a reflective account of the methods you use to ensure that you maintain the trust of your staff. Include a critical incident which demonstrates the way in which you maintain accountability and trust in your work.

1.7 Compare methods of addressing conflict within a team

In Chapter 8 we look at Larson and LaFasto's CONECT model (2001) for resolving conflict and it would be useful for you to look at this later to achieve this outcome.

Conflict within teams is not uncommon but can be unpleasant and lead to disruption in performance. However, when resolved effectively, conflict can lead to personal and professional growth since it can be creative and productive.

There are two types of conflicts: those which revolve around the disagreements in relation to approaches to work and those conflicts which may arise between individual members of the team stemming from differences in personal values and beliefs.

Badly managed conflict leads to ineffective team work and people start to avoid each other and rifts develop. This inevitably leads to ineffectual care of service users, clients and patients.

Larson and LaFasto (2001) suggest an effective way of solving this sort of conflict (see Chapter 8).

Thompson's (2006) RED approach to managing conflict is for situations with a high degree of tension associated with them:

> **R** – **R**ecognise the conflict; do not sweep it under the carpet
>
> **E** – **E**valuate the conflict to see how detrimental it would be if it was allowed to develop
>
> **D** – **D**eal with the conflict; keep open communication

The two destructive extremes, either pretending the conflict does not exist or overreacting to the situation, are according to Thompson best avoided.

In the next section a number of practical ways of managing conflict and promoting a positive team environment are suggested.

Activity 7.1.7

Show how you have dealt with conflict within the workplace and evaluate the impact of your style. Describe how a different way of dealing with the same conflict may have changed the outcome. You might use Larson and LaFasto's CONECT model or Thompson's RED model.

---

2 Be able to support a positive culture within the team for a health and social care or children and young people's setting

2.1 Identify the components of a positive culture within own team

An effective team works towards the same goals and the team members will cooperate with the decisions made. When properly managed and developed, teamwork improves processes and produces results quickly and economically through the free exchange of ideas and information. See the following website for more information:

www.businessballs.com/dtiresources/TQM_development_people_teams.pdf

The organisation which promotes openness and creativity, encouraging the team members to share information, to innovate and take calculated risks, will provide a positive climate in which to work. Wheelan provides a useful list of characteristics of high performing teams. How far does this reflect your own team?

The characteristics of high performance teams

1. Members are clear about and agree with the team's goals.
2. Tasks are appropriate to team versus individual solution.
3. Members are clear about and accept their roles.
4. Role assignments match members' abilities.
5. The leadership style matches the team's development level.
6. An open communication structure allows all members to participate.
7. The team receives, gives and utilises feedback about its effectiveness and productivity.
8. The team spends time defining and discussing problems it must solve or decisions it must make.
9. Members also spend time planning how they will solve problems and make decisions.
10. The team uses effective decision-making strategies.
11. The team implements and evaluates its solutions and decisions.
12. Task-related deviance is tolerated.
13. Team norms encourage high performance, quality, success and innovation.
14. Subgroups are integrated into the team as a whole.
15. The team contains the smallest number of members necessary to accomplish its goals.
16. Team members have sufficient time together to develop a mature working unit and to accomplish the team's goals.
17. The team is highly cohesive and cooperative.
18. Periods of conflict are frequent but brief, and the group has effective conflict management strategies.

(Wheelan, 2005, p.40)

2.2 **Demonstrate how own practice supports a positive culture in the team**

 2.3 **Use systems and processes to support a positive culture in the team**

Activity 7.2.1

Describe a situation which demonstrates how you cultivate openness and innovation within your team.

Keep the notes in your portfolio.

 2.4 **Encourage creative and innovative ways of working within the team**

As we have seen above, effective teams are cohesive; they share goals and vision and operate in an atmosphere of openness and co-operation.

The manager and leader who wants to encourage the team to be innovative and creative needs to adopt a management style that can transform the team further. The Transformational Leadership approach is one in which the leader sets out to create change by empowering the team to try new things.

James MacGregor Burns developed the concept of transformational leadership in 1978. He believed that positive change could be created in teams by fostering a culture of interest in each other and in the interests of the group as a whole. Motivation, morale and performance of the group were enhanced by a leader who was 'energetic, enthusiastic and passionate'. If you have ever been in the presence of somebody who is enthusiastic and passionate about what they do, you will recognise just how powerful an influence this can be.

As Burns suggested, it is through the strength of the leader's vision and personality that such leaders are able to inspire team members to change their expectations and motivations to work towards common goals. Bass developed the theory further and defined transformational leaders as those people who could:

'broaden and elevate the interests of their employees, when they generate awareness and acceptance of the purposes and the mission of the group and when they stir their employees to look beyond their own self-interest for the good of the group.'

(Bass, 1990)

Transformational leadership then goes beyond more traditional methods of leadership. Such leaders have a clear collective vision which they manage to communicate effectively to all the team. As effective role models, they inspire their team members to put the good of the whole organisation above self-interest and are not afraid to use unconventional methods to achieve the collective vision. (Adapted from Epitropaki (2001), accessed 16/8/11.)

Activity 7.2.2

Problems which are unusual or out of the norm require an innovative or creative response. How do you encourage the staff in your setting to adopt creative and innovative ways of working? Give an example.

3 Be able to support a shared vision within the team for a health and social care or children and young people's setting

 3.1 **Identify the factors that influence the vision and strategic direction of the team**

Skills for Care in their Adult Social Care Management Induction Standards (2008) identify seven common principles to support self-care and specifically highlight the need for leaders and managers to have a 'clear vision and be committed to making a positive difference'.

The factors that influence the vision and direction for care work are those imposed by legal and professional groups and changes which come about as the result of research and new development.

The Department of Health provides guidance for health care in this country and shapes the delivery of adult social care services through leadership and policy. In addition, local councils with social services have a responsibility to commission public, private and voluntary sector providers to deliver services that meet the needs of their local population. This whole process shapes the shared vision for the delivery of care services and your work is directly influenced by these things.

In the White Paper *Equity and Excellence: Liberating the NHS* (2010), the emphasis is placed on collaborative working within the public sector.

'The Department will continue to have a vital role in setting adult social care policy. We want a sustainable adult social care system that gives people support and freedom to lead the life they choose, with dignity. We recognise the critical interdependence between the NHS and the adult social care system in securing better outcomes for people, including carers. We will seek to break down barriers between health and social care funding to encourage preventative action.'

(Department of Health, 2010)

The Government White Paper, *Our Health, Our Care, Our Say: A new direction for community services,* sets out a number of key priorities for health and social care. The responses address key statements posed by local communities in relation to the delivery of health and social care services.

Through such initiatives, your organisation's vision needs to reflect adherence to these guidelines and as such, at a team level, you will also be looking to meet the standards set out at a national level.

Health, social care and children and young people's professionals work together at three levels (Department of Health, 1998):

■ Strategic – planning and sharing information

■ Operational management – policies that demonstrate partnership

■ Individual care – joint training and a single point of access to health care.

Effective working in health, social care and Children and Young People (CYP) settings require that we collaborate together in order to achieve the national outcomes and to influence the achievement of a shared vision, both nationally and locally.

3.2 Communicate the vision and strategic direction to team members

3.3 Work with *others* to promote a shared vision within the team

We may not always agree with what we are expected to do in health care and occasionally there are decisions made at national level which impact on local delivery of care. For example, recent cutbacks in budgets in the public sector have left many organisations with fewer resources at their disposal and little option but to reduce the number of staff to save money. These sorts of decisions are less than conducive to good team relationships but as a manager you are likely to be involved in making such changes and you need to be able to ensure the staff are also fully aware of the need for change.

Managing change in this situation is crucial to keeping the team focused on the vision and the strategic direction.

In health care, change happens for various reasons – new research in practice becomes available, new policies and regulations appear, overspending on budgets and occasionally the need to update buildings or premises leads to disruption in the working day. The turnover of staff also constitutes a change to team working and can be a challenge.

Any change is a challenge and can cause anxiety for some, so managers need to be aware of how to minimise this and keep the team focused. Managing change requires a planned and systematic approach to ensure that the team's motivation is maintained.

John P. Kotter's (1995) 'eight steps to successful change' provides a useful starting point. Each stage recognises how individuals respond to and approach change, and Kotter identifies this through how we see, feel and then act towards change.

Kotter's eight-step change model can be summarised as:

1. **Increase urgency** – Inspire people to move, make objectives real and relevant.

2. **Build the guiding team** – Get the right people in place with the right emotional commitment and the right mix of skills and levels.

3. **Get the vision right** – Get the team to establish a simple vision and strategy, focus on emotional and creative aspects necessary to drive service and efficiency.

4. **Communicate for buy-in** – Involve as many people as possible, communicate the essentials simply, and appeal and respond to people's needs. De-clutter communications – make technology work for you rather than against.

5. **Empower action** – Remove obstacles, enable constructive feedback and lots of support from leaders – reward and recognise progress and achievements.

6. **Create short-term wins** – Set aims that are easy to achieve, in bite-size chunks. Have manageable numbers of initiatives. Finish current stages before starting new ones.

7. **Don't let up** – Foster and encourage determination and persistence. On-going change – encourage on-going progress reporting – highlight achieved and future milestones.

8. **Make change stick** – Reinforce the value of successful change via recruitment, promotion, new change leaders. Weave change into culture.

From www.businessballs.com/changemanagement.htm

Kotter's model shows well how managers can motivate people to buy into the change by 'owning' the change and this is the important element of any successful change.

We can reduce the model above down to four major factors:

- The urgency factor
- The vision factor
- The resource factor
- The action factor.

The urgency factor

The pressure to change is on the organisation and you need to get the team behind you to ensure successful outcomes.

The vision factor

A clear shared vision is an imperative and, as managers, it is necessary to ensure that team members are with you and not against you. Motivation is the key here and you need to be aware of what motivates your team.

Activity 7.3.1

Think about the members of your team and what you know about them. What is it that motivates each person (e.g. recognition, pride, money)?

Talk to the staff to find out if you are correct.

You may have identified some of the following motivators for your staff. Some of your staff may take huge **pride** in the work they do, but if this goes unrecognised, motivation will drop. Such members of the team are more likely to perform well and provide new ideas for improving the organisation's own well-being if they do not feel they are being taken for granted.

Being **happy** in work is also a motivating force and if you care about your team's well-being you are likely to have a happy team.

By **treating others as we would wish to be treated ourselves** we are likely to improve relationships between everyone at all levels in the organisation.

Some of our team may thrive on being given **responsibility** as this demonstrates to them that they are trusted. If you are able to delegate responsibility and provide support this can be a useful motivator for some.

Being **valued** and feeling as though you are part of the organisation's success is also a huge motivating force. Think about the last time you said 'thank you' to your team for their individual contributions and for a job well done. Can you risk losing the support of the team when all it requires is a small gesture to say how much you appreciate their work? Our staff and employees are as valuable as the clients who use the service and there is a tendency to forget this.

The fear of the consequences of change can have a damaging effect on the morale of the team. Ensuring that staff feel secure in their roles is a management task to maintain motivation. Honest and open communication is essential and it should be provided on a continuous basis.

Change raises the level of stress and takes us out of our comfort zone. We start to fear not only for our jobs but also for the upset in our routine and the status quo. As a manager, the need to communicate to the team that the change will bring about a new 'comfort zone', once implemented, will be most welcome.

Money as a motivator must also be considered, but is surprisingly way down on the list for most people. Any change that requires low paid staff to do more for little recompense is likely to be viewed negatively and staff will feel under-valued. If more pay cannot be part of the agreed changes, then the other motivators and perhaps other packages can be implemented to improve motivation.

The resource factor

The resources you need to implement change have to be identified before you proceed and you need to ensure these are provided. Without the necessary tools, your team cannot be expected to do the job.

The action factor

When all else is in place, the next part of any change is to act. Having planned for change, and implemented it, you then need to check that it is working and act if it is not.

If the change is working, then maintaining the effectiveness and appropriateness of the change is good practice. By monitoring and analysing data produced you are in a position to evaluate the success or otherwise and to keep the team informed of progress.

3.4 Evaluate how the vision and strategic direction of the team influences team practice

The evaluation phase of any project involves a sequence of stages that includes:

- **forming** objectives, goals and hypotheses of the project;

- **conceptualising** the major components of the project, the participants, the setting, and how you will measure the outcomes;

- **designing** the evaluation and giving **details of** how these components will be coordinated;

- **analysing** the information, in both qualitative and quantitative ways;

- **using** what is learned through the evaluation process.

(Adapted from www.socialresearch
methods.net/kb/pecycle.php)

You might also use a model of reflection in your evaluative process which you and the team are likely to be aware of. Kolb's (1984) cycle of experiential learning can be adapted well here.

Kolb recommends that we need to recall our observation of an event or the change, in this case, reflect on those observations, develop and research some theories about what we saw and then decide on some action as a result of the process (Jasper, 2003).

What happened?
What changes have been implemented?

What would you change?
What is your action plan?

What did you become aware of?
What went well/less well?

What sense do you make of the situation?
What have you learnt?

Figure 7.6 A reflective cycle based on the work of Kolb (1984)
From Tilmouth *et al.*, 2011

4 Be able to develop a plan with team members to meet agreed objectives for a health and social care or children and young people's setting

 **Identify team objectives**

Facilitate team members to actively participate in the planning process

Encourage sharing of skills and knowledge between team members

To enable the achievement of a 'shared vision', the team will need to work to a set of objectives. You are likely to have met the team's aims and objectives before as they are often linked, but they are distinctly different.

Aims are the goals you hope to achieve or, in this case, may be the overall shared vision.

Objectives are the activities you undertake in order to reach that goal.

Figure 7.7 Aim for your goal

Activity 7.3.2

Write a reflective account of a recent change you have been forced to make as a result of funding cuts in the public sector.

How did you manage the change and, on reflection, what might you do differently next time?

Activity 7.4.1

Look at the following example of an overall aim and specific aims and then see if you can identify the objectives to meet those aims.

The overall aim of the project:

- To improve the quality of care for the young people/elderly in our care setting.

Specific aims:

- To increase our clients' quality of life.
- To increase our clients' comfort and well-being.
- To increase our clients' confidence and motivation.
- To empower our clients to engage in their own care to enhance well-being.

Perhaps you had something along these lines:

- To provide information and advice on care packages available.
- To provide an excellent living space and health care for all.
- To offer a variety of activities to enhance well-being and health and fitness.
- To support clients in accessing clubs, jobs, external activities and training.
- To facilitate a support group for clients.
- To enable clients to be represented at staff meetings.
- Encourage open communication between staff and clients to undertake problem solving.

One of the best ways to get staff involved in these sorts of activities is to allow time during the regular team meeting for the team to express their views. So often, our team meetings become a mere information-giving session and this does not provide an adequate venue for the exchange of ideas. If this is the case, then valuable expertise, the skills and knowledge of the staff will not be accessed.

A meeting is an opportunity to communicate with the whole team present and can be a useful vehicle by which to encourage the staff to discuss the overall aims of the team with the shared vision in mind.

Meetings afford the opportunity for the team to get to know each other and to open discussion and make action points. Day (2006) suggests that the success of a meeting can depend on the way it is chaired and this is an important role for the manager to learn.

You will have attended badly managed meetings, where the start and end times are not adhered to, where some people talk a lot and others just sit, and where there is little or no control about what is happening or indeed, what is being accomplished. You may come away wondering what the meeting had actually achieved!

By starting the meeting on time and agreeing to stick to an end time, you will have a more

focused group. It is also important to remind the people attending the meeting of the purpose of the meeting. As the chair leading the meeting, you need to ensure that you encourage participation from the entire group using open questions and occasionally directing your attention to one person in particular. In this way you are giving everybody in the team the chance to express what they know and to demonstrate their skills, which may be useful to achieving the whole team's outcomes. It is very important to come away from the meeting with some action points or objectives, if appropriate. Day (2006, p.91) suggests some ground rules for team members:

- Be prepared for the meeting.
- Attend the meeting on time.
- Start and end the meeting on time.
- Respect and value the diversity of team members.
- Participate in the meeting.
- Actively listen to the discussions.
- Make decisions by consensus.

(From Tilmouth *et al.*, 2011)

4.2 Analyse how the skills, interests, knowledge and expertise within the team can meet agreed objectives

You will now be more familiar with the roles your staff take on in their work and have been encouraged to identify what motivates them through the previous activities in this chapter. You are likely to have also noticed the types of skills that they have. For example, you may know a member of staff who is particularly good at dealing with conflict, whereas others are much more creative and tend to be able to engage with the clients in this way.

The success of the team will depend on bringing together people with diverse skills and knowledge and if they lack these, encouraging them to undertake training and education. For example, the skills of doctors, nurses, occupational therapists and physiotherapists working together in an orthopaedic ward to best meet the needs of the patients on the ward is called a multi-disciplinary team (MDT).

Your team will also work with other members of wider groups of professionals and you may find yourselves liaising with and calling on the services of those who work in social work, community nursing staff, infection control teams, the justice system and education staff.

In the past, groups of staff from the same discipline rarely communicated with other specialists around patient issues and this led to a number of problems in service provision. The push towards multi-disciplinary team working has been encouraged over the last 20 years or so and the Laming Report (2003) highlighted the importance of working closely with people from other professional groups and agencies (see also Chapter 2).

One of the advantages of teamwork is the abundance and quality of ideas. However, some teams can start to think in the same way and the ideas from individuals become subsumed into the team view. For the team to perform successfully, it is essential that they do not become side-tracked with unimportant issues, or take too much time discussing small details or get caught up in team conflict. An effective team supports its individual team members and recognises that the skills and knowledge of each team member, although varied, are of equal value.

4.5 Agree roles and responsibilities with team members

Activity 7.4.2

Agenda an item for the next team meeting in which you discuss the roles and responsibilities of team members for a particular task.

Place a copy of the minutes of the meeting in your portfolio and provide a reflective account to show how you agreed the roles and responsibilities.

It is possible that you may have had to make some uncomfortable decisions and staff members may not have been fully on board with the responsibilities you agreed with them. An assertive approach to dealing with difficult issues will go a long way to ensuring the team remains focused and motivated.

Working towards a win/win outcome shows that you respect the person and the differences they have. In this way they are likely to be more prepared and committed to work towards an outcome which is mutually acceptable.

5 Be able to support individual team members to work towards agreed objectives in a health and social care or children and young people's setting

5.1 Set personal work objectives with team members based on agreed objectives

In Chapter 8 where we look at supervision, we deal in more depth with this particular point and you are advised to read that in conjunction with this outcome. You can also cover the outcome in the activity to follow the next section.

5.2 Work with team members to identify opportunities for development and growth

5.3 Provide advice and support to team members to make the most of identified development opportunities

In any team effort there will be times when training is required if the team members are to be able to perform well. The use of coaching as a strategy to enhance team performance is now a well respected factor in team development.

Parsloe and Wray defined coaching as:

> 'a process that enables learning and development to occur and thus performance to improve. To be successful, a coach requires a knowledge and understanding of process as well as the variety of styles, skills and techniques that are appropriate to the context in which the coaching takes place.'
>
> (Parsloe and Wray, 2000)

Clutterbuck and Megginson (2006) have further identified four main styles that coaches have defined themselves. These are:

- Assessor
- Tutor
- Demonstrator
- Stimulator.

Figure 7.8 The GROW model

On a continuum between directive and non-directive, Assessor and Tutor tend to be more directive whilst Demonstrator and Stimulator tend to be more non-directive. As a manager providing coaching, you need to be able to move between styles and to use a high degree of reflection to recognise when and how to use the styles.

The GROW model developed by Whitmore (2002) and further adapted by Alexander and Renshaw (2005) is a useful framework to adopt.

Activity 7.5.1

Using the GROW model (as expressed in the diagram and in the list to follow), work with a team member to identify opportunities for their own development and growth and set personal work objectives to which they can work.

Topic

- Goal (**G**)
- Current situation (**R** = Reality)
- Options (**O**)
- Obstacles (**W** = Wrap Up).

Hawkins and Shohet (2009) suggest supervision is an important part of taking care of the team members and we cover this subject in more depth in Chapter 8.

Supervision involves education, support, self-development and self-awareness but is sometimes seen in a negative way with a certain amount of suspicion and a lack of trust. There

may be a feeling that supervision is management's way of judging individuals and their performance and the team may feel defensive and uncomfortable.

The main advantage of supervision is that team members are able to continue to learn and move forwards at work and it can help people use their resources better. It needs to be viewed therefore as a positive tool for change in the team.

5.4 Use a solution focused approach to support team members to address identified challenges

The solution-focused approach to management started with a psychotherapy background. Insoo Kim Berg, a young American therapist in the 1960s, was dissatisfied with the traditional way of carrying out therapy and looked to developing a new way of looking at problems. Together with Steve de Shazer in the 1980s, a new way of approaching problems was favoured and they switched to studying 'solution behaviour'.

This has led to further models being put forward and The Four-Step Method of Solution-Focused Management is now a favoured approach in management circles

- Step One – Acknowledge the problem
- Step Two – Describe the success – what do you want to achieve?
- Step Three – Identify and analyse positive exceptions. When did this happen in the past? And what did you do differently that time to achieve that?
- Step Four – Take a small step forward. Try it out!

Step One – Acknowledge the problem

You may ask the following questions to identify the problem. What is the problem and how does it hinder and affect you? What do you want instead of the problem? For example, what is it about the member of staff that causes you to feel they are difficult to manage? By focusing on the problem you have with that team member, you will be able to address the issue in a more constructive manner.

Step Two – Describe the success

What do you want to achieve? What kind of success are you looking for? In asking the following questions you will begin to focus on the solution. How will you know that the success happens? What will be better then? How will you be able to change your own behaviour when the success happens?

If we look back at our example again, the success may be that the difficulty you have had with managing the team member will become a thing of the past and you are more able to move forward in a positive way. You want a constructive member of the team and will notice that this success has happened when the member of staff becomes more helpful in moving a project forward.

Step Three – Identify and analyse positive exceptions

In this section you recognise that the member of your team has not always been difficult and start to seek out times in the past when they have been helpful and constructive. The sort of questions you need to ask here are: When did this happen in the past? And what was it that you did differently that time to achieve that? What was different and what caused this success to happen? Which aspects of the positive exceptions could you use again? It might be that you recall a time when the team member was particularly positive and if you think about what you did to contribute to that, you may be able to reconstruct this behaviour again. For example, perhaps you said something that moved the team member to behave differently. You may have been firm about what you expected of them or perhaps you gave a word of encouragement or thanks. Whatever you did, repeating it could change the behaviour for the better.

Step Four – Take a small step forward. Try it out!

(Adapted from © 2004 Coert Visser and Gwenda Schlundt Bodien http://articlescoertvisser.blogspot.com/2007/11/4-step-method-of-solution-focused.html)

Activity 7.5.2

Using the above four points identify a solution focused approach to support a team member to address a challenge.

6 Be able to manage team performance in a health and social care or children and young people's setting

6.1 Monitor and evaluate progress towards agreed objectives

In section 3.4 we looked at ways in which the vision and strategic direction of the team influence team practice and you are advised to revisit this now. There is little difference in the way you will monitor and evaluate progress and you may decide to use a reflective model to do this as suggested previously.

Activity 7.6.1

Using the evidence gained from documents such as patient satisfaction surveys, staff supervision records, complaints and compliments and any other records you collect, provide a report to evaluate the team's progress towards meeting the organisation's strategic goals and objectives.

6.2 Provide feedback on performance to:

■ the individual

■ the team

6.3 Provide recognition when individual and team objectives have been achieved

We all need to know how we are progressing in anything we do and feedback, whether positive or negative, is a necessary part of managing people well. Providing feedback means we acknowledge what the team members are doing and this in itself can be a huge motivator. It also helps the team to stay focused and on track.

The following is a useful model to adopt for both individuals and teams. See Figure 7.9.

> ### BOOST feedback
> - **Balanced:** focus not only on areas for development, but also on strengths
> - **Observed:** provide feedback based only upon behaviours that you have observed
> - **Objective:** avoid judgements and relate your feedback to the observed behaviours, not personally
> - **Specific:** back up your comments with specific examples of observed behaviour
> - **Timely:** give feedback soon after the activity to allow learner the opportunity to reflect on the learning

Figure 7.9 BOOST feedback
From Tilmouth et al., 2011

Good practice demands we feed back to staff our views on how they are progressing and performing.

A good starting point is to ask the member of staff to evaluate their own performance and, in so doing, you will be able to gain an understanding of how they perceive their level of performance. You may find they are critical of themselves but this will give you the chance to praise them and give them some good news about their performance. However if there is an issue with the performance of the staff member, they may actually find it difficult to express this themselves and this might cause issues. In the next section we look at how we might approach the more challenging issues associated with poor performance.

Activity 7.6.2

Using the report compiled for Activity 7.6.1, give feedback to the staff via the team meeting and in individual sessions. Demonstrate the techniques you have used to provide the staff with positive feedback and recognition of a job well done.

6.4 Explain how team members are managed when performance does not meet requirements

Occasionally it is necessary to give negative feedback to staff in order to address issues with unsatisfactory performance. This inevitably causes conflict and can be quite uncomfortable.

Individuals receive criticism in different ways and you need to ensure that you are sensitive to how they will be feeling at this time. In Chapter 8 we look at the feedback sandwich and you are directed to this now.

A good approach is to provide a positive point initially and to say clearly what was good about it. You can stress how well they did and what you liked about their performance. The feedback about the performance that is not being well done can then be given with a developmental slant to it. Again, you must specifically highlight what you expect the team member to do and give a clear indication of how they might achieve this. You then constructively give advice on how they can change. Finally, by ending with a positive point you can do much to rebuild self-esteem in what can often be a rather uncomfortable situation.

The following points might help:

- Do not make it a personal issue. Keep a clear picture of the person and yourself separate from the issue. It is the behaviour not the person you have issues with.

- Do not blame and accuse, just point out what changes you feel need to be made.

- Be clear and specific about your perception of the issue to be addressed and your desired outcome.

- Look and listen to each other.

(If this becomes a conflict issue then often we start to avoid looking directly at each other and stop listening to each other. We need to look and listen to each other so that we can respond appropriately.)

- Ensure that you understand each other and if you are unclear or confused about the issue, ask open questions and paraphrase back what you think you hear.

- Choose your place and time carefully when you need to give negative feedback. Make sure both parties feel comfortable and set a time limit.

- Following the feedback acknowledge and show appreciation of one another.

Activity 7.6.3

Being mindful of confidentiality and anonymising your records, provide evidence of a meeting with a member of your staff who is underperforming. Describe how you prepared for the meeting before you met the member of staff and how you approached the subject. Evaluate your own performance by writing a reflective account of what you did, why you did it in that way and the outcome of the whole meeting.

Summary

In this chapter we have addressed how effective team performance requires the development of a positive and supportive culture in an organisation and only in this way can we expect staff to be supportive of a shared vision to meet the agreed objectives for a health and social care or children and young people's setting.

How teams function and the roles that members adopt in teams have been examined, together with a variety of models of leadership relevant to the health and care sector. The strategies for effective team working and leadership have been reviewed through the activities you have been requested to undertake for your portfolio.

Team working means taking responsibility for your own work, as well as respecting the contributions of all your colleagues, and good communication is essential to effective team working.

Learning outcomes	Assessment criteria
1 Understand the features of effective team performance within a health and social care or children and young people's setting	(1.1) **Explain the features of effective team performance** **See p.111 for guidance.**
	(1.2) **Identify the challenges experienced by developing teams** **Activity 7.1.1, p.113**
	(1.3) **Identify the challenges experienced by established teams** **Activity 7.1.2, p.115**
	(1.4) **Explain how challenges to effective team performance can be overcome** **Activity 7.1.3, p.116**
	(1.5) **Analyse how different management styles may influence outcomes of team performance** **Activity 7.1.4, p.117** **Activity 7.1.5, p.118**
	(1.6) **Analyse methods of developing and maintaining:** ■ trust ■ accountability **Activity 7.1.6, p.119**
	(1.7) **Compare methods of addressing conflict within a team** **Activity 7.1.7, p.120**

2 Be able to support a positive culture within the team for a health and social care or children and young people's setting	**(2.1)** Identify the components of a positive culture within own team **Activity 7.2.1, p.121**
	(2.2) Demonstrate how own practice supports a positive culture in the team **Activity 7.2.1, p.121**
	(2.3) Use systems and processes to support a positive culture in the team **Activity 7.2.1, p.121**
	(2.4) Encourage creative and innovative ways of working within the team **Activity 7.2.2, p.121**
3 Be able to support a shared vision within the team for a health and social care or children and young people's setting	**(3.1)** Identify the factors that influence the vision and strategic direction of the team **See p.121 for guidance.**
	(3.2) Communicate the vision and strategic direction to team members **Activity 7.3.1, p.123**
	(3.3) Work with others to promote a shared vision within the team **Activity 7.3.1, p.123**
	(3.4) Evaluate how the vision and strategic direction of the team influences team practice **Activity 7.3.2, p.124**

Learning outcomes	Assessment criteria
4 Be able to develop a plan with team members to meet agreed objectives for a health and social care or children and young people's setting	**4.1** Identify team objectives **Activity 7.4.1, p.124** **4.2** Analyse how the skills, interests, knowledge and expertise within the team can meet agreed objectives **See p.125 for guidance.** **4.3** Facilitate team members to actively participate in the planning process **Activity 7.4.1, p.124** **4.4** Encourage sharing of skills and knowledge between team members **Activity 7.4.1, p.124** **4.5** Agree roles and responsibilities with team members **Activity 7.4.2, p.126**
5 Be able to support individual team members to work towards agreed objectives in a health and social care or children and young people's setting	**5.1** Set personal work objectives with team members based on agreed objectives in a health and social care or children and young people's setting **See p.126 for guidance.** **5.2** Work with team members to identify opportunities for development and growth **Activity 7.5.1, p.127** **5.3** Provide advice and support to team members to make the most of identified development opportunities **Activity 7.5.1, p.127** **5.4** Use a solution focused approach to support team members to address identified challenges **Activity 7.5.2, p.128**

6 Be able to manage team performance in a health and social care or children and young people's setting

 Monitor and evaluate progress towards agreed objectives
Activity 7.6.1, p.128

 Provide feedback on performance to:
- the individual
- the team

Activity 7.6.2, p.129

 Provide recognition when individual and team objectives have been achieved
Activity 7.6.2, p.129

 Explain how team members are managed when performance does not meet requirements
Activity 7.6.3, p.129

References

Adair, J. (1983) *Effective Leadership*. New York: Pan Books.

Alexander, G. and Renshaw, B. (2005) *Supercoaching*. London: Random House Business Books.

Allport, G. W. and Odbert, H. S. (1936) 'Trait-names: A psycho-lexical study', *Psychological Monographs,* 47(211).

Bass, B. M. (1990) 'From transactional to transformational leadership: Learning to share the vision', *Organizational Dynamics.* Winter, pp.19–31.

Belbin, M. (1981) *Management Teams: Why they succeed or fail.* London: Heinemann.

Burns, J. M. (1978) *Leadership.* New York: Harper & Row.

Clutterbuck, D. and Megginson, D. (2006) *Making Coaching Work.* London: CIPD.

Coert Visser and Gwenda Schlundt Bodien (2004), http://articlescoertvisser.blogspot.com/2007/11/4-step-method-of-solution-focused.html

Day, J. (2006) *Interprofessional Working.* Cheltenham: Nelson Thornes.

DOH (1998) *Our Health, Our Care, Our Say: a New Direction for Community Services.* London: HMSO.

DOH (2010) *Equity and Excellence: Liberating the NHS.* London: HMSO.

Epitropaki, O. (2001) *What is Transformational Leadership.* Sheffield: Institute of Work Psychology, University of Sheffield. http://esrccoi.group.shef.ac.uk/pdf/whatis/transformational.pdf

Fiedler, F. E. (1967) *A Theory of Leadership Effectiveness.* New York: McGraw-Hill.

George, B. (2003) *Authentic Leadership: Rediscovering the secrets to creating lasting value.* San Francisco: Jossey Bass.

Hawkins, P. and Shohet, R. (2009) *Supervision in the Helping Professions* (3e). Berkshire: Open University Press.

Jasper, M. (2003) *Beginning Reflective Practice.* Cheltenham: Nelson Thornes.

Kotter, J.P. (1995) 'Leading Change: Why Transformation Efforts Fail', *Harvard Business Review OnPoint* (March–April), 1–10.

Kouzes, J. M. and Posner, B. Z. (2003) *The Leadership Challenge* (3e). San Francisco: Jossey-Bass.

Larson, C. E. and LaFasto, F. M. J. (1989) *Teamwork: What Must Go Right/What Can Go Wrong.* London: Sage Publications.

Larson, C.E. and LaFasto, F.M.J. (2001) *When Teams Work Best: 6,000 team members and leaders tell what it takes to succeed.* London: Sage.

Lewin, K., Lippit, R. and White, R. K. (1939). 'Patterns of aggressive behavior in experimentally created social climates'. *Journal of Social Psychology,* 10, pp.271–301.

McKibbon J., Walter, A. with Mason, L. (2008) *Leadership and Management in Health and Social Care for NVQ/SVQ Level 4*. London: Heinemann.

Martin, V., Charlesworth, J. and Henderson, E. (2010) *Managing in Health and Social Care* (2e). London: Routledge.

Parsloe, E. and Wray, M. (2000) *Coaching and Mentoring: Practical methods to improve learning*. London: Kegan Paul.

Pearson, P. and Spencer, J. (1997) *Promoting Teamwork in Primary Care: A research-based approach*. London: Arnold.

Skills for Care (2008) *Adult Social Care Management Induction Standards*.

Stewart, R. (1997) *The Reality of Management* (3e). Oxford: Butterworth-Heinemann.

Terry, R. W. (1993) *Authentic Leadership: Courage in Action*. New York: John Wiley.

Tilmouth, T., Davies-Ward, E. and Williams, B. (2011) *Foundation Degree in Health and Social Care*. London: Hodder Education.

Thompson, N. (2006) *People Problems:* Basingstoke: Palgrave Macmillan.

Tuckman, B. (1965) 'Developmental sequence in small groups', *Psychological Bulletin*, 63(6), pp.384–99.

Wheelan, S. A. (2005) *Creating Effective Teams: A guide for members and leaders* (2e). London: Sage.

Whitmore, J. (2002) *Coaching For Performance: GROWing People, Performance and Purpose* (3e), London: Nicholas Brealey Publishing

Yoder-Wise, P. S. (2003) *Leading and Managing in Nursing* (3e). St Louis, Missouri: Mosby.

www.businessballs.com/changemanagement. htm

www.businessballs.com/dtiresources/TQM_ development_people_teams.pdf

Insoo Kim Berg and Steve de Shazer at www. solutionmind.com/approach/solution_focused_ origins.html

8 Unit LM2c Develop professional supervision practice in health and social care or children and young people's work settings

Supervision has been introduced into practice to provide professional support and learning for staff, to enable them to develop knowledge, skills and competence in their work. This enhances the experience of the service user/patient/ client and in turn improves quality and safety in the care setting.

In this chapter we will cover the purpose and processes of professional supervision together with performance management and dealing with conflict.

Throughout the chapter you are advised to undertake the activities in order to provide evidence of your completion of the outcomes below.

Learning outcomes

By the end of this chapter you will:

1. Understand the purpose of professional supervision in health and social care or children and young people's work settings.

2. Understand how the principles of professional supervision can be used to inform performance management in health and social care or children and young people's work settings.

3. Be able to undertake the preparation for professional supervision with supervisees in health and social care or children and young people's work settings.

4. Be able to provide professional supervision in health and social care or children and young people's work settings.

5. Be able to manage conflict situations during professional supervision in health and social care or children and young people's work settings.

6. Be able to evaluate own practice when conducting professional supervision in health and social care or children and young people's work settings.

1 Understand the purpose of professional supervision in health and social care or children and young people's work settings

1.1 Analyse the principles, scope and purpose of professional supervision

Supervision is a process whereby a manager or supervisor oversees, supports and develops the knowledge and skills of a supervisee. It is the way in which a manager can enable a worker to carry out their role in an effective way.

Carroll (2007), in his article *One More Time: What is Supervision?*, provides us with a fantastic potted history about the development of what we now know is supervision, from its inception during Freud's time to now. His definition:

'At its simplest, supervision is a forum where supervisees review and reflect on their work in order to do it better. Practitioners bring their actual work practice to another person (individual supervision), or to a group (small group or team supervision), and with their help review what happened in their practice in order to learn from that experience. Ultimately, supervision is for better quality service.'

(Carroll, 2007)

A further definition put forward by the United Kingdom Central Council (UKCC) in 1996 is also worthy of note:

'Supervision aims to identify solutions to problems, improve practice and increase understanding of professional issues.'

(UKCC, 1996)

A different type of supervision is that which exists with the counsellor and their supervisor. The British Association of Counselling states that the:

'primary purpose of supervision is to protect the best interests of the client.'

So, in this instance, it is the client who features at the heart of the process.

The definitions should be nothing new to you and as a care worker and manager, you will have your own ideas as to what you see supervision as. It is as well though to focus on the purpose of the activity, as well as the main principles.

The scope and purpose of supervision

All social care workers and managers in care settings are required to undergo supervision and meet particular standards and requirements. In another part of this chapter we look in more detail at the legal aspects of this practice. The General Social Care Council states clearly that:

'As a social care worker, you must be accountable for the quality of your work and take responsibility for maintaining and improving your knowledge and skills.'

Equally, you are expected to:

'Meet relevant standards of practice and work in a lawful, safe and effective way.

'Seek assistance from your employer or the appropriate authority if you do not feel able or adequately prepared to carry out any aspect of your work or you are not sure how to proceed in a work matter.'

In order to do this, there should be policies and procedures to enable such working to take place, as well as a vehicle for you to discuss your practice and to support you in changing any deficiencies in practice.

The whole purpose of this clear directive is to improve the quality of the work we do in order to achieve agreed objectives and outcomes. Our intention through supervision is to ensure that all people who use services in social care and children's settings have the capacity to lead independent and fulfilling lives. It also ensures that staff themselves feel supported in their work and have recourse to a system of help should they require it.

The British Association of Social Workers and the College of Social Work (BASW/CoSW) England Code of Good Practice for Supervision in Social Work highlights the purpose as being:

'to support social workers to provide good quality services. Social work is a complex and demanding profession. Effective supervision of social workers enables social workers to maximise their effectiveness.'

The NHS Management Executive (1993) further defines the scope of supervision as:

'...a formal process of professional support and learning which enables individual practitioners to develop knowledge and competence, assume responsibility for their own practice and enhance consumer protection and safety of care in complex situations.'

Clinical supervision therefore allows the registered nurse access to professional supervision by a skilled supervisor.

The NHS Management Executive goes on to show that:

'Clinical supervision enables registered nurses to:

■ identify solutions to problems

■ increase understanding of professional issues

■ improve standards of patient care

■ further develop their skills and knowledge

■ enhance their understanding of their own practice.'

People involved and principles of supervision

Whilst there are a number of models for supervision including one-to-one supervision, group supervision, and peer group supervision, the approach used will depend on a number of factors, including personal choice, access to supervision, length of experience, qualifications and availability of supervisory groups.

The supervisor, and it is likely to be you in your own area, is usually a skilled professional who assists staff to develop their own skills and helps them to attain knowledge and professional values. You are also required to give advice in supervisory situations and to counsel staff on practice guidelines and policy.

The person being supervised or the supervisee is a practitioner who receives professional advice, support and guidance from a supervisor. In the case of an experienced person, the supervisor may impart support and guidance on reflective practice. We occasionally manage people who have more experience than ourselves and in this case we may be used more as a source of support in their practice.

The Royal College of Nursing (RCN) provides seven general principles for the supervisor and these are helpful to know when carrying out this role.

1. People must always understand clearly what is expected of them.

2. People must have guidance in their work (information, techniques enabling better work, coaching, and personality improvement suggestions).

3. Good work always should be recognised.

4. Poor work deserves constructive criticism.

5. People should have opportunities to show that they can accept greater responsibility.

6. People should be encouraged to improve themselves.

7. People should work in a safe and healthful environment.

(www.rcn.org.uk/development/learning/
transcultural_health/clinicalsupervision)

Activity 8.1.1

What policies and procedures for supervision are available in your own setting? Evaluate the effectiveness of your practice.

1.2 Outline theories and models of professional supervision

Professional supervision has in the past been likened to the apprentice system or the 'student learning at the feet of a master'.

Figure 8.1 Learning at the feet of a master

As a supervisor you are certainly engaged with observing and assisting staff in delivering good quality care and then giving feedback. However, as we mentioned earlier, you may have less experience in terms of the number of years in practice than the member of staff and, in this situation, it is evident that additional training is required in supervision practice.

There is also the implication that a hierarchy exists if we subscribe to this sort of framework and therefore a power relationship is built up. We cover this later in the chapter.

Clinical and professional supervision is now recognised as a complex exchange between supervisor and supervisee, with supervisory models/theories developed to provide a frame for it.

Supervision is an ethical requirement of professions where one-to-one contact with clients is an on-going process and the models which have been developed lend themselves more to this type of process.

As a process for learning, three models are apparent. These are:

- developmental models
- integrative models
- orientation-specific models.

(www.mentalhealthacademy.com.au)

Developmental models

Developmental models of supervision simply define progressive stages of supervisee development from novice to expert (Bernard and Goodyear, 1998).

This sort of supervision has been a dominant model for a number of years and focuses on stages within the process (Hogan, 1964; Holloway, 1987).

Supervisees at the beginning or novice stage have limited skills and are presumed to have a lack of confidence. At this stage the supervisee is likely to be highly dependent upon the supervisor and may feel quite insecure.

At the middle stage supervisees have built on their skills and confidence and there may be a tendency to question more and to move between feeling dependent and at the same time fairly autonomous. In contrast, the supervisee, who is at the expert end of the developmental spectrum, is likely to demonstrate good problem-solving skills and reflection. The supervisee is more confident and begins to integrate theory into their practice and is able to reflect on why they are practising in the way they are.

These models require the supervisor to have an accurate picture of the current stage of the person being supervised and the job they are doing. They then need to facilitate progression to the next stage and in this model the term 'scaffolding' has been used to describe this (Stoltenberg and Delworth, 1987; Zimmerman and Schunk, 2003).

Figure 8.2 Scaffolding

'Scaffolding' means the supervisee uses knowledge and skills they already have to produce new learning. As they gain skills at this stage they are encouraged to incorporate these skills and some from the next stage and, in doing so, build up a more advanced repertoire. This continual growth is a two-way process in that the supervisor–supervisee relationship changes as they both progress in their learning. For Stoltenberg and Delworth (1987) their developmental model has three levels for supervisees – beginning, intermediate and advanced – and the focus in each level is on the development of self-awareness, motivation and autonomy.

In this particular model, the supervisee starts working in a dependent manner imitating the supervisor in their role. As they gain in confidence they become more self-assured and so move to the intermediate level where the dependence on the supervisor is restricted to a certain extent on more difficult clients and cases. Stoltenberg and Delworth report conflict happening in this stage as the supervisee's self-concept is threatened when they start to question the actions of the supervisor. Independence occurs at the advanced level and supervisees start to be accountable for the decisions they make.

The three processes (awareness, motivation, autonomy) involved in this model are further enhanced by eight growth areas. The eight areas are: intervention, treatment goals and plans skills competence, interpersonal

assessment, assessment techniques, client conceptualisation, individual differences, theoretical orientation and professional ethics.

Stoltenberg and Delworth (1987) believed that if supervisees could start to identify their own strengths and growth areas, they would become accountable for their own life-long learning development as therapists and supervisors.

Integrative models

These types of models utilise a number of theories and models and tend to integrate several types of approach. Many of these models refer to the supervision that exists for counsellors and the requirement they have to seek supervision in order to maintain their practice. We will look later at the more clinical models in use.

Some examples of integrative models are those developed by Stoltenberg and Delworth (1987), who suggested a three-stage integrated developmental model, Bernard (1979) with the discrimination model, Holloway (1987) and the systems approach to supervision, and Ward and House's (1998) reflective learning model. We will look at two of these models.

Bernard's discrimination model was published in 1979 and later developed in 1998. It identified three parts of supervision, namely intervention, conceptualisation and personalisation, and three possible supervisor roles, that of teacher, counsellor and consultant (Bernard and Goodyear, 1998). It focuses on the relationship a counsellor would have with their supervisor and promotes effective skill building through the three areas shown above.

Within the roles taken on by the supervisor, the 'teaching' role occurs when the supervisor lectures or instructs the supervisee. Counselling happens when they assist supervisees in noticing how they may be responding to a client's issues and need to be more objective in their approach. They may have been caught up in a problem of their client's which they feel empathy for but cannot move on from. The consultant role occurs when co-therapy is required and the supervisee works with the supervisor and client.

In addition to the three roles taken on by the supervisor, there are within these three different types of supervision:

- Intervention, the supervisee's intervention skills are the main focus.

- Conceptualisation, or how the supervisee understands what is going in the session.

- Personalisation, or how the supervisee deals with the potential issues of counter-transference responses and how they deal with their own personal issues.

In Holloway's systems approach model, the emphasis is on the relationship between the supervisor and supervisee. Holloway describes seven aspects of supervision, all connected by the supervisory relationship which takes centre stage. These aspects are the functions of supervision, the tasks of supervision, the client, the trainee, the supervisor and the institution (Holloway, from Smith, 2009).

Orientation specific models

In these types of models of supervision, there is a firm belief that the supervisor and supervisee should share the same theoretical orientation in order to optimise the relationship. For example, if the supervisor favours a particular approach to psychoanalysis/therapy such as behavioural or client-centred therapy, for effective supervision to occur, the supervisee should understand the concepts of the theory. In this way orientation specific models of supervision often mimic the therapy itself with the terminology, focus and techniques from the counselling session becoming part of the supervision as well.

As we mentioned previously, you will note how all of the above models lend themselves to the counsellor or psychotherapist role and as such may not be appropriate for you in your setting.

Mark Smith (1996, 2005) gives an account of Alfred Kadushin's discussion of supervision in social work. Using the work of John Dawson (1926), Kadushin restates the functions of supervision as being:

- **Administrative** – the promotion and maintenance of good standards of work, co-ordination of practice with policies of administration, the assurance of an efficient and smooth-running office. In this role the primary concern is to ensure adherence to policy and procedure and is therefore one of control and authority.

- **Educational** – the educational development of each individual worker on the staff in a manner calculated to encourage them fully to realise their possibilities of usefulness. The primary goal in this role is to improve the skill of the worker and to encourage reflection.

- **Supportive** – the maintenance of harmonious working relationships, the cultivation of *esprit de corps*. (This is Kadushin's (1992) rendering of Dawson (1926, p.293) cited by Smith (1996, 2005).) Within this role the supervisor must attempt to improve morale and job satisfaction. With staff facing job-related stress, there is a need to help them and enable them to face the potential problem of 'burnout'.

Similarly, the Open University (1998) and Proctor (undated) outlined three components of clinical supervision, namely:

- **Formative educative function** which refers to the part of supervision which encourages the professional development of the practitioner through reflection on practice and self-awareness.

- **Restorative supportive function** which is the supportive relationship between the supervisor and the supervisee, dealing with the emotional stress arising from practice.

- **Normative managerial function** – this aspect deals with the responsibility of the employer or manager to put in place the means for developing competence and supporting employees in the interest of clinical governance and risk management.

These types of model may fit much better in an organisation where the manager's supervisory role is determined by performance standards and quality. But which model can we use? Interestingly, the Nursing and Midwifery Council (NMC), whilst supporting the principle of clinical supervision, does not:

'advocate any particular model of clinical supervision and we do not provide detailed guidance about its nature and scope. Instead, the NMC has defined a set of principles, which we believe should underpin any system of clinical supervision that is used.'

So rather than specifying a framework for our use, they would ask us to look to the principles of supervision and use those to guide our practice. These principles are set out in the box below.

- Clinical supervision supports practice, enabling registered nurses to maintain and improve standards of care.

- Clinical supervision is a practice-focused professional relationship, involving a practitioner reflecting on practice guided by a skilled supervisor.

- Registered nurses and managers should develop the process of clinical supervision according to local circumstances. Ground rules should be agreed so that the supervisor and the registered nurse approach clinical supervision openly, confidently and are aware of what is involved.

- Every registered nurse should have access to clinical supervision and each supervisor should supervise a realistic number of practitioners.

- Preparation for supervisors should be flexible and sensitive to local circumstances. The principles and relevance of clinical supervision should be included in pre-registration and post-registration education programmes.

■ Evaluation of clinical supervision is needed to assess how it influences care and practice standards. Evaluation systems should be determined locally.

■ The NMC supports the establishment of clinical supervision as an important part of clinical governance and in the interests of maintaining and improving standards of care.

Activity 8.1.2

Which model of supervision do you use in your own practice? Highlight how you undertake the process and determine where it fits with the models shown. Write a reflective piece to show your understanding of the models and frameworks.

1.3 Explain how the requirements of legislation, codes of practice and *agreed ways of working* influence professional supervision

From a legal point of view, supervision is a requirement for all staff. The Skills for Care Council in its document *Providing Effective Supervision* (2007) states that:

'High quality supervision is one of the most important drivers in ensuring positive outcomes for people who use social care and children's services. It also has a crucial role to play in the development, retention and motivation of the workforce.'

Not only is it good practice to supply supervision, the *National Minimum Standards for Care Homes for Older People and for Adults* also make this a requirement.

Standard 36 states the following:

'36.1 The registered person ensures that the employment policies and procedures adopted by the home and its induction, training and supervision arrangements are put into practice.

36.2 Care staff receive formal supervision at least six times a year.

36.3 Supervision covers:

■ all aspects of practice

■ philosophy of care in the home

■ career development needs.

36.4 All other staff are supervised as part of the normal management process on a continuous basis.

36.5 Volunteers receive training, supervision and support appropriate to their role and do not replace paid staff.'

Whilst the standards outline the minimum requirements, it goes without saying that you may well need to see and supervise staff on other occasions. Effective management demands that you support your staff to develop areas of practice in which they are deficient or not coping well.

However, recently the way we work with supervision has been under scrutiny and the Social Care Institute for Excellence (SCIE) offers the following insight from their online document to be found at www.scie.org.uk/publications/guides/guide01/supervision/supervision.asp

'"Supervision" has fallen into disrepute in recent years, for a number of reasons:

It has acquired a bad reputation as a semi-private activity, focused on the individual supervisee's needs and not on the outcomes for the service user.

Conversely, supervision has become procedurally driven, checking compliance rather than positively challenging accepted custom and practice. The relationship between practitioner and supervisor is therefore likely to be a prescriptive one, as managers oversee compliance with procedural and fiscal requirements.'

(SCIE)

As a manager you are responsible for the effectiveness of the work the team undertakes and for the quality of that work. This is likely then to affect the way in which supervision is carried out and by focusing more on the outcomes for the organisation and not, for example, on the supervisee and their development, supervision becomes a tick-box exercise at best, checking compliance with policy and procedure. At worst it may not be done at all and be left out of your role!

In support of supervision as a vital management tool for improving the practice in a team and questioning practice and custom, the Harkness Report (Harkness and Hensley, 1991) examined the relationship between social work supervision and its effect on client outcomes and concluded that client satisfaction was affected positively when practitioners had access to supervision which allowed them to improve communication and problem-solving skills.

In addition, the Skills for Care and the Children's Workforce Development Council (CWDC) have promoted the widespread provision of high quality supervision across adult and children's social care, by providing a supervision tool. This tool links to the Skills for Care and Children's Workforce Development

Council's social care leadership and management strategy suite of products and provides links to other frameworks, including the Championing Children Framework (2006).

As the document suggests:

> 'Professional supervision can make a major contribution to the way organisations ensure the achievement of high quality provision and consistent outcomes for people who use services (adults, children, young people, families, carers). High quality supervision is also vital in the support and motivation of workers undertaking demanding jobs and should therefore be a key component of retention strategies. Supervision should contribute to meeting performance standards and the expectations of people who use services, and of carers and families, in a changing environment.'

The above quote therefore addresses not only the need to meet standards and quality provision through supervision, but also how this practice can motivate and retain the staff in the setting.

The codes of practice, legal requirements and the way in which we address the quality of the care in our settings is influenced, undoubtedly, by the supervision we can give our staff.

As the Skills for Care and CWDC document (2006) points out:

> 'For supervision to be effective it needs to combine a performance management approach with a dynamic, empowering and enabling supervisory relationship. Supervision should improve the quality of practice, support the development of integrated working and ensure continuing professional development.'

We will look further at performance management in section 2 of this chapter.

Activity 8.1.3

Read the Skills for Care Council's document *Providing Effective Supervision* (2007) or the Children's Workforce Development Council's guidance on supervision and determine how the guidance has been worked into the practice in your own area.

Ask yourself the following questions:

Does our code of practice reflect current thinking about supervision?

Do we need to change our policy on supervision to bring it up to date?

The next section will help you to see why it is necessary to keep up to date with research.

1.4 Explain how findings from research, critical reviews and inquiries can be used within professional supervision

As practitioners we are duty-bound to perform care in a safe way and in a way in which we are able to question the practice. Alternately, we may be asked to account for why we undertake a particular practice and therefore the skills and knowledge for doing so need to be up to date. To 'do no harm' then is the essential premise of evidence-based practice and the need to be able to demonstrate that the care we provide is safe and effective is a reasonable expectation. It is no different in our practice with respect to supervision.

As an effective practitioner accountable for your own safe practice, you need to have access to and be up to date with the research related to your own area and be able to critically appraise such work. As a manager of staff in your setting, you are no less accountable when it comes to ensuring that the staff have embraced the notion of evidence-based practice.

Evidence-based practice is about incorporating evidence, making professional judgements and applying our knowledge to formulate care decisions and, in supervision, staff need to be informed of how they can achieve this.

Activity 8.1.4

How might you help a member of staff during supervision to undertake a piece of work for a course?

In the activity above you might have encouraged the member of staff to access evidence-based practice journals, either online or through the NHS website, for example. Also, the Cochrane Library, an international body, is dedicated to gathering and disseminating published research and the National Electronic Library for Health can also be a useful resource. Bandolier is a free full text journal library available online and is useful for accessing information from systematic reviews, trials and observational studies. The NHS also has an online library where you can obtain Clinical Knowledge summaries.

The reforms we have seen in the NHS over the last 30 or so years have changed the performance of the health service enormously. The need to conduct research which provides evidence for our practice became a major agenda item for all health authorities and professionals and led to the development of the research and development or R & D initiative.

Figure 8.3 Resources for study

In making a decision about how and what care is to be given, it is important to have an accurate picture of the research available and to construct sufficient evidence from it to support our actions. In supervising staff we need to ensure that their practice is based on good sound evidence and that they are informed as to how they might be able to improve their own practice consistent with new initiatives in care which are constantly coming on line.

The use of the best available evidence and research is an ethical consideration not only from an individual practitioner's view but also from the organisational view. In supervising staff you need to ensure that the member of staff is practising in an informed way and is aware of the need to contribute to their knowledge base by accessing Continuing Professional Development (CPD) and knowledge updates. In this way you can be assured that your staff are delivering enhanced care that is safe. For the organisation, safe practice contributes to reduced numbers of incidents surrounding patients and their care and risks in the workplace and thus the potential for litigation. It can also raise the profile of the organisation.

1.5 Explain how professional supervision can protect the:

■ **individual**

■ **supervisor**

■ **supervisee**

The Royal College of Nursing in their document *A Vision for the Future* (1993) defined supervision as:

> 'a formal process of professional support and learning which enables individual practitioners to develop knowledge and competence, assume responsibility for their own practice and enhance consumer protection and safety of care in complex clinical situations.'

This definition clearly points out how the process of supervision protects not only the person who is undergoing it, but also the recipient, in this case the patient or client. It follows that the supervisor will also benefit, not only from being supervised themselves but also through enabling the staff in the setting to be able to work in an efficient and safe way.

As a manager and leader in a health and social care or children's services setting, supervision at its very best can benefit all those working in the area. To enable you to monitor and review the work, supervision can prove to be one of the main ways in which your organisation can do this. It ensures that all staff are being properly supported and developing their skills and you can be assured that the clients and patients in your care are being safely cared for by competent and knowledgeable staff.

2 Understand how the principles of professional supervision can be used to inform performance management in health and social care or children and young people's work settings

2.1 Explain the Performance Management Cycle

The Chartered Institute of Personnel Development (CIPD, 2006) describes the Performance Management Cycle as 'a systematic approach' which includes:

■ setting objectives

■ using relevant performance indicators and other measures

■ regularly monitoring and appraising individuals and teams to identify achievements

■ teasing out training and development needs

■ using the knowledge gained to modify plans.

This approach can be represented in a four-stage Performance Management Cycle. See Figure 8.4.

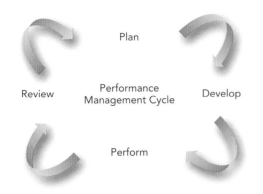

Figure 8.4 The four-stage Performance Management Cycle

Stage One – Plan

At the planning stage of the Performance Management Cycle, you will need to evaluate an employee's current role and performance in order to ascertain where areas of improvement may be needed and to set realistic goals and aims.

Stage Two – Develop

In this stage the focus is on improving expertise by allowing the employee to develop new skills and knowledge through CPD. As the manager you will need to be able to identify opportunities for staff and to provide coaching and mentoring as needed.

Stage Three – Perform

When we think of performance we often imagine actors playing out a scene or perhaps we might think about a musician playing or performing a piece of music. Whatever comes to mind, it is evident that at this stage 'something is done' and there are things to consider here. For example, making plans becomes meaningless when they do not relate to the needs of the staff, clients or the organisation. Also, in the performance of those plans, job satisfaction, and therefore improved staff morale, comes with doing the job well and a good manager will ensure that staff are working to their strengths in order to achieve this. It is important at this stage that the staff are enabled to do this by having access to the resources they need. It is unreasonable to expect improved performance with lack of resources or poor resources.

Stage Four – Review

The final stage is the evaluation by both parties to consider what has been done and what has been achieved. It is here that we can ascertain whether the goals have been reached. By assessing the results of the planned changes, it is possible to determine what next needs to be done, hence the cyclical nature of the process.

Activity 8.2.1

With a member of your staff complete the following activity.

With the staff member, clearly identify what change or task is required and how it will be measured. (PLAN)

Develop the staff member by identifying needs they have in order to complete the task. (DEVELOP)

Encourage the member of staff to perform to the required standard and provide support and development. (PERFORM)

Review the whole process and assess and evaluate performance against a set of measures. (REVIEW)

2.2 Analyse how professional supervision supports performance

When you read further about performance management, you will notice that there are numerous ways in which it is expressed and there are many cycles, all with varying stages. This is not important. By using a Performance Management Cycle you impose structure and process to the management of staff and their training and development needs.

In any organisation the aim is to produce and deliver high-quality services and to ensure that all opportunities for improvement, change and innovation are clearly identified and worked towards.

To achieve that end, the organisation must realise its potential against performance targets, and equally ensure that the performance management systems in place get the best out of people in the workplace, and deliver the best for people who use services. This can be monitored through the supervision process.

The national minimum standards for services in social care and children's services, together with national occupational standards and codes of practice, are all helping to change the performance management framework in the social care sector and this is something to celebrate. The inspection process and even the supervisory framework you adopt should be seen as an opportunity to improve performance and service delivery rather than used as a punitive measure to be feared. Critics argue that performance management is not a good thing for this very reason and, as we saw earlier in the chapter, there are also some people who do not value supervision. However, effective performance management and supervision can promote good quality service delivery and result in more highly motivated staff (SCIE, 2011).

As a supervisor there is a need to measure performance against results and not merely focus on behaviours and activity. The employee who always appears to be busy and working hard may not necessarily be contributing to the goals of the work setting. Think for a moment about the member of staff who always seems to have a lot to do but rarely accomplishes what actually should be done. In this instance, the employee needs to be made aware of the organisational goals together with methods by which those goals may be achieved and this can be achieved through good supervision. In the next section we shall look closely at how we can achieve this.

2.3 Analyse how performance indicators can be used to measure practice

The objectives of your organisation are the starting point when it comes to setting targets for performance. You will also be aware of the job descriptions of the staff and the competencies required to carry out certain roles.

Staff must understand what is expected of them and how what they do contributes to the continued success of the work setting. As the manager of staff, you need to ensure that the first step you take in performance management is to define clearly what the staff are required to do, why they need to do it and to what standard.

A good way in which to do this is to have a set of performance criteria which are made up of measures and standards which clearly state the level of performance required in areas such as:

- deadlines
- cost
- quality
- quantity.

You also need to ensure that the objectives you set are:

- consistent with the member of staff's job description
- consistent with the organisational goals
- clearly expressed
- supported by measurable performance criteria
- challenging.

Setting objectives is not an easy task by any means, but you may be familiar with SMART targets and this will help.

S – Specific
M – Measurable
A – Achievable
R – Realistic
T – Time-bound

Figure 8.5 SMART objectives

Objectives which are Specific, Measurable, Achievable and agreed, Realistic and Time-bound or SMART are a useful way to start.

Specific – Being specific means we have a much greater chance of success and the way to set such a goal is to plan with these questions in mind.

- Who: Who is involved?
- What: What do I want to accomplish?
- Where: Where will this happen?
- When: In what timescale?
- Which: Identify requirements and constraints.
- Why: Do we need to do this?

Example: TT to rewrite the Safeguarding Policy by the end of (date).

Although we have not specified here the reason for doing this, it can be assumed that safeguarding being a huge area in care work is a firm enough reason.

Measurable – To ensure your target is measurable, you might ask questions such as:

- How much?
- How many?
- How will I know when it is accomplished?

In the case of our example, we will know it is done when it is written!

Achievable and agreed – An achievable target for a member of staff is one which they agree is needed and one that they can actually do. In helping a member of staff in this part of target setting, you need to help them plan their steps and establish a timeframe for carrying out those steps.

Realistic – To be realistic, the member of staff and you as the manager must believe that the person can actually accomplish the task.

It is wise to check that the individual has done something similar in the past and is given the opportunity to identify what they might need in terms of support to accomplish the target.

Time-bound – Without a timeframe, the target loses urgency and momentum so by setting a date for completion, there is a given point when the task is to be completed and delivered.

Activity 8.2.2

Set a SMART target for yourself in which you show how you intend to complete the work for this particular unit.

Write the target in to your portfolio.

In summary then, professional supervision in health and social care or children and young people's work settings is about ensuring that there is accountability for the quality of the work undertaken and that staff are responsible for maintaining and improving their knowledge and skills. In doing so, they need to meet relevant standards of practice and work in a lawful, safe and effective way, seeking assistance if they do not feel adequately prepared to carry out any aspect of their work. Performance management is the means by which staff can be helped to achieve this. This is done through the setting of objectives, using relevant performance indicators and other measures and regularly monitoring and appraising individuals and teams to identify achievements and training and development needs.

3 Be able to undertake the preparation for professional supervision with supervisees in health and social care or children and young people's work settings

3.1 Explain factors which result in a power imbalance in professional supervision

The concept of power brings to mind negative connotations of abuse and harassment and this kind of thinking about what managers do can lead us to distrust anybody who is in such a position of power. This then can affect supervision.

If you are the manager in a work setting, you are already in a position of power. It is quite possible that you may even have recruited the people who you manage. You have influence and authority over those people. Furthermore, the concept of 'master–apprentice' in supervision evokes a hierarchy of power that favours the master and this is likely to affect the supervisory relationship.

Two main types of power, namely personal and organisational, are worthy of further investigation here.

When we refer to personal power, we are noting the knowledge, skills and competence associated with an individual which makes them an expert. As an expert, the individual can exert a certain amount of power in various situations. Think about the teacher–learner relationship.

Ascribed or status power is that which is given to a person by others based on their position in society, or even such things as attractiveness, status, reputation or wealth.

Organisational power can be of four types.

Reward power is the ability of the leader to give inducements such as pay, promotion or praise to move an organisation forward. Coercive power is a negative form of the above, with the leader imposing punishment such as disciplinary procedures.

Legitimate power is that which comes with a role or rank in an organisation and one in which the incumbent has authority. Information power is that based on access to information or data that is valued and not open to all (from Gopee and Galloway, 2009).

Being the manager in a work setting means you invariably supervise the work of the team and this in itself may lead to power imbalance. As we saw in the last section, the role of supervision in care has become one of the ways in which it is possible to monitor the work of employees, ensuring that performance indicators are being met and this in itself leads to conflict which we come back to later on in the chapter. Supervision has thus moved from the formative–educative and restorative–supportive function to favour the normative–managerial function only (see page 139). With this in mind, we need to look at ways to address the imbalance.

3.2 Explain how to address power imbalance in own supervision practice

If you recognise that a power imbalance exists in the supervision relationship then you can start to address it. What do we mean by this?

Activity 8.3.1

Reflect on how you as a manager address the power imbalance in your own setting. What sorts of actions do you take, for example, when an important decision needs to be made and one which you know is likely to be unpopular?

As a manager with responsibility for the smooth running of a department or organisation, your staff will be looking to you to lead with respect for them and honesty. You will always have the power in the relationship by virtue of the fact that you are accountable for the actions of the staff, that is, the buck stops with you! However, there is no need to take an authoritarian approach to how you lead. Having a conscious awareness of how being 'in charge' can make or break a relationship means you can take control of decisions and set the tone for the work group. Whilst it is good to be 'one of the team' and adopt a friendly manner towards staff, there is a fine line between this and taking control of the situation when you need to. With respect to the activity you have just completed it is always best policy to act with integrity, fairness and respect for others. I once worked with a manager who always blamed the difficult, unpopular decisions on higher management with the line 'it's not my decision, it's what they have told me to do' and then took credit for the more palatable ones. He soon lost credibility with staff who saw through his lack of integrity. By acknowledging that there is a difference between the role you have as a manager and leader and the staff, you recognise that a power relationship is in force and ultimately you will have to step up to the mark when action needs to be taken and decisions made. By not acknowledging the power relationship you are in danger of losing the goodwill of the team.

3.3 Agree with supervisee confidentiality, boundaries, roles and accountability within the professional supervision process

In planning supervision sessions, the right balance between an informal and structured approach needs to be created. Effective supervision is about sharing experiences in a safe environment, and informality will enable both parties to feel comfortable and safe. But if no structure is imposed, there is a danger that the session will not be viewed as meaning much and learning may not occur at all.

The best way to impose structure on the proceedings is to first of all ensure there is a supervision policy in place. If this is the case then you will be expected to undertake this aspect of staff development and there will be guidelines as to how you can do this.

The whole process of supervision needs to be 'owned' not only by the organisation but also by the supervisee. Everybody needs to feel part of the process if the merits of such an activity are to be achieved.

Thompson (2000) writes:

> 'Some people unfortunately adopt a narrow view of supervision and see it primarily... as a means of ensuring that sufficient quantity and quality of work is carried out... a broader view of supervision can play a significant role in promoting learning and developing a culture of continuous professional development.'

You may wish to adopt the following framework to manage your sessions:

- Establish ground rules and boundaries, reminding the supervisee of these at the start of each session.

- Remind supervisee of the need for confidentiality on both sides and to agree the boundaries of such and areas that may have to be divulged.

CONTRACT FOR SUPERVISION IN THE CARE SETTING

Student: _____

Supervisor: _____

Setting : _____

Dates: _____

The supervisor listed above has agreed to provide clinical supervision of the named member of staff.

The supervisor agrees:

1. to follow the guidelines required by the care setting

2. to directly observe the staff member at least once in the practical setting over the next three months

3. to give the member of staff written and verbal feedback suggestions, and reinforcement;

4. to provide a minimum of two meetings for discussion of role and work assigned.

The member of staff agrees to:

5. follow format and procedures suggested by the supervisor for daily plans, progress notes, reports, etc;

6. complete assignments and work in a timely manner.

7. advise the supervisor of any changes to role or work pattern.

Signatures:

_____

(student)

_____

(Supervisor)

_____

(Director of Clinical Education)

Date: _____

Figure 8.6 An example of a contract

■ Agree that the session will not be interrupted unless an emergency occurs and agree what constitutes an emergency. This will really help to confirm the importance of the process.

■ Agree the appropriate reason for cancelling the session.

■ Identify the agenda for discussion at the start of each session. Both you and the supervisee should do this. These should fit within the categories of:

– clinical issues/reflections on role

– what support is needed/professional issues

– educational issues/workload discussions

– management issues.

■ Ensure appropriate allocation of time and agree that you, the supervisor, should act as timekeeper.

■ Agree an action plan following each item discussed.

■ A brief record of the contents of the session should be kept by the supervisor.

3.4 Agree with supervisee the frequency and location of professional supervision

With a policy in place, together with a supervision agreement, the frequency and location of the supervision can be agreed.

A suitable meeting room needs to be identified and booked in advance. To ensure the supervisee is confident that the whole process will take place in a calm and also a confidential manner, the room must afford privacy and you will need to ensure that mobile phones are switched off or landlines re-routed to another line for the duration of the meeting.

How often you meet will depend upon the policy in your organisation but you may agree to meet on a monthly basis for one to two hours.

3.5 Agree with supervisee sources of evidence that can be used to inform professional supervision

3.6 Agree with supervisee actions to be taken in preparation for professional supervision

The evidence you require a member of staff to bring to supervision will very much depend on the agreement you have made and the agenda set at the last meeting. An action plan which had previously been drawn up may require the

supervisee to do something before the next meeting and to bring the finished piece. For example, the supervisee may be undertaking a course of study and will require some support in course work. In this instance, they may bring with them copies of work so far, course content and reflective accounts of their learning so far. You need to ensure that you do not fall into the trap of becoming a 'surrogate course tutor' for the staff member but allow them to reflect on their learning with respect to how it is affecting or changing their practice.

In preparing for the supervisory meeting, staff need to be aware of the agenda set at the previous meeting and if this required work to be completed, they should get into the habit of bringing with them evidence to support the work done.

Activity 8.3.2

This activity will take you some time to complete and requires you to present a case study.

Being mindful of confidentiality and anonymising your records, compile a case study from your encounter in supervision with one member of staff.

Ensure that the following is part of the study:

■ Show how you agreed the confidentiality, boundaries, roles and accountability issues within the relationship. Give examples.

■ Record how frequently you met and where.

■ Describe what you discussed with respect to the sources of evidence that you required the supervisee to collect in order to inform professional supervision.

■ Say how you and the supervisee prepared for each session.

■ Provide evidence to show how you recorded agreed supervision decisions.

4 Be able to provide professional supervision in health and social care or children and young people's work settings

4.1 Support supervisees to reflect on their practice

This process of reflection is extremely important to you as a manager since it enables you to bring together practice and theory. Reflection on practice enables us to take a step back from what we are learning and assess what was good and what we might have done differently in any one situation.

In helping your staff to be more reflective about their work, there are a number of very useful reflective tools such as the one developed by Gibbs (1988).

Gibbs (1988) refers to stages of reflection namely:

Description – You may ask yourself where you were, who you were with, what happened and what the result was.

Feelings – Recollecting what you were thinking/ feeling at the start and if the feelings changed during the event.

Evaluation – What was good and bad about the experience? How do you judge the event?

Analysis – What sense can you make of the situation? Break the situation down.

Conclusion – What else could have been done? How can you learn from the experience?

Action plan – If it arose again would you do the same?

(Adapted from Jasper, (2003))

Figure 8.7 The process of reflection
Gibbs, 1988

Activity 8.4.1

Prepare a PowerPoint presentation detailing the process of reflection and showing the key elements of this for your staff.

You may have highlighted the key elements of reflection as follows:

■ **Reflection** is associated with deep thought, and helps us to achieve a better understanding of ourselves and the roles we carry out. It helps us to **make sense of experience**. We don't always learn from experiences. Reflection is where we actively analyse experience, attempting to 'make sense' or find the meaning in it.

■ **Stand back**. It can be hard to reflect when we are caught up in an activity. 'Standing back' gives a better view or perspective on an experience, issue or action.

■ **Undertake repetition**. Reflection involves 'going over' something, often several times, in order to get a broad view and check nothing is missed.

■ **Gain a sense of deeper honesty**. Reflection is associated with 'striving after truth'. Through reflection, we can acknowledge things that we find difficult to admit in the normal course of events.

■ **'Weigh up'**. Reflection involves being even-handed or balanced in judgement. This means taking everything into account, not just the most obvious.

■ **Achieve clarity**. Reflection can bring greater clarity, like seeing events reflected in a mirror. This can help at any stage of planning, carrying out and reviewing activities.

■ **Gain understanding**. Reflection is about learning and understanding on a deeper level. This includes gaining valuable insights that cannot be just 'taught'.

■ **Make judgements**. Reflection involves an element of drawing conclusions in order to move on, change or develop an approach, strategy or activity.

4.2 Provide positive feedback about the achievements of the supervisee

The definition of feedback is an open two-way communication between two or more parties.

Feedback needs to be provided on a regular basis and should be a daily part of your work as a manager. In a formal supervision session, the best way to approach this task is to ask the supervisee how they perceived their performance of a task before you launch in with your assessment.

In this way you can see what they understand about how well they are doing their job and you are also encouraging them to be reflective about their performance.

Occasionally we are very critical about what we do and it is therefore nice to hear some positive praise for how we have completed a particular job.

Figure 8.8 A pat on the back

Figure 8.9 The praise 'sandwich'

In this way, the unpalatable news is sandwiched by good news and the blow of receiving it is softened. Here's how it might work.

4.3 Provide constructive feedback that can be used to improve performance

Think about the following.

Your manager wants to give you some constructive feedback and has called a meeting for that purpose. How are you feeling? We would guess that you are probably approaching the meeting in a negative way, thinking that you are about to be criticised in some way. The term 'feedback' is often confused with criticism and how we might have done a job in a better way and, for that reason, we view the whole concept less than positively.

So if that's how you feel about it, chances are your staff and supervisees share the same negative vibes! We cannot go through life without making any mistakes and without requiring some guidance on aspects of our work and, although the content of feedback may be negative, it can always be given in a constructive and encouraging way. When done in such a way, you can help the member of staff to solve a problem, or even to address a part of their behaviour and work towards organisational goals. We give such feedback to ensure that the supervisee is helped to develop, grow and to improve.

So how do you go about giving constructive feedback? You may have heard of the 'feedback sandwich' and although it has come in for criticism (ironically) from some writers, it is a good way for new managers and supervisors to deliver news that may otherwise be seen as negative.

The feedback sandwich is a three-step procedure to help provide constructive feedback, consisting of praise followed by the problem area or criticism, followed by more praise.

Activity 8.4.2

Jenny is a member of staff who is undertaking a teaching qualification and has been asked to undertake some staff development. Her manager is aware that she does not fully engage all the staff in the room when she teaches and has noticed some staff members not paying attention.

Praise: 'Jenny, I really enjoyed your presentation to the staff this morning. I thought your PowerPoint presentation was very clear and you had some great hand-outs for the staff. This is such an important subject, isn't it? We need to ensure that all staff are clear about this.'

Criticism: 'Did you notice that two of the staff were using their mobile phones whilst you were talking and I think they got rather muddled about some of the points you were making? I think this might mean that they have not fully understood how important safeguarding is. Can you be sure they are going to be able to cope with the work you set them to do? Perhaps you could ask more questions of individuals to get them to voice their concerns.'

Allow for discussion.

Praise: 'I am pleased that your teaching seems to be going really well at the moment and the staff obviously enjoy it too. Well done.'

Figure 8.10 Providing feedback

You will see here that the area for Jenny to work on has been highlighted but she has also been praised for the good points in her teaching. Hearing what someone likes about us or our performance is always encouraging and being specific about what is good about us is also a useful tool. We need to know what it is that is good. By making reference to the issue you have a concern with and offering ways in which it can be addressed, the criticism is seen as more constructive and useful.

Activity 8.4.3

Provide an example of constructive feedback you have used to help improve the performance of a member of staff.

4.4 Support supervisees to identify their own development needs

On-going staff development is just one discussion you will have with your supervisees during the supervision session. These needs are likely to reflect their job role and the long term goals of the organisation.

If the member of staff is seeking new responsibilities in the work setting, they may be helped to identify courses to enable them in a new role.

It is important that you as a manager and supervisor are up to date with policy changes, national initiatives and legal requirements for the setting in order to specify the sort of training needed.

Professional development requirements attached to various roles and required by regulatory bodies such as the General Social Work Council, NMC or HPC (Health Professional Council) change over time and you need to have a good understanding of those required for your work setting.

4.5 Review and revise professional supervision targets to meet the identified objectives of the work setting

Staff appraisals, performed at the end of an annual cycle for managing staff, are a vehicle for reviewing the goals set throughout the supervision process and planning for the year to come.

Activity 8.4.4

What is the purpose of staff appraisal in your own setting?

You may have highlighted the following:

- Review the job description and role.
- Look at individual performance and achievement and reward (performance-related pay or other incentives).
- Plan on-going professional development.
- Give feedback.

The object of appraisal is to set goals for the coming year and to identify ways in which the staff member can improve their performance over the next year. It should be a positive process in which the member of staff can be provided with details about their performance and can start to plan for the forthcoming year. Staff who have been underperforming should have been made aware of this during supervision and at appraisal will be identifying ways in which they can meet the required standards in the year to come. They should not be surprised to learn of the problems with their performance at this stage in the proceedings since they will have received feedback in the previous supervision sessions.

The process of appraisal is similar to supervision. The meeting needs to be planned in advance, a room booked and time allocated to ensure the main points on the prepared agenda are covered and agreed. In some settings the person undergoing appraisal is asked to complete their own evaluation of how they have performed and what they have achieved to bring with them to the meeting to be discussed. This can then be part of the recorded notes of the meeting.

The following website takes you to a useful booklet produced by ACAS (the Advisory, Conciliation and Arbitration Service) which details the whole process of staff appraisal and you are recommended to read this through for further information: www.acas.org.uk/media/pdf/o/q/B07_1.pdf

In addition to the above, the following website provides a useful template for staff appraisal: www.businessballs.com/performanceappraisalform.pdf

4.6 Support supervisees to explore different methods of addressing challenging situations

In dealing with any challenging situation, your supervisees must be directed to the policies in the workplace and should be given the opportunity to undergo training. Any challenging behaviour, either by a visitor, another staff member or a client, can be frightening and staff need to be given the opportunity to talk about the situation and to discuss the triggers which may have led to the outburst.

It is a good idea to discuss with new staff and to remind experienced staff of the types of challenging behaviour your work setting might come across and to ensure they are aware of how they are to deal with such incidents.

Activity 8.4.5

Remind yourself of your policies with respect to how you would help staff to deal with challenging behaviour.

4.7 Record agreed supervision decisions

All supervision meetings need to be properly recorded in order to identify and support agreed actions and their completion within agreed timescales. Without records we cannot be sure we have actually set tasks and actions and this can lead to confusion.

The way in which you do this will vary but you may decide that you will take brief notes at the meeting and then write up the whole meeting later. If you have a lot of supervisees, it might be more appropriate for you to complete handwritten notes during the meeting and this means that you have the opportunity for the exact wording to be agreed at the time and then there is an accurate record of what was said. A signature from both yourself and the supervisee on the record is good practice and a copy of the record can be given to the supervisee immediately.

However you choose to record the meeting, the following are points to consider:

- record decisions and actions which you agree on
- have clear timescales
- detail responsibilities.

5 Be able to manage conflict situations during professional supervision in health and social care or children and young people's work settings

5.1 Give examples from own practice of managing conflict situations within professional supervision

5.2 Reflect on own practice in managing conflict situations experienced during professional supervision process

Activity 8.5.1

Identify an example of a conflict situation you have had to deal with and write a reflective account of what happened and how you managed it.

Conflict can disrupt performance but within teams it is a common occurrence. When the resolution of the conflict is effective, then it can have a positive effect leading to personal growth and development.

If managed effectively it can be 'creative and productive and creative solutions to difficult problems can often be found through positive conflict resolution' (Tilmouth et al., 2011).

You may come across two types of conflict:

- **Task-based conflict** – which are disagreements related to approaches to work, processes and structural issues within the team and the organisation.

- **Relationship-based conflict** – which are conflicts between individual members of the team and are usually caused by differences in personal values and beliefs.

In Activity 8.5.1 above you may have identified areas of conflict such as:

■ Lack of clarity around team roles and responsibilities

■ Unfair distribution of work

■ Lack of clear vision on the part of the supervisee

■ Lack of understanding of the role of others

■ Poor communication.

It is imperative to handle such conflict effectively since bad handling of these situations will lead to an ineffective team. Staff start to avoid each other and rifts occur, with staff taking sides. The ultimate downside of this happening is that this most certainly leads to poor and ineffectual care of service users, clients and patients.

The most effective way of solving conflict in a team is for people concerned to have constructive conversation (Larson and LaFasto, 2001). By doing so, each person will be helped to see the perspective of the other person and will gain some understanding about the way the other person feels about the situation. The conversation must result in each party committing to making improvements in the relationship (in Tilmouth *et al.*, 2011).

These conversations might be initiated by the staff members themselves or they may require the services of a neutral facilitator and this can be set up in supervision.

Larson and LaFasto's CONECT model for resolving conflict by conversation is useful:

■ **Commit** to the relationship by discussing the relationship, and not the problem causing concern. Each person should say why they feel change should occur and what they hope to gain. This is a very positive approach.

■ **Optimise** safety, with both parties committing to maintain confidentiality and create an atmosphere of trust.

■ **Neutralise** defensiveness, with each person explaining what they have observed, how it made them feel, and the long-term effects of the other person's actions.

■ **Explain** each perspective.

■ **Change** one behaviour and ask each person to change.

■ **Track** the change and decide how improvements will be measured. Agree to meet to discuss whether changes have been successful (in Tilmouth *et al.*, 2011).

In resolving conflict, when people's needs are discovered, then a solution can be found. We may be tempted to compromise but compromise means that people's needs are still not fully met and this can lead to resentment (West, 2004).

6 Be able to evaluate own practice when conducting professional supervision in health and social care or children and young people's work settings

6.1 Gather feedback from supervisee/s on own approach to supervision process

The only way in which you can evaluate your work as a supervisor is to ask for feedback and this may be quite difficult to do. However, if you are to improve your practice, you do need evidence of what you can do to achieve this.

You might decide to ask staff to complete an anonymous questionnaire about your work. Perhaps the following questions might be useful:

1. How did you find my approach to the session?

2. Was it positive?

3. How might I have improved it?

4. What was the best aspect of my approach?

5. And the worst?

6. What are the areas I need to improve?

Activity 8.6.1

Following the next supervision session, ask the member of staff to comment on your work. Collect the data and reflect on the comments.

6.2 Adapt approaches to own professional supervision in light of feedback from supervisees and others

Activity 8.6.2

Comment on the changes you intend to make as a result of your feedback.

Summary

Supervision is one way of providing professional support and learning for staff, to enable them to develop knowledge, skills and competence in their work. This chapter has covered the various aspects of supervision and has shown how the process enhances the work of the staff member and leads to improved care and safety in the care setting for our clients and patients.

Learning outcomes	Assessment criteria
1 Understand the purpose of professional supervision in health and social care or children and young people's work settings	(1.1) Analyse the principles, scope and purpose of professional supervision **Activity 8.1.1, p.137** (1.2) Outline theories and models of professional supervision **Activity 8.1.2, p.140** (1.3) Explain how the requirements of legislation, codes of practice and agreed ways of working influence professional supervision **Activity 8.1.3, p.141** (1.4) Explain how findings from research, critical reviews and inquiries can be used within professional supervision **Activity 8.1.4, p.141** (1.5) Explain how professional supervision can protect the: ■ individual ■ supervisor ■ supervisee **See p.142 for guidance.**
2 Understand how the principles of professional supervision can be used to inform performance management in health and social care or children and young people's work settings	(2.1) Explain the Performance Management Cycle **Activity 8.2.1, p.143** (2.2) Analyse how professional supervision supports performance **See p.143 for guidance.** (2.3) Analyse how performance indicators can be used to measure practice **Activity 8.2.2, p.145**

Learning outcomes	Assessment criteria
3 Be able to undertake the preparation for professional supervision with supervisees in health and social care or children and young people's work settings	**(3.1)** Explain factors which result in a power imbalance in professional supervision **See p.145 for guidance.**
	(3.2) Explain how to address power imbalance in own supervision practice **Activity 8.3.1, p.145**
	(3.3) Agree with supervisee confidentiality, boundaries, roles and accountability within the professional supervision process **Activity 8.3.2, p.147**
	(3.4) Agree with supervisee the frequency and location of professional supervision **Activity 8.3.2, p.147**
	(3.5) Agree with supervisee sources of evidence that can be used to inform professional supervision **Activity 8.3.2, p.147**
	(3.6) Agree with supervisee actions to be taken in preparation for professional supervision **Activity 8.3.2, p.147**
4 Be able to provide professional supervision in health and social care or children and young people's work settings	**(4.1)** Support supervisees to reflect on their practice **Activity 8.4.1, p.148**
	(4.2) Provide positive feedback about the achievements of the supervisee **See p.148 for guidance.**
	(4.3) Provide constructive feedback that can be used to improve performance **Activity 8.4.2, p.149 Activity 8.4.3, p.150**
	(4.4) Support supervisees to identify their own development needs **See p.150 for guidance.**
	(4.5) Review and revise professional supervision targets to meet the identified objectives of the work setting **Activity 8.4.4, p.150**
	(4.6) Support supervisees to explore different methods of addressing challenging situations **Activity 8.4.5, p.151**
	(4.7) Record agreed supervision decisions **Activity 8.3.2, p.147**

5 Be able to manage conflict situations during professional supervision in health and social care or children and young people's work settings	(5.1) Give examples from own practice of managing conflict situations within professional supervision **Activity 8.5.1, p.151**
	(5.2) Reflect on own practice in managing conflict situations experienced during professional supervision process **Activity 8.5.1, p.151**
6 Be able to evaluate own practice when conducting professional supervision in health and social care or children and young people's work settings	(6.1) Gather feedback from supervisee/s on own approach to supervision process **Activity 8.6.1, p.152**
	(6.2) Adapt approaches to own professional supervision in light of feedback from supervisees and others **Activity 8.6.2, p.152**

References

Bernard, J. M. (1979). 'Supervisor Training: A discrimination model', *Counsellor Education and Supervision,* 19, pp.60–8.

Bernard, J. M. and Goodyear, R. K. (1998) *Fundamentals of Clinical Supervision* (2e). Needham Heights, MA: Allyn & Bacon.

Carroll, M. (2007) 'One More Time: What is Supervision?' *Psychotherapy in Australia,* Vol. 13, no. 3, May. www.supervisioncentre.com/docs/kv/one%20more%20time.pdf

CIPD (2006) *Coaching Supervision: Maximising the potential of coaching.* The Bath Consultancy Group.

Department of Health (2003) *National Minimum Standards: Care Homes for Older People,* DOH 2003b Standard 36. London: TSO.

DfES (2006) *Championing Children. A shared set of skills, knowledge and behaviours for those leading and managing integrated children's services.* London: DFES.

DfES (2007) *Providing Effective Supervision.* Skills for Care and the Children's Workforce Development Council (CWDC). London: TSO.

General Social Care Council (2010) *The General Social Care Council – Code of Practice.*

Gibbs, G. (1988) *Learning by Doing: A guide to teaching and learning methods.* Oxford: Further Education Unit, Oxford Brookes University.

Godden, J. (undated) (BASW/CoSW England) *Code of Practice to Support Social Workers.*

Gopee, N. and Galloway, J. (2009) *Leadership and Management in Health Care.* London: Sage.

Harkness, D. and Hensley, H. (1991) 'Changing the focus of social work supervision: effects on client satisfaction and generalised contentment', *Social Work* 36 (6), pp.506–12.

Hogan, R. A. (1964) 'Issues and Approaches in Supervision', *Psychotherapy, Theory, Research & Practice.* 1, pp.139–41.

Holloway, E. L. (1987) 'Developmental Models of Supervision: Is it development?' *Professional Psychology: Research and Practice.* 18 (3), pp.209–16.

IDEA (2008) *Performance Management: don't measure for pleasure.* http://www.ideasnetwork.be/consulting-services/performance-management,en,119.html

Jasper, M. (2003) *Beginning Reflective Practice.* Cheltenham: Nelson Thornes.

Kadushin, A. (1992) *Supervision in Social* Work (3e). New York: Columbia University Press.

Larson, C. E. and LaFasto, F. M. J.(2001) *When Teams Work Best: 6,000 team members and leaders tell what it takes to succeed.* London: Sage.

NHS Management Executive (1993) as cited at www.nmc-uk.org/Nurses-and-midwives/Advice-by-topic/A/Advice/Clinical-supervision-for-registered-nurses/

Nursing & Midwifery Council (2008) *The Code: Standards of conduct, performance and ethics for nurses and midwives.*

The Open University, School of Health and Social Welfare (1998) *Clinical Supervision: A development pack for nurses.* Milton Keynes: Open University.

Proctor, B. (undated) 'Supervision: a co-operative exercise in accountability' in Marken, M. and Payne, M. (eds), *Enabling and Enduring.* Leicester: National Youth Bureau/ Council for Education and Training in Youth and Community Work.

Royal College of Nursing (1993) 'A vision for the future', *Guidance for Occupational Health Nurses.*

SCIE (2011) www.scie.org.uk/workforce/ peoplemanagement/staffmanagement/ performance/index.asp

Skills for Care and CWDC (2007) *Providing Effective Supervision: A workforce development tool, including a unit of competence and supporting guidance.* SCF01/0607.

Smith, K. L. (2009) *A Brief Summary of Supervision Models.* www.gallaudet.edu/ documents/academic/cou_ supervisionmodels%5B1%5D.pdf

Smith, M. K. (1996, 2005) 'The functions of supervision', *The Encyclopedia of Informal Education.*

Stoltenberg, C. D. and Delworth, U. (1987) *Supervising Counsellors and Therapists.* San Francisco: Jossey-Bass.

Stoltenberg, C. D., McNeill, B. and Delworth, U. (1998) *IDM Supervision: An integrated developmental model of supervising counselors and therapists.* San Francisco: Jossey-Bass.

Thompson, N. (2000) *Promoting Workplace Learning.* BASW policy press.

Tilmouth, T., Davis-Ward, E. and Williams, B. (2011) *Foundation Degree in Health and Social Care.* London: Hodder Education

UKCC (1996) *Position Statement on clinical supervision for nursing & health visiting.* London: UKCC.

Ward, C. C. and House, R. M. (1998) 'Counseling supervision: A reflective model', *Counselor Education and Supervision,* 38, pp.23–33.

West, M. (2004) *Effective Teamwork.* Oxford: Blackwell.

Zimmerman, B. J. and Schunk, D. S. (eds) (2003) *Educational Psychology: A century of contributions.* Mahwah, NJ: Lawrence Erlbaum Associates.

http://cdn.basw.co.uk/upload/basw_13603-1.pdf

www.mentalhealthacademy.com.au

www.rcn.org.uk/development/learning/ transcultural_health/clinicalsupervision

www.skillsforcare.org.uk

9

Unit M3 Manage health and social care practice to ensure positive outcomes for individuals

The purpose of this chapter is to assess the learner's knowledge, understanding and skills required in the process of planning and achieving positive outcomes that underpin the personalisation agenda. This unit covers the key areas of practice that support the implementation of personalisation. This agenda is further covered in Chapters 2 and 6.

The unit also explores the role of the manager/senior worker in providing a supportive environment for individuals to achieve positive outcomes.

Learning outcomes
By the end of this chapter you will:

1. Understand the theory and principles that underpin outcome based practice.

2. Be able to lead practice that promotes social, emotional, cultural, spiritual and intellectual well-being.

3. Be able to lead practice that promotes individuals' health.

4. Be able to lead inclusive provision that gives individuals choice and control over the outcomes they want to achieve.

5. Be able to manage effective working partnerships with carers, families and significant others to achieve positive outcomes.

1 Understand the theory and principles that underpin outcome based practice

 Explain 'outcome based practice'

In an attempt to ensure that all individuals requiring care are dealt with holistically and with their needs being met, the 'personalisation' agenda has been introduced into a lot of recent government documentation. A system of care and support tailored to meet the needs of the individual has replaced the 'one size fits all' approach previously in vogue.

Outcome based practice, also referred to as outcomes management, and outcomes-focussed assessment, is one such approach to achieving desired patient care goals. It involves a combination of teamwork, quality improvement, which is continually evaluated, and process and outcome measurement.

Based upon the social model of disability and empowerment, this approach has been hailed as a better option to the needs-led assessment, and research supports this (Harris *et al.*, 2005).

Three dimensions of the model have been put forward as being:

■ Outcomes involving change, such as those that focus on developing self-confidence, or skills which enable self-care.

■ Outcomes maintaining quality of life, occasionally referred to as maintenance outcomes.

■ Outcomes associated with the process of receiving services, or those which involve being valued and listened to in the care process.

Harris *et al.* (2005) categorised the dimensions into a four-part framework which might also be seen as showing how needs may be met. See Table 9.1.

Table 9.1 The outcomes framework

Autonomy outcomes	Personal comfort outcomes
Access to all areas of the home	Personal hygiene
Access to locality and wider environment	Safety/security
Communicative access	Desired level of cleanliness of home
Financial security	Emotional well-being
	Physical health
Economic participation outcomes	**Social participation outcomes**
Access to paid employment as desired	Access to mainstream leisure activities
Access to training	Access to support in parenting role
Access to further/higher education/ employment	Access to support for personal secure relationships
Access to appropriate training for new skills (e.g. lip reading)	Access to advocacy/peer support
	Citizenship

From Maclean et al., 2002

Seen as a user-centred approach to care, it involves the care worker acting as a facilitator in care pathways.

Activity 9.1.1

Explain what you understand by 'outcome based practice' to a member of your staff.

1.2 Critically review *approaches to outcome based practice*

Outcome based practice was a new way of working and replaced the needs-led approach. The reasons for this focus on the problems with 'needs', both conceptually and practically.

One of the problems is that the identification of 'needs' is highly subjective. Also, working with clients in a needs-led approach meant that professionals focussed on the immediate situation and support requirements that would be provided by the care professional.

Another problem with focussing on 'needs' is that they change over time, and there is no specified point at which the work can be said to have been achieved. The work frequently lacks direction and purpose and it is almost impossible to measure success or failure. Needs have a tendency to become moveable feasts in that once they are identified, others also become apparent and there appears to be no end to the work being done for the client.

The idea of 'outcomes' in care was seen as a different approach to which the focus on achievement was a more meaningful way to assist with care. The focus of the work is on the goals or desired achievements of the service user and this has been seen as a very different approach to that of the needs-led assessment of care.

In using this approach, the care worker takes on the role of assisting the client to identify immediate, medium-term and long-term goals. Rather than leading the client's care, the health professional:

> 'steers, guides, (and) pronounces the identification of "needs" and the proposed "intervention" towards practice driven by the service user, who is encouraged and facilitated to identify their "outcomes", a set of immediate, medium- and long-term goals that they wish to achieve. The focus on outcomes overcomes many of the deficiencies of the "needs" model described above.'
>
> (Qureshi et al., 2000, quoted in Barnes and Mercer, 2004)

With this renewed focus on outcomes, the work becomes target driven and specific, and there is a goal in mind. It is the client in this type of care who sets review dates and monitors their achievement, thus moving the focus away from the care professionals' 'assessment of the service user's needs'.

The client then remains in complete control of the entire process, from the identification of outcomes, to their achievement and evaluation of the success or failure of the venture. In this type of approach, the role of the care professional is to assist the service user in the achievement of their outcomes only.

Whilst this approach would seem to provide the ultimate in person-centred care, it is not without its critics. A study carried out by Qureshi *et al.* in 2000 for York University highlights some of the issues with it.

One of the problem areas was the struggle with the concept of outcomes that care professionals seemed to have, together with the professional and organisational culture which did not accept the introduction of such innovations (Qureshi *et al.* 1998). Previous research and development work did find, however, that as staff gained a clearer understanding of the outcomes concept, the outcomes focus provided a clearer basis for care planning.

A further area of concern was with the whole notion of 'expert power'. With the client at the centre of the assessment process identifying their own aims and objectives in negotiation with care professionals, control and responsibility for the achievement sat very much with the client. This meant that the professional felt their role had been reduced to one of facilitator and this did not sit well with some who believed that, as experts, they should have a bigger part in the decision-making mechanism.

This somewhat radical approach to care meant that professionals needed to change their perceptions of care and embrace a newer way of working. The change by care professionals to using the term 'outcome' rather than 'need' was one which helped to change perceptions, although the research showed this was not easy as evident in the quotation below:

> 'However, some staff experienced difficulty in moving from "needs" to "outcomes"... Where the outcomes are to be recorded we had examples under "health" stating "to use the toilet" and the planned action to achieve the outcome being "raised toilet seat"... Depressingly, staff in these instances failed to grasp the difference between the identification of a need and an outcome... The staff in these instances, however, were making these functional items the whole focus of their work and this reduces the possibilities of exploring the whole context of the service user's aspirations (their outcomes), and demeans service users by focusing solely upon bodily functions in this way and reinstates (and in many ways reinforces) the expert power of the professional over the service user.'

> (Qureshi *et al.*, 2000, quoted in Barnes and Mercer, 2004)

Further issues with this type of approach seemed to stem from the care professional's need to reach a service solution instead of listening to the client's desired outcomes. This was reported as a need to take responsibility on the part of the professional and was also linked to pressure of work. A number of professional practice issues have been noted in the research and the challenge of introducing an outcomes approach has been raised. Amongst some issues has been the tendency of the care professionals to fall back into a provider service mode instead of thinking and acting creatively with clients. Also some professionals claimed to be unable to grasp the outcomes concept, a claim the research team felt was not believable, citing the 'least trained, less professionally educated staff' as those who managed to understand and embrace the concept. Conversely, the research did show that clients valued the outcomes approach and 'appear comfortable with setting goals and working towards them'.

Activity 9.1.2

Consider the needs-led and the outcome-based approach to care and compare the two. Show examples of how you have used the latter approach in your own care.

1.3 Analyse the effect of legislation and policy on outcome based practice

As we noted in the last section, the whole practice of social care has been concerned in the past with identifying clients' needs and assessing care packages.

Since the NHS and Community Care Act 1990 (Section 47(1)) was passed, local authorities are duty bound to carry out assessments of need for community care services with individuals who appear to need them. This act developed the use of a 'needs-led approach', together with assessment and 'individually tailored packages of care'. The emphasis was to be on providing flexible care in people's own homes so that they might live 'as normal a life as possible'. Prior to that, the National Assistance Act of 1948 and the Chronically Sick and Disabled Persons Act of 1970 (Section 2) had duties of assessment of individual needs for everyone who fell within Section 29, as well as a duty to provide care and support services for disabled people.

The legislation with respect to outcome based practice is part of the personalisation agenda so favoured by health professionals and government over the last 40 years or so. Dissatisfaction with the care system saw the development of the civil rights movement of the 1960s and 1970s and the medical model came under scrutiny and the social model of disability became more accepted in practice.

In the 1980s and 1990s, there was a move towards a more individualistic, consumer-led approach to social care and the Conservative government talked of the 'dependency culture' that was in evidence and the need to address this.

The Social Security Act of 1986 saw Supplementary Benefit being replaced with Income Support and the Disabled Persons Act (1986) brought about assessment of needs for disabled persons. The provision of an Independent Living Fund (ILF) which aimed to increase choice and control in order to promote independent living was brought in.

The 1988 Griffiths Report on Community Care advised that social services should use a variety of providers to prevent a 'monopoly' on the provision of care and support and the concept of the 'mixed economy of care' was introduced. The 1989 *Caring for People* White Paper paved the way for community care and care management in social work.

In the late 1990s, new legislation allowing for direct payments came about as a result of the Community Care and Direct Payments Act 1996. This was to enable social service authorities/departments to make cash payments to disabled people for community care services, and in later years, this was also made available to older people, people with mental health problems, carers and parents of disabled children. This major development to ensure that all groups requiring care were empowered and had choice and control was picked up by the New Labour government in the years 2001–9 who were keen to promote independent living. 'Individual budgets' introduced in 2003 brought about a new model of social care provision.

The *Valuing People* White Paper (2001) made direct payments available to more people with a learning disability and it is in this paper that we first officially come across the term 'person-centred planning'.

Several other papers are worthy of note. *Improving the Life Chances of Disabled People* (2005) brought about the introduction of individual budgets to improve choice and control over the mix of care and support.

In addition, the paper *Independence, Wellbeing and Choice* (2005) obligated social care services to help people to maintain their independence by 'giving them greater choice and control over the way their needs are met'.

It was in *Our Health, Our Care, Our Say: A new direction for community service* (2006) that the concept of personalised care was introduced. *Putting People First: A shared vision and commitment to transformation of adult social care* was a commitment to enable people to manage and control their own support through individual/personal budgets. *Care, Support, Independence: Shaping the future of care together* (2009) provided a consultation on how personalised social care and support can be delivered and funded.

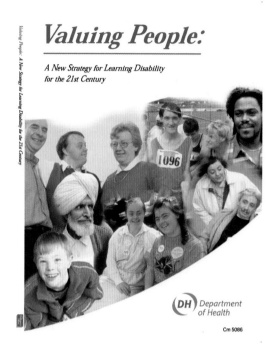

Figure 9.1 *Valuing People*

The introduction of the personal health budget to allow people to have more choice, flexibility and control over the health services and care they receive came about as a result of the White Paper *Personal Health Budgets: First steps* (2009).

One of the newest papers is that provided by the White Paper *A Vision For Adult Social Care: Capable communities and active citizens*, which was published in November 2010, and set out the plans for a new direction for adult social care, putting personalised services and outcomes centre stage.

Activity 9.1.3

Write a reflective account that shows how your own practice with respect to outcome based practice has been affected by the legislation.

1.4 Explain how outcome based practice can result in positive changes in individuals' lives

Activity 9.1.4

What are the positive changes that can come about with outcome based practice that are not apparent in a service-led approach? Compare the two approaches.

Outcome-based care puts the person firmly at the centre of the care service and delivers meaningful individual outcomes. You may have highlighted the following points as being the key benefits of such care:

■ The client is able to express their aspirations for a more fulfilling life and their abilities and talents are explored and used.

■ Care workers are empowered to work more closely with clients to understand how to enable them to become more independent.

■ Changing needs and preferences can be responded to.

■ Clients are able to exercise more choice and have more flexibility in the day-to-day delivery of their service.

■ Partnership working between all stakeholders is encouraged.

■ Funding and time are used to a greater effect.

■ It provides a basis for evaluating the effectiveness of services.

(Adapted from Care UK website)

2 Be able to lead practice that promotes social, emotional, cultural, spiritual and intellectual well-being

2.1 Explain the psychological basis for well-being

A subjective view of psychological well-being would be to say that we are happy or satisfied with our lives. But this is fraught with difficulty since what makes you happy is unlikely to be the same for your clients or other care workers, perhaps. So although our emotions and how we feel is a part of psychological well-being, it is not enough. In order to feel really good and to have fulfilling lives, we need to experience purpose and meaning, in addition to positive emotions. The psychologist Carol Ryff has developed a clear model of psychological well-being that breaks it down into six key parts and these are:

1. Self-acceptance

2. Positive relations with others

3. Autonomy

4. Environmental mastery

5. Purpose in life

6. Personal growth.

(From Ryff's 1989 *Psychological Well-being Inventory*)

If we are to lead practice that promotes social, emotional, cultural, spiritual and intellectual well-being, we need to be aware of the factors that can contribute to this. Writers sometimes speak of well-being along with health and there has been much debate over the years about what constitutes a good definition of health and also mental health.

The World Health Organization (1946) defines health as:

'a state of complete physical, mental and social well-being and not merely the absence of disease or infirmity.'

Mental health is described as:

'a state of well-being in which the individual realises his or her own abilities, can cope with the normal stresses of life, can work productively and fruitfully, and is able to make a contribution to his or her community.'

(WHO, 2002)

These definitions speak of well-being as a multi-dimensional entity, much more than just being happy or satisfied. It includes health in social, physical, mental domains, and implies emotional, career and spiritual domains.

In ensuring the 'well-being' of our clients and even our staff, as managers we need to be aware of how we might measure the state of well-being to ensure that clients are getting their overall needs met to provide us with a sense of how happy and healthy someone is. When things are not going well and our joy with life and general sense of calm is lacking, we start to experience stress, worry and anxiety. Our psychological well-being becomes compromised and this will inevitably lead to our quality of life being reduced. For the people in our care, this can lead to depression and its subsequent effects on the physical well-being and health.

Psychological well-being is about enabling our clients to experience a well rounded and balanced life with all the attendant emotions that go with this.

Activity 9.2.1

Explain the psychological basis for well-being.

The concept of holistic health and well-being incorporates several different facets including:

■ physical

■ intellectual/mental

■ emotional

■ social

- spiritual
- sexual.

(Ewles and Simnett, 1999)

Briefly define each of the terms and say how you promote psychological well-being in your clients.

Perhaps you answered in this way:

Physical health refers to the bodily functions and fitness etc. and describes the ability of the body to function in an efficient way.

Intellectual and mental health concerns the sense of purpose we have in life and the ability to feel good and to cope. If we can think clearly and coherently, then we are more likely to be intellectually healthy. It also deals with the need to grow and learn and our capacity to become self-actualising.

Self-actualisation is worth mentioning since it is a term much used by psychologists. Kurt Goldstein (1878–1965) and Carl Rogers (1961) referred to this as a 'basic drive', and one which would enable us to reach our full potential. Maslow's hierarchy of needs (1970) has 'self-actualisation' at the apex of the pyramid and refers to creativity, motivation and development of problem-solving skills.

Emotional health is about our capacity to love and feel loved, and to be able to voice our emotions in a responsible manner in order to maintain relationships with others.

Being involved in these sorts of relationships and having a sense of support in our lives is all about **social health**. Our ability to make friends and to be involved in activities with others is incorporated here as well.

Spiritual health is often a difficult one to recognise since not all of us have a belief in a god or a religion. Some individuals have a strong need to belong to a group or organised religion and feel they are not complete without a belief of this kind. But spiritual health can also be about our moral principles and the way in which we live and have purpose in our lives. For these people, the concept of a god or a need to be part of a religion is unnecessary, they just want to live 'good' lives.

Sexual health is about how we accept and express our own sexuality.

All of the above represent our individual dimensions of health but clearly we are also affected by external influences. For example, the wider society in which we live, where we live and the sort of environment we live in will all have influences on our health and well-being (from Tilmouth *et al.*, 2011).

2.2 Promote a culture among the workforce of considering all aspects of individuals' well-being in day-to-day practice

2.3 Review the extent to which systems and processes promote individual well-being

In order to promote psychological well-being, let's take as our starting point Ryff's 1989 Psychological Well-being Inventory. In engendering a culture that promotes well-being in our day-to-day practice, we need to ensure we have an awareness of the aspects of well-being and what it is our clients may need.

Self-acceptance

The way in which we view our own lives and ourselves is a major source of well-being. If we are satisfied with who we are, and can live with our past experiences without bitterness or regret, then we can have contentment with our current situation. Self-acceptance is about coming to terms with what we can't change or control and so often we meet people who are unable to do this. This may lead them into undertaking therapy to make the change or they may simply continue along the same path not realising the potential for change.

Positive relations with others

Loving relationships and friendships where care and trust are apparent are so important to all of us and yet there may be a tendency to forget this in the workplace. Just as we value closeness and support of others, so too will our clients, but this can be neglected when we merely attend to physical needs. The need to be able to connect to others and have the opportunity to make friendships is just as important in long-term care as it is to us who can return home to our families each night.

Autonomy

We all value our independence and can possibly remember how it felt to be truly free of certain constraints when we were younger. Being free to make choices and our own decisions is a liberating time in our lives. Being in control of our own destiny is what autonomy refers to. Yet when a person goes into a care home or is ill for a long period of time, it is sometimes this aspect of their lives that is taken from them and often because care workers think this is the right thing to do. As unique people with our own identity, values and goals in life, we need to be able to maintain the ability to think and act for ourselves and this is part of care work, to empower our clients to do the same.

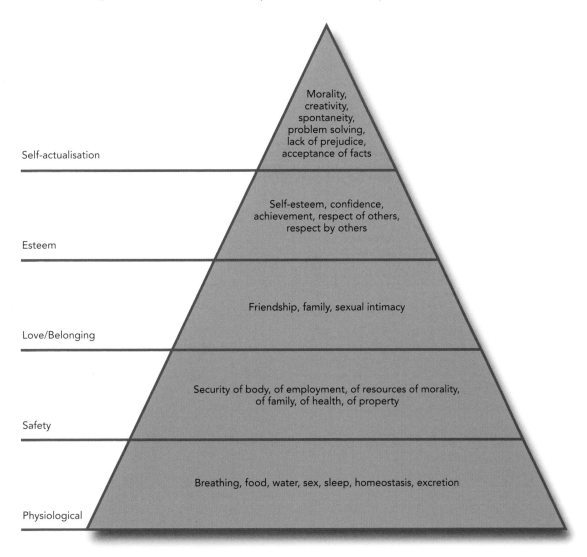

Figure 9.2 Maslow's hierarchy of needs

Mastery

Autonomy is about making decisions for ourselves and keeping control of our own lives and mastery is a similar concept. Being masters of our own environment and adapting to and modifying our situations in order to progress and achieve what we need is a vital part of this concept. It can be easy to see how this aspect of life can be taken from a person who is in long-term care. Although it may seem to be difficult to achieve in a long-term care situation, as care professionals it is imperative to keep the lines of communication open and to access the client's wishes and desires as to how they wish to live and what they need to do to control their circumstances as much as possible. This in turn will give them confidence and belief in our abilities which brings with it a sense of pride and success.

Purpose in life

Can you imagine a life without a purpose? Some of our clients may actually feel that once they are in long-term care or have a disability that prevents them from living the way they used to, life is not worth living. They need to be empowered to feel that there is something to strive for, even in changed circumstances. By enabling the client to continue to use their strengths and talents, to develop relationships and to pursue their goals, they can find real purpose in living.

Personal growth

We never stop learning so long as we are willing to be open to new experiences and seek out our potential. Just because our client is elderly or has to be in long-term care, as care professionals we need to encourage them to continue to be curious about aspects of life and to seek out opportunities to expand as a person.

The whole concept of well-being is about being comfortable in our lives where everything has come together. But the question is, how can you enable the people you care for to feel in this way?

The systems you have in place for managing care may seem to be counter-productive to promoting the things we talked about above. How, for example, are you able to allow a client to have mastery over their own environment when that environment is one in which a number of constraints operate with respect to the way it is managed and the procedures it operates? Or how much autonomy can a person have if they live in a care home?

We recognise there are constraints to enabling clients to live full and purposeful lives when it comes to service delivery and, of course, some things may be difficult to achieve. But a positive outcome for an individual is only possible if they are fully involved in deciding what that positive outcome will be. In planning the care of our clients, we need to have systems in place which allow the client to be at the centre of that care meeting and an equal partner in the decisions that are made.

Activity 9.2.2

In your own care setting how do you promote a culture among the workforce which shows consideration of all aspects of individuals' well-being? Write a case study which shows the systems and processes in place that promote individual well-being.

In the last activity you may have referred to the following sorts of things: An approach which does something more for the client than simply allowing them to have choice is one in which the person is valued, has dignity and is treated as the unique person they truly are (see Chapter 5).

Respect for the person comes about when care staff take the time to really get to know the person and take into account all the cultural and religious choices, values and preferences the person has.

Care work in this respect is not about humouring the client or ignoring certain aspects of the client's life that do not fit well with us; it is about equality in a relationship and supporting the client to live the life they want to in the circumstances they find themselves in. It's about them, not us!

3 Be able to lead practice that promotes individuals' health

3.1 Demonstrate the effective use of resources to promote good health and healthy choices in all aspects of the provision

As we saw in the last section, our overall health and well-being is a multi-faceted state and although we talk a lot about physical health, the other factors of emotional, social, spiritual and mental health are equally important and can positively affect almost every area of an individual's life: education, employment, family and relationships. It can help the individual to 'achieve their potential, realise their ambitions, cope with adversity, work productively and contribute to their community and society' (DOH, 2010a).

Figure 9.3 Promoting good health

The Department of Health in 2009 published their *New Horizons* document as part of a continuing programme of action to improve the mental health and well-being of the population. Two key objectives were identified within the publication:

1. Improving the mental health and well-being of the population.

2. Improving the quality and accessibility of services for people with poor mental health.

As a nation we spend 11% of the NHS annual budget on mental health services and recent estimates put the annual wider economic costs of mental health problems at around £77 billion.

It goes without saying that, in order to reduce such costs, promoting mental health and well-being in all aspects of our lives will significantly help. Research has shown a tangible link between poor mental health and wider health inequalities associated with increased health-risk behaviours and increased morbidity and mortality from physical ill health.

Promoting good mental health, therefore, has significant potential benefits – not only the improvement to health outcomes and life expectancy, but also improving educational and economic outcomes.

Evidence also points to the fact that half of all mental illness (excluding dementias) start by the age of 14, so by ensuring a positive start in life through interventions in the early years, there is a potential to decrease mental health issues by a quarter to a half.

The report goes on to suggest that:

'lifelong learning promotes resilience and thereby reduces the risk of mental illness, in particular in later life (p.13). It is also noted that early interventions are a key way of preventing mental ill health and promoting well-being, and that learning is a key method of intervention, with lifelong learning also noted as a key element in strategies to keep people active and participating.' (p.14)

Mental well-being is defined in *New Horizons* as a:

'positive state of mind and body, feeling safe and able to cope, with a sense of connection with people, communities and the wider environment.'

So rather than mental health being seen as the absence of mental illness, it takes on a much wider meaning. Good mental health and well-being are associated with improved outcomes for individuals in all walks of life, whatever their age.

A further guidance paper, published in 2010 entitled *Confident Communities and Brighter Futures: A framework for developing well-being*, outlined the mental health policy further.

The vision, to create confident communities and brighter futures through well-being for all, is supported by a number of strategies to enable achievement. The framework for action included the following areas:

■ Taking a life course approach – ensuring a positive start in life by developing personal resilience and educational and social skills. For the elderly, suggestions for maintaining mental health in later years include reducing poverty, keeping active, keeping warm, lifelong learning, social connections and community engagement, such as volunteering.

■ Building strength, safety and resilience – through interventions aimed at preventing violence, reducing poverty, debt, unemployment, poor housing and homelessness, and mitigating the impacts of climate change.

■ Developing sustainable, connected communities – by reducing social exclusion and addressing stigma and discrimination. Enhance sustainable communities by promoting social and ecological engagement to develop connected, inclusive communities.

■ Integrating physical and mental health. The key interventions suggested in the government guidance include targeting health improvement programmes and physical health checks for people with mental health problems. By improving the early intervention and treatment of mental health problems, including referral for psychological therapies, the health outcomes for people with physical illnesses can be improved.

■ Promoting purpose and participation. In this outcome, the guidance suggests that well-being can be enhanced through a balance of physical and mental activity, a positive outlook, creativity and purposeful community activity.

Activity 9.3.1

In your own workplace how do you promote good health and healthy choices in all aspects of the provision?

Demonstrate how you put your resources to effective use with respect to this aspect of well-being.

(3.2) Use *appropriate methods* to meet the health needs of individuals

Services for our clients are provided by a range of professionals and in a variety of ways. In planning care for positive outcomes, the care worker needs to work with the client to ensure that the best services are offered to meet the needs of the client. Care planning is about what the client needs and wants, not about what the care worker can arrange for them. Sometimes this may led to conflict. For example, we, as care professionals, recognise that obesity can cause all sorts of health issues and may believe that it is in our client's best interests to diet. However, the choice remains with them and we can only investigate services that may be of use to them with this issue. We are not at liberty to insist they use them.

Some of the things you may be asked to help with are outlined below:

- Agreed therapeutic/development activities
- Regular health checks
- Administering prescribed medication/treatment
- Promoting/supporting healthy lifestyle choices.

As you will be aware, there are national minimum standards for different services and you should familiarise yourself with these. These can be accessed at www.cqc.org.uk.

Standard Two of the National Framework for Elderly People outlines person-centred care and gives us guidance as to how we should go about meeting the health needs of the elderly. We paraphrase some of the guidance in the box below and have tried to highlight just a couple of the main points with respect to meeting the health needs of the elderly client.

Standard 2

NHS and social care services treat older people as individuals and enable them to make choices about their own care. This is achieved through the single assessment process, integrated commissioning arrangements and integrated provision of services, including community equipment and continence services.

Rationale

2.1 Older people and their carers should receive person-centred care and services which respect them as individuals and which are arranged around their needs. Person-centred care requires managers and professionals to:

- listen to older people
- respect their dignity and privacy 57 (C1) 58 (U) 59 (D/C2)
- recognise individual differences and specific needs 60 (C1/D) including cultural and religious differences 61 (P)
- enable older people to make informed choices, involving them in all decisions about their needs and care 62 (P)
- provide co-ordinated and integrated service responses
- involve and support carers whenever necessary.

2.3 Proper assessment of the range and complexity of older people's needs and prompt provision of care (including community equipment) can improve their ability to function independently; reduce the need for emergency hospital admission; and decrease the need for premature admission to a residential care setting 65 (A1).

2.5 The NHS and local councils should ensure that services meet the assessed needs of older people in ways that value and respect their individuality, their dignity and their privacy. This starts with:

- appropriate personal and professional behaviour by staff in all care settings, which can be particularly important at the end of life;
- providing information so the service user and, where appropriate their carer, can be involved in decisions about their own care.

2.6 Person-centred care needs to be supported by services that are organised to meet needs. The NHS and councils should deploy the 1999 Health Act flexibilities to:

- establish joint commissioning arrangements for older people's services, including consideration of a lead commissioner and the use of pooled budgets;
- ensure an integrated approach to service provision, such that they are person centred, regardless of professional or organisational boundaries.

Personal and professional behaviour

2.8 Service users and their carers should be able to expect that 75 (P) 76 (D/C2):

- staff are polite and courteous at all times, for example, using the older person's preferred form of address and relating to them as a competent adult;
- procedures are in place to identify and, where possible, meet any particular needs and preferences relating to gender, personal appearance, communication, diet, race or culture, and religious and spiritual beliefs 77 (P) 78 (P);
- staff communicate in ways which meet the needs of all users and carers, including those with sensory impairment, physical or mental frailty, or learning disability or those whose first or preferred language is not English. Interpreting and translation services should be made available 79 (B3) 80 (P).

2.12 Older people need information about:

- their own health – how they can improve their health through the promotion of health and well-being and the prevention of illness 94 (C1) 95 (B3);
- their assessment, investigation, diagnosis, treatment, rehabilitation and care;
- any referral procedures or eligibility criteria;

- the range of local health and social services and housing services available, for example, from local *Better Care, Higher Standards*;

- charters; the range of services and equipment available to meet their needs; and, where needed, training on appropriate use of equipment. As more information about the performance of services locally is being made available, this too will help to inform older people's choices.

2.13 Older people should be involved in making their own decisions, where this is possible and is what they wish, about the options available to them. Last year, direct payments for social services were extended to older people giving them more choice and control over their care options. It is also for the older person to determine the level of personal risk they are prepared to take when making decisions about their own health and circumstances 96 (C2).

2.14 In order to make decisions about their care older people need:

- to understand their care – letters between clinicians about an individual patient's care will be copied to the patient if that is their wish 97 (P), and service users will be given a copy of their care plan;

- the opportunity to ask questions including about their medicines, why they have been prescribed, and any possible side-effects;

- contact points for further information and support, such as local voluntary organisations and independent advocacy services;

- a named contact in case of problems or emergencies;

- to know how to complain 98 (P) 99 (U).

2.15 All information should be provided in appropriate formats. This may include providing information:

- in a range of languages, depending on local needs 100 (B3) 101 (P) 102 (P), or as visual or spoken information, as well as the written word;

- for people with sensory impairment through languages such as the British Sign Language and the deaf blind manual; and in accessible formats, for example via large print letters, telephone, e-mail, or textphone;

- in formats accessible to those with literacy or learning difficulties, for example, easy-read versions of leaflets using simple language and pictures 103 (C1) 104 (B3) 105 (C1/C).

One of the essential factors in any care planning and provision is to adopt a holistic approach, recognising that all clients, young,

older or disabled either physically or with a learning disability, are individuals with needs which impact upon their lives. It is important to give individuals choice and doing so requires you to have information about services which are available and to give out that information in an unbiased way. You may often be asked 'What would you do or what would you choose?'; the answer to which has to be, 'I am not you and it is for you to decide'!

Figure 9.4 All clients are individuals

Activity 9.3.2

Supervise a member of staff carrying out a care assessment and evaluate the extent to which the member of staff used appropriate methods to meet the health needs of individuals.

How might they improve on the assessment and how can you ensure as a manager that all staff are fully aware of what is required of them with respect to the national minimum standards for your own setting?

3.3 Implement practice and protocols for involving appropriate professional health care expertise for individuals

3.4 Develop a plan to ensure the workforce has the necessary training to recognise individual health care needs

4.4 Develop a plan to ensure the workforce has the necessary training to support individuals to achieve outcomes

This section is a self-directed assessment activity. The box on the following page contains a list of websites that might be useful for staff training purposes.

Policy websites

National policies on learning disabilities

Equal Lives (Northern Ireland) www. rmhldni.gov.uk

Fulfilling the Promises (Wales) www.wales. gov.uk

The Same as You (Scotland) www.scotland. gov.uk

Valuing People (England) www.dh.gov.uk/ en/Publicationsandstatistics/Publications/ PublicationsPolicyandGuidance/DH_4009153

Law on consent to treatment

Office of the Public Guardian: Mental Capacity Act (2005) www.publicguardian. gov.uk

Northern Ireland: Guidance on Consent to Treatment (2003) www.dhsspsni.gov.uk

Scottish Executive: Adults with Incapacity Act (2000) www.scotland.gov.uk

Other laws and policies

Carers and Disabled Children's Act (2000) www.opsi.gov.uk

Disability Discrimination Act (1995) www. opsi.gov.uk

Human Rights Act (1998) www.opsi.gov.uk

Mental Health Act (2007) www.dh.gov.uk

Mental Health (Care and Treatment) (Scotland) Act 2003 www.opsi.gov.uk

NHS and Community Care Act (1990) www. opsi.gov.uk

Activity 9.3.3

For your portfolio, list and evaluate the policies and protocols for involving appropriate professional health care expertise for individuals in your work setting.

Develop and implement staff training to ensure the workforce is able to recognise individual health care needs and can support individuals to achieve outcomes.

---

4 Be able to lead inclusive provision that gives individuals choice and control over the outcomes they want to achieve

4.1 Explain the necessary steps in order for individuals to have choice and control over decisions

In any decision being made, the person who is at the centre of making that decision has to feel they are actively doing so. Too often a client may feel they are merely a passive attendant at a meeting, with little say in what goes on. We take for granted the work we do with all its related administration, meetings and bureaucracy. For a client, this may seem rather overwhelming and it would take a lot of confidence on their part to question anything you may put forward. The following steps may help:

Step 1

The client needs to be clear about who they want involved in their care but may rely on you to help them to identify the specialist help. For example, a client who is being cared for at home by their spouse may not realise that special equipment to help her and her husband cope at home is available.

Step 2

Monitor the process of the care arrangements as you go along and check that the client is clear about what has happened so far. It is important that the communication method is suitable for the client. If, for example, the client has trouble with reading documents of small print, you need to ensure that they have access to large print versions. The client may also need extra assistance if English is not their first language and interpreters may be required at each meeting.

Step 3

It may be that your client has previous case notes with another agency and, in this step, you need to obtain your client's consent to obtain these notes. The client needs to be informed of all aspects of their care, including the need to contact others for additional information.

Step 4

Recording the above step is necessary and your client may be asked to sign to confirm that they have agreed for certain information to be released. If at any point your client does not give consent for any action, this must be respected.

Step 5

Just as you need to monitor the process throughout, you must also ensure that feedback from the client and family and friends is forthcoming regularly. Positive feedback will mean that, of course, the process is running well. However, any concerns must always be dealt with in an efficient and non-judgemental way. If the client wishes to make a complaint, then it is up to you to support them in accessing the correct procedures to do so.

Activity 9.4.1

Show how the assessment in Activity 9.3.2 enabled the client to exercise choice and control over decisions. Provide the care plan with annotations to show where each step has been accomplished.

4.2 Manage resources so that individuals can achieve positive outcomes

4.3 Monitor and evaluate progress towards the achievement of outcomes

Any plan of care produced needs to be resourced in terms of finances, as well as the availability of services, which may of course change over time. This is why a continual check on what is happening with the client's care needs to be made.

Funding may be reduced or demand for a particular service may increase, thus making it more difficult for your client to access the service. Adjustments to the plan should be and in accordance with how it is progressing.

Activity 9.4.2

How does your organisation monitor the resources and evaluate progress towards the achievement of outcomes for your clients? Write a reflective account of the process undertaken and place copies of relevant documentation into your portfolio.

In answer to the above activity, it is likely that you have in place an evaluation system to enable all involved in the care to comment and document how that care is working.

Lay carers, the client themselves and the service providers all need to be regularly providing feedback about the circumstances of the care package and any need for adjustment. At the start of the whole care planning process, you will have put into place a means for providing feedback. You will also have identified some key people in the process; these being the:

- individual receiving the care
- family and friends involved in the care
- health care professionals
- service provider.

Individual receiving the care

Being the central figure in the care process, there needs to be a clear process for the client to record how they experience the care they are receiving. This can be achieved by the use of a checklist, perhaps on a weekly or monthly basis, regular contact via e-mail, telephone or meetings with the care manager or the person facilitating the care, and recording the care given on a daily basis on the care plan.

Family and friends involved in the care

Feedback from these individuals is valuable but form filling can be laborious and time consuming. They may feel overwhelmed with having to provide a regular feedback form so you need to be able to obtain their views in different ways. Perhaps a weekly phone call may be the way in which to do this and can be part of the care package.

Health care professionals

By agreeing what will trigger a contact at the start of the care process, you can ensure that again contact is maintained and care is monitored. For example, you may agree to notification only if the client's condition changes.

Any problems with taking medication or medication being ineffective may also trigger a response. If mobility problems change or the client starts to refuse certain aspects of the care, this will also be a sign that contact with the care manager needs to be made. In between regular review meetings, these instances will ensure the seamless delivery of care and that the client is not at risk of inadequate care.

The service provider

As the care manager, you are in the best position to monitor the client's care and to notice any change. You can tell whether a service requires changing or increasing by being in close contact with the client on a daily basis.

4.5 Implement systems and processes for recording the identification, progress and achievement of outcomes

5.2 Implement systems, procedures and practices that engage carers, families and significant others

The whole process of monitoring and evaluating the care package is about recognising and documenting changes to circumstances. You will already have in place systems that record the care to be provided and also evaluate that care. As a service provider, you are also duty bound to regularly ask for feedback from clients and their family about how well you do in the delivery of your service.

Activity 9.4.3

Collect together the documentation you use to show how you go about recording progress in care and the achievement of client outcomes and which show the systems and practices that engage others.

5 Be able to manage effective working partnerships with carers, families and significant others to achieve positive outcomes

5.1 Analyse the importance of effective working relationships with carers, families and significant others for the achievement of positive outcomes

In the course of our working life, we interact with many people and it should come as no surprise that the quality of these interactions can have a profound effect, not only on our own health and well-being, and our enjoyment of work, but also for those with whom we interact. For our client, we have a responsibility to ensure that these working relationships promote their best interests and work towards positive outcomes in their care package.

To remind ourselves of the role of the health and social care worker, we turn to Standard One in the Common Induction Standards which clearly outline the responsibilities and limits of your relationship with an individual in your care.

Citing the General Social Care Council's Code of Conduct, your responsibilities are to:

■ Protect their rights and promote their interests.

■ Establish and maintain their trust and confidence.

■ Promote their independence and protect them as far as possible from danger or harm.

■ Respect their rights and ensure their behaviour does not harm themselves or other people.

■ Uphold public trust and confidence.

■ Be accountable for the quality of your work and take responsibility for maintaining and improving your knowledge and skill.

Whilst you may feel confident that you do all of the above and maintain good working relationships with all individuals you come into contact with, we need to be mindful of the actual relationship between health care professionals and those requiring care.

For example, look at the language the standards use and note the use of the word 'their'. This seems to imply a passive relationship in which the health professional is 'doing something' to the individual. For us, it conjures up a relationship in which the health professional takes on the responsibility of ensuring that the individual is 'cared for' rather than a major part of their own care.

The difficulty we believe is in the hierarchical nature of the relationship between health professional and the client which, try as we might to diminish, is still prevalent. The power the health care professional possesses in terms of knowledge and expertise, the language used in care work, professional autonomy and the environment in which we work will all have an effect on the relationship if not carefully handled. It is the transfer of the power to the client which is fraught with difficulty and one which needs to be worked on constantly.

Positive benefits come from effective team work and by seeing the client as the central figure in the team working towards their own care package, the relationship forged will be effective. The Health Care Commission in 2006 outlined the characteristics of a good team as having the following in place:

■ Clear objectives

■ Close working relationship towards those objectives

■ Regular meetings to discuss ways of improving and outcomes achieved

■ No more than 15 members.

Although these characteristics are more often applied to teams in health care settings, we make no apologies by applying it to the team that makes up the care providers for the client. By adopting this sort of strategy, we can expect the working relationship between all parties to be improved.

Activity 9.5.1

Provide a case study which outlines how you have achieved effective working relationships with carers, families and significant others for the achievement of positive outcomes.

5.3 Use *appropriate approaches to address conflicts and dilemmas* that may arise between individuals, staff and carers, families and significant others

In Chapter 7 we cited Thompson's (2006) RED approach to managing conflict and revisit it here.

R – **R**ecognise the conflict; do not sweep it under the carpet

E – **E**valuate the conflict to see how detrimental it would be if it was allowed to develop

D – **D**eal with the conflict; keep open communication

Appropriate ways in which to deal with any barriers and conflicts which arise can be on a one-to-one basis or in group discussion. Providing information to enable the client and the team involved in their care to make informed decisions may also help the process and reduce the conflict. Conflict may sometimes be the result of lack of information which causes distress and may lead to angry outbursts.

The way in which you deal with and resolve conflict comes from your favoured leadership approach. The skills approach developed by Mumford *et al.* (2000) lists within its five components social judgement skills as one of the competencies required in dealing with conflict. The capacity to understand people and social systems serves to enable leaders to work with others to solve problems and to implement change. Part of this competency is *social performance* and this refers to the skill of persuasion in communicating with others. Any

conflict can be resolved if the leader acts as a mediator in the process.

A further useful approach in dealing with conflict is that proposed in Heifetz's approach to ethical leadership (1994). In this approach, the solution to conflict is to effect a change. Heifetz puts forward the view that leadership involves the use of authority to deal with conflicting values. In the conflict situation, the ethical leader will inspire trust, empathy and nurture in order to help others feel safe in facing difficult situations. In this model, leaders act to:

- enable others to pay attention to the issues
- give information
- manage and frame the issues
- look at the conflicting issues
- facilitate decision making.

(Adapted from Northouse, 2010)

Activity 9.5.2

Demonstrate the approach you use to deal with conflict and say which model you favour and why

5.4 Explain how *legislation and regulation influence working relationships with carers, families and significant others*

5.5 Implement *safe and confidential recording systems and processes to provide effective information sharing and recording*

This section is covered in Chapter 1 and you are asked to re-read this now.

Activity 9.5.3

Complete a case study to show how you deal with clients' confidential information with respect to person-centred care and positive outcomes.

Summary

All individuals requiring care must be dealt with holistically, with their individual needs being met. One of the problems experienced in care over the past 60 years or so is that the identification of 'needs' is highly subjective. Working with clients in a needs-led approach has often meant that professionals were focussing on the immediate situation and support requirements and care planning thus became a 'one size fits all' approach. This meant the client used the services that were available and offered to them by care workers rather than receiving care that was more suited to their own individual needs and wants. Clients were passive recipients of care and not involved in the care planning process. As a result of much research and change within the health care system, the 'personalisation' agenda was introduced so that a system of care and support tailored to meet the needs of the individual replaced the former system.

For positive outcomes for all those we care for as care workers and managers we need to work *with* the client to ensure that the best services are offered to meet the needs of the client.

Learning outcomes	Assessment criteria
1 Understand the theory and principles that underpin outcome based practice	(1.1) **Explain 'outcome based practice'** **Activity 9.1.1, p.158**
	(1.2) **Critically review approaches to outcome based practice** **Activity 9.1.2, p.159**
	(1.3) **Analyse the effect of legislation and policy on outcome based practice** **Activity 9.1.3, p.160**
	(1.4) **Explain how outcome based practice can result in positive changes in individuals' lives** **Activity 9.1.4, p.160**
2 Be able to lead practice that promotes social, emotional, cultural, spiritual and intellectual well-being	(2.1) **Explain the psychological basis for well-being** **Activity 9.2.1, p.161**
	(2.2) **Promote a culture among the workforce of considering all aspects of individuals' well-being in day-to-day practice** **Activity 9.2.2, p.164**
	(2.3) **Review the extent to which systems and processes promote individual well-being** **Activity 9.2.2, p.164**

3 Be able to lead practice that promotes individuals' health	**3.1** Demonstrate the effective use of resources to promote good health and healthy choices in all aspects of the provision **Activity 9.3.1, p.165**
	3.2 Use appropriate methods to meet the health needs of individuals **Activity 9.3.2, p.167**
	3.3 Implement practice and protocols for involving appropriate professional health care expertise for individuals **Activity 9.3.3, p.168**
	3.4 Develop a plan to ensure the workforce has the necessary training to recognise individual health care needs **Activity 9.3.3, p.168**
4 Be able to lead inclusive provision that gives individuals' choice and control over the outcomes they want to achieve	**4.1** Explain the necessary steps in order for individuals to have choice and control over decisions **Activity 9.4.1, p.169**
	4.2 Manage resources so that individuals can achieve positive outcomes **Activity 9.4.2, p.169**
	4.3 Monitor and evaluate progress towards the achievement of outcomes **Activity 9.4.2, p.169**
	4.4 Develop a plan to ensure the workforce has the necessary training to support individuals to achieve outcomes **Activity 9.4.3, p.168**
	4.5 Implement systems and processes for recording the identification, progress and achievement of outcomes **Activity 9.4.3, p.170**

Learning outcomes	Assessment criteria
5 Be able to manage effective working partnerships with carers, families and significant others to achieve positive outcomes	**(5.1)** **Analyse the importance of effective working relationships with carers, families and significant others for the achievement of positive outcomes** **Activity 9.5.1, p.171**
	(5.2) **Implement systems, procedures and practices that engage carers, families and significant others** **Activity 9.4.3, p.170**
	(5.3) **Use appropriate approaches to address conflicts and dilemmas that may arise between individuals, staff and carers, families and significant others** **Activity 9.5.2, p.171**
	(5.4) **Explain how legislation and regulation influence working relationships with carers, families and significant others** **Activity 9.5.3, p.171**
	(5.5) **Implement safe and confidential recording systems and processes to provide effective information sharing and recording** **Activity 9.5.3, p.171**

References

Barnes, C. and Mercer, G. (eds) (2004) *Disability Policy and Practice: Applying the social model.* Leeds: The Disability Press.

Department of Health (1989) *Caring for People: Community care in the next decade and beyond.* London: HMSO.

Department of Health (2000) *National Service Framework – for Older People.* London: HMSO.

Department of Health (2001) *Valuing People: a new strategy for learning disability for the 21st century.* London: HMSO.

Department of Health (2005) *Independence, Wellbeing and Choice: Our Vision for the future of social care for adults in England.* London: HMSO.

Department of Health (2006) *Our Health, Our Care, Our Say: A new direction for community service.* London: HMSO.

Depatment of Health (2007) *Putting People First: A shared vision and commitment to transformation of adult social care.* London: HMSO.

Department of Health (2009) *Personal Health Budgets: First steps.* London: HMSO.

Department of Health (2009) *Care, Support, Independence: Shaping the future of care together.* London: HMSO

Department of Health (2010a) *New Horizons: Confident communities, brighter futures: A framework for developing wellbeing.* London: HMSO.

Department of Health (2010b) *A Vision for Adult Social Care: Capable communities and active citizens.* London: HMSO.

Ewles, L. and Simnett, I. (1999) *Promoting Health: A practical guide to health education* (4e). Edinburgh: Harcourt.

Harris, J., Foster, M., Jackson, K. and Morgan, H. (2005) *Outcomes for Disabled Service Users.* York: Social Policy Research Unit, University of York.

Heifetz, R (1994) *Leadership without easy answers.* Cambridge, Mass.: The Belknap Press of Harvard University Press.

HM Government (2009) *New Horizons: A shared vision for mental health*. London: HMSO.

HM Government (1990) *The NHS and Community Care Act 1990*. London: HMSO.

HM Government (2005) *Improving the Life Chances of Disabled People*. A joint report with Department of Work and Pensions, Department of Health, Department for Education and Skills, Office of the Deputy Prime Minister. London: HMSO.

Kishida, Y., Kitamura, T., Gatayama, R., Matsuoka, T., Miura, S. and Yamabe, K. (2004) 'Ryff's Psychological Well-Being Inventory: Factorial structure and life history correlates among Japanese university students.' *Psychological Reports*, 94(1) pp.83–103.

Maclean, I., Maclean, S. and Pardy McLaughlin, L. (2002) *A Handbook of Theory for Social Care*. Volume Two. London: City and Guilds.

Maslow, A. H. (1970) *Motivation and Personality* (2e). New York: Harper and Row.

Mumford, M.D., Zaccharo, S.J., Connolly, M.S. and Marks, M.A (2000) 'Leadership Skill: Conclusions and future directions'. *Leadership Quarterly*, 11(1), pp.155–70.

Northouse, P. (2010) *Leadership Theory and Practice* (5e). Thousand Oaks, CA: Sage.

Qureshi, H., Patmore, C., Nicholas, E. and Bamford, C. (1998) *Overview: Outcomes of social care for older people and carers*, Outcomes in Community Care Practice No. 5. York: Social Policy Research Unit, University of York.

Qureshi, H., Bamford, C., Nicholas, E., Patmore, C. and Harris, J. (2000) *Outcomes in Social Care Practice: Developing an outcome focus in care management and user surveys*. York: Social Policy Research Unit, University of York.

Rogers, C. (1961) *On Becoming a Person: a Therapist's View of Psychotherapy*. Boston: Houghton Mifflin.

Thompson, N. (2006) *People Problems*. Basingstoke: Palgrave Macmillan

Tilmouth, T., Davies-Ward, E. and Williams, B. (2011) *Foundation Studies in Health and Social Care*. London: Hodder & Stoughton.

World Health Organizaion (1946) *Consititution of the World Health Organization*. http://whqlibdoc.who.int/hist/official_records/constitution.pdf

World Health Organizaion (2002) *Mental Health Policy and Service Guidance Package: Workplace Mental Health Policies and Programmes*. Draft document, Geneva: World Health Organization, Department of Mental Health and Substance Development (unpublished document)

Unit P1 Safeguarding and protection of vulnerable adults

The purpose of this chapter is to enable you to engage with issues related to the protection and safeguarding of vulnerable adults. The unit requires that you understand the legal and regulatory basis for safeguarding and know the actions to take and procedures to follow and the chapter will introduce you to the legal framework and the best practice with respect to handling situations where abuse may be suspected. One of the key steps in safeguarding is to work in partnership with other organisations in order to achieve the best possible outcomes and this chapter will help you to address this area of your work.

Learning outcomes

By the end of this chapter you will:

1. Understand the legislation, regulations and policies that underpin the protection of vulnerable adults.

2. Be able to lead service provision that protects vulnerable adults.

3. Be able to manage inter-agency, joint or integrated working in order to protect vulnerable adults.

4. Be able to monitor and evaluate the systems, processes and practice that safeguard vulnerable adults.

1 Understand the legislation, regulations and policies that underpin the protection of vulnerable adults

1.1 **Analyse the differences between the concept of safeguarding and the concept of protection in relation to vulnerable adults**

Safeguarding was defined in the Children Act of 1989 and the Joint Chief Inspectors Report on Arrangements to Safeguard Children (2002) as meaning that:

'Agencies [and organisations] working with children and young people take all reasonable measures to ensure that the risks of harm to the individual's welfare are minimised; and where there are concerns about children and young people's welfare, all agencies [and organisations] take all appropriate actions to address those concerns, working to agreed local policies and procedures, working in partnership with other local agencies.'

The term 'safeguarding practices' is most commonly applied to children and young people under the age of 18 and is further differentiated in some texts where 'children' refers to those under the age of 18 who are still in full-time education, and 'young people' as those under the age of 18 who have left full-time education. We deal more fully with the legislation for children in Chapter 12.

With respect to adults, key aspects of legislation include similar standards of protection to 'vulnerable adults'. A vulnerable adult is defined as an individual aged 18 or over who depends on others for assistance with respect to the performance of basic functions or who has a severe impairment in the ability to communicate and therefore a reduced ability to protect themselves from assault, abuse or neglect. But there is a debate about the difference in definitions which seem to surround this subject.

The Department of Health's definition of a vulnerable adult refers to a person who:

'may be in need of community care services by reason of mental or other disability, age or illness; and who is or may be unable to care of him or herself, or unable to protect him or herself against significant harm or exploitation.'

(DOH, 2000, pp.8–9).

This definition does seem to identify groups of people such as the elderly as being vulnerable and we may find this unacceptable. It is, after all, the situation in which the person finds themselves that makes them vulnerable not the actual individual, necessarily. There are many elderly people who would be most upset to be termed vulnerable just by virtue of the fact that they happen to be over 65, for instance.

CSCI in their 2008 document *Raising Voices: Views on safeguarding adults* further addressed the definition debate, going as far as commenting that such a lack of clarity with respect to the terms used also led to confusion over the roles and responsibilities of care workers responding to concerns (McKibbin *et al.*, 2008).

There does not seem to be a commonly accepted definition for 'safeguarding adults' and, as such, your own policies need to clarify the terms for your staff in order to ensure that a shared understanding is at least possible for your workplace. A useful exercise is to discuss the terms with the staff to check their own understanding.

1.2 **Evaluate the impact of *policy developments* on approaches to safeguarding vulnerable adults in own service setting**

1.3 **Explain the legislative framework for safeguarding vulnerable adults**

Our work in the care system is governed by the legal system and you will be familiar with the laws to which we work. However, with respect to protecting vulnerable adults in care, the legal framework provides only guidelines with respect to rights and service provision but does not specifically mention protection. Children are protected from abuse under the Children Act 1989.

The following laws provide guidance as to the rights and requirements for service provision but there was limited mention of protection *per se* until the Care Standards Act was published in 2000. This Act set out the Protection of Vulnerable Adults (POVA) scheme which was then implemented on a phased basis from 26 July 2004.

- National Assistance Act 1948

- Mental Health Act 1983

- Mental Health Bill 2004

- Mental Capacity Act 2005

- Chronically Sick and Disabled Persons Act 1986

- Disability Discrimination Act 1995

- NHS Community Care Act 1990

- Safeguarding Vulnerable Groups Act 2006

- Adult Support and Protection Act (Scotland) 2007.

These laws have developed over a number of years and occasionally come about as a response to cases of concern being highlighted in the media. This has led to an alarming number of changes to law over time as a result

of investigations into abuse in institutions and towards individuals. Clearly things had to change and the response by government was to address the protection of adults through guidelines and policy documents. The year 2000 and a couple of years leading up to this date saw several publications from the government all seeking to address the issue of adult abuse.

The Human Rights Act of 1998 aimed to protect adults from abuse and, if we have a role in the public sector, we also have responsibility to comply with this Act. It does not, however, apply to those who work for private providers or who provide services to direct payment users. These services are not liable for prosecution under this Act for abuses of human rights although the government is expected to review this situation soon.

The government's White Paper *Modernising Social Services*, published at the end of 1998, sought to provide better protection for individuals needing care and support but it was with the express intention of addressing the need for greater protection to victims and witnesses of abuse that the government actively implemented the measures proposed in *Speaking Up for Justice*, a report on the treatment of vulnerable or intimidated witnesses in the criminal justice system. Recognising that there was a difficulty expressing concern about abuse because of the potential consequences to the informant of reporting abuse crime, it was agreed that local multi-agency codes of practice would be the best way forward.

The *No Secrets* (2000) government publication came about as a response to the ever increasing media coverage of adult abuse. The guidance ensured that local authorities were responsible for coordinating the development of policy to protect the vulnerable individual through multi-agency working and setting up Safeguarding Adults Boards and Vulnerable Adults Safeguarding policies and procedures. In addition, the Care Standards Act of the same year set out the Protection of Vulnerable Adults (POVA) scheme to be rolled out on a phased basis, being fully implemented by 2004. The Welsh assembly also published their guidance *In Safe Hands, Implementing Adult Protection Procedures in Wales* (July 2000) as a response to the Welsh White Paper *Building for the Future* (1999) which identified the protection and promotion of the welfare of vulnerable adults as a priority and reinforcing the Welsh Assembly's respect for human rights and the provisions of the Human Rights Act 1998.

The White Paper *Valuing People: A new strategy for learning disability in the 21st century* published in 2001 was a landmark paper for people with learning disability and set out ways in which services would be improved, highlighting four main principles: namely civil rights, independence, choice and inclusion.

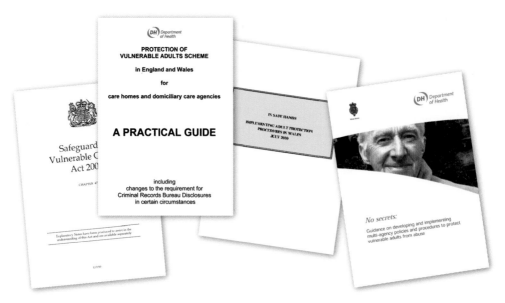

Figure 10.1 Some of the documents mentioned in this section

Quality of care for vulnerable adults was set to improve in a marked way because of these new initiatives, not least because of the changes to staff training, quality controls and the response by professional bodies to address codes of practice to bring them into line with National Minimum Standards.

It was the POVA scheme set out in the Care Standards Act 2000 and implemented in 2004 that went further to protect those in care from abuse by care providers. Central to the POVA scheme is the POVA list of care workers who have harmed vulnerable adults in their care. In appointing people to care work, it became a legal requirement from July 2004 to undertake checks through the Standard or Enhanced Disclosure application process from the Criminal Records Bureau (CRB).

Changes to the reporting system by way of the Vetting and Barring Scheme ('the Scheme') came about following the publication of the Bichard Inquiry (2004) which recommended a new scheme under which everyone working with children or vulnerable adults should be checked and registered. The Bichard Inquiry was commissioned following the murders of Holly Wells and Jessica Chapman and revelations that certain checks had been missed. More of this in Chapter 12.

Recognising the need for a single agency to vet and register individuals who want to work or volunteer with vulnerable people, the Independent Safeguarding Authority (ISA) was set up and the Criminal Records Bureau was made responsible for managing the system and processing the applications for ISA registration. The inquiry led to the Safeguarding Vulnerable Groups Act 2006 ('the Act') and the Safeguarding Vulnerable Groups Order (Northern Ireland) 2007 ('the Order') which set up the scheme.

Activity 10.1.1

All of the above legislation and guidelines changed the way in which care was being delivered, recognising the real threat of abuse and its impact. The CSCI, in association with the Association of Chief Police Officers (ACPO), the Association of Directors of Social Services (ADSS) and the DOH amongst others, published *Safeguarding Adults: A National Framework of standards for good practice and outcomes in adult protection work* (2005).

Obtain a copy of this now and evaluate the impact of this policy document and the subsequent standards outlined therein on approaches to safeguarding vulnerable adults in your own service setting. The list in the box below may be useful to you.

The National Framework of 11 sets of good practice standards are listed below:

Standard 1 Each local authority has established a multi-agency partnership to lead 'Safeguarding Adults' work.

Standard 2 Accountability for and ownership of 'Safeguarding Adults' work is recognised by each partner organisation's executive body.

Standard 3 The 'Safeguarding Adults' policy includes a clear statement of every person's right to live a life free from abuse and neglect, and this message is actively promoted to the public by the Local Strategic Partnership, the 'Safeguarding Adults' partnership, and its member organisations.

Standard 4 Each partner agency has a clear, well publicised policy of Zero-Tolerance of abuse within the organisation.

Standard 5 The 'Safeguarding Adults' partnership oversees a multi-agency workforce development/training sub-group. The partnership has a workforce development/training strategy and ensures that it is appropriately resourced.

Standard 6 All citizens can access information about how to gain safety from abuse and violence, including information about the local 'Safeguarding Adults' procedures.

Standard 7 There is a local multi-agency 'Safeguarding Adults' policy and procedure describing the framework for responding to all adults *who is[are] or may be eligible for community care services'* **and** who may be at risk of abuse or neglect.

Standard 8 Each partner agency has a set of internal guidelines, consistent with the local multi-agency 'Safeguarding Adults' policy and procedures, which set out the responsibilities of all workers to operate within it.

Standard 9 The multi-agency 'Safeguarding Adults' procedures detail the following stages: Alert, Referral, Decision, Safeguarding assessment strategy, Safeguarding assessment, Safeguarding plan, Review, Recording and Monitoring.

Standard 10 The safeguarding procedures are accessible to all adults covered by the policy.

Standard 11 The partnership explicitly includes service users as key partners in all aspects of the work. This includes building service-user participation into its membership; monitoring, development and implementation of its work; training strategy; and planning and implementation of their individual safeguarding assessment and plans.

1.4 Evaluate how serious case reviews or inquiries have influenced quality assurance, regulation and inspection relating to the safeguarding of vulnerable adults

In the 1960s Erving Goffman, an eminent sociologist, published his work entitled *Asylums: Essays on the Social Situation of Mental Patients and other Inmates*. This work proved to be a far-reaching one in that the findings highlighted the effects on individuals who were institutionalised due to mental illness. The ways

in which the staff worked served to maintain the status quo in the institution and affected the behaviour of the 'inmates' who took on the role of 'captor' rather than an individual requiring medical care. This led to the patient becoming 'institutionalised', a term we still use today. This dehumanising effect on patients led to further work in this area which started to uncover how such treatment could lead to abuse.

The task-focused way of care that was so prevalent in the 1970s and 1980s was brought under the spotlight as researchers made claims that rigid routines and treating individuals in the same way was poor practice.

As a student nurse in the mid-1970s, I can well recall the way in which the end of the night shift became a concerted effort by all night staff to ensure that patients were out of bed sitting in chairs by the time the Sister entered the ward at the start of the early shift. These patients were often out of bed by 6 a.m. and had to sit there until breakfast at 8.30 or 9, irrespective of how they were feeling or the condition they presented with. Our focus as nurses was to present a tidy ward, with tidy patients sat by tidy beds! Lee-Treweek's (2008) work on these sorts of practices showed how the needs of the staff and organisation were being met at the expense of the patients.

You may be forgiven for thinking that these sorts of practices, whilst poor, were not actually abuse but as research has shown, in treating individuals in this manner, little respect was being shown for them and this led to the dehumanising effects on people. This lack of recognition of individuals as thinking, feeling human beings led to more serious incidents being uncovered. We are well aware of some of these cases, not least the regime of abuse at the Winterbourne View unit, in Hambrook, near Bristol, which was exposed by the BBC *Panorama* programme.

Efforts to address such abuse has been on-going for a number of years. The House of Commons Report of 2003–4 on elder abuse highlighted the plight of the elderly and other vulnerable groups with respect to addressing issues of abuse. Recognising that abuse of older people is a hidden and often ignored phenomenon, the group identified the need to address these issues through a more robust system of care. Although precise figures to determine the extent of the problem were unavailable, at the time it was estimated that 500,000 older people in England could be subject to abuse.

Abuse occurring in institutional settings and in the home by care staff, relatives and friends, in the form of sexual and financial abuse, abuse of medication to control and sedate, physical abuse, neglect and behaviour designed to degrade and humiliate was fast becoming known through media coverage and reporting as a result of the changes brought about by the *No Secrets* document.

Failure to report abuse was found to be as much due to fear and embarrassment as ignorance of reporting procedures. In addition, the lack of training in identifying abuse for care staff was an issue and served to increase the difficulties in determining the true scale of the problem. Recommendations from the report included the need to apply an accurate definition of abuse which would be shared by all government departments, statutory agencies, independent bodies, charities and organisations. Further, performance indicators were to be established in order to enable accurate measurement of the problem to be undertaken. There was a move to ensure that the National Minimum Standards for domiciliary care were required to report adverse incidents, and the frequency and effectiveness of the inspection of NHS establishments providing care for older people was to be improved.

Activity 10.1.2

Download and read the report *Elder Abuse* on www.publications.parliament. uk/pa/cm200304/cmselect/ cmhealth/111/111.pdf

Write 500 words for your portfolio on how this report has influenced quality assurance, regulation and inspection relating to the safeguarding of vulnerable adults in your care setting.

Without doubt the serious cases reported in various research have moved government and health care organisations to address the issues relating to the vulnerable person in care.

In January 2006 the White Paper *Our Health, Our Care, Our Say* set a new direction for the whole health and social care system. With a radical move in the way services were delivered, there was a keen effort to ensure that a more personalised service was available, giving people a stronger voice to enable them to become the major drivers of service improvement.

In 2007 this was taken a step further with the *Putting People First: A shared vision and commitment to the transformation of adult social care* document. Recognising that the key elements of a reformed adult social care system in the UK had been outlined in several papers since 2000, this paper intended to set out a care system that addressed the demographic changes presented by an ageing population who would depend on long-term care way into the future. In implementing the guidance, targets for 2011 were set for local councils to provide a wide range of personalised services to improve the lives of people who need care and support at all levels. You would be correct in observing that the idea of individualised care is nothing new but the *Putting People First* paper represented a shift in culture responding in a more radical way to the changing demands of an ageing society.

The 'personalisation agenda' outlined in the paper supported this shift by recognising the need to view people as unique individuals rather than group them together and define them as a 'vulnerable client group'.

Local councils were to move the agenda along by providing individual budgets and self-directed support planning, along with services to help advise, recommend and coordinate things for those who were unable to arrange their own care. The key idea was that the vulnerable individual would be supported financially by the state and would have control over who provides their services.

The Department of Health Care shows that progress has been made in 148 out of 150 local councils in England. Some of the performance indicators are listed below:

- On 31 March 2009, almost 93,000 people were receiving Personal Budgets equating to over £681m of council expenditure.

- By the end of March 2010 it was expected this would rise to around 206,000 people.

- Four out of five authorities feel that the range and flexibility of provision has already improved, and over three-quarters believe that the development of preventative services in their area has significantly impacted on outcomes.

We have addressed the safeguarding arrangements for adults in this section but serious incidents relating to children have led to a number of inquiries being carried out and changes to the system have been put in place as a result. We cover these more fully in Chapter 12.

1.5 Explain the protocols and referral procedures when harm or abuse is alleged or suspected

Abuse is defined in *No Secrets* as:

> 'a violation of an individual's human or civil rights by any other person or persons.'

It may consist of a single or repeated act and may be physical, verbal, sexual, psychological, or an act of neglect or an omission to act. If a vulnerable person is persuaded to enter into a financial or sexual transaction to which he or she has not consented, or cannot consent, this is also abuse.

Action on Elder Abuse defines abuse as:

'A single or repeated act or lack of appropriate action, occurring within any relationship where there is an expectation of trust, which causes distress and harm to an older person.'

The protocols and procedures for reporting abuse are laid out in Standards 6, 7, 8 and 9 of the *Safeguarding Adults* document and are addressed briefly here.

Standard 6 makes provision for individuals to access information about how to remain safe from abuse in an attempt to uphold human rights. It ensures that any organisation receiving reports that an adult may be experiencing abuse or neglect responds in a positive and proactive manner and lays down procedures and timings for that reporting.

Standard 7 deals with the agencies involved in situations of abuse and highlights procedures for information sharing amongst multi-agencies.

Standard 8 identifies the partner agency systems and the internal reporting procedures for all partner agencies, together with protocols for accurately recording facts, together with the actions taken as a result. This standard also highlights the need for each organisation to have a 'whistle-blowing' policy and procedure that is linked to that of safeguarding adults, and is disseminated to staff and volunteers.

Standard 9 identifies a checklist for effective procedures detailing the stages that should be followed.

The table on the next page has been compiled from the actual guidelines.

Activity 10.1.3

Explain the protocols and referral procedures when harm or abuse is alleged or suspected in your own work setting.

In answering the above, you may have highlighted the safeguarding policy you have in place, together with the complaints procedure. In both cases these protocols need to be accessible and publicised to enable individuals ease of use. If anyone, care worker or client, suspects abuse they should be encouraged to use the protocols.

Confidentiality needs to be assured for all parties involved, and all complaints need to be taken seriously. The following checklist will be of help:

- Is everybody in your organisation aware of the existence of the policy?

- Is it located in an easily accessible place?

- Is it clearly written and available in other languages or other formats if necessary?

- Does it describe what will happen and the responses the person may expect?

The standard in the *Safeguarding Adults* document clearly recommends the appointment of safeguarding managers who receive specific training and support for the role. It goes on to point out that the worker who first becomes aware of concerns of abuse or neglect needs to ensure that emergency assistance, where required, is summoned immediately and if there is evidence of criminal activity, the police are contacted. Any information given directly by the adult concerned is listened to and recorded carefully, but the person is not questioned at this stage. Such questioning may create unnecessary stress and can also risk the contamination of evidence.

A referral to the multi-agency 'safeguarding adults' process is made and a record of the abuse, with the person making the report stating their name clearly, signing and dating it, is collated.

Figure 10.2 A care worker talking to a client

Consent is gained for the referral from an adult who is deemed mentally capable and is thought to be experiencing abuse, and a clear and concise report is compiled before any further action is taken.

Table 10.1 Guidelines from the *Safeguarding Adults* document

Action	Time frame
Alert Reporting concerns of abuse or neglect which are received or noticed within a partner organisation. Any immediate protection needs are addressed	**Alert** Immediate action to safeguard anyone at immediate risk
Referral Placing information about that concern into a multi-agency context	**Referral** Within the same working day
Decision Deciding whether the 'safeguarding adults' procedures are appropriate to address the concern	**Decision** By the end of the working day following the one on which the safeguarding referral was made
Safeguarding assessment strategy Formulating a multi-agency plan for assessing the risk and addressing any immediate protection needs	**Safeguarding assessment strategy** Within five working days
Safeguarding assessment Co-ordinating the collection of the information about abuse or neglect that has occurred or might occur. This may include an investigation, e.g. a criminal or disciplinary investigation	**Safeguarding assessment** Within four weeks of the safeguarding referral
Safeguarding plan Co-ordinating a multi-agency response to the risk of abuse that has been identified	**Safeguarding plan** Within four weeks of the safeguarding assessment being completed
Review The review of that plan	**Review** Within six months for first review and thereafter yearly

2 Be able to lead service provision that protects vulnerable adults

2.1 Promote service provision that supports vulnerable adults to assess risks and make informed choices

As we saw in the last section, the 'safeguarding adults' national framework provides national standards which address all issues pertaining to the protection of vulnerable adults. Underpinning all service provision should be the recognition of human rights as laid out in the Human Rights Act, particularly in relation to Article 2, 'the Right to Life', Article 3 'Freedom from Torture' (including humiliating and degrading treatment), and Article 8 'Right to Family Life'.

In all decision-making processes, human rights must be considered paramount. Your workplace should have in place a comprehensive risk assessment strategy which identifies risks relating to the workings of the organisation, how it provides its services, together with its delivery of individual activities and any strategy associated with its guardianship responsibility.

We look more closely at this in section 2.3 but in the meantime please undertake the following activity.

Activity 10.2.1

Obtain and read a copy of your organisation's risk assessment and safeguarding procedure.

2.2 Provide information to others on:

■ indicators of abuse

The NHS Choices: Your health, Your Choices website clearly details indicators of abuse in vulnerable adults whilst recognising that it is not always easy to spot the symptoms. As highlighted in the *No Secrets* document, reporting abuse is no easy thing to do and, due to embarrassment or fear, a vulnerable person may not wish to speak out. They may make excuses for why they have bruises or why they are always short of money. As the NHS website shows, waiting for the person to share their concerns with you may only delay matters and allow the abuse to continue.

There are, of course, behavioural signs to consider and these include:

■ becoming quiet and withdrawn

■ being aggressive or angry for no obvious reason

■ looking unkempt, dirty or thinner than usual

■ sudden changes in their normal character, such as appearing helpless, depressed or tearful

■ physical signs of abuse, such as bruises, wounds, fractures and other untreated injuries

■ the same injuries happening more than once

■ not wanting to be left on their own or alone with particular people

■ being unusually light-hearted and insisting there's nothing wrong.

(www.nhs.uk/CarersDirect/guide/vulnerable-people/Pages/vulnerable-adults.aspx)

Also changes in the individual's financial circumstances which result in debts arising or financial documents going missing should also alert the care worker to something being amiss.

■ measures that can be taken to avoid abuse taking place

It is a difficult task to take care of a vulnerable adult where there are a variety of needs and this increases the risk of abuse, both intended and unintended. By being aware of the situation and the needs of the vulnerable adult, the care professional can be forewarned as to the risk factors.

The responsibilities and demands of care-giving can be extremely stressful, leading to mental and physical health problems in the person undertaking the care role. Among carers, then, significant risk factors for abuse of vulnerable adults might include the following:

■ inability to cope with stress of the situation

■ depression

■ lack of support from others within the family or in a care organisation

■ substance abuse.

By recognising these sorts of signs in carers, we can provide support to ensure that the risk of abuse does not become an issue.

Support in the form of financial help and physical help from carers coming into the home may be of use to a family who can feel isolated in looking after vulnerable adults. For staff in care situations, either in organisations or working in the community, working in isolation and little training are also risk factors for abusive situations to arise. Inadequate resources or lack of other staff for support and heavy workloads are also factors that require addressing to prevent abuse.

Figure 10.3 A potentially abusive situation

Figure 10.4 Providing support

Activity 10.2.2

Think of your own workplace and indicate areas of concern with respect to the following:

- lack of staffing
- lone workers
- lack of training
- stress amongst staff
- staff becoming depressed or taking time off work due to stress
- heavier workloads due to cuts.

How do you intend to address these sorts of issues as a manager? Write a piece for your portfolio.

Abuse occurs because individuals are not valued and the abuser shows little regard for the victim. By encouraging a person-centred approach to care, we can be assured that our clients are given choice, independence and are actively involved in their own care. This is best practice and by ensuring that the individual's rights are upheld, we can go a long way to reducing the likelihood of abuse happening.

CSCI (the Commission for Social Care Inspection, now known as the Care Quality Commission) (2007) identifies factors that can help to prevent abuse from happening. These are:

- **Operating a culture of openness and dignity.** This enables the families and clients in care homes to raise any concerns they have about their care.

- **Visible and clear complaints procedures.** Clients must be able to understand that they have a right to complain and that they will not be coerced or intimidated in any way.

- **Roles and responsibilities of staff and managers are clear with respect to handling complaints.**

- **Training for all staff in adult protection.**

■ steps that need to be taken in the case of suspected or alleged abuse

'Abuse is a violation of an individual's human and civil rights by any other person or persons.'

No Secrets (DOH, 2000)

Any suspicion of abuse or discovery of abuse happening must be dealt with immediately. It may also transpire that an individual approaches you or a member of your staff and tells you/them that they are being abused.

This is called 'disclosure' and you are duty-bound to believe what you are being told and act on it. If the person wants to tell you in confidence, you need to inform them that if they are at risk of harm, then you have a duty to put a stop to it and will need to inform others in order to help them. You cannot keep a 'secret' of abuse.

If you are put into such a position, you will need to ensure that you undertake to:

- Reassure the person.

- Not take a detailed report just yet but listen and avoid questioning.

- Report the disclosure immediately to a senior person.

- Access the procedures in your workplace dealing with suspected abuse.

- Write down when the report was made to you, date etc., who was involved, names of witnesses, what happened and the facts of the conversation.

- Not discuss the incident further.

- Keep the report safe until it can be investigated further.

- Keep the individual who reported the abuse safe.

The flow chart shown in Figure 10.5 highlights the stages involved in responding to concerns about abuse.

2.3 Identify the policies and procedures in own work setting that contribute towards safeguarding and the prevention of abuse

One of the policies your workplace will have is a risk assessment specifically for examining potential cases of abuse.

A risk assessment of this type will examine the potential causes of harm to vulnerable adults, staff, volunteers or others in your organisation with respect to the activities and services provided, as well as the interactions with and between vulnerable adults and the wider community.

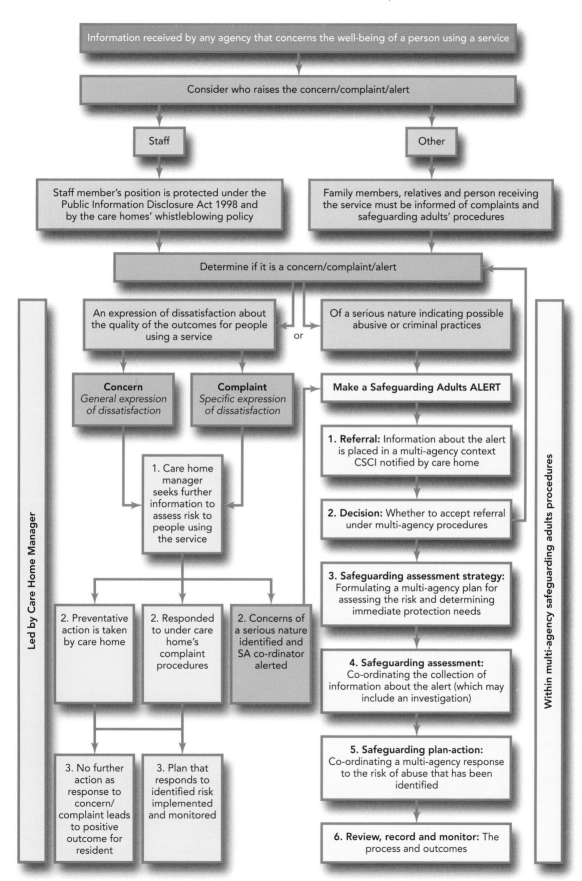

Figure 10.5 Stages in responding to concerns about abuse
Flowchart developed by CSCI

In your organisation's risk assessment there should be details of the risk of harm that might be posed in different situations such as:

- threatening behaviours or intimidation
- behaviours which might result in injury, neglect or exploitation by self or others
- the use and misuse of medication
- the misuse of drugs or alcohol
- aggression and violence
- suicide or self-harm
- the type of impairment or disability of individual in your setting
- the potential for accidents, for example, whilst out in the community or participating in a social event or activity.

As well as a risk assessment for abuse, you are also likely to have access to a safeguarding policy and this is linked to the standards we mentioned earlier.

> ### Activity 10.2.3
>
> Remind yourself of the standards now.

Each local authority has established a multi-agency partnership to lead 'safeguarding adults' work and the set of standards outlines the multi-agency framework within which planning, implementation and monitoring of 'safeguarding adults' work should take place, including a list of suggested partner agencies. Your own organisation will have a copy of that policy and as a manager you need to be aware of its contents.

2.4 Monitor the implementation of policies and procedures that aim to safeguard vulnerable adults and prevent abuse from occurring

2.5 Provide feedback to others on practice that supports the protection of vulnerable adults

The following activity will provide you with the evidence you need for these outcomes.

> ### Activity 10.2.4
>
> Undertake a small-scale study to evaluate how the policies in your organisation are being implemented and write a report to show how your own area is responding to the protection of vulnerable adults.

> Ensure the report is published to all staff and any recommendations being made are acted upon.

3 Be able to manage inter-agency, joint or integrated working in order to protect vulnerable adults

3.1 Follow *agreed protocols* for working in partnership with other organisations

The *No Secrets* document outlined its requirement for multi-agency working and this has been summarised in the National Minimum Standards for care and subsequently into local authority planning and the development of Safeguarding Adults Boards and safeguarding procedures.

Safeguarding Adults Boards are made up of the local social services authority, the police, the NHS and all groups involved in protecting at-risk adults. In order to ensure that the public are able to have a say in decision making, the boards also include members of the local community.

The standards outlined in the safeguarding adults national framework specifically detail how the partnerships should work and be set up. It puts the onus on the local authority to establish a multi-agency partnership to lead 'safeguarding adults' work and to include representation from all the appropriate statutory agencies such as Adult Social Services, Housing, Welfare Rights/Benefits, Education Services, Legal Services, Primary Care Trusts, other NHS Care Trusts, Commission for Social Care Inspection, Health Care Commission, Strategic Health Authority and the Department of Work and Pensions.

Figure 10.6 A committee

The established partnership then brings together an executive management team to oversee strategic development of the work in the form of a strategic/forward plan. The strategic plan includes:

- Safeguarding adults policy – development and review.

- Safeguarding adults procedures for reporting and responding to concerns of abuse or neglect – monitoring, development and review.

- Equal access strategy.

- Information-sharing agreement – development and review.

- Training strategy for all staff and volunteers.

- Training strategy for service users and carers.

- Strategy to disseminate information about adult abuse and 'safeguarding adults' work to staff, volunteers, service users, carers and members of the public.

- A commissioning strategy for services for people who are at risk of or have experienced abuse or neglect.

- A commissioning strategy for responses to and services for perpetrators of abuse/neglect.

- Strategies for reducing risk of abuse and neglect across a range of settings, including care settings and the community.

- Review of the strategic plan and publication of an annual report.

(ADSS, 2005)

3.2 Review the effectiveness of systems and procedures for working in partnership with other organisations

Activity 10.3.1

Obtain a copy of the protocols for working in partnership with the organisations you deal with and write a short review of how effective the systems and procedures are. You need to evaluate the performance of your own organisation and that of your partners and make an assessment of how you might improve the service for your clients.

4 Be able to monitor and evaluate the systems, processes and practice that safeguard vulnerable adults

4.1 Support the participation of vulnerable adults in a review of systems and procedures

In an earlier section we highlighted the need to promote person-centred practice in order to reduce the risks of abuse and this is covered further in Chapter 2. Good practice demands that the client is the 'central' part in the process of care and is part of the decision-making process. With respect to vulnerable adults, the *Valuing People* White Paper (2001) argued that service users should be at liberty to plan their own lives, make their own choices and be involved in all decisions pertaining to their care. The 'safeguarding adults' national framework in Standard 11 supports this, stating:

- 11.1 The partnership explicitly includes service users as key partners in all aspects of the work.

- 11.2 Partner organisations build service user involvement into the design and delivery of safeguarding services.

- 11.3 The policy is explicit in its promotion of the core values of promoting independence, respect, dignity and choice and interventions carried out under the procedures are consistent with this.

- 11.4 Feedback is sought from all individual service users and carers about the delivery and outcomes of safeguarding work for them. There is a mechanism for this feedback to inform improvements and developments.

- 11.5 The partnership recognises and promotes the value of community and neighbourhood networks in preventing abuse and protecting those who are at risk.

Activity 10.4.1

Describe how your service supports the participation of vulnerable adults in a review of systems and procedures.

An example of good practice has been supplied in the *Safeguarding Adults* document (see box overleaf) Perhaps your own area has a similar example.

Figure 10.7 Blowing the whistle

4.2 **Evaluate the effectiveness of systems and procedures to protect vulnerable adults in own service setting**

Activity 10.4.2

How effective are the systems and procedures in your own setting? Audit the complaints procedure and the staff in your area to determine whether changes need to be made.

4.3 **Challenge ineffective practice in the promotion of the safeguarding of vulnerable adults**

Unfortunately, as managers you may come across practice which is not only ineffective but also unsafe and you will be expected to challenge this. Reporting any concerns about practice is known as 'whistle-blowing' and all staff are protected by means of the Public Interest Disclosure Act of 1998 which clearly encourages people to report poor practice without fear of reprisals should they do so.

In the 1990s there was a lengthy and protracted debate regarding whistle-blowing in the NHS following the case of Graham Pink, who had been dismissed from his post as a staff nurse when he blew the whistle on what he regarded as poor standards of care of elderly patients in a Stockport hospital.

CSCI (2011) have defined whistle-blowing as:

'Employees draw[ing] attention to bad practice where they work...'

But what actually constitutes poor practice? Look at the following scenarios and then say which you think are unsafe in terms of safeguarding vulnerable adults.

1. Joan refuses to take her medication and staff have decided to mix it in with her food.

2. A member of staff has recently become an agent for Avon. She brings in the catalogue for the elderly clients and often takes orders from them.

3. The staff are very busy and often leave some of the more ill clients until the last minute. This occasionally results in having less time to complete the dressings effectively. Occasionally a wet bed is also the result of having to wait for the care staff.

4. A non-English speaking client is accompanied to outpatients for her regular diabetic check-ups and staff communicate through her husband. They notice bruising on her arm and comment about it, to be told she is clumsy due to her condition.

5. Jim wants to watch the football on TV and there is a planned trip to the local shopping centre. He does not wish to go and has always said he dislikes shopping but the staff encourage him to do so since he would not be able to stay behind.

Although some of the above situations may seem particularly unsafe or potentially abusive, namely 3 and 4, all of the others would also require challenging. In situation 1, the hiding of medication in food is a breach of rights and refusal to take the medication must be discussed with the client and their family to try to deal in another way with the problem.

Situation 2 puts the clients in a difficult situation and they may feel obliged to buy from the member of staff. They may believe that not doing so may jeopardise their care in some way. The last situation is a case of staff meeting their own needs and not Jim's. It will be difficult if Jim is the only person who does not wish to go shopping but they need to respect his views and, by persuading him otherwise, this is not happening.

In *all* of the situations the staff are not providing good care and should be challenged. They may be unaware of this and therefore a diplomatic approach needs to be taken. They may also be overworked and under-resourced to carry out heavy workloads and again this needs to be addressed. In most of the above cases a simple word with the staff member involved may suffice. With situation 4, it may be that domestic abuse is suspected and this therefore requires a more delicate approach but cannot be ignored.

When unsafe practice is uncovered you need to resort to the system you have in place to address it and you must be familiar with your own organisation's safeguarding policy. It would be useful also to refer to the CSCI flow chart shown on page 185 to determine whether to deal with the issue as a:

- complaint
- concern
- alert.

A complaint or a concern, according to CSCI, is a 'general expression of dissatisfaction'; and an alert is 'an issue of a serious nature indicating possible abuse'.

Any information you have been given must be carefully recorded, using the words and phrases of the person who is disclosing the information, and recording facts only and not your opinions. You also need to record the event as soon is possible and sign, date and give timings of what has happened.

If the situation means an allegation is made against a member of staff, then your action must be swift and you need to determine whether or not the police need to be involved and the member of staff suspended from duty. In doing so, it needs to be clear to the staff

member and those who work with them that this is termed a 'neutral activity' and in no way implies guilt of any kind. It is only following an inquiry that action against staff may need to be taken using the disciplinary framework or capability procedures.

Activity 10.4.3

How would you challenge ineffective practice according to your organisation's safeguarding of vulnerable adults policy?

4.4 Recommend proposals for improvements in systems and procedures in own service setting

In all the aforementioned activities you will have accessed the policies and procedures you use in your own organisation and may have identified areas that require improvement. Please complete the following activity and then say how you would address any of the issues your research has raised with respect to safeguarding vulnerable adults.

Activity 10.4.4

The following website has an excellent set of training film clips which might be used for staff training: www.nmc-uk.org/ Nurses-and-midwives/safeguarding-film-one-an-introduction/

Review these now and determine where you might use them to help staff to understand more fully safeguarding issues for vulnerable adults.

Report on how you might improve the safeguarding process within your own organisation and ensure these recommendations are made known to staff and management.

Summary

In this chapter we have seen how the protection and safeguarding of vulnerable adults has historically been flawed. This has largely been addressed by changes in law and has led to more coherent and streamlined ways in which care professions work together. One of the key

changes in safeguarding has been to develop the way in which professional bodies work in partnership with other organisations, rather than as isolated agencies, and in this way it has been possible to achieve the best possible outcomes for vulnerable people.

Learning outcomes	Assessment criteria
1 Understand the legislation, regulations and policies that underpin the protection of vulnerable adults	**1.1** Analyse the differences between the concept of safeguarding and the concept of protection in relation to vulnerable adults **See p.176 for guidance**
	1.2 Evaluate the impact of policy developments on approaches to safeguarding vulnerable adults in own service setting **Activity 10.1.1, p.178**
	1.3 Explain the legislative framework for safeguarding vulnerable adults **Activity 10.1.1, p.178**
	1.4 Evaluate how serious case reviews or inquiries have influenced quality assurance, regulation and inspection relating to the safeguarding of vulnerable adults **Activity 10.1.2, p.180**
	1.5 Explain the protocols and referral procedures when harm or abuse is alleged or suspected **Activity 10.1.3, p.181**
2 Be able to lead service provision that protects vulnerable adults	**2.1** Promote service provision that supports vulnerable adults to assess risks and make informed choices **Activity 10.2.1, p.182**
	2.2 Provide information to others on: ▓ indicators of abuse ▓ measures that can be taken to avoid abuse taking place ▓ steps that need to be taken in the case of suspected or alleged abuse **Activity 10.2.2, p.184**
	2.3 Identify the policies and procedures in own work setting that contribute towards safeguarding and the prevention of abuse **Activity 10.2.3, p.186**
	2.4 Monitor the implementation of policies and procedures that aim to safeguard vulnerable adults and prevent abuse from occurring **Activity 10.2.4, p.186**
	2.5 Provide feedback to others on practice that supports the protection of vulnerable adults **Activity 10.2.4, p.186**

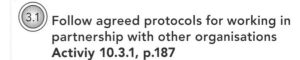

3 Be able to manage inter-agency, joint or integrated working in order to protect vulnerable adults	**(3.1)** Follow agreed protocols for working in partnership with other organisations **Activiy 10.3.1, p.187**
	(3.2) Review the effectiveness of systems and procedures for working in partnership with other organisations **Activiy 10.3.1, p.187**
4 Be able to monitor and evaluate the systems, processes and practice that safeguard vulnerable adults	**(4.1)** Support the participation of vulnerable adults in a review of systems and procedures **Activity 10.4.1, p.187**
	(4.2) Evaluate the effectiveness of systems and procedures to protect vulnerable adults in own service setting **Activity 10.4.2, p.188**
	(4.3) Challenge ineffective practice in the promotion of the safeguarding of vulnerable adults **Activity 10.4.3, p.189**
	(4.4) Recommend proposals for improvements in systems and procedures in own service setting **Activity 10.4.4, p.189**

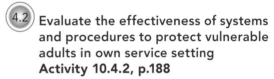

References

ADSS (2005) *Safeguarding Adults: A National Framework of Standards for good practice and outcomes in adult protection work.* London: ADSS. www.adass.org.uk/images/stories/Publications/Guidance/safeguarding.pdf

CSCI (2005) *Safeguarding Children: The second joint Chief Inspectors' Report on arrangements to safeguard children. A summary.* London: CSCI.

CSCI (2007) *Rights, risks and restraints: An exploration into the use of restraint in the care of older people.* http://www.cqi.org.uk/_db/documents/restraint[1].pdf

CSCI (2008) *Raising Voices: Views on safeguarding adults.* London: CSCI.

CSCI (2011) *Whistleblowing Guidance for providers who are registered with the Care Quality Commission.* CQC

DOH (1998) *Modernising Social Services.* London: HMSO.

DOH (1999) *Building for the Future: A White Paper for Wales.* London: HMSO.

DOH and the Home Office (2000) *No Secrets: Guidance on developing and implementing multi-agency policies and procedures to protect vulnerable adults from abuse.* London: DOH and the Home Office. www.dh.gov.uk/en/Publicationsandstatistics/Publications/PublicationsPolicyAndGuidance/DH_4008486

DOH (2001) *Valuing People: A new strategy for learning disability in the 21st century.* London: HMSO.

DOH (2006) The White Paper *Our Health, Our Care, Our Say: a new direction for community services: A brief guide.* London: HMSO.

DOH (2007) *Putting People First: A shared vision and commitment to the transformation of adult social care.* London: HMSO.

Goffman, E. (1961) *Asylums: Essays on the social situation of mental patients and other inmates.* New York: Anchor Books.

Home Office (1989 and 2004) The Children Act 1989. London: HMSO.

Home Office (1998) *Speaking Up for Justice*. London: HMSO

Home Office (1999) *Action for justice (implementing the Speaking up for justice report on vulnerable or intimidated witnesses in the criminal justice system in England and Wales)*. London: HO Communication Directorate.

House of Commons (2004) *The Bichard Inquiry Report*. London: HMSO.

House of Commons (2005) *Elder Abuse – Second Report of Session 2003–04*. London: HMSO.

Lee-Treweek, G. (2008) 'Bedroom Abuse: The hidden work in a nursing home' in Johnson, J. and De Souza, C. (eds) *Understanding Health and Social Care: An introductory reader* (2e). London: Sage.

McKibbin, J., Walton, A. and Mason, L. (2008) *Leadership and Management in Health and Social Care for NVQ/SVQ Level 4*. London: Heinemann.

National Assembley for Wales (2000) *In Safe Hands: Implementing Adult Protection Procedures in Wales*. National Assembly for Wales and Home Office.

Action on Elder Abuse (2006) www.elderabuse.org.uk/

http://www.nhs.uk/CarersDirect/guide/vulnerable-people/Pages/vulnerable-adults.aspx

11 Unit P3 Lead and manage group living for adults

In this chapter we look at the skills and knowledge required for managing group living. By undertaking the activities, you will build upon your knowledge base to enable you to lead group living environments that provide individuals with the opportunities to achieve positive outcomes.

Learning outcomes
By the end of this chapter you will:

1. Be able to develop the physical group living environment to promote positive outcomes for individuals.

2. Be able to lead the planning, implementation and review of daily living activities.

3. Be able to promote positive outcomes in a group living environment.

4. Be able to manage a positive group living environment.

1 Be able to develop the physical group living environment to promote positive outcomes for individuals

1.1 Review current theoretical approaches to group living provision for adults

The emphasis on person-centred care has seen a rise in a number of initiatives to enable people to live as independently as possible. There are, however, some groups of people who may require support of a more substantial nature and who therefore need to move into residential accommodation and group living arrangements.

In previous chapters we looked at the rise of institutions in the eighteenth century, when the Industrial Revolution led to the upset of the status quo with respect to family life with the movement of large numbers of people into cities and towns to find work. Traditional help systems were put at risk and the only way in which people could access care was through the workhouse system or in large asylums.

These large asylums soon became a sort of 'holding place' for those with mental illness, learning disability and physical disability. People

were housed for much of their lives in these institutions and it became apparent that the treatment within was largely of an inhumane nature. Incidents of abuse and neglect in these establishments became high profile in the 1960s and 1970s when the media reported on various places, highlighting the plight of the 'inmates', and this led to a major closure programme. The result was a move to a more community-based arrangement of care, given support by the 1990 NHS and Community Care Act.

Today there are various options for care, not only for the elderly adult but also for children and young people. In this chapter we will confine ourselves to that offered to adults. From small residential homes for the elderly or young people with learning disabilities to sheltered accommodation or Extra Care housing, there are numerous options available now for group living. As an alternative to residential accommodation, the latter option is becoming increasingly popular. Individuals can buy or rent accommodation which is self-contained but has the option of communal living arrangements where shared restaurant facilities offer the chance for the community to meet. There are also care facilities on hand to ensure that residents have extra help should they require it. You may be familiar with other terms used to describe the various types of housing with care for the older adult and these include 'very sheltered housing', 'enhanced sheltered housing', 'supported housing', 'integrated care', 'extra care', 'and 'assisted living'.

Figure 11.1 A modern care establishment

A literature review by Croucher *et al.* (2006) for the Joseph Rowntree Foundation, entitled *Housing with Care for Later Life*, suggests that the numerous definitions we see today reflect the way in which housing with care has developed in the UK within the past 20 years. It shows the response by housing providers, both local authority housing departments and housing associations, to the changing needs of the tenants in their sheltered housing schemes.

More recently, social and health care professionals have become more interested in housing with care models, in order to reduce the need for residential care and to facilitate the maintenance of independence. The literature review goes on to reveal the differences in the schemes with regard to the type of needs being met and the services that residents can access and the levels of dependency that can be accommodated (see, for example, Greenwood and Smith, 1999).

The Department of Health's Housing Learning and Improvement Network (LIN) has promoted the term 'extra care housing', and describes it as:

'... a concept rather than a housing type that covers a range of specialist housing models. It incorporates particular design features and has key guiding principles. It can be referred to by several different names.'

Although the definitions may be flexible, some authors have pointed to the main features of such housing. Oldman (2000) highlights three key points that distinguish 'very sheltered housing' from 'traditional sheltered housing':

- the provision of a meal
- the provision of additional services
- the possibility of a more barrier-free environment.

'Extra Care' schemes, on the other hand, offer not just care services, but support with domestic tasks and opportunities for social interaction, both within and outside the scheme (Baker, 2002).

The primary function of any housing scheme or group living for adults is the promotion of independence; but the major difference to that of the residential care home is that residents are tenants or owners, with their own front door, living in barrier-free environments with use of assistive technologies should they require them. They are clearly meant to be an alternative to residential or institutional models of care, with the emphasis on housing rather than the care.

They do, however, share certain common features with residential care settings in that there is the provision of a meal, together with communal facilities or shared spaces, all residents are from one age group, and there is 24-hour staffing.

Activity 11.1.1

Compare your own setting with a sheltered housing setting. How does the group living provision for your clients differ?

1.2 Evaluate the impact of legal and regulatory requirements on the physical group living environment

As we noted in the first section, there have been considerable changes to the way in which care has been provided over the last 150 years or so. Historically, the delivery of health care in this country has had an uncomfortable journey through the years and governments have tried to address the growing need for help for those who could not work, for whatever reason. The Poor Laws of 1834 and the development of the Charity Organisation Society (COS) in 1869 were an attempt to address the poverty experienced by some at the time. The rise of the workhouse in response to this need, with its terribly dehumanising regime and the institutionalisation of people who were disabled or who had mental health problems or learning disabilities, was a classic example of the institutionalisation of those individuals who could not care for themselves in the community.

In the 1940s, the Poor Laws were abolished and in 1948, the Welfare State and National Assistance Act was introduced. National Assistance Boards dealt with financial support and local authorities provided basic residential accommodation to disabled and older people. With a public welfare system becoming established as a result of the Beveridge Report, the aim was to provide a 'cradle to grave' system of social insurance and benefits for the disadvantaged in society.

It was the rising tide of dissatisfaction with the care system that saw the development of the civil rights movement of the 1960s and 1970s. There was also an emerging 'anti-psychiatry' movement in the late 1960s which criticised the medical model in mental health, wanting individuals with mental health problems to have a greater say in decisions about their lives and choices. The closure of psychiatric institutions and former asylums was to become a major government issue, particularly when there were several media reports of inhumane treatment in such places.

Figure 11.2 An old-style ward

Laws such as the Chronically Sick and Disabled Persons Act (1970) place a duty on local authorities to provide care and support services for disabled people and the passing of this Act was hailed as a ground-breaking step towards equality.

The move towards a more individualistic, consumer-led approach to social care in the 1980s and 1990s saw the Conservative Government suggesting that a 'dependency culture' was in evidence and there was a need to address this.

The assessment of needs for disabled persons came about as a result of the passing of the Social Security Act (1986) and Supplementary Benefit being replaced with Income Support. The Disabled Persons Act (1986) brought about the movement of people out of long-term institutions, together with provision of an Independent Living Fund (ILF), which was brought in to promote independent living. In the late 1980s the concept of the 'mixed economy of care' was introduced and the 1988 Griffiths Report on Community Care advised that social services should use a variety of providers to prevent a 'monopoly' on the provision of care and support. At this time the use of private sector providers, particularly in small groups homes, domiciliary and day care services was encouraged and a market economy was introduced.

The 1989 *Caring for People* White Paper paved the way for community care and care

management in social work and this gathered momentum with the NHS and Community Care Act (1990). The emphasis was to be on providing flexible care in people's own homes so that they might live 'as normal a life as possible'.

In 2000 the Care Standards Act 2000 (CSA) was published and within it the National Care Standards Commission (NCSC), an independent non-governmental public body that regulates social and health care services, identified minimum standards for care. This far-reaching Act set out a broad range of regulation-making powers covering the management, staff, premises and conduct of social and independent health care establishments and agencies.

It was this Act that published the National Minimum Standards for care of elderly people under which we now work and it is within these standards that we are given the most direct guidance as to how we need to conduct the living arrangements within care establishments.

More recently the DOH (2010) paper *Healthy Lives, Healthy People: Our strategy for public health in England* made recommendations about 'designing communities for active ageing and sustainability'. In this paper there is a commitment to:

> 'make active ageing the norm rather than the exception, for example, by building more Lifetime Homes, protecting green spaces and launching physical activity initiatives, including a £135 million Lottery investment in a Mass Participation and Community Sport legacy programme and a volunteer-led walks programme. We will protect and promote community ownership of green spaces and improve access to land so that people can grow their own food...'

Activity 11.1.2

Show how your own care setting has responded to the changes in law in the development of a person-centred group living environment.

1.3 Review the balance between maintaining an environment that is safe and secure and promoting freedom and choice

Risk assessment and risk management are an essential part of adult social care but it is often difficult to balance empowerment with the duty of care we owe our clients. If individuals are to be enabled to lead independent lives, then they need to be able to take the risks they choose to take, but this constantly needs to be weighed against the likelihood of significant harm arising from that choice.

In assessing the seriousness of risk, you may like to address the following areas in your workplace:

- The sorts of factors that increase exposure to risk, e.g. environmental, social, financial, communication and recognition of abuse.

- The existence of support to minimise risk.

- The nature, extent and length of time of the risk.

- The impact the risk may have on the individual and on others.

In addition to the above, you are also bound by law as stated in Section 3(1) of the Health and Safety at Work etc. Act 1974, which clearly states:

'It shall be the duty of every employer to conduct his undertaking in such a way as to ensure, so far as is reasonably practicable, that persons not in his employment who may be affected thereby are not thereby exposed to risks to their health or safety.'

Unfortunately, this can make us risk averse and will undoubtedly lead to a lack of choice for the clients, together with a loss of control and independent living leading to an adverse effect on care.

Care settings and housing vary in type and the risks associated with them will differ. The rights of individuals in our care can occasionally be in conflict with health and safety issues and we need to be prepared to address such occasions. Whilst the client is clearly not imprisoned in the home, occasionally we may have concerns as to the client's safety when they are not in our care. The CSCI document *Rights, Risks and Restraints: An exploration into the use of restraint in the care of older people* (2007), although concerned mainly with how some older people have been restrained in some care settings, does, however, make some useful points.

Respecting people's basic human rights to dignity, freedom and respect underpin good quality social care. People may need support in managing their care and making decisions but they have the right, whether in their own home or in a care home, to make choices about their lives and to take risks.

Social care services have responsibilities to keep people safe from harm and to ensure their safety. It is this need to balance people's rights to freedom and to make choices with ensuring people are safe that is at the heart of this exploration into the use of restraint in the care of older people.

Our attitudes to risk are likely to be different when it comes to risking our own personal safety, but as care professionals, we are bound by law and have a duty of care to our clients and this is likely to change our attitude to risk management. We may be more careful when dealing with clients and take the view that as 'vulnerable adults' they need to be protected in some way. We may occasionally take a 'safety first approach' and focus upon what the client cannot do.

This type of approach focuses on the person's physical problems and disability and tends to ignore other needs. Treatment of this kind may lead to loss of self-esteem and denies the right to choice and an increase in independence. In this way, there is a danger that the care worker becomes more controlling of the client and person-centred approaches become less of a reality.

Risk in this instance then is thought of in terms of danger, loss, threat, damage or injury and the positive benefits of risk-taking are lost and therefore a more balanced approach needs to be adopted.

The Department of Health agrees with this. In their paper of 2007, *Independence, Choice and Risk: A guide to best practice in supported decision making*, they make the point that a 'safety first approach' may 'not be necessarily the best option for the person and may be detrimental to quality of life and a risk to maintaining independence'.

In Titterton's 'Positive Risk Approach', risk is seen as positive and enhancing, and recognises the needs of individuals. It demonstrates that choice and autonomy are important and promotes the rights of vulnerable people. Steve Morgan (2004) summarises the approach:

'Positive risk-taking is: weighing up the potential benefits and harms of exercising one choice of action over another. Identifying the potential risks involved, and developing plans and actions that reflect the positive potentials and stated priorities of the service user. It involves using available resources and support to achieve the desired outcomes, and to minimise the potential harmful outcomes. It is not negligent ignorance of the potential risks… it is usually a very carefully thought-out strategy for managing a specific situation or set of circumstances.'

If we are to provide real choice and control for our clients, we need to enable individuals to take the risks they choose, with support from the staff. This means allowing the individuals using our service to define their own risks and to plan and monitor any activity they wish to undertake which may entail some form of risk.

Activity 11.1.3

Write a short reflective piece outlining how you maintain an environment that is safe and secure but still manage to promote freedom and choice.

1.4 Explain how the physical environment can promote *well-being*

1.5 Justify proposals for providing and maintaining high-quality decorations and furnishings for group living

Figure 11.3 A traditional care setting

Figure 11.4 A modern care setting

So, which setting do you prefer? There can be little doubt that the picture showing a more vibrant and modern set-up is going to enhance the quality of life of those who live there. The somewhat sterile picture of previous types of care settings we would hope is very much a place of the past. The Mind website offers the following insight:

'Good quality, affordable, safe housing is essential to our well-being. Poor housing or homelessness can contribute to mental ill health or can make an episode of mental distress more difficult to manage. This may also be compounded by the fact that poor housing and homelessness are often linked to other forms of social exclusion, such as poverty.'

(www.mind.org.uk/help/social_factors/ housing_and_mental_health)

Although this particular quote mentions homelessness and housing, it can be applied to the care setting. A poor setting with respect to the accommodation in a care home may lead to mental distress.

Judd *et al.* (1998) in their work *Design for Dementia* point out two main principles for designing care homes which can be applied to all settings, not just those dealing with dementia.

1. The design should encourage independence, confidence and raise self-esteem. It should welcome relatives and reinforce personal identity.

2. Key design features should include familiar, domestic, homely styles, with single rooms enabling the individual to bring personal belongings to their living space. Furniture and fittings should be age-appropriate and encourage residents to take part in various activities in different spaces.

The Government described 'decent homes' and these are not references to care homes per se, but again we can apply the sentiment as:

'homes that support the health and well-being of those who live in them. Decent Homes should be:

- warm
- weatherproof
- equipped with modern facilities
- in a good state of repair

and should provide:

- access to clean, safe, green spaces
- access to public services.

(National Audit Office, The Decent Homes Programme, 2010)

With respect to the internal state of decoration and furnishings, the National Minimum Standards 19 to 26 are specific in their guidance.

In the preamble to this set of standards, they write:

'The links between the style of home, its philosophy of care and its size, design and layout are interwoven. A home which sets out to offer family-like care is unlikely to be successful if it operates in a large building with high numbers of resident places. It would need special design features – being divided into smaller units, each with its own communal focus, for example, to measure up to its claim to offer a domestic, family-scale environment. On the other hand, someone looking for a "hotel"-style home may prefer a large home with more individual facilities than could be offered by the small family-style home.'

The text goes on to describe various differences and changes that would need to be made to the accommodation to enhance the living space for individuals with special needs.

It firmly places the onus on the home owners and proprietors to make clear which clientele their homes are aimed at and to make sure the physical environment matches their requirements. The philosophy of care is therefore an important consideration in determining how you might go about designing and decorating the home.

The box below shows the standards which deal with the living environment.

Premises

Standard 19

19.1 The location and layout of the home is suitable for its stated purpose; it is accessible, safe and well-maintained; meets service users' individual and collective needs in a comfortable and homely way and has been designed with reference to relevant guidance.

Shared facilities

Standard 20

20.1 In all newly built homes and first time registrations, the home provides sitting, recreational and dining space (referred to collectively as communal space) apart from service users' private accommodation and excluding corridors and entrance hall amounting to at least 4.1 square metres for each service user.

Lavatories and washing facilities

Standard 21

21.1 Toilet, washing and bathing facilities are provided to meet the needs of service users.

Adaptations and equipment

Standard 22

22.1 The registered person demonstrates that an assessment of the premises and facilities has been made by suitably qualified persons, including a qualified occupational therapist, with specialist knowledge of the client groups catered for, and provides evidence that the recommended disability equipment has been secured or provided and environmental adaptations made to meet the needs of service users.

Individual accommodation: space requirements

Standard 23

23.1 The home provides accommodation for each service user which meets minimum space requirements.

Individual accommodation: furniture and fittings

Standard 24

24.1 The home provides private accommodation for each service user which is furnished and equipped to assure comfort and privacy, and meets the assessed needs of the service user.

24.2 In the absence of service users' own provision, furnishings for individual rooms are provided to the minimum as follows:

- a clean comfortable bed, minimum 900 mm wide, at a suitable, safe height for the service user, and bed linen

- curtains or blinds

- mirror

- overhead and bedside lighting

- comfortable seating for two people

- drawers and enclosed space for hanging clothes

- at least two accessible double electric sockets

- a table to sit at and a bedside table

- wash-hand basin (unless en-suite wc and whb provided).

24.3 Adjustable beds are provided for service users receiving nursing care.

24.4 The service user's room is carpeted or equivalent.

24.5 Doors to service users' private accommodation are fitted with locks suited to service users' capabilities and accessible to staff in emergencies.

24.6 Service users are provided with keys unless their risk assessment suggests otherwise.

24.7 Each service user has lockable storage space for medication, money and valuables and is provided with the key which he or she can retain (unless the reason for not doing so is explained in the care plan).

24.8 Screening is provided in double rooms to ensure privacy for personal care.

Services: heating and lighting

Standard 25

25.1 The heating, lighting, water supply and ventilation of service users' accommodation meet the relevant environmental health and safety requirements and the needs of individual service users.

Services: hygiene and control of infection
Standard 26

26.1 The premises are kept clean, hygienic and free from offensive odours throughout and systems are in place to control the spread of infection, in accordance with relevant legislation and published professional guidance.

- personal hygiene
- dressing and undressing
- self-feeding
- mobility and transfers (getting from bed to wheelchair, or the ability to get onto or off toilet, etc.)
- bowel and bladder management.

Activity 11.1.4

Explain how the physical environment in your own care setting promotes well-being. Write an account of one service user's adjustment to living in a group setting.

Using your care home prospectus or marketing material, evaluate how it shows that you are providing and maintaining high-quality decorations and furnishings for group living.

Figure 11.5 A daily activity

1.6 Develop an inclusive approach to decision making about the physical environment

Decision making about the day-to-day running of the home and the general state of repair and decorations should not only be the decision of the staff but should include the residents in discussion as well. Most care establishments now run a weekly or monthly service user meeting in which such things can be discussed.

Activity 11.1.5

Collect together information from such meetings to show how you have developed an inclusive approach to such decisions.

2 Be able to lead the planning, implementation and review of daily living activities

2.1 Evaluate the impact of legislation and regulation on daily living activities

In health care we use the term 'daily living activities' to refer to daily self-care activities such as:

As health professionals, our clients undergo assessment as to their ability or inability to perform these daily living activities. By measuring in this way, we gain knowledge of the client's functional status and can determine how independent a client is.

Government policy and law have identified the need to assess individuals as to the care they require. From as far back as the National Assistance Act in 1948, local authorities were required to promote the welfare of individuals with sensory, physical or mental difficulties by making an accurate assessment of their needs. This practice has been further implemented in the 1986 Disabled Persons Act, the NHS and Community Care Act (1990) and the Care Standards Act (2000).

The legal requirements that these set out for care workers are the need to assess individual needs, risks and access to services, which need to be set out in a Care Plan of which daily living activities are a part.

In Standards 7 to 11 of the National Minimum Standards (Care Standards Act 2000), the requirements are clearly laid out as to the assessment and care planning of all clients within the home which will be used to make judgements on the quality of care delivered. The standards require the care plans to be drawn up in consultation with the client and to meet relevant clinical guidance. They must be signed by the client or a representative, if the resident is not capable, and reviewed monthly to reflect changing needs.

With respect to daily living and social activities, Standards 12 to 15 require the home to demonstrate that it complies with good practice in relation to dignity and choice and there is a responsibility to demonstrate that routines and activities of daily living are flexible and reflect the needs and aspirations of the people who live in them. By stating the client's wishes and needs on the care plan, this standard can easily be met.

Activity 11.2.1

Show how legislation and regulation on daily living activities has changed your own practice in the care setting over the last five years or so. How have you developed the assessment process to take into account any changes in the law?

The next three sections in this part of the chapter require you to work with a member of staff and to evaluate the assessment process undertaken with one client.

2.2 Support others to plan and implement daily living activities that meet individual needs and preferences

2.3 Develop systems to ensure individuals are central to decisions about their daily living activities

2.4 Oversee the review of daily living activities

Activity 11.2.2

Using a case study approach and working with a staff member, undertake the assessment of daily living activities for one client and evaluate the approach.

Show the systems you have in place for ensuring that the client remains the central figure in the assessment process.

After one week return to the client and review the process. Prepare an evaluative account of the whole process.

Write a reflective piece to show the effect of the systems you have in place and comment on the strengths and weaknesses of the whole process.

3 Be able to promote positive outcomes in a group living environment

3.1 Evaluate how group living can promote positive outcomes for individuals

3.2 Review the ways in which group activities may be used to promote the achievement of individual positive outcomes

The ageing process brings with it challenges with respect to every aspect of our lives. Elderly people may find that they are unable to move as freely as they once did or they may develop a disability which brings with it restrictions of varying types. Also, younger adults who may have a learning disability may find they require a lot more help if they are to continue to live as independently as they can. It may be that the daily living activities become increasingly stressful or difficult to undertake alone. Such difficulties bring with them the possibility of isolation. If the person is unable to move freely, they may opt to stay at home, becoming more socially isolated. The resulting loneliness can then lead to depression and helplessness. In addition, the worry about safety and being alone at home is also a problem for some individuals. With limited mobility, the potential to fall is very real to some people and this is also an area that can cause stress and anxiety.

There is some support from research to suggest that living alone is linked with the experience of different emotions, including anger, loneliness and depression. Russell (2011) in the Ph.D. thesis *Distress in Context* suggested that people living alone expressed more loneliness, particularly when they suffered physical limitations making it difficult to leave the house to meet others. Spending a great deal of time on one's own also means social support is lost and this can lead to depression. For those who have been recently widowed and live alone for the first time in years, depression becomes a very real threat. A study by Bright, Baker and Neimeyer (1999) found that mutual support groups were generally just as effective as trained therapists at alleviating moderate levels of depression. Roberts *et al.* (1999) also found that individuals with serious mental health problems who were taking part in mutual support groups showed improved psychosocial adjustment over the course of the study.

There is little doubt that support groups for various conditions have positive outcomes for those in attendance, not only in the advice or support received, but also because they can give support to others in the same position.

Group living for such individuals will thus pay dividends with respect to their health and happiness. Having an active social life is vital to our well-being whereas being alone for much of the time is a recipe for depression. This may be what brings clients to the care setting – the opportunity to make new friends and the offer of facilities with a range of social and recreational activities.

We can also turn to research within the educational field to show how group activity can promote the achievement of personal outcomes. Cooperative learning theory posits the view that people working together to achieve shared goals were more successful in attaining outcomes than those who strived independently to complete the same goals. If this is indeed the case, then group activities in which there is a cooperative environment will motivate the individual within the group to succeed.

John Dewey (1859–1952) was an American philosopher and psychologist who believed that students would do well to develop knowledge and social skills that could be used outside of the classroom. His contributions to cooperative learning were based on the ideas of establishing relationships within the group members so that they could all successfully carry out and achieve the learning goal. Since Dewey's work, David and Roger Johnson (1975) have contributed to the cooperative learning theory and further identified that cooperative learning promoted mutual liking, improved communication, high acceptance and support, as well as an increase in a variety of thinking strategies among individuals.

Although we are talking here about the adults within our care, the application is similar. Working together as a group engenders a feeling of belonging and is also a huge motivator.

Activity 11.3.1

Undertake a small piece of research within the care setting to determine how group living has promoted positive outcomes for your clients. Develop a questionnaire or interview the clients to evaluate how you have measured the outcomes for the client. In addition, show how group activities have been used to promote the achievement of individual positive outcomes.

3.3 Ensure that individuals are supported to maintain and develop relationships

We form attachments throughout our lives because this is a basic human need. Relationships are an integral part of our lives and create an interdependent state or dependence between two or more people. This sort of dependence therefore impacts on individuals and can lead to conflict if the relationship should falter at any time. From early childhood we are subject to interactions with various people and groups, and these interactions may be of an intimate nature or friendly or part of family life. We learn how to relate in different ways in relationships and also identify those with whom we do not get on and those sorts of people we like.

George Levinger (1980), a psychologist, described relationships as having five stages. His ABCDE model is shown below. According to Levinger, these five stages relate to any relationship, regardless of whether it is a significant other, friend or family.

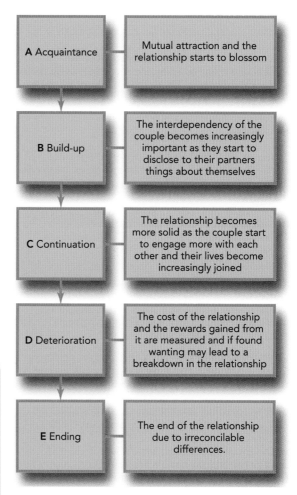

Figure 11.6 George Levinger's five-stage relationship model

George Levinger's ABCDE model

A – Attraction stage

When we first see somebody, we observe certain things about them and make a judgement about whether or not we like them. Regardless of whether they are of the opposite sex or the same sex, we may be attracted by their appearance, dress or the sort of body language they use. We can also be attracted from a distance by the stories and descriptions of the person from a third party. Similar interests, life philosophies and personality are all attractive features at the start of a relationship.

B – Building stage

At this stage in the relationship, common ground in personality, attitude and interests is found and it is here that the relationship may terminate before it even starts. If we do not share a common ground with the person, we may terminate our connection with them.

C – Continuation stage

If, after the building stage, the individuals feel that the relationship is worth pursuing, they enter the continuation stage, and it is here that efforts are made to enhance the positive factors of the relationship. There may be demonstrations of affection, trust and commitment.

D – Deterioration stage

If one or both parties no longer wish to remain in the relationship, then deterioration steps in. If good interpersonal communication is maintained to resolve conflicts in a meaningful way, this can stop the deterioration of the relationship.

E – Ending stage

The ending stage is when the deterioration stage has not been stopped and, although it can be painful for all those involved, it might be viewed positively since it can allow growth and maturity and a new start.

In your own work setting, the people you care for will be going through these stages all the time. They will be interacting with staff and other clients, family, friends and visitors and will be forming attractions and likes and dislikes. You may even be aware that there are some clients whom you feel closer to and others with whom you find interaction a little difficult. As a professional care worker, though, you need to ensure that all relationships within the care setting between staff and clients have integrity and are based on the values and attitudes that underpin best practice. This can be difficult to do since disclosure of your own personal information can be inappropriate; however, by

asking about the client's family or making reference to certain events and their plans for the future, you deepen the relationship and such interest shown in the client can also make you seem more human!

A research study by Hubbard *et al.* (2003) entitled 'Meaningful social interactions between older people in institutional care settings' showed the important influence of social relationships in older age on the health dimensions of the quality of life, including life satisfaction and emotional, subjective and psychological well-being.

In the literature review, the study also revealed reports that institutional care settings occasionally lack high levels of social interaction and social activity and cited the work of Bowie and Mountain (1993); Godlove *et al.* (1982); and Mattiasson and Andersson (1997). Even in care, the individual may feel isolated. Other literature showed caring relationships between residents, in addition to conflict. Also reference is made to the lack of understanding about sexuality and intimate relationships in care settings (Berger, 2000), the predominate view being that:

> 'older people in institutional care settings are without sexual interests, identities, needs or capabilities, and that expressions of sexuality among residents ought to be repressed.'
>
> (Brown 1989; Glass *et al.* 1986)

Activity 11.3.2

What policies and procedures are in place in your care setting that show that the organisation ensures individuals are supported to maintain and develop relationships?

Write a short account of how you have helped somebody to develop good relationships within the home.

3.4 Demonstrate effective approaches to resolving any conflicts and tensions in group living

The research study by Hubbard *et al.* (2003) also found that within care settings there was open hostility amongst residents leading to angry exchanges and conflict.

Read the extract in the following Case Study box.

Case Study

Some residents obviously disliked one another and told each other so. As a male resident of D4 entered the lounge, a female resident retorted, 'I don't like you.' He replied, 'I don't like you either.' The behaviour of some residents aroused anger. When one resident started to moan aloud, another became increasingly agitated and shouted, 'Oh, for Jesus's sake.' One female resident of D4, who repeatedly asked to go to the toilet, obviously got on another's nerves, who shouted, 'You're not needing the toilet at all; go and give her a slap in the mouth.' As a resident sang in the dining room of D4, another said, 'I wish she'd shut up, it sounds terrible.' A female resident pulled a face as she watched another wipe her nose on her sleeve. She mimed the actions, looked at the researcher, raised her eyes in disgust, and said, 'I wouldn't dream of doing that myself. I looked the other way.' Still at D4, a male resident laughingly explained why he did not like a particular female resident: 'There's a lady with a ghastly voice which goes on incessantly. I assume she's a widow 'cause no man could stand it [laughs]. I just know her

voice which conquers space [laughs]. Once when I was in the dining room that woman was spouting away as usual when a chap who was completely off his legs, very military looking, told her to shut up … It was really funny, he got up and shouted "shut up".' Some residents' behaviour aroused deep hostility and they were "labelled" by others as idiots, stupid, clowns, funny types, mental and confused.

Some of the residents vented their dislike by segregating themselves so that they did not have to interact with those residents with whom they did not want to socialise… Other residents of A1 placed gates on their doors to prevent others from entering. One male resident with a gate on his door sat in his room all day because he did not like to socialise with others. A female resident who liked to walk up and down corridors and enter rooms in the dementia unit explained, 'He's greetin' [crying] when you goes to the room with the gate. Who doesn't want [pause], lonely [pause]. He forces us away.'

We cannot hope to get on with everybody we come into contact with and it is the same for our clients. However, how might you deal with a similar situation as that shown above? There is clearly a lot of tension within the care home under scrutiny and there are certainly ways in which such conflict can be dealt with. We have covered this in other chapters, but to recap, here are the principles dealing with conflict:

- Maintain a mutual respect.
- Keep the lines of communication open.
- Aim to gain the viewpoint of all parties involved.
- Keep an open mind.
- Be willing to compromise and negotiate.

Activity 11.3.3

Prepare a flow chart to show how you would deal with resolving conflicts and tensions in group living. Ensure that you reference theorists on conflict resolution in your chart.

4 Be able to manage a positive group living environment

4.1 Evaluate the effects of the working schedules and patterns on a group living environment

4.2 Recommend changes to working schedules and patterns as a result of evaluation

Activity 11.4.1

Analyse the rota system in place in your care setting and evaluate the effect this has on the continuity of care in the environment.

Collect evidence from clients and staff as to how they view the system and how it impacts on the care given and the relationships within the group living environment.

Make recommendations as to changes you wish to make, then implement those changes.

The off-duty rota is bound to have an effect on the relationships between carer and client and the continuity of care within the environment. Carers are not at work for 24 hours a day and unless there has been careful planning with respect to care, clients may be left in a difficult position.

Haggerty *et al.* (2003) conducted a multi-disciplinary review and suggested three types of continuity in care:

1. **Informational continuity** – The use of information on past events and personal circumstances to make current care appropriate for each individual.

2. **Management continuity** – A consistent and coherent approach to the management of a health condition that is responsive to a patient's changing needs.

3. **Relational continuity** – An on-going therapeutic relationship between a patient and one or more providers.

(Haggerty *et al.*, 2003)

The first type, informational continuity, refers to the thread that links the care from one provider to another. This is the information contained in the care plan which documents the medical condition, patient's preferences, and values.

In chronic clinical diseases which are complex, management continuity is important, particularly when several providers are working with the client. It is imperative that shared plans and care protocols are in place to ensure care is continuous.

Relational continuity refers to the need to have a consistent core of staff to provide clients with a sense of coherence.

For continuity to exist, care must be experienced as connected and coherent. For clients and their families, the experience of continuity of care demonstrates that the care provider knows about the client's care and is familiar with everything about them, and this leads to confidence in the care others will be supplying when their key worker is off duty.

4.3 Develop a workforce development plan for the group living environment

The Social Care Institute for Excellence (SCIE) tells us that workforce planning is about addressing two basic premises in terms of the workforce: How many and what sort of staff? As manager you will be well aware of the need to determine what skills each staff member has and to ensure that, during a span of duty, you have the right people in place for the care that needs to be given.

In developing your own workforce plan, you will need to analyse your current workforce and identify the skills mix required in your own setting to deliver the sort of service you provide. It is not only about your current provision, though. You need to be aware that changes in the future will need to be considered so that your plan can highlight gaps to be filled. When the Care Standards Act 2000 came into force, a lot of care homes failed to plan for the training of staff and this resulted in a number of closures of homes due to the lack of qualified staff as set out by the Act. As an employer of staff, you are bound by the National Minimum Standards for Care Homes to show that you make appropriate plans for your workforce.

In developing your plan, the stages outlined by SCIE are useful and these follow.

Audit of current provision

You need to have up-to-date records of all staff working in your setting with details such as working hours, training undertaken, retirement ages and turnover. You would also do well to look at the diversity of your staff to see whether the workforce matches that of the clientele you have. If not, you may wish to plan for future campaigns to bring in more diverse staff. An example of this happening is the current police campaign to attract more ethnic groups to the force.

The context of your service

In this section of the plan you make reference to the trends in the business: whether it is expanding or otherwise; the changing needs of service users; new regulations or legal initiatives that may change the service delivery.

Forecasting

This refers to the identification of gaps in the service that you have identified from stages one and two. You may have realised that, with the growth of the elderly population in your area, not only will more staff be needed but there may be a need to recruit qualified nurses if these clients come with chronic conditions requiring nursing care.

Planning

Three areas are shown by SCIE as being necessary in this part of your plan:

- recruitment and succession planning (i.e. replacing staff who leave or retire)
- career development plans for staff and retention plans
- changes to remuneration packages or benefits to staff.

Implementation

In this stage, the plan needs to be integrated into the strategic plan of the organisation and should then be reviewed in line with it.

Workforce development helps to identify current trends and forecast future workforce structures to meet service delivery requirements. The health care system is concerned with productivity and outcomes and, with changing structures in health and social care, workforce development planning is critical to maintaining a good service and achieving positive outcomes for people.

Activity 11.4.2

Develop a workforce development plan for your own setting.

4.4 Support staff to recognise professional boundaries whilst developing and maintaining positive relationships with individuals

New staff in the care setting may be unaware of the sort of boundaries under which professional carers operate and it is part of their induction to ensure these boundaries are clear. Boundaries are the framework within which the care worker and the client relationship occurs. They ensure that the carer and the client remain in a safe situation because parameters are set within which services can be delivered.

The sorts of things a new staff member may need to be aware of are how they stand with respect to personal disclosure, the use of touch and the limits to that, and the general tone the professional relationship may take. Uppermost in our minds should always be that any relationship has to be with the best interests of the client in mind.

In order to protect the carer–client relationship the following checklist may be useful:

- As a care professional you are obliged to maintain healthy professional boundaries and not to cross the social barrier. The professional role is one that ensures professional caring and social relationships are not confused with one another.

- Romantic or sexual relationships are never appropriate during the course of a professional relationship.

- In dealing with vulnerable people in care, any discomfort expressed about a relationship with a carer must be taken seriously and investigated.

- If a boundary has been crossed, then staff need to be aware that this will constitute professional misconduct and that it must be reported to protect client care.

- A professional carer must be made aware that they are not to receive personal gain of any kind at the client's expense, even if the client has expressed that they wish this to be so. They need to seek advice from you, the manager, if this happens.

Activity 11.4.3

What systems do you have in place to support your staff in recognising professional boundaries?

4.5 Use appropriate methods to raise staff awareness of the group dynamics in a group living environment

In Chapter 7 on teamwork we cover the various roles that people may undertake in the course of interactions within the team and you are advised to review these now. In this section we look at the sort of group dynamics that may be seen with some of our clients in the group setting.

We all exhibit certain characteristics in our interactions and, in a group setting, our behaviour can help or hinder the way in which the group works. Anyone who is working in a setting where there are groups will benefit from looking at the ways in which groups operate.

We would hope that one of your aims in a group living setting is to make everyone feel comfortable and happy in the living environment. It is crucial that all in the setting are involved in the activity and general day-to-day running of the environment. The levels of involvement will, of course, vary, with some clients being more active and willing to participate in all activity offered, whilst others may be more withdrawn and reluctant to do so. There are factors which will affect participation and these are listed below.

The **physical environment** – is it a comfortable physical or social space?

The **psychological atmosphere** – is it non-threatening?

Client's **personal thoughts and preoccupations** – is there anything worrying the client and therefore preventing them from taking a more active part in group living?

The **level of interaction** – is information provided which everyone understands?

Familiarity – do clients know each other sufficiently well to feel safe and valued in the environment?

A group constitutes two or more people interacting with one another in such a way that each individual influences and is influenced by another. You can see how this might affect the way in which the care setting operates.

The theory of group dynamics came about as a result of the work of Lewin (1951) in his research on field theory and refers to the collective interactions that take place within a group (Reber and Reber, 2003). Lewin's work concerned the types of leadership he observed and the effects of 'democratic, autocratic and *laissez-faire*' methods/styles of leadership on group structure and the behaviour of group members.

The results were interesting since they expressed how groups work under such leadership. For example, the democratic leader in the study was seen to gain superior group results from the team as change was more easily accepted. The encouragement within this leadership style to allow all individuals to participate and therefore become an identifiable part of the group was seen to be part of that success. The more authoritarian group structures, because of the rigidity of the approach, led to dysfunctional decision making which seemed to reduce creativity. Inefficiency was noticed with the groups that had *laissez-faire* styles of leadership.

This is interesting since it appears that the type of leader we may be will undoubtedly affect the ways in which the groups we lead and manage will function. Of the three leadership styles, it is the democratic leaders who can expect a more friendly setting in which groups can function. Autocratic and *laissez-faire* leadership style groups seem to engender feelings of discontent, hostility, scapegoating and aggression (Daniels, 2003).

We would hope in our care setting to encourage friendships to develop amongst the clients and for all to get along well with each other. But let's consider how a friendship might actually affect the rest of the larger group. On the positive side, strong friendships mean that there is communication going on and this can mean that others are drawn into the discussion, resulting in a more sociable atmosphere. On the other hand, friendships may also exclude others with the development of so-called cliques and subgroups, and this can damage the group's cohesion. Perhaps you have noticed this with some of the clients in your own care setting.

In raising staff awareness about group dynamics, they need to be familiar with the way in which groups are formed and how they function. One of the main areas for groups not being able to get along, and this can apply to teams of professionals and your clients, is poor communication. This is covered in Chapter 3 but here is a reminder.

Groups are formed for various reasons. For your clients, the group they have been assigned to is not necessarily through their own choice and so they will need to have some help to establish good relationships for a harmonious living environment. Being able to share experiences and gain some support and reassurance from others is a good starting point and group discussion can help this along.

Communication within a group deals with verbal and non-verbal communication and your staff should be aware of the explicit and the implied messages that can be seen if they pay attention to the person.

When people move into the care setting, they bring much of their own experience with them and this can have a major effect on group dynamics. For example, clients bring their past experiences, with their own perceptions, attitudes and values, which can sometimes cause contention. They may also come with a particular set of expectations about the setting and how they will be living and these expectations can influence the manner in which the group develops over a period of time.

Staff need to be aware of the way in which they can help the group to work in harmony and they need to make a conscious effort to not only understand what is happening within the group, but also to be aware of how their own personality may affect the status quo. For example, you may have noticed that there are some issues with the group in the setting and that not everyone wants to participate in some of the pre-arranged activities and they show little interest. A potential cause might be that some of the clients are being intimidated by others and feel insecure simply because of stronger members in the group.

You might also notice that some of the clients are consistently ignored when they voice their opinions or try to join in with activities and this may be due to others being nervous of their contribution. Perhaps their educational background is different and others feel threatened.

Staff need to be aware of the personalities of everyone in the setting in order to be able to promote a harmonious and welcoming atmosphere for all. There will be dominant personalities – those with ideas and those who take on the role of the joker or clown. You will also have people who always take the alternative view and constantly act as devil's advocate, never agreeing with the group. All these are roles that people play in groups and care professionals need to be able to handle these types of clients in a meaningful and sympathetic manner.

Activity 11.4.4

Prepare a staff training session on group dynamics to raise their awareness of the group dynamics in your own group living setting.

Evaluate the presentation and check learning has occurred.

4.6 Review the effectiveness of approaches to resource management in maintaining a positive group living environment

Effective businesses need business plans and as a manager you will have been asked to prepare such a document. The Department of Health requires all care establishments to have business and financial plans in place for external inspection.

You may have been asked to present financial accounts to the Care Standards Commission to demonstrate that clients' fees are being used in an effective way towards their care and that you are providing the best value in your service delivery. In order to do this, you need to be aware of how to set budgets and also monitor the expenditure of your own department. This expenditure is likely to be in relation to supplies, staffing, equipment and overhead expenses.

A budget refers to the allocation of finances for specific purposes and will form a part of your action plan for the future. If you are part of a large organisation, you will be allocated a small part of the overall financial income and will be expected to audit the expenditure you undertake and to keep within the limits of your budget for a specific length of time, usually known as the financial year. If, however, you work within a small care home and are in total control of the whole income and outgoings, then you need to ensure that the budget is carefully allocated to various areas and to avoid overspending.

Budgeting is a continuous process and to manage the process effectively requires the ability to see beyond the barriers of the yearly divisions and to project future trends with respect to the business. In preparing a budget, the expected income for the year needs to be predicted, along with the predicted expenditure for the year. There are several ways in which this can be accomplished.

■ **Incremental budgeting** is a method which looks at the previous year's budget, allows for inflation and then forecasts income and expenditure for the coming year and sets the budget according to that found.

■ **Programme budgeting** is a process which looks at the costs of the whole organisation and then allocates funds on the basis of the aims and objectives of the setting.

■ **Zero-based budgeting** begins each year from scratch. There is no recourse to previous years' budgets but planning is based on accurate assessment of needs for the coming year.

Whichever way you choose to set your budget, variations may occur and you need to be aware of the potential to overspend. What you paid for services last year may now be far more expensive and accuracy is the key to managing the finances effectively.

You may also need to undertake a cost–benefit analysis which is weighing the effectiveness of the resources and services you wish to purchase against alternatives. For example, you may have decided that the setting needs to be updated and decorated and new furniture purchased. However, if the washing machine breaks down and a new one is needed, you might have to change the plans or at least re-assess the needs with respect to the decorative update. Planning therefore needs to be both on a long-term and a short-term basis.

The flow chart in Figure 11.7 may be helpful in the planning process.

Access the aims and objectives of the organisation

↓

Access last year's income and expenditure

↓

Prepare a statement for the team as to the spending plans for the coming year

↓

Supervise and monitor the control of the budget
Ascertain who is responsible for what

↓

Evaluate your performance against the aims and objectives

Figure 11.7 Planning

Regular monitoring of the budget is essential as the amount you spend throughout the year is likely to vary. In the winter time, the expense of heating and lighting is likely to be much more than during the summer months, so seasonal fluctuations need to be taken into account. Such planning for this is called budgetary profiling and if you do not take this into account, you are likely to introduce cash flow problems which can be most stressful. Your staff may not understand how the budget is set and why sometimes they are unable to purchase certain items or undertake activities with clients. It is important therefore to ensure that the team is aware of how the budget functions. You will need to discuss changes with your team and clarify the costs of any changes. For example, some staff may not understand why they are now being asked to finance their own university courses when in the past these costs have been met by the organisation. Clear discussions in an open and transparent manner can help to clarify this for them.

Activity 11.4.5

Review the effectiveness of your own approach to resource management in maintaining a positive group living environment by completing a case study based on last year's financial activity. How did you ensure staff were kept aware of the financial state of the organisation and how effectively do you think this was managed? Would you make any changes in the next year and why?

Summary

To enable people to live as independently as possible there has been much emphasis placed on person-centred care and this has seen a rise in the number of initiatives. In this chapter we have looked at the varied groups of people who require support of a substantial nature and who move into residential accommodation and group living arrangements.

From small residential homes for the elderly or young people with learning disabilities to sheltered accommodation or Extra Care housing, there are numerous options available now for group living. One alternative to residential accommodation is the availability of buying or renting self-contained accommodation which has the option of communal living arrangements with shared restaurant facilities and the chance for the community to meet. We also came across terms such as 'very sheltered housing', 'enhanced sheltered housing', 'supported housing', 'integrated care', 'extra care', and 'assisted living'.

In addition to the group living arrangement, the chapter also addressed the basic human need to form relationships and the effects these have on well-being. The way in which we *all* live affects our well-being, and whether we live alone with support coming on a daily basis or in a group living environment, as care workers we need to be diligent in ensuring that positive outcomes are afforded to all individuals.

Learning outcomes	Assessment criteria
1 Be able to develop the physical group living environment to promote positive outcomes for individuals	**1.1** Review current theoretical approaches to group living provision for adults **Activity 11.1.1, p.194**
	1.2 Evaluate the impact of legal and regulatory requirements on the physical group living environment **Activity 11.1.2, p.195**
	1.3 Review the balance between maintaining an environment that is safe and secure and promoting freedom and choice **Activity 11.1.3, p.196**
	1.4 Explain how the physical environment can promote well-being **Activity 11.1.4, p.199**
	1.5 Justify proposals for providing and maintaining high-quality decorations and furnishings for group living **Activity 11.1.4, p.199**
	1.6 Develop an inclusive approach to decision making about the physical environment **Activity 11.1.5, p.199**
2 Be able to lead the planning, implementation and review of daily living activities	**2.1** Evaluate the impact of legislation and regulation on daily living activities **Activity 11.2.1, p.200**
	2.2 Support others to plan and implement daily living activities that meet individual needs and preferences **Activity 11.2.2, p.200**
	2.3 Develop systems to ensure individuals are central to decisions about their daily living activities **Activity 11.2.2, p.200**
	2.4 Oversee the review of daily living activities **Activity 11.2.2, p.200**

Learning outcomes	Assessment criteria
3 Be able to promote positive outcomes in a group living environment	(3.1) Evaluate how group living can promote positive outcomes for individuals **Activity 11.3.1, p.201** (3.2) Review the ways in which group activities may be used to promote the achievement of individual positive outcomes **Activity 11.3.1, p.201** (3.3) Ensure that individuals are supported to maintain and develop relationships **Activity 11.3.2, p.202** (3.4) Demonstrate effective approaches to resolving any conflicts and tensions in group living **Activity 11.3.3, p.203**
4 Be able to manage a positive group living environment	(4.1) Evaluate the effects of the working schedules and patterns on a group living environment **Activity 11.4.1, p.203** (4.2) Recommend changes to working schedules and patterns as a result of evaluation **Activity 11.4.1, p.203** (4.3) Develop a workforce development plan for the group living environment **Activity 11.4.2, p.205** (4.4) Support staff to recognise professional boundaries whilst developing and maintaining positive relationships with individuals **Activity 11.4.3, p.205** (4.5) Use appropriate methods to raise staff awareness of the group dynamics in a group living environment **Activity 11.4.4, p.207** (4.6) Review the effectiveness of approaches to resource management in maintaining a positive group living environment **Activity 11.4.5, p.208**

References

Baker, T. (2002) *An Evaluation of an Extracare Scheme – Runnymede Court.* Estover, Plymouth: Hanover Housing Association.

Berger, J. (2000) 'Sexuality and Intimacy in the Nursing Home: A romantic couple of mixed cognitive capacities'. *Journal of Clinical Ethics,* 11, 4, pp.309–13.

Bowie, P. and Mountain, G. (1993) 'Using Direct Observation to Record the Behaviour of Long-Stay Patients with Dementia'. *International Journal of Geriatric Psychiatry,* 8, pp.857–64.

Bright, J. I., Baker, K. D. and Neimeyer, R. A. (1999) 'Professional and Paraprofessional Group Treatments for Depression: A comparison of cognitive-behavioral and mutual support interventions'. *Journal of Consulting and Clinical Psychology,* 67(4), pp.491–501.

Brown, L. (1989) 'Is There Sexual Freedom for our Aging Population in Long-Term Care Institutions?' *Journal of Gerontological Social Work,* 13, 3/4, pp.75–93.

Croucher, K., Hicks, L. and Jackson, K. (2006) *Housing with Care for Later Life.* University of York: Joseph Rowntree Foundation.

CSCI (2007) *Rights, Risks and Restraints: An exploration into the use of restraint in the care of older people.* London: CSCI.

Daniels, V. (2003) *Kurt Lewin Notes.* Sonoma State University. www.sonoma.edu/users/d/daniels/lewinnotes.html

DOH (1989) *Caring For People: Community care for people in the next decade and beyond.* London: HMSO

DOH (2007) *Independence, Choice and Risk: A guide to best practice in support decision making.* London: HMSO

DOH (2010) *Healthy Lives, Healthy People: Our strategy for public health in England.* London: HMSO.

Glass, J., Mustian, R. and Carter, L. (1986) 'Knowledge and Attitudes of Health-Care Providers toward Sexuality in the Institutionalized Elderly'. *Educational Gerontology,* 12, pp.465–75.

Godlove, C., Richard, L. and Rodwell, C., (1982) *Time for Action: An Observation Study of Elderly People in Four Different Core Environments.* Social Services Monographs, Research in Practice, Joint Unit for Social Service Research, University of Sheffield, Sheffield.

Greenwood, C. and Smith, J. (1999) *Sharing in ExtraCare.* Staines: Hanover.

Haggerty, J. L., Reid, R. J. Freeman, G. K., Starfield B. H. , Adair, C. E. and McKendry, R. (2003) 'Continuity of Care: A multi-disciplinary review'. *BMJ,* 327, pp.1219–21.

Hubbard, G., Tester, S. and Downs, M. G. (2003) 'Meaningful Social Interactions Between Older People in Institutional Care Settings'. *Ageing & Society,* 23, pp.99–114. Cambridge: Cambridge University Press.

Johnson, D., Johnson, R. (1975) *Learning Together and Alone, Cooperation, Competition and Individualization.* Englewood Cliffs, NJ: Prentice-Hall.

Judd, S., Marshall, M. and Phippen, P. (1998) *Design For Dementia.* London: Hawker Publications

Lewin, K. (1951) *Field Theory in Social Science: Selected theoretical papers,* Cartwright, D. (ed.). New York: Harper & Row.

Mattiasson, A. and Andersson, L. (1997) 'Quality of Nursing Home Care Assessed By Competent Nursing Home Patients'. *Journal of Advanced Nursing,* 26, pp.1117–24.

Morgan, S. (2004) *Positive risk-taking: an idea whose time has come.* practicebasedevidence.squarespace.com/storage/pdfs/OpenMind–PositiveRiskTaking.pdf

Oldman, C. (2000) *Blurring the Boundaries: A fresh look at housing and care provision for older people.* Brighton: Pavilion Publishing in association with JRF.

Reber, A., and Reber, E. (2003) *The Penguin Dictionary of Psychology.* London: Penguin Books

Roberts, L. J., Salem, D., Rappaport, J., Toro, P. A., Luke, D. A. and Seidman, E. (1999) 'Giving and Receiving Help: Interpersonal transactions in mutual-help meetings and psychosocial adjustment of members'. *American Journal of Community Psychology,* 27(6), pp.841–868.

Russell, D. (2011) *Distress in Context.* Ph.D. thesis. From www.psychologytoday.com/experts/david-russell-phd

www.scie.org.uk/workforce/Peoplemanagement/leadership/workforcedev/index.asp

www.mind.org.uk/help/social_factors/housing_and_mental_health

You may not work directly with children but you are required to have some understanding of the safeguarding protocols and procedures with children. In this chapter you will be introduced to the policies and procedures for safe working with children and the ways in which to respond to evidence of abuse and harm in children.

Learning outcomes

By the end of this chapter you will:

1. Understand the policies, procedures and practices for safe working with children and young people.

2. Understand how to respond to evidence or concerns that a child or young person has been abused or harmed.

1 Understand the policies, procedures and practices for safe working with children and young people

1.1 Explain the policies, procedures and practices for safe working with children and young people

It was following the horrific murders of Jessica Chapman and Holly Wells by a school caretaker that the whole issue of safeguarding children came under the spotlight once again. Prior to

Every child matters

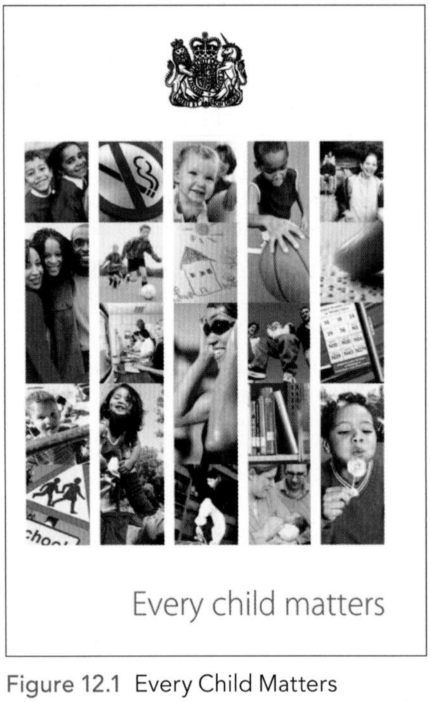

Figure 12.1 Every Child Matters

this event, the Children Act of 1984 and subsequently 2004 highlighted the obligations of professionals working with children to report suspected abuse. However, following some serious incidents, most notably the death of Victoria Climbié in 2000, a public inquiry was set up to address the failure of the law to uphold the protection of vulnerable children. As a result of the inquiry carried out by Lord Laming into Victoria's death, major changes in child protection policies came about.

The Every Child Matters (ECM) initiative was launched in 2003 by the government, and has become one of the most far-reaching policy initiatives to be released in the last ten years. Covering children and young adults up to the age of 19, or 24 for those with disabilities, it led to changes in the Children Act as shown in the 2004 version and provided a detailed framework for working with children within multi-agency partnerships. The themes:

- Be healthy
- Stay safe
- Enjoy and achieve
- Make a positive contribution
- Achieve economic well-being

were to be adopted by all agencies working with children, including early years children's centres, schools, social work services, primary and secondary health services, play workers, and Child and Adolescent Mental Health services (CAMHS).

One of the main criticisms of the services for children in the past had been the failure of professionals to understand each other's roles or to work together in a multi-disciplinary manner. This was highlighted by the Laming Inquiry and the ECM initiative sought to change this. Despite huge changes being made to the way in which professionals were to work with children and to safeguard them, the murders of

Jessica Chapman and Holly Wells prompted a further inquiry. The Bichard Inquiry recommended a new scheme under which everyone working with children or vulnerable adults should be checked and registered.

The new Vetting and Barring Scheme (the Scheme) focused public attention on the way that people who work with children are screened as to their suitability and led to the Safeguarding Vulnerable Groups Act 2006 and the Safeguarding Vulnerable Groups Order (Northern Ireland) 2007.

Recognising the need for a single agency to vet and register all individuals who want to work or volunteer with children, the Independent Safeguarding Authority (ISA) was set up, with the Criminal Records Bureau being made responsible for managing the system and processing the applications for ISA registration. The ISA utilises the POVA (Protection of Vulnerable Adults) and the POCA (Protection of Children Act) lists and List 99 (a list of teachers who have been considered unsuitable to work with children) to assess those wishing to work with children and can then either give registration to work or put them onto the ISA barred list. It needs to be stressed that, although these systems have improved the safeguarding of children, the need for employers to have robust recruitment procedures remains paramount.

Figure 12.2 Safety in the care setting

Further policy documents you need to be aware of are *Working Together to Safeguard Children* 2006 (updated in 2010) and *The Protection of Children in England: A progress report* (Laming, 2009) which continue to promote the sharing of data between those working with vulnerable children. If you are working in Scotland you may well need to familiarise yourself with the paper *Protecting Children – A shared responsibility* (Scottish Executive, 1998) and for Northern Ireland you may like to look at *Co-operating to Safeguard Children* (Department of Health, Social Services and Public Safety, 2003)

The statutory guidance *Working Together to Safeguard Children* (2006) created the role of Local Authority Designated Officer or 'LADO'. This officer is responsible for managing allegations of abuse against adults who work with children (teachers, social workers, church leaders, youth workers, etc.).

In addition, local Safeguarding Children Boards (LSCBs) have been set up to ensure that agencies and professionals in the area promote the welfare of children. In the event of the death or serious injury of a child, a Serious Case Review is initiated to identify failings and improve future practice.

Activity 12.1.1

Write short notes on the policies shown in the above section to demonstrate your understanding of safe working with children and young people.

2 Understand how to respond to evidence or concerns that a child or young person has been abused or harmed

2.1 Describe the possible signs, symptoms, indicators and behaviours that may cause concern in the context of safeguarding

Your local safeguarding board will have guidance in place which details the sorts of signs and symptoms of abuse that you need to be aware of. Another useful organisation to which you can turn for information is the NSPCC and we encourage you to look at this website now: www.nspcc.org.uk/inform. The fact sheet compiled by NSPCC Consultancy Services provides guidance for individuals who work in voluntary, community and commercial organisations and provides information on how they can recognise the signs of child abuse, so that they can alert the appropriate authorities.

Any maltreatment of a child, whether it is direct or indirect, constitutes abuse and must be remedied. Children are vulnerable to abuse from adults and other children and we should be aware of this.

The UK Government guidance *Working Together to Safeguard Children 2010* (1.33–1.36) identifies four types of abuse as being:

1. Physical abuse
2. Emotional abuse
3. Sexual abuse
4. Neglect.

Physical abuse

This is any action that results in a child being hurt in a physical manner such as hitting, shaking, burning, drowning or suffocating and resulting in harm.

The physical signs of abuse may include:

- unexplained bruising or injuries on any part of the body
- multiple bruises – on the upper arm or on the outside of the thigh
- cigarette burns
- human bite marks
- fractures
- scalds
- multiple burns with a clearly demarcated edge such as those made by cigarettes.

Changes in behaviour which might indicate physical abuse include the following:

- fear of parents being approached
- aggressive behaviour or temper outbursts
- flinching when approached or touched
- reluctance to get changed, for example, in hot weather
- depression
- withdrawn behaviour.

Emotional abuse

Any action that leaves a child feeling worthless, unloved or inadequate constitutes emotional abuse. This can include not giving the child opportunities to express their views, deliberately silencing them or 'making fun' of what they say or how they communicate. It is interesting to note what the NSPCC guidelines say about this type of abuse:

> 'It may feature age or developmentally inappropriate expectations being imposed on children. These may include interactions that are beyond the child's developmental capability, as well as overprotection and limitation of exploration and learning, or preventing the child participating in normal social interaction. It may involve seeing or hearing the ill-treatment of another. It may involve serious bullying (including cyber-bullying), causing children frequently to feel frightened or in danger, or the exploitation or corruption of children. Some level of emotional abuse is involved in all types of maltreatment of a child, though it may occur alone.'

Unfortunately it is difficult to measure or recognise emotional abuse but indications such as failure to thrive and grow or developmental issues may indicate problems. It is also the case that children who are well cared for physically may be emotionally abused by being put down or belittled by parents or other siblings. Receiving little attention or love and affection from parents or carers should also alert the care worker to abuse.

Changes in behaviour which might indicate emotional abuse include the following:

- sulking, hair twisting, rocking or behaviour which is neurotic in nature
- being unable to play
- fear of making mistakes
- speech disorders which develop suddenly
- self-harm such as cutting
- fear of parent being approached or involved in discussion
- developmental delay in terms of emotional progress.

Sexual abuse

This sort of abuse can include forcing a child to take part in sexual activity and may also include non-contact activities, such as involving children in looking at sexual images or encouraging children to behave in sexually inappropriate ways.

Changes in a child's behaviour may cause you to become concerned and physical signs can also be present. Children may also tell you about sexual abuse and they do this because they want it to stop. It is important that you listen and take them seriously.

The physical signs of sexual abuse may include:

- pain or itching in the genital region
- bruising or bleeding near genital region
- sexually transmitted disease
- vaginal discharge or infection
- stomach pains
- discomfort when walking or sitting down
- pregnancy.

Changes in behaviour which can also indicate sexual abuse include the following:

- becoming aggressive or withdrawn
- fear of being left with a specific person or group of people
- having nightmares
- trying to run away from home
- sexual knowledge which is beyond their age, or sexual drawings or use of sexual language
- bedwetting
- eating problems such as overeating or anorexia
- self-harm or mutilation, or suicide attempts
- saying they have secrets they cannot reveal

- substance or drug abuse
- suddenly having unexplained sources of money or consumer items
- not allowed to have friends (particularly in adolescence)
- acting in a sexually explicit way towards adults.

Neglect

Any failure to meet a child's basic physical and/or psychological needs is termed neglect and is likely to result in the child's health or development becoming impaired. A pregnant woman who continues to abuse substances during her pregnancy may also be guilty of neglect.

The physical signs of neglect may include:

- the child being constantly hungry, sometimes resorting to stealing food from other children
- constantly dirty or 'smelly'
- loss of weight, or being constantly underweight
- inappropriate clothing for the conditions, e.g. lack of coat or jumper in winter, etc.

Figure 12.3 Neglect

Changes in behaviour which can also indicate neglect may include:

- complaining of tiredness all the time
- not attending to medical needs and/or failing to attend appointments
- having few friends, being a 'loner'
- mentioning being left alone or unsupervised.

For children, bullying can also be a problem and, although we may see it as part of physical or emotional abuse, it is not included in many texts as a specific type of abuse.

Under the Children Act 1989, a bullying incident should be addressed as a child protection issue, particularly when there is 'reasonable cause to suspect that a child is suffering, or is likely to suffer, significant harm'. Bullying is deliberately hurtful behaviour, and usually takes place over a prolonged period of time. The forms it takes can vary from physical (e.g. fighting, hitting, theft of money or other items), verbal (e.g. racist or homophobic remarks, name calling, threatening behaviour) and emotional (e.g. excluding an individual from the activities and social acceptance of their peer group).

Schools are now required to comply with the new Equality Duty which has come about as a result of the Equality Act 2010 which replaced previous anti-discrimination laws. This came into being on 5 April 2011 and has three aims. It requires public bodies to:

- Address and eliminate unlawful discrimination, harassment and victimisation.
- Advance equality of opportunity between people who share a protected characteristic and people who do not share it.
- Foster good relations between people who share a protected characteristic and people who do not share it.

(DfE, 2011)

Although bullying is not always easy to recognise, a child who exhibits signs of depression, low self-esteem, shyness, poor academic achievement or is constantly on their own and threatens or attempts suicide should alert staff to potential harm. For parents or residential care workers dealing with children, the following may also need to be addressed:

- coming home with cuts and bruises
- torn clothes
- asking for possessions to be replaced because they have 'lost' them
- losing dinner money or reporting not having had any dinner
- falling out with previously good friends
- changes in mood and becoming bad tempered
- wanting to avoid leaving their home and being ill and not wanting to attend school
- aggression with younger brothers and sisters
- doing less well at school or failing

- sleep problems
- anxiety
- becoming quiet and withdrawn.

(Adapted from *Working Together to Safeguard Children*, 2006)

Figure 12.4 Bullying

Activity 12.2.1

Prepare a staff training session using the above information and present a PowerPoint presentation showing your understanding of the signs, symptoms, indicators and behaviours that may cause concern in the context of safeguarding of children.

2.2 Describe the actions to take if a child or young person alleges harm or abuse in line with policies and procedures of own setting

As we have noted above, recognising child abuse is not easy and it is not your responsibility to decide whether or not abuse has taken place or if a child is at significant risk of harm from someone. But you do have a responsibility and duty of care to act in order that the appropriate agencies can investigate and take any necessary action to protect a child and this will be set out in your organisation's child protection or safeguarding procedures.

The DFES guidance entitled *What To Do If You're Worried a Child is being Abused – Summary* supplies useful information as to how to deal with such a situation. It highlights the following points that everyone working with children and families should familiarise themselves with:

- Follow your organisation's procedures and protocols for promoting and safeguarding the welfare of children.
- Know who to contact in your organisation to express concerns about a child's welfare.
- Remember that an allegation of child abuse or neglect may lead to a criminal investigation, so don't do anything that may jeopardise a police investigation.
- Do not ask a child leading questions or attempt to investigate the allegations of abuse.
- Ensure that you are aware of who is responsible for making referrals.
- If you are the person who makes the referral, make sure you know who to contact in the police, health, education, school and children's social care.
- Record full information about the child at first point of contact, including name(s), address(es), gender, date of birth, name(s) of person(s) with parental responsibility (for consent purposes) and primary carer(s), if different.
- Keep this information up to date.
- Record in writing all concerns, discussions about the child, the decisions that were made and the reasons for those decisions.

Activity 12.2.2

Describe the actions you would take if a child or young person alleges harm or abuse in line with the policies and procedures of your own setting. Keep your notes in your portfolio.

2.3 Explain the rights that children, young people and their families have in situations where harm or abuse is suspected or alleged

As we have seen from the preceding text, child abuse is a social problem and as such our children need to be protected. Every child therefore has a right to live free of physical and emotional harm, neglect and bullying.

In 1991 the United Nations Convention on the Rights of the Child 1989 was ratified in the UK and included the following rights for children:

- the right to protection from abuse
- the right to express their views
- the right to be listened to

- the right to care and services for disabled children or children living away from home.

- the right to protection from any form of discrimination

- the right to receive and share information as long as that information is not damaging to others

- the right to freedom of religion although they should also be free to examine beliefs

- the right to education.

In June 2010, the Welsh Assembly laid down the Proposed Rights of Children and Young Persons (Wales) Measure. Children are also covered by the Human Rights Act 1998 which incorporates the European Convention on Human Rights. Although children are not specifically mentioned in this Act, it is unlawful for public authorities to act in a manner which is incompatible with the rights and freedoms contained in the Act and these rights include the right to respect for private and family life.

The first Children's Commissioner post was created in 2001 as a result of the Children's Commissioner for Wales Act 2001. The aim of this post is to safeguard and promote the rights and welfare of children and other parts of the UK soon followed with the creation of further commissioners for Northern Ireland (Commissioner for Children and Young People (NI) Order 2003), Scotland (Commissioner for Children and Young People (Scotland) Act 2003) and England (sections 1–9 of the Children Act 2004).

Further rights for children are evidenced in the Education Act 2002 which includes a provision in Section 175 which requires school governing bodies, LEAs and further education institutions to make arrangements to safeguard and promote the welfare of children. In addition, the Adoption and Children Act 2002, which amended the Children Act 1989, included witnessing domestic violence as a further definition of 'harm'.

What the law has done over the last decade or so is to give children a voice and this is made clear in the Children Act of 2004, which states that the interests of children and young people are 'paramount' in all considerations of welfare and safeguarding and that safeguarding children is everyone's responsibility. By providing legislation to improve children's lives, there is now a more integrated service delivery to ensure that children are given the services they require for health, education and safety.

Anyone who works with children and young people must recognise that the needs and rights of the child are the main focus and, as the law says, 'paramount', irrespective of what their parents think. This can cause tension, however, and there is also a need to recognise and acknowledge the needs of parents and their right to parent their child.

Where appropriate the care worker should enable the child to exercise their rights and help them to take decisions. When working with children, you have a duty to safeguard and protect them from harm and occasionally this can mean breaking confidences by sharing information.

Activity 12.2.3

Check your policy on safeguarding and, if your organisation has any connection with children in care, ensure that the policy has a section detailing how you would safeguard children and young people.

Summary

This chapter has shown how the law has given a voice to children and, in particular, the Children Act of 2004 clearly states that the interests of children and young people are 'paramount' in all considerations of welfare. Whether you are directly involved in the care of children and young people or not, you need to be aware of the issues which surround safeguarding children. There is now a more integrated service delivery to ensure that children are given the services they require for health, education and safety. In addition, this chapter has shown how you need to respond to any issues that may arise with respect to the suspected abuse of children.

Learning outcomes	Assessment criteria
1 Understand the policies, procedures and practices for safe working with children and young people	**1.1** Explain the policies, procedures and practices for safe working with children and young people **Activity 12.1.1, p.213**
2 Understand how to respond to evidence or concerns that a child or young person has been abused or harmed	**2.1** Describe the possible signs, symptoms, indicators and behaviours that may cause concern in the context of safeguarding **Activity 12.2.1, p.216** **2.2** Describe the actions to take if a child or young person alleges harm or abuse in line with policies and procedures of own setting **Activity 12.2.2, p.216** **2.3** Explain the rights that children, young people and their families have in situations where harm or abuse is suspected or alleged **Activity 12.2.3, p.217**

References

Department of Health, Social Services and Public Safety (2003) *Co-operating to Safeguard Children*. Belfast: Northern Ireland Executive.

DfES (2003) *Every Child Matters: Summary*. London: HMSO.

DfES (2006) *What To Do If You're Worried a Child is Being Abused: Summary*. London: HMSO.

DfE (2006, updated in 2010) *Working Together to Safeguard Children: A guide to inter-agency working to safeguard and promote the welfare of children*. London: HMSO.

DfE (2011) *Preventing and Tackling Bullying. Advice for Head Teachers, Staff and Governing Bodies*. London: HMSO.

The Home Office (2004) *The Bichard Inquiry Report HC653*. London: The Stationery Office.

Laming, W.H. (2009) *The Protection of Children in England: A progress report*. London: House of Commons.

NSPCC (2010) *Child Protection Fact Sheet. The definitions and signs of child abuse* at www.nspcc.org.uk

Scottish Executive (1998) *Protecting Children – A shared responsibility*. Edinburgh: The Scottish Government.

13 Unit SS 5.1 Assess the individual in a health and social care setting

This chapter should be read in conjunction with Chapter 9 'Manage health and social care practice to ensure positive outcomes for individuals' and Chapter 2 'Work in partnership in health and social care or children and young people's settings'.

It addresses the different forms of assessment in the context of partnership working and looks at how you can manage the whole process of carrying out, reviewing and planning assessment for clients. Reference is made to three models of assessment and their uses and the Single Assessment Process, as suggested by the National Service Framework for Older People (2001), is introduced and discussed. Throughout the chapter a series of activities will help you to build a portfolio of evidence to cover the learning outcomes of the unit.

Learning outcomes

By the end of this chapter you will:

1. Understand assessment processes.

2. Be able to lead and contribute to assessments.

3. Be able to manage the outcomes of assessments.

4. Be able to promote *others'* understanding of the role of assessment.

5. Review and evaluate the effectiveness of assessment.

1 Understand assessment processes

1.1 **Compare and contrast the range and purpose of different forms of assessment**

4.1 **Develop others' understanding of the functions of a range of assessment tools**

The Social Care Institute for Excellence has this to say about assessment:

> 'Although assessment has been recognised as a core skill in social work and should underpin all social work interventions, there is no singular theory or understanding as to what the purpose of assessment is and what the process should entail.'
>
> (SCIE, 2004)

With no one theory to support it, the process of assessment then becomes a huge subject and one which potentially might differ with each service in a partnership group. This situation could lead to fragmentation of a client's care with many differing approaches to assessing their needs being used at the same time. It becomes imperative then to determine how we as care providers will assess the client and to simplify the process.

The care planning process is a good place to start. In any assessment of a client's needs the following 'basic helping cycle' as suggested by Taylor and Devine (1993) is useful.

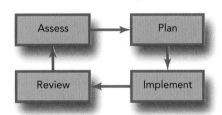

Figure 13.1 Basic Care Cycle

In this basic cycle, the client and care professional work together to assess the needs of the client. The care to meet those needs is then planned and put into action at the third stage and finally evaluated or 'reviewed', starting the cycle again.

In 2005 Thompson described what he called the 'ASIRT' model of care planning:

AS – Assessment phase which is the start of the process and the first part of an action plan leading onto the …

I – Intervention stage when aims and objectives for the intervention are selected

R – Review when the evaluation of what has happened takes place, before finally

T – Termination, when the intervention is no longer needed and can be stopped.

The care planning process, however we approach it, is just one part of assessment. Three different models of assessment have been suggested in research by Smale *et al.* (1993):

The Questioning Model – in which the care worker leads the process and questions and listens, before processing the information. This means that the process is service led.

The Procedural Model – in which information is gathered by the care professional who then makes a judgement as to 'best fit' for the service. This is criterion based and a range of checklists is used to determine which service is best for the client.

The Exchange Model – in which the care workers view the clients as the expert in their own care needs and is really the most person-centred approach of the three. This model seems to describe the most holistic form of assessment with the care professional managing a more client-centred approach.

The types of assessment we carry out will differ according to the setting we are in or according to the type of needs the person has.

If the person living in their own home is having difficulty with their personal care, they might consider getting support by having a community care assessment of their needs. These assessments are carried out by social services in order that services can be provided by the social services department of a local authority. The assessment considers what type of services are needed by the person being assessed and can vary, depending on the particular needs of the person who needs help.

Older people

Community care assessments for older people are carried out under the 'Single Assessment Process'. This is explained more fully in the next section.

People with mental health problems

Assessments for people in need of mental health services are carried out under the 'Care Programme Approach', which assesses:

- risk and safety
- psychiatric symptoms and experiences
- psychological thoughts and behaviours.

Mental health issues require the help of mental healthcare professionals and the community care assessment entitles the individual to a care plan that is regularly reviewed by the professional.

If the person has a range of needs and is considered to have severe mental health problems, their care may be co-ordinated under a Care Programme Approach (CPA) and a CPA

care co-ordinator will be appointed to co-ordinate the assessment and planning process. The co-ordinator is usually a nurse, social worker or occupational therapist.

People with learning disabilities

For clients with learning disabilities, assessment is governed by the principles set out by the 'Valuing People' plan which aims to improve services for people with learning disabilities by treating them all as individuals. This 'person-centred approach' considers the client's ability to exercise choice and control over their lives.

Activity 13.1.1

Reflect on the different forms of assessment used in your own care setting. How useful are they and what changes might be made to improve what you are doing?

Undertake a staff training session to ensure that others have an understanding of the assessment tools in use.

1.2 Explain how partnership work can positively support assessment processes

All care agencies need to work together so that assessment and the resultant care plan is effective and coordinated. The Single Assessment Process (SAP) was introduced in the National Service Framework for Older People (2001) in Standard 2: Person-centred care, the aim of which was to ensure that the NHS and social care services treat older people as individuals, enabling them to make choices about their own care.

Many older people have wide ranging needs and, in recognition of that, care must be holistic and centre on the whole person. The requirement to develop a Single Assessment Process was based on just this fact, to provide a person-centred health and social care framework, which includes entry into the system, holistic assessment, care planning, care delivery and review.

In working with partners to deliver care there is always the potential for repetition of work and overlap of delivery. SAP aims to ensure that the individual's needs are assessed thoroughly and accurately, without duplication by different agencies. By sharing the information appropriately between all relevant agencies, SAP coordinates the assessment and ensures effective delivery of care.

Joint working necessitates the effective sharing of information and there is a range of approaches to implement electronic SAP (e-SAP) across the country currently being looked at. The Health and Social Care Integration Programme, an NHS Connecting for Health project, is working to enable the sharing of electronic records between the NHS and social care systems, subject to the individual's consent.

There is also available a National SAP Resource which has been commissioned by the Department of Health to create and host an online resource for health and social care professionals implementing SAP. This free resource holds material to assist multi-agency working and aims to provide access to information to enable the sharing of good practice and reduce duplication of effort.

To download information on this resource look at National CAF/SAP Learning and Development Resource at the Centre for Policy on Ageing website: www.cpa.org.uk/sap

Activity 13.1.2

Access the SAP and determine how you might use it to work with partners in developing care packages. Write a short reflective piece on how you currently work with partners in assessing clients.

2 Be able to lead and contribute to assessments

2.1 Initiate early assessment of the individual

2.2 Support the active participation of the individual in shaping the assessment process

Recently there have been media articles about the need for early assessment with respect to memory loss in patients and signs of stroke. With respect to memory loss, the National Institute for Health and Clinical Excellence (NICE) recommends that early assessment should take place, to enable planning for the future or, if treatment is to be given, to enable its institution at an early stage. In the case of stroke, the quicker the condition is assessed, the sooner the person can access treatment and the possibility of full recovery. In these cases then, early assessment is crucial to enable a better outcome for the client.

In all other cases of need, the assessment process should be initiated immediately or as soon as the care requirements of the client change. Early assessment enables the care plan to be implemented with speed and meet the needs of the clients as they arise.

When the assessment takes place, the client needs to be the central figure in the negotiation and this is recognised in legislation as being the optimum process for care planning. The NHS and Community Care Act (1990) and the Carer Recognition Act (1995) led the way in this type of care planning. The 'care professional knows best' way of operating takes away choice and limits the client's ability to make their own decisions and should therefore be a thing of the past. Any care plan that is developed without the client is meaningless since it is the client who experiences the discomfort of their condition and has the expert opinion of what they need.

To aid the client in the assessment process the best way to proceed is to ask the questions 'what do you want, what do you need, and how are you feeling at the moment?' By actively encouraging the client to voice their needs, concerns and wants with respect to their care, a good rapport is developed and the client will feel actively involved in all decisions.

Occasionally we may find that the client is not fully able to engage with the process due to conditions that prevent understanding or sensory impairments which may make the process difficult. In this case, an advocate needs to be called in to act on behalf of the client and to ensure that they are fully represented.

Figure 13.2 Helping a client with their assessment

Activity 13.2.1

Present a case study to show how you ensure that clients are assessed early and are a central part of the assessment process. Show the paperwork for one client, ensuring that confidentiality is maintained.

2.3 Undertake assessments within the boundaries of own role

2.4 Make recommendations to support referral processes

Your role in the assessment process may be as a key worker undertaking the whole process and referring the client to various other services or you may be a care professional who delivers care in another capacity. Whatever part you are playing, you do need to ensure that you are able to successfully negotiate with others and refer clients on if you cannot fulfil their needs.

The Commission for Social Care Inspection in their National Minimum Standards publishes standards for your own particular setting and, as such, you should make yourself and your staff aware of the regulations for assessment and the updating of clients' care plans. For example, Standard 6.9 states that:

'The service user is made aware of the respective roles and responsibilities of the care manager/CPA care co-ordinator, key worker and/or advocate and knows how to contact them.'

The client needs to be fully aware of the roles of each person involved in their care and you must ensure that you explain to them what your role is. You need to make sure that:

■ as far as possible, the needs of the client are being met

■ any information obtained from the client is relevant to meet their needs

■ the information you provide is coherent and meets the individual needs of the clients.

At times you may be required to refer the client to another care professional and this can mean a delay in treatment or service delivery. It may be that the service required has a waiting list or it may be simply that the way in which the referral system works is cumbersome or confusing for the client. Clients are often told that a referral to another service will be made, only then to realise they have little or no influence over the process or any knowledge about who they will be referred to or how long they can expect to wait. This inevitably leads to increased dissatisfaction with the care being given and you are likely to end up with a very unhappy client.

As a manager you can pre-empt this by implementing referral agreements. In the event that referrals need to be made between the partners delivering the client's care, you can undertake the following.

Develop referral guidelines which define the conditions that should be referred

The partnership group should work together to draw up a set of guidelines that outlines the conditions best managed by the setting and the conditions that need to be referred. With each group undertaking this work, there will be information about local practice habits, previous patterns of referral and availability of specialists, as well as current information on how each condition should be managed.

Any referrals to other services should be discussed with the client in advance and the client's consent obtained to disclosing information.

You then need to ensure that the recipient of the referral is able to provide the required service and that any confidential information disclosed will be protected.

Activity 13.2.2

Give evidence to show how referrals are made in your own setting and write a reflective piece about the boundaries within your own role in the assessment process.

3 Be able to manage the outcomes of assessments

3.1 Develop a care or support plan in collaboration with the individual that meets their needs

3.2 Implement interventions that contribute to positive outcomes for the individual

The responsibility for organising the care planning meeting with the client may lie with you as the manager of the care setting and therefore you need to have gathered all the information for the meeting to take place. This needs to be done in advance of the actual meeting to enable people to read about and understand the services that may be on offer. Only then can informed choices and decisions be made.

Before the meeting you need to ensure that contact is made to all who should attend and you also need to be aware of the professional with whom you will be working in order to support this client. For the client, the meeting may be quite a daunting process. They may lack the confidence to be part of a meeting where there are GPs, health visitors and housing officers present and, as such, may not participate fully. It is good practice then to meet with the client and the family before the meeting to help them through the process and to discuss what will happen and who will be there.

You might also help them to prepare what they wish to say and perhaps they might make some notes to help them.

It is possible that you may need to act as an advocate for the client or you might enlist the help of an independent person to do this job, particularly if you are chairing the meeting. This is a difficult situation since it is quite easy to make suggestions as to what you or the advocate thinks is best for the client and yet may be far from what they actually want and would be the best outcome for them. Care must be taken to listen to what the client is saying and to put forward their views, not your own.

Activity 13.3.1

Provide evidence that you have developed a care or support plan in collaboration with a client in your care that meets their needs.

Describe and analyse the interventions that were implemented, detailing how they contributed to positive outcomes for the client.

4 Be able to promote *others'* understanding of the role of assessment

4.2 **Develop others' understanding that assessment may have a positive and/or negative impact on an individual and their families**

The main aim of any assessment has to be to improve the quality of life of the client but so often care workers focus merely on the *needs* of the client and fail to recognise their strengths. If we continually focus on what the client is unable to do, we negate the fact that they have strengths in certain areas and they can miss out on optimising their well-being.

In helping others in the care process to understand this, a reminder can be made as to the positive and negative definitions of health. If we hold a negative view of health then we subscribe to the notion that 'health is the absence of disease' (WHO, 1946). A more positive way to look at health is to focus on what the individual *can* do, irrespective of any condition they have. In this respect, the focus is more on optimising the health of the client and recognising the fact that, despite having an illness and needs, they can still live an independent and full life.

4.3 **Develop others' understanding of their contribution to the assessment process**

Look at the following case study and answer the questions.

Case Study

Mrs Jones is 75 years old and has recently lost her husband. She is currently feeling lonely and has problems with her mobility following a stroke four years ago. Her husband used to drive her to the shops and helped her with the weekly food shop. She is able to cook and clean her house with no problems and manages to go to a local lunch club once a week as the bus stops outside her house every Tuesday. Her children and their families all live over 100 miles away and cannot therefore offer any support to her, but she has caring neighbours who pop in from time to time and help with the garden, which was her husband's domain.

Mrs Jones enjoys baking and is an active member of the WI and regularly bakes for sales. She also likes to swim but has found it difficult to get to the pool since her husband's death. Bathing at home is also a bit of a problem and she has no shower fitted so is 'strip washing' every day.

Care worker A comes to assess Mrs Jones and asks her what her needs are. The care worker notices that Mrs Jones has a mobility problem. Mrs Jones says she has trouble with getting to the shops and is a little lonely.

The care worker puts into place home help to aid Mrs Jones with her housework and arranges a regular supermarket delivery for her main food needs. A care worker also comes in once a week to help Mrs Jones with her bath.

1. What are your views on this outcome for Mrs Jones?

2. How do you think she will be feeling about the services that have been put into place?

It is possible that you have noticed that, although Mrs Jones's needs may be met in this scenario and with these services, there are major limitations in the outcomes.

Activity 13.4.1

Using the case study above, prepare a staff training session to address the needs of Mrs Jones in a more positive manner and encourage the staff to undertake a further assessment of Mrs Jones which results in a positive outcome for her.

5 Review and evaluate the effectiveness of assessment

5.1 Review the assessment process based on feedback from the individual and/or *others*

5.2 Evaluate the outcomes of assessment based on feedback from the individual and/or *others*

Once the care plan is in place and being implemented, it is most important to monitor its effectiveness and to make changes as and when necessary.

At the outset you will have agreed on the following:

- How often should we monitor the plan?
- What methods will we use?
- Who will be expected to contribute to the evaluation?

How often? This largely depends upon the complexity of the plan and the needs of the client. If the client has severe needs to be met, then changes are likely to happen with more regularity, in which case a weekly meeting may need to be planned to monitor how the plan is working. If, however, the client needs very little support, the need to monitor the plan may become necessary only when a change occurs.

Methods? This can be in written form or at case meetings but whatever method is used, it is wise to document what has been said, so a verbal report would not be best practice since there is no record.

Who? The more people involved in the care of the client, the more evidence there will be to check the outcomes. There is a danger that too much information may be forthcoming so you may limit the evaluation to key people. It is also not good practice to overload a lay carer with forms to fill

out on a regular basis since they may already feel overwhelmed with the care they are giving.

Once you have the information on how the plan is working, you need to collate the evidence and respond to the changes that are identified.

Some examples of the sorts of things that might become evident from your monitoring are shown in the box below.

Deterioration of the client's physical condition
Deterioration of the client's mental condition
Change in support from neighbours, friends or family
Change in housing
Change in finances
Change in local services on offer
Change in staff in agencies being used

Whatever changes have been noted for your client need to be recorded and then acted on. The information about the changes must be shared with all involved in the care and action taken as to how the changes will impact on the care and the client.

In reviewing the process there should be a planned meeting in order for all involved in the process to be present to discuss the changes and how they can be dealt with. As the care manager, it is likely that you will be responsible for organising the meeting and drawing up an agenda or a checklist of things that need to be discussed.

Activity 13.5.1

Using the care plan of the client you have recently assessed, provide evidence of the most recent review and the feedback from those involved in the evaluative process.

5.3 Develop an action plan to address the findings

At the end of the review meeting, you will need to ensure that the care plan is revised and updated with respect to the changes that have been discussed. The client needs to understand how the changes will impact on their care and the significance of the changes.

Revisions to the plan can be as follows:

Outcome achieved

In this case, the client's condition has changed and they no longer require an intervention to help. For example, perhaps they had been suffering from bronchitis which necessitated additional care being put into place. Their recovery means this care is no longer needed.

Reduction in support

This links in with the first outcome and, as the client becomes more independent, they may need a reduced level of support and this can be planned for here.

Increase in support

Sometimes the client may require more care in certain areas, for example, a change in the client's family circumstances. Perhaps a family member moving from the area may mean that they need other care put into place to fill this void.

Increase in the type of support needed

In this case, if the client has become more disorientated or forgetful, then they may need a different type of service put into place. Also the onset of a physical disability may also require a change in care.

Changing the method of support

Occasionally, a service provider may go out of business or be unable to offer the service due to resource limitations. In this instance, a new service provider needs to be provided and the change noted in the action plan.

The care planning process is an important one and every step of the way needs to be documented, reviewed and accurately recorded. Good practice demands that confidentiality is respected and that records are maintained in good order. Written reports must be included in the care package. Minutes of meetings with staff in attendance must also be kept and a record of the pre-review meeting should also be available to show how the client was prepared for the meetings.

Changes to the package should be identified clearly and the revised plan made available to all involved in the care to be delivered.

Activity 13.5.2

Using the care plan and the recent review notes of the client you have, develop an action plan to address the findings.

Summary

This chapter has shown the different forms of assessment in the context of partnership working and has looked at how you can manage the whole process of carrying out, reviewing and planning assessment for clients. Three models of assessment and their uses were described, together with the Single Assessment Process, as suggested by the National Service Framework for Older People (2001). In order to lead meaningful and full lives, despite the presence of illness and debilitating conditions, managing the assessment of individuals in a positive way is essential for positive outcomes to be achieved.

Learning outcomes	Assessment criteria
1 Understand assessment processes	**1.1** Compare and contrast the range and purpose of different forms of assessment **Activity 13.1.1, p.220**
	1.2 Explain how partnership work can positively support assessment processes **Activity 13.1.2, p.221**
2 Be able to lead and contribute to assessments	**2.1** Initiate early assessment of the individual **Activity 13.2.1, p.221**
	2.2 Support the active participation of the individual in shaping the assessment process **Activity 13.2.1, p.221**
	2.3 Undertake assessments within the boundaries of own role **Activity 13.2.2, p.222**
	2.4 Make recommendations to support referral processes **Activity 13.2.2, p.222**
3 Be able to manage the outcomes of assessments	**3.1** Develop a care or support plan in collaboration with the individual that meets their needs **Activity 13.3.1, p.223**
	3.2 Implement interventions that contribute to positive outcomes for the individual **Activity 13.3.2, p.223**
4 Be able to promote others' understanding of the role of assessment	**4.1** Develop others' understanding of the functions of a range of assessment tools **Activity 13.1.1, p.220**
	4.2 Develop others' understanding that assessment may have a positive and/or negative impact on an individual and their families **Activity 13.4.1, p.224**
	4.3 Develop others' understanding of their contribution to the assessment process **Activity 13.4.1, p.224**

5 Review and evaluate the effectiveness of assessment findings	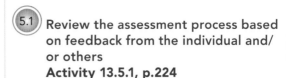 **5.1** Review the assessment process based on feedback from the individual and/ or others **Activity 13.5.1, p.224**
	5.2 Evaluate the outcomes of assessment based on feedback from the individual and/or others **Activity 13.5.1, p.224**
	5.3 Develop an action plan to address the findings **Activity 13.5.2, p.225**

References

Department of Health (2001) *National Service Framework for Older People.* London: HMSO.

SCIE (2004) *Leading Practice: A development programme for first line managers.* (online www.scie.org.uk/publications/guides/guide27/files/lp-participants.pdf)

Smale, G., Tuson, G., Biehal, N. and Marsh, P. (1993) *Empowerment, Assessment, Care Management and the Skilled Worker.* London: HMSO.

Taylor, B. and Devine, D. (1993) *Assessing Needs and Planning Care in Social Work.* London: Arena Press.

Thompson, N. (2005) *Understanding Social Work: Preparing for practice.* Basingstoke: Palgrave Macmillan.

World Health Organization (1946) *Preamble to the Constitution of the World Health Organization as adopted by the International Health Conference,* New York, 19–22 June 1946.

Glossary of terms

Advocate – A person who speaks on behalf of another, to enable them to meet their needs.

Appraisal – The assessment, at regular intervals, of an employee's performance in their work role and an evaluation of the support that may be required to sustain and develop an employee's competence.

Appreciative inquiry – An evaluative model of performance analysis that directs energy on identifying and building on strengths rather than trying to compensate for or to rectify weaknesses.

AQAA – Annual Quality Assurance Assessment.

Audit – An evaluation of a person, organisation, system, process, project or product.

Barriers – Actual, or perceived, blocks to desired outcomes.

Benchmarks – A point of reference by which something can be measured. Benchmarks are often used as a means to compare performance against that of similar organisations.

'Best kept secret' – Skills, knowledge or good practice that a staff member has, but which have not been shared more widely with others.

Bullying – The use by an individual, or group of individuals, of persistent, aggressive or unreasonable behaviour against a co-worker.

Care Programme Approach (CPA) (1990) – Similar to the SAP, this applies to the individual with mental health problems and ensures that they are fully involved in their own care plan.

Care Quality Commission (CQC) – The independent regulator of Health and Social Care Services in England.

Champion – An individual, often an enthusiast, who is able to raise the profile and lead on a specific issue.

Coaching – A process through which one individual supports and enables another individual to unlock and maximise their own potential, in order to develop and improve their performance.

CONECT model – Larson and LaFasto's 2001 model for resolving conflict.

COSHH – Control of Substances Hazardous to Health Regulations 2002.

CSCI – Commission for Social Care Inspection.

DDA – Disability Discrimination Act 1995.

Dehumanisation – To treat an individual as less than human, to fail to respect their individuality and personal requirements.

Discrimination – Treatment or consideration of, or making a distinction in favour of or against, a person or thing based solely on the group, class, or category to which that person belongs rather than on their own merits.

Discrimination model of supervision – Published in 1979 by Bernard and later developed in 1998. It identifies three parts of supervision, namely, intervention, conceptualisation and personalisation, together with three possible supervisor roles: teacher, counsellor and consultant.

Diversity – Acceptance and respect of difference.

DOH – The Department of Health.

DPA – The Data Protection Act 1998.

Duty of care – A legal and moral obligation owed to those with whom you hold a care relationship that requires the care giver to provide care that is reasonable and of an accepted standard.

ELP or Essential Lifestyle Planning – A guided process for learning how someone wants to live and developing a plan to help make it happen.

Emotional intelligence – The capacity for recognising our own feelings and those of others, for motivating ourselves, for managing emotions in ourselves, as well as others.

Empathy – The ability to 'put yourself in the shoes of others'.

Equality – Refers to achieving equal rights for people regardless of what factors they might have that make them different.

Equal opportunities – Offering the same or similar opportunities in life, regardless of different characteristics such as race, gender, age.

Ethical dilemma – A moral problem for which there is no easy solution.

Fairness – The quality of treating people equally or in a way that is right or reasonable.

GP commissioning consortia – The devolvement of funds from Primary Care Trusts to local consortia for use at local level.

GROW model – Developed by Whitmore (2002) in which a Goal (**G**), Current situation (**R** = Reality), Options (**O**) and Obstacles (**W** = Wrap Up) are identified to help a person maximise their full potential.

Harassment – Deliberate behaviour that annoys or upsets someone.

HASAWA – The Health and Safety at Work Act, 1974.

HSC – The Health and Safety Commission.

HSE – The Health and Safety Executive.

Incident analysis – Formally reflecting on and analysing an incident.

Inclusion – A deliberate shift in organisation culture to ensure that all individuals feel respected and valued.

Independent Safeguarding Authority (ISA) – The Independent Safeguarding Authority's (ISA) role is to help prevent unsuitable people from working with children and vulnerable adults.

Industrial tribunals – Courts which deal with employment cases and claims of religious or political discrimination.

Infantilisation – Unreasonably treating another as if they were a child.

Institutionalisation – A theory that describes how individuals become habituated to certain ways of doing things which then become the norm. In care settings this can mean the person loses their independence and self-esteem as they start to accept the carer's way of doing things.

Invisibilisation – The deliberate act of disregarding and ignoring another.

Learning organisations – An organisation that facilitates the learning of its members and continuously transforms itself.

List 99 – A list of teachers who have been considered unsuitable to work with children.

MA – Master of Arts – A higher level educational qualification.

The McGill Action Planning System (MAPS) – A planning process for children with disabilities to enable their integration into the school community. The team in this process includes the child, family members, friends, and regular and special education personnel.

Marginalisation – The social process of relegating an individual or group to the fringes and acceptance of these people as unimportant.

Medicalisation – The process of identifying difference as a medical or pathological condition.

Mentoring – A helping relationship between an individual with potential and an individual with expertise.

MHOR – Manual Handling Operations Regulations 1992.

MHSWR – Management of Health and Safety at Work Regulations 1999.

Multi-disciplinary team – The skill mix of a variety of professionals such as doctors, nurses, occupational therapists and physiotherapists, working together to meet the needs of the patient/client.

M.Sc. – Master of Science – See above, MA.

Needs-led approach – The focus of assessment of an individual's needs.

Normalisation – Also known as Social Role Valorisation. Describes a set of principles that underlies the idea that people with a learning disability should experience the 'normal' patterns of everyday life by living in ordinary places, doing ordinary things, with ordinary people.

Objective – A measureable outcome that can be reasonably achieved within an expected timeframe and with available resources.

Oppression – The unjust exercise of power or authority over an individual or group.

Paralinguistic communication – The study of voice and how words are said; the tone and pitch which help to reveal the emotions behind the words.

PATHS (Planning Alternative Tomorrows and Hope) – A system developed by Jack Pearpoint, Marsha Forest and John O'Brien which focuses on a person's 'North Star' or their dream for the future.

PCT – Primary care trust.

Performance management cycle – 'A systematic approach' which includes: setting objectives, using relevant performance indicators, monitoring and appraising individuals and teams, and identifying training and development needs using the knowledge gained to modify plans.

Person-centred practice – A process of life planning for individuals based around the principles of inclusion and the social model of disability.

Personal development planned activities – Enable an individual to enhance their skills and attributes and increase their personal potential in order to contribute to the realisation of dreams and aspirations.

Personal Futures Planning – This process suggests a series of tasks and provides a set of tools to help us begin the process with people to uncover their capacities, to discover opportunities in the local community, and to invent new service responses that help, more than get in the way.

Glossary of terms

Personalisation agenda – Allowing individuals to build a system of care and support tailored to meet their own individual needs and designed with their full involvement.

POCA – Protection of Children Act.

Policy – A formal statement of actions drawn up in relation to particular circumstances to guide future actions and decisions.

Positive Risk Approach – Risk is seen as positive, enhancing, and recognises the needs and choices of individuals.

POVA – The Protection of Vulnerable Adults.

Power – To exercise authority.

PPE – Personal Protective Equipment at Work Regulations 1992.

Prejudice – A preconceived, unjust judgement based on erroneous or limited knowledge.

Professional development – Refers to planned acquisition of skills and knowledge attained for both personal development, professional competence and career advancement.

Professional development plan – A formal plan of action to meet professional development objectives.

PUWER – Provision and Use of Work Equipment Regulations 1998.

RED approach –Thompson's (2006) model for managing conflict with a high degree of tension.

Reflection in-action – To critically reflect on what one is doing whilst one is doing it and to revise actions in the light of that reflection.

Reflection on-action – A retrospective activity that requires interpretation and analysis of recalled information.

Reflective practice – A structured process of looking back at something in order to understand it and learn from it.

RIDDOR – Reporting on Injuries, Diseases, and Dangerous Occurrences Regulations 1995.

Risk – The chance of an event happening, normally associated with adverse events.

Risk assessment – The formal assessment of the likelihood and impact of an adverse event.

Risk management – Strategies put in place to manage or minimise a risk.

Safety first approach – The approach to risk assessment which focuses upon what the client cannot do.

Scaffolding – The facilitation of progression to a higher stage of learning or professional development.

Self-awareness – Knowing our own emotions and recognising those feelings as they happen.

Single assessment process – A person-centred approach which includes entry into the care system, holistic assessment, care planning, care delivery and review.

Skill set – The qualifications, knowledge and competencies necessary to fulfil a particular role.

Solution-focused approach – A four-step method of solution-focused management to deal with problems in a dynamic way.

Standards – Statements specifying the expected level of performance for specific activities.

Stereotype – To unfairly attribute individuals from specific groups with the same characteristics.

Supervision – A means of providing professional support and learning for staff.

Systems approach model – The author Holloway describes this model which emphasises the relationship between the supervisor and supervisee.

Transformational leadership – A leadership approach in which the leader sets out to create change by empowering the team to try new things.

Trivialisation – To deliberately minimise the seriousness of an issue or event.

Vulnerable adult – A person over 18 who is or may be in need of community care services by reason of mental or other disability, age or illness and may be unable to take care of him or herself, or is unable to protect him or herself from significant harm or serious exploitation.

360° feedback – Performance data collected from an employee's manager, colleagues, subordinates, clients, etc.

Index